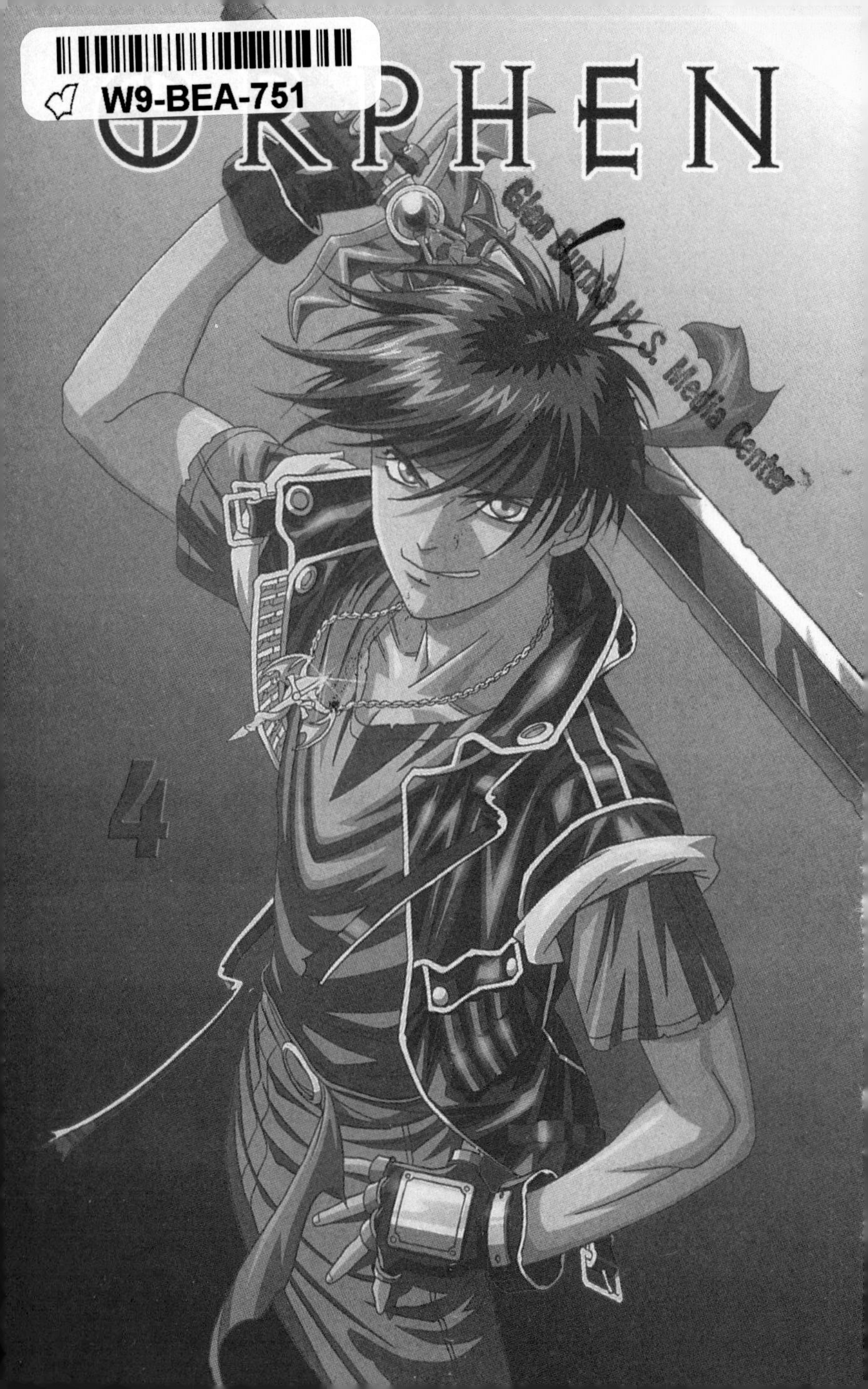
ORPHEN
4

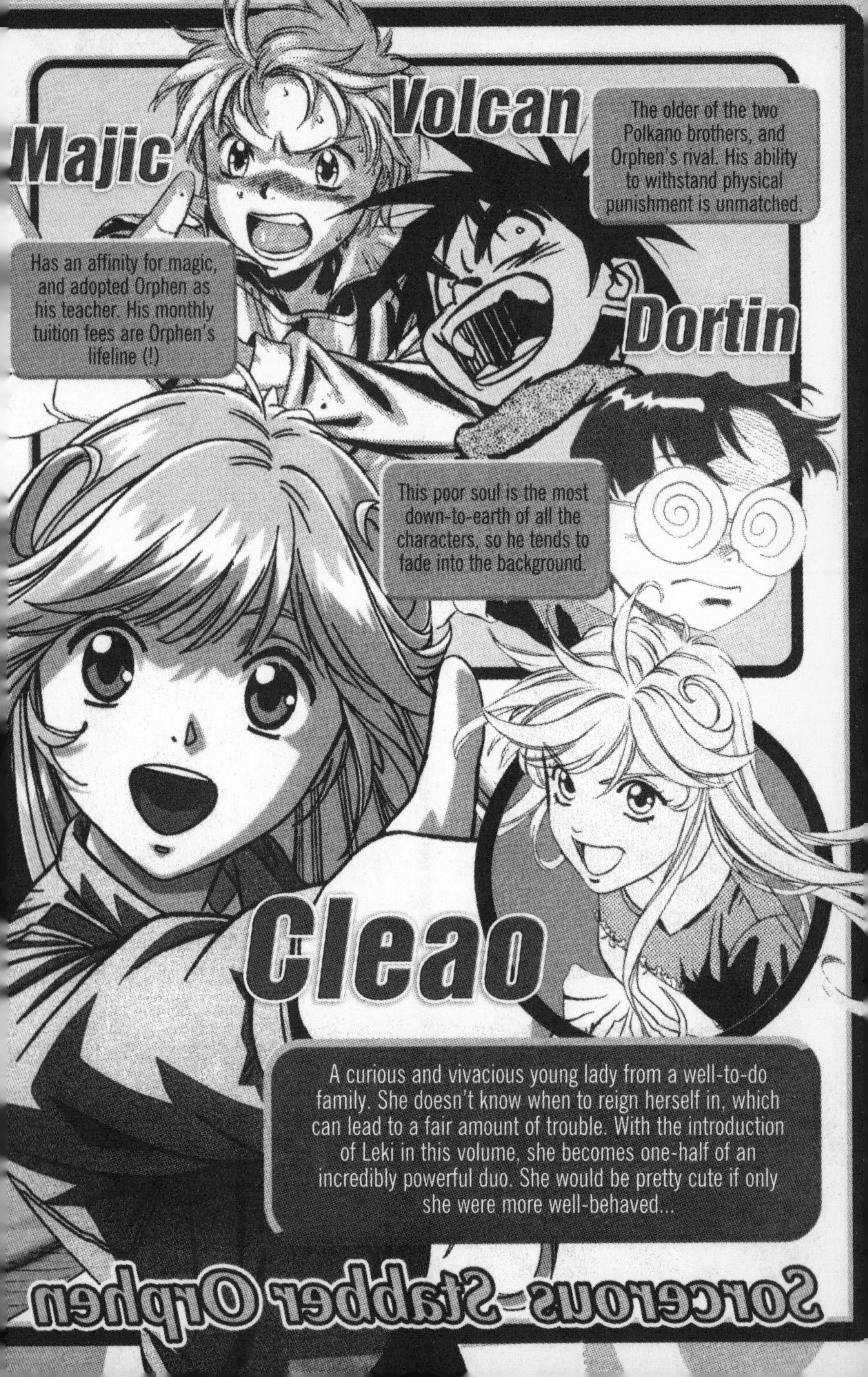
Majic
Has an affinity for magic, and adopted Orphen as his teacher. His monthly tuition fees are Orphen's lifeline (!)
Volcan
The older of the two Polkano brothers, and Orphen's rival. His ability to withstand physical punishment is unmatched.
Dortin
This poor soul is the most down-to-earth of all the characters, so he tends to fade into the background.
Cleao
A curious and vivacious young lady from a well-to-do family. She doesn't know when to reign herself in, which can lead to a fair amount of trouble. With the introduction of Leki in this volume, she becomes one-half of an incredibly powerful duo. She would be pretty cute if only she were more well-behaved...
Sorcerous Stabber Orphen

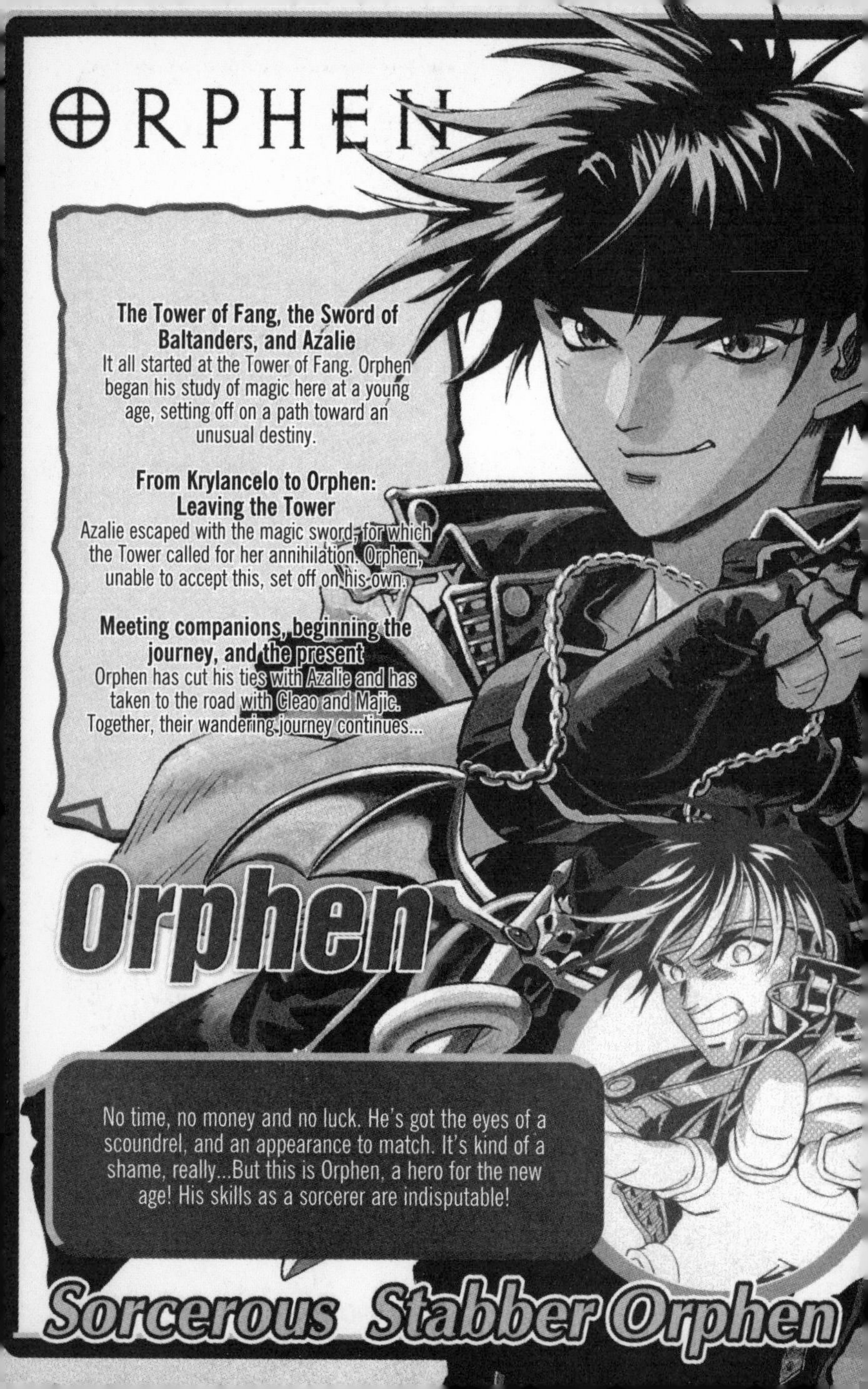
ORPHEN
The Tower of Fang, the Sword of Baltanders, and Azalie
It all started at the Tower of Fang. Orphen began his study of magic here at a young age, setting off on a path toward an unusual destiny.
From Krylancelo to Orphen: Leaving the Tower
Azalie escaped with the magic sword, for which the Tower called for her annihilation. Orphen, unable to accept this, set off on his own.
Meeting companions, beginning the journey, and the present
Orphen has cut his ties with Azalie and has taken to the road with Cleao and Majic. Together, their wandering journey continues...
Orphen
No time, no money and no luck. He's got the eyes of a scoundrel, and an appearance to match. It's kind of a shame, really...But this is Orphen, a hero for the new age! His skills as a sorcerer are indisputable!
Sorcerous Stabber Orphen

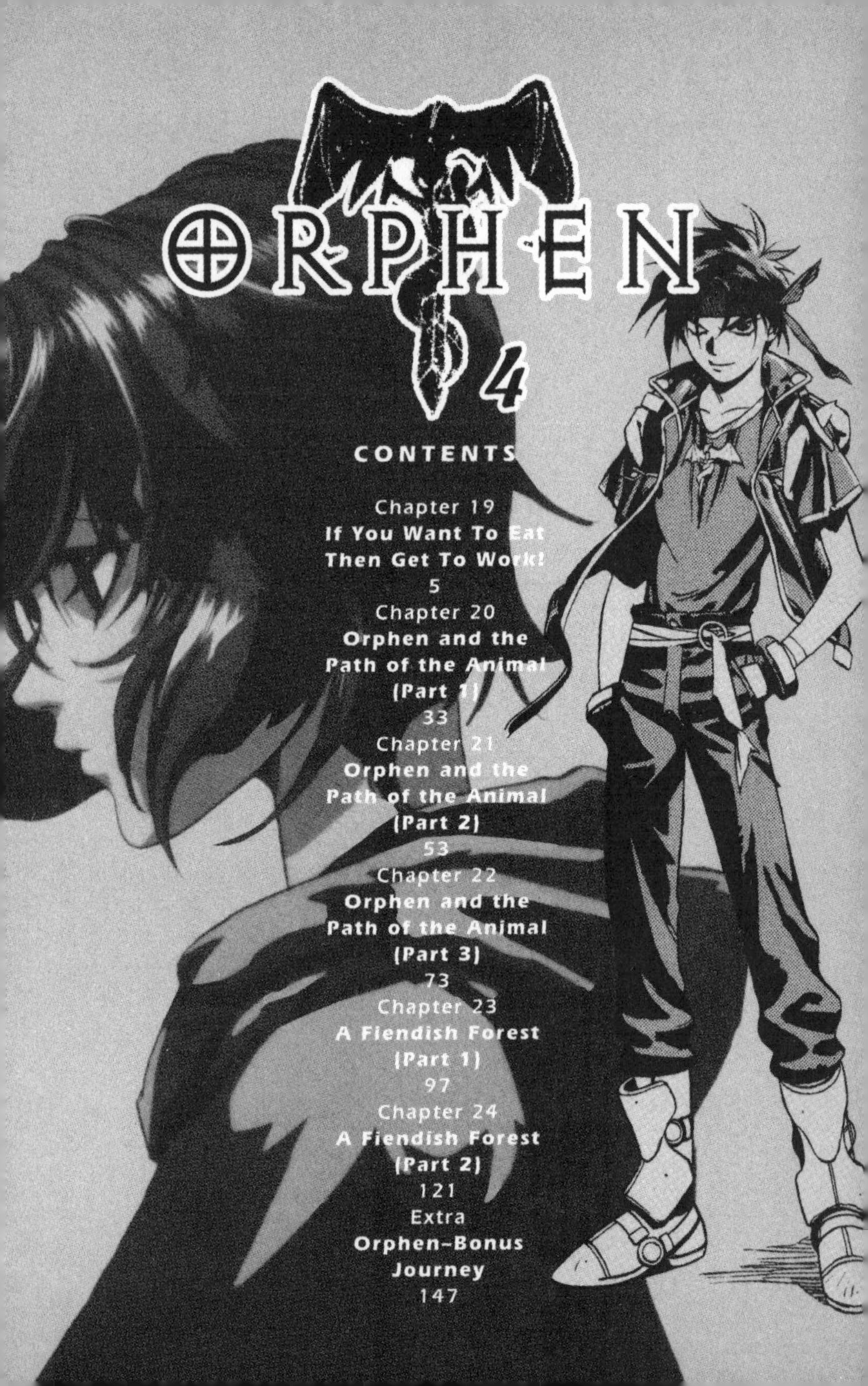

ORPHEN 4

CONTENTS

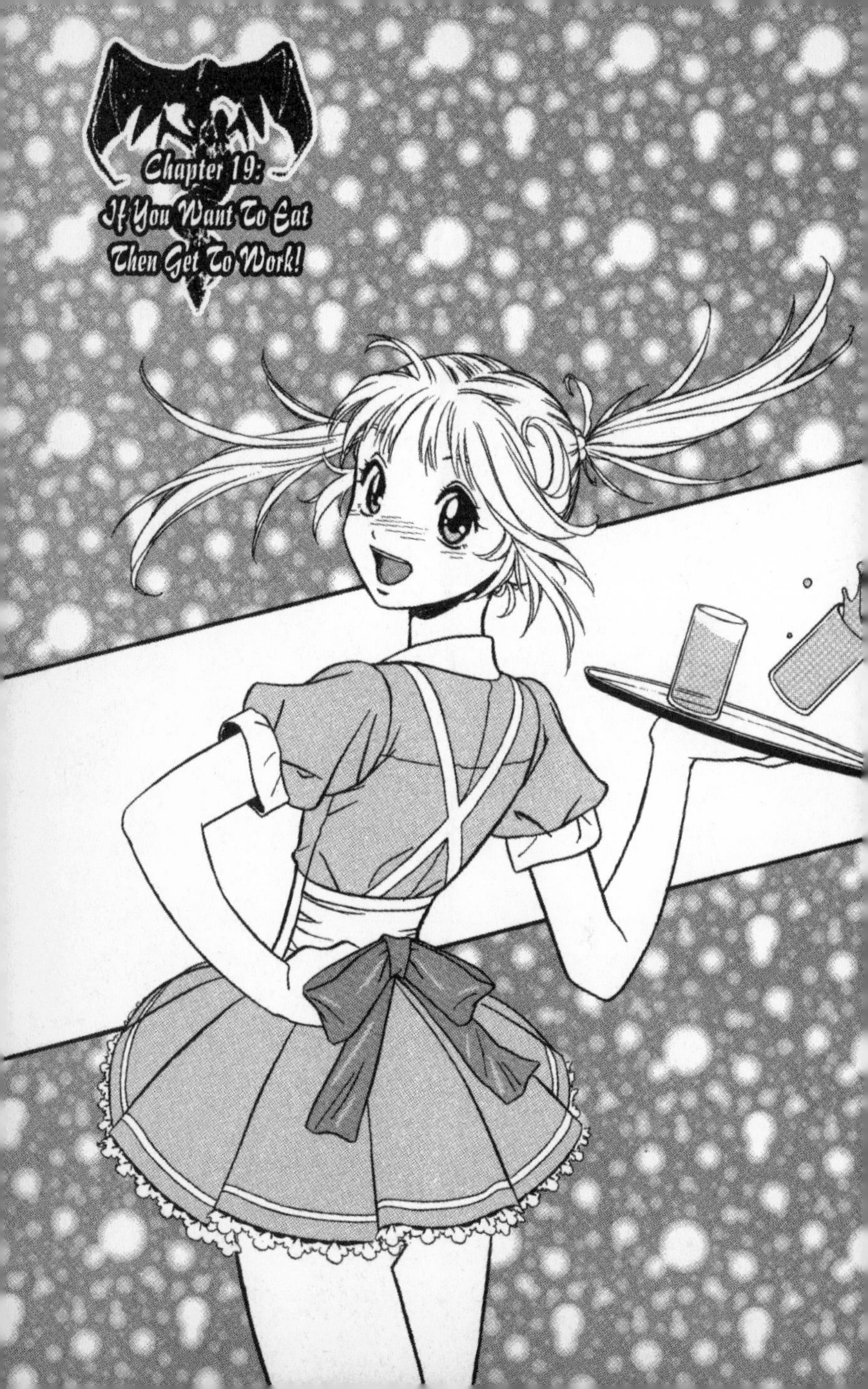
Chapter 19:
If You Want To Eat
Then Get To Work!

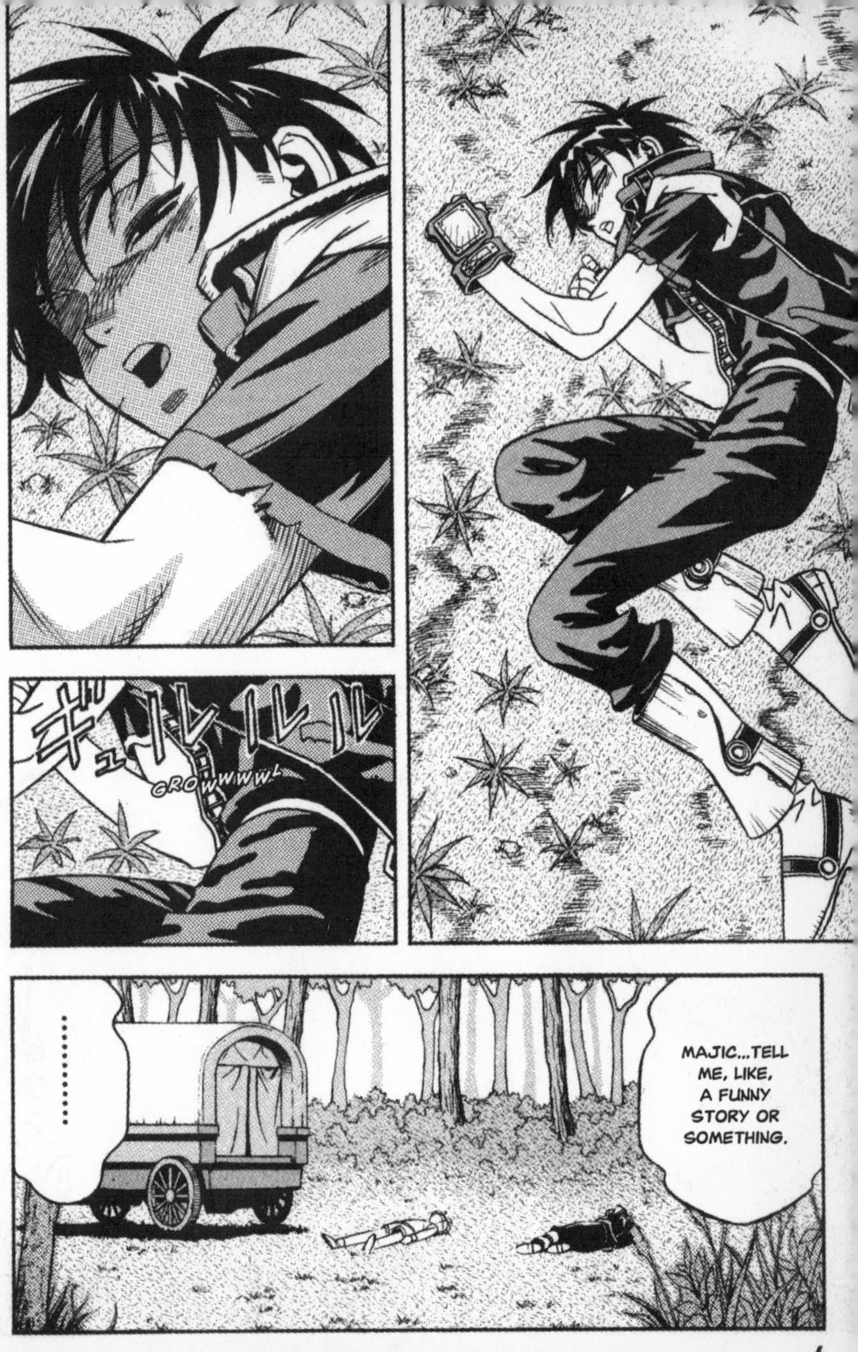
ギュルルル
GROWWWWL
MAJIC...TELL ME, LIKE, A FUNNY STORY OR SOMETHING.
......

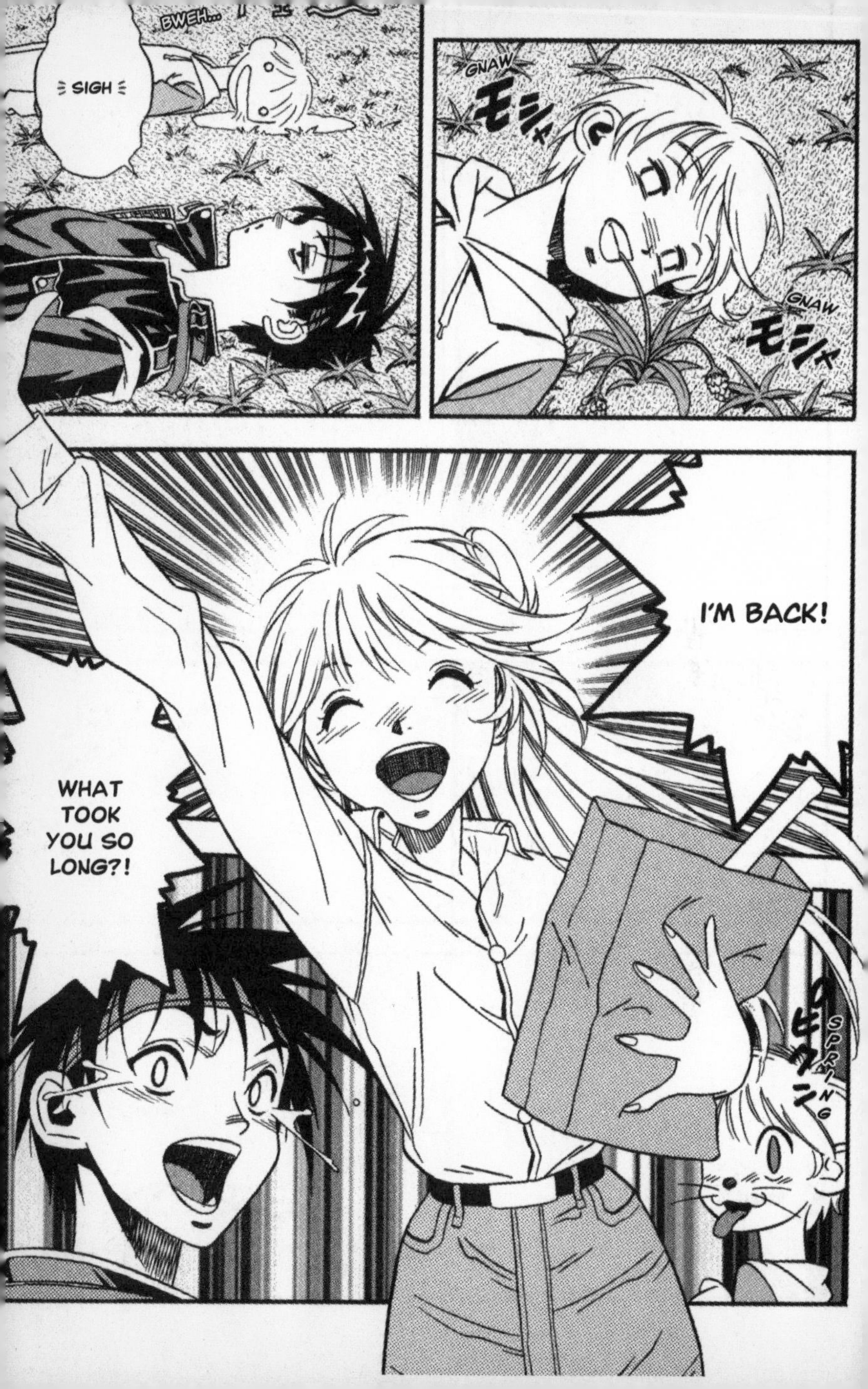
GNAW
モシャ
GNAW
モシャ
BWEH...
SIGH
I'M BACK!
SPRING
WHAT TOOK YOU SO LONG?!

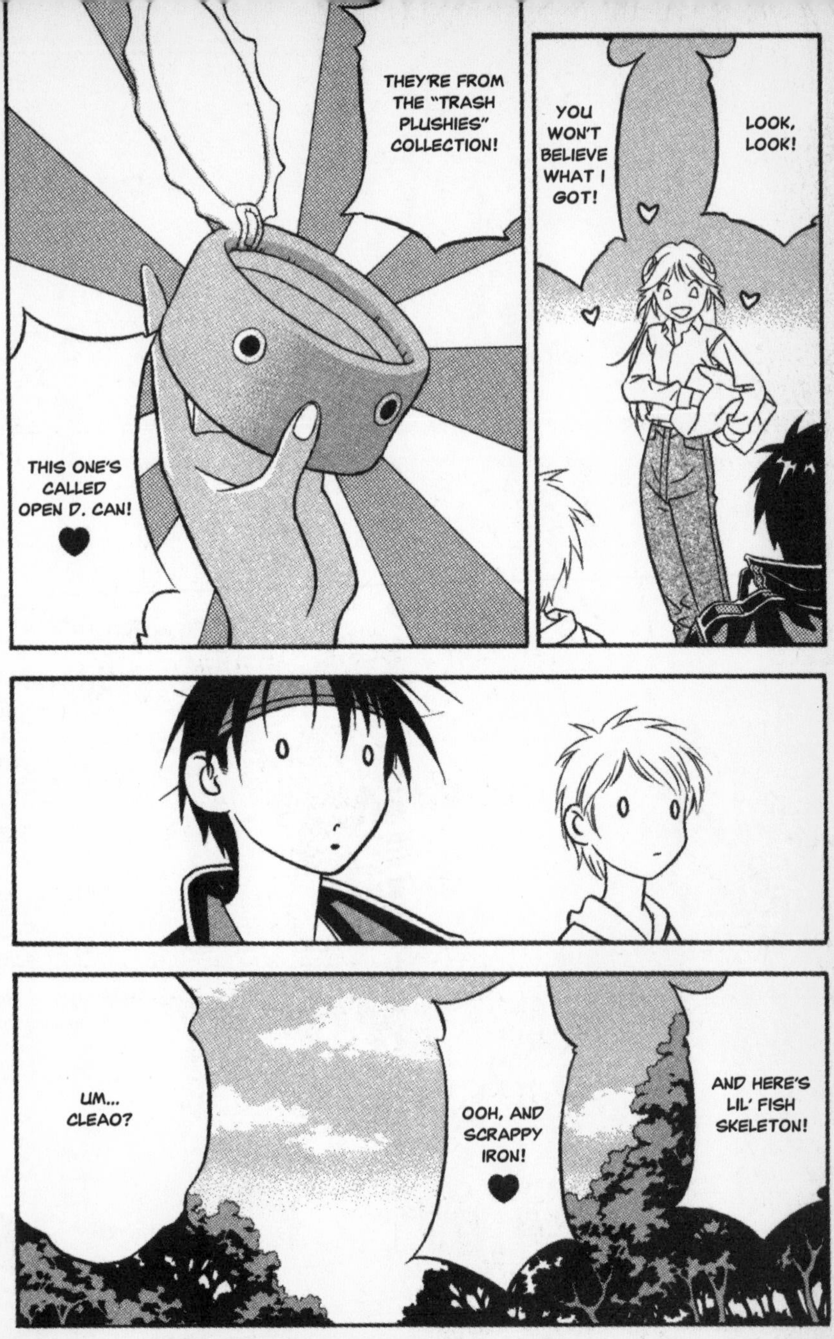
LOOK, LOOK!
YOU WON'T BELIEVE WHAT I GOT!
THEY'RE FROM THE "TRASH PLUSHIES" COLLECTION!
THIS ONE'S CALLED OPEN D. CAN!
AND HERE'S LIL' FISH SKELETON!
OOH, AND SCRAPPY IRON!
UM... CLEAO?

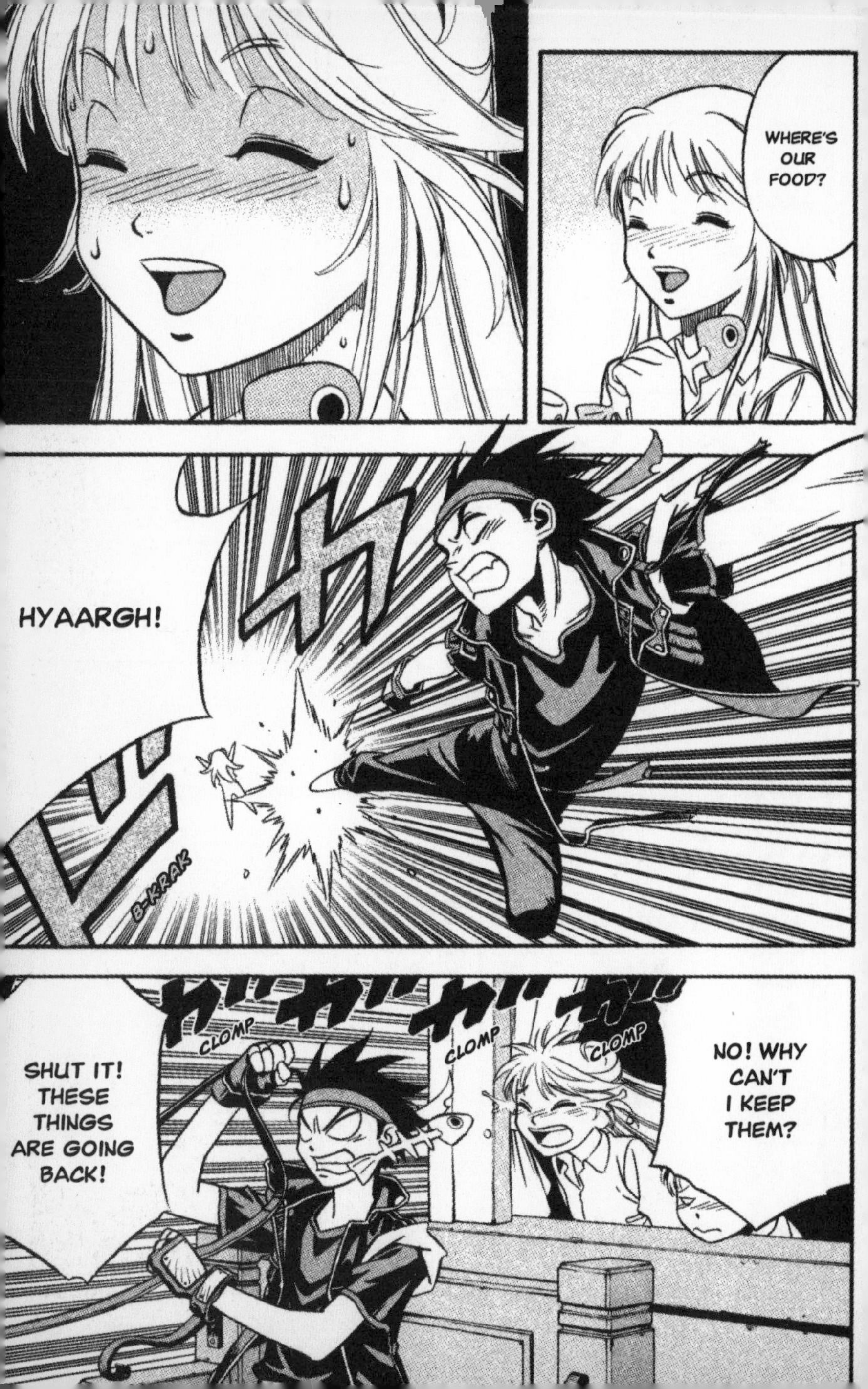
WHERE'S OUR FOOD?
HYAARGH!
B-KRAK
NO! WHY CAN'T I KEEP THEM?
CLOMP
CLOMP
CLOMP
SHUT IT! THESE THINGS ARE GOING BACK!

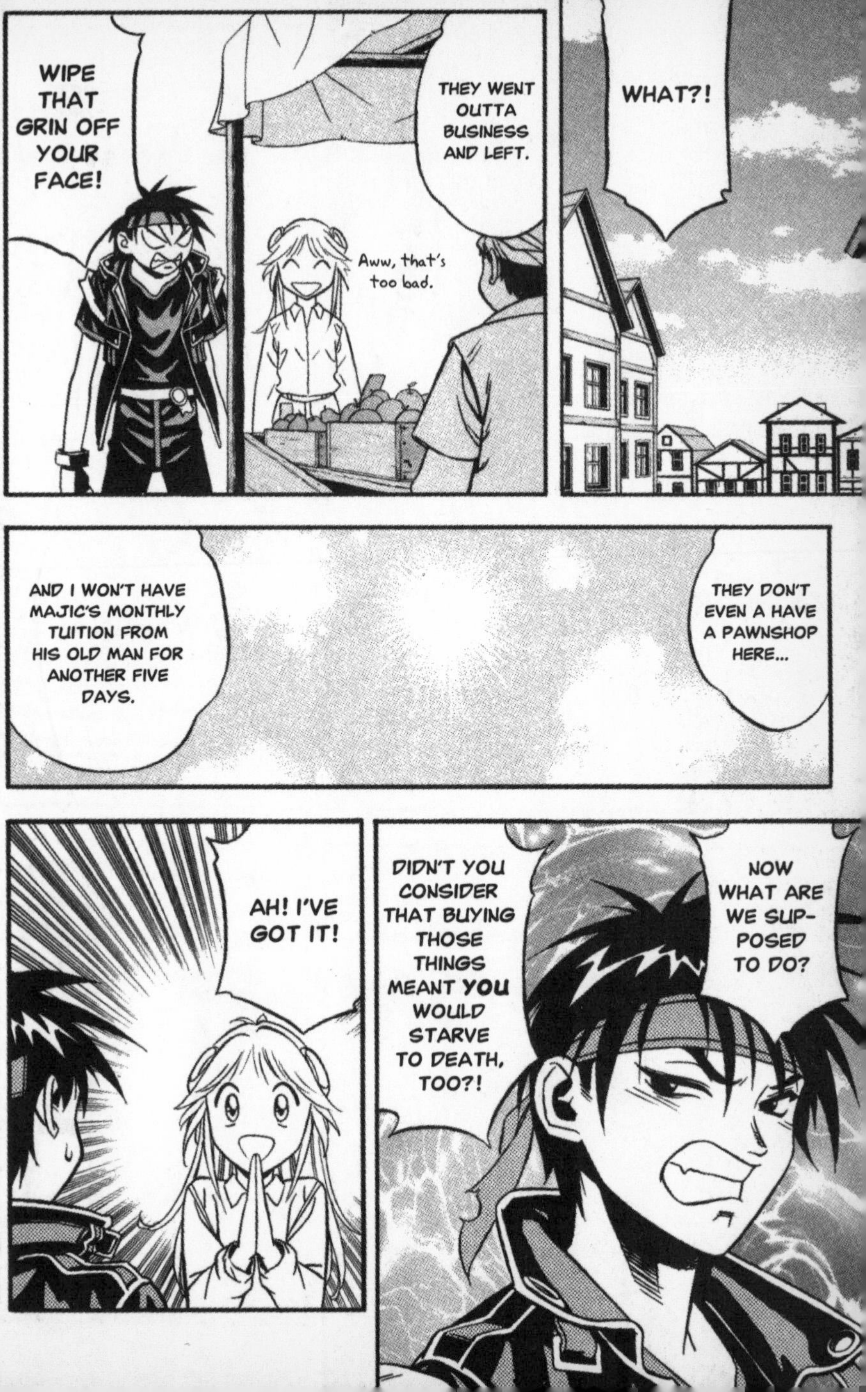
WHAT?!
THEY WENT OUTTA BUSINESS AND LEFT.
Aww, that's too bad.
WIPE THAT GRIN OFF YOUR FACE!
THEY DON'T EVEN A HAVE A PAWNSHOP HERE...
AND I WON'T HAVE MAJIC'S MONTHLY TUITION FROM HIS OLD MAN FOR ANOTHER FIVE DAYS.
NOW WHAT ARE WE SUP-POSED TO DO?
DIDN'T YOU CONSIDER THAT BUYING THOSE THINGS MEANT **YOU** WOULD STARVE TO DEATH, TOO?!
AH! I'VE GOT IT!

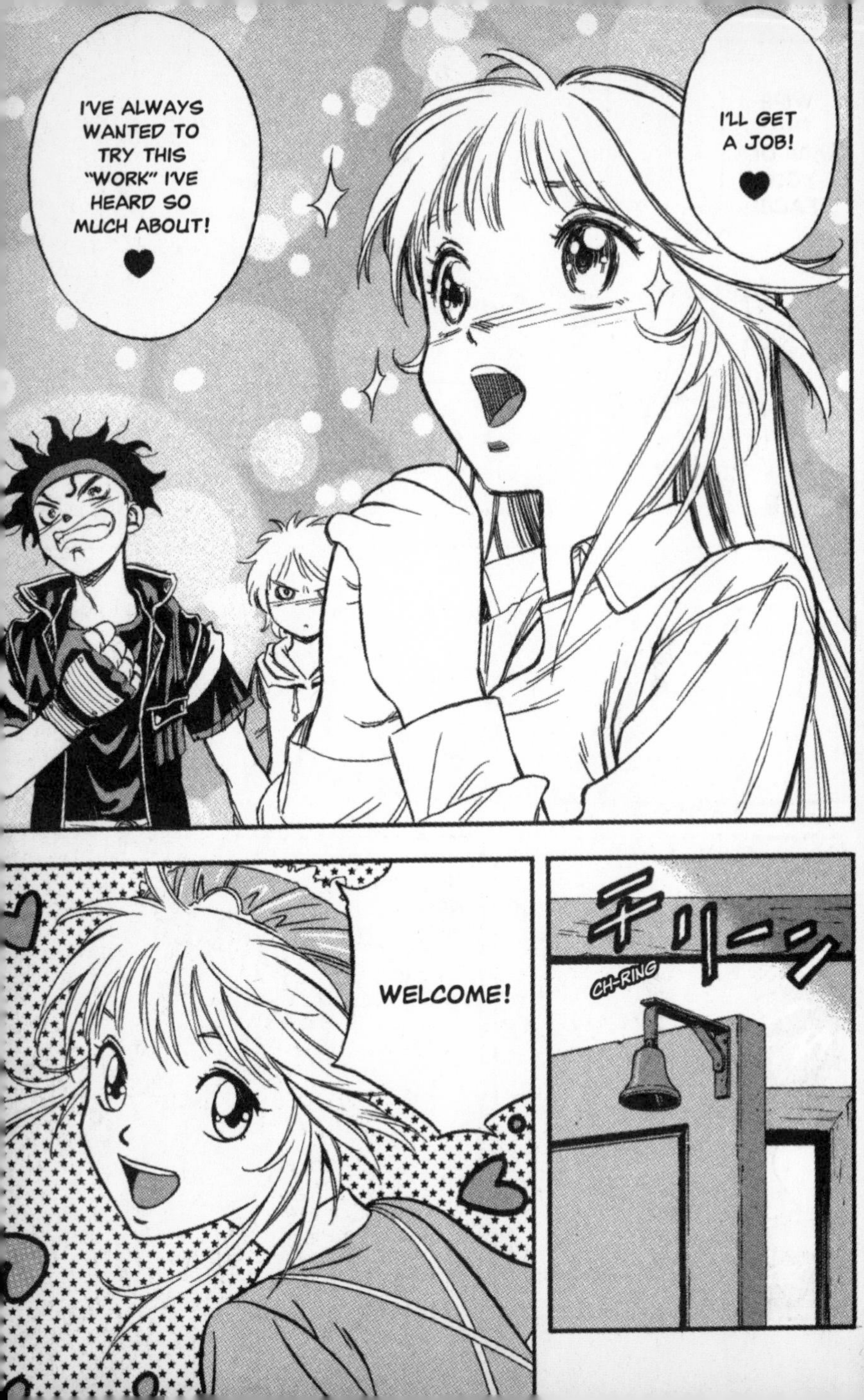
I'LL GET A JOB! ♥
I'VE ALWAYS WANTED TO TRY THIS "WORK" I'VE HEARD SO MUCH ABOUT! ♥
チリーン
CH-RING
WELCOME!

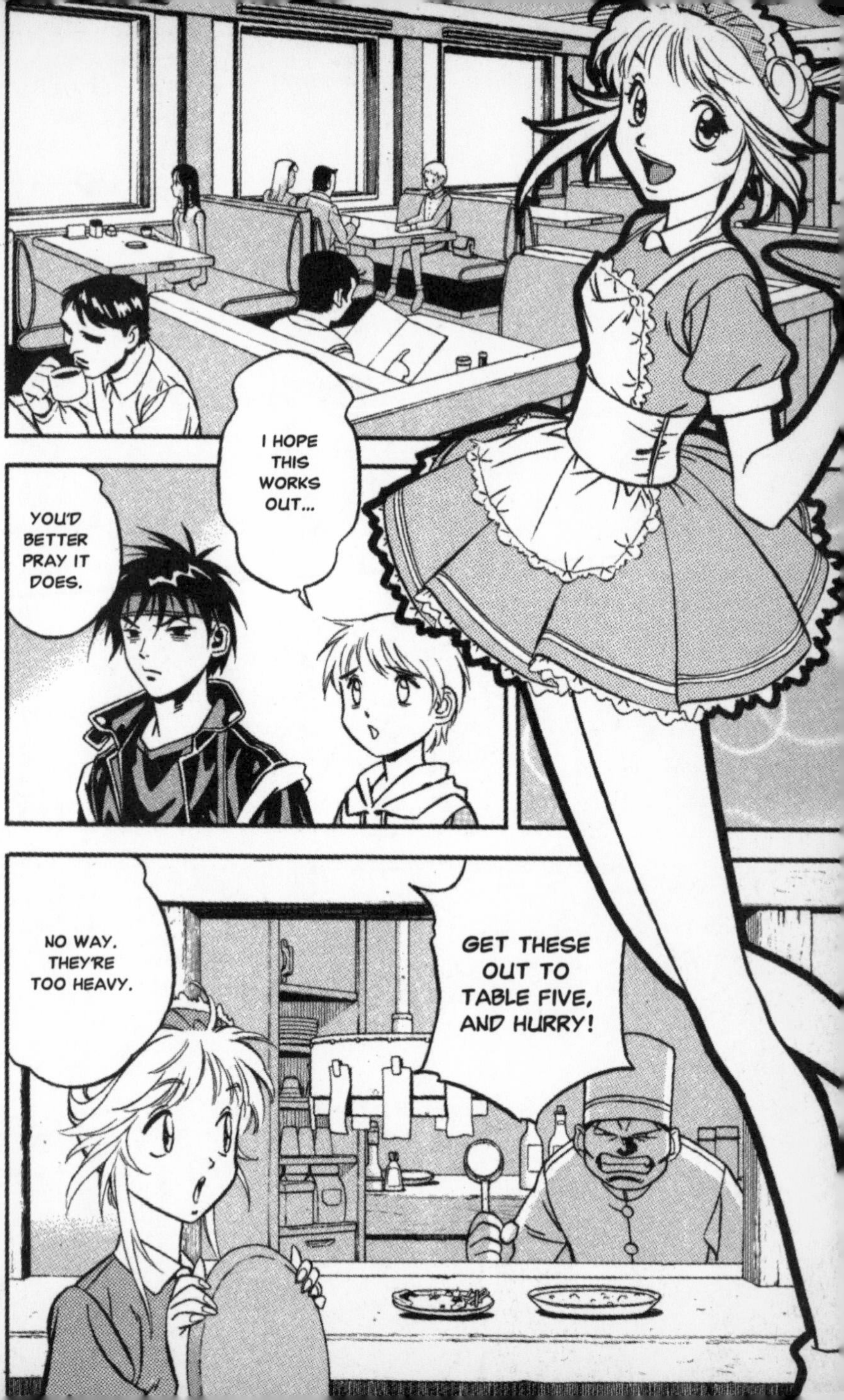
I HOPE THIS WORKS OUT...
YOU'D BETTER PRAY IT DOES.
GET THESE OUT TO TABLE FIVE, AND HURRY!
NO WAY. THEY'RE TOO HEAVY.

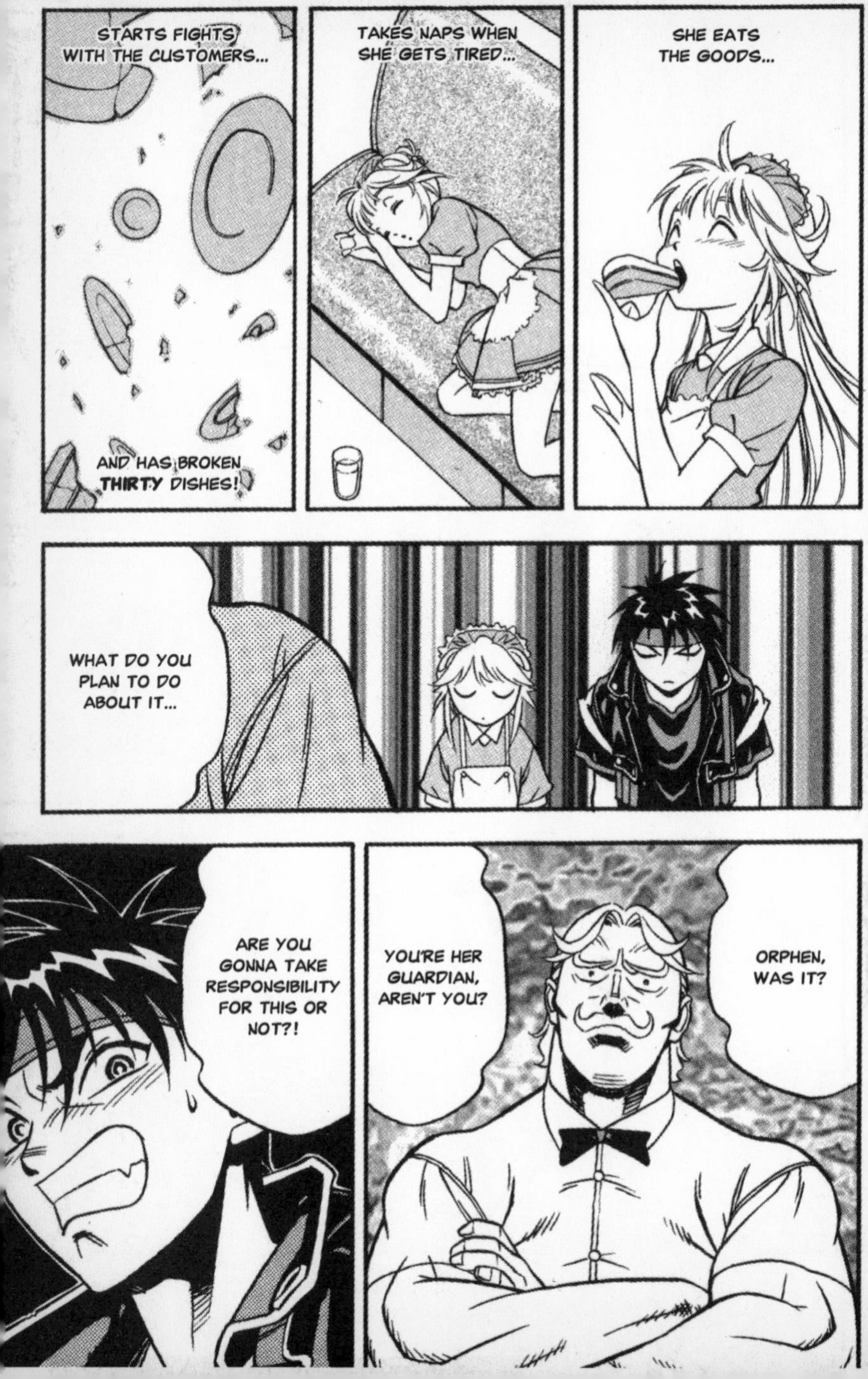
SHE EATS THE GOODS...
TAKES NAPS WHEN SHE GETS TIRED...
STARTS FIGHTS WITH THE CUSTOMERS...
AND HAS BROKEN THIRTY DISHES!
WHAT DO YOU PLAN TO DO ABOUT IT...
ORPHEN, WAS IT?
YOU'RE HER GUARDIAN, AREN'T YOU?
ARE YOU GONNA TAKE RESPONSIBILITY FOR THIS OR NOT?!

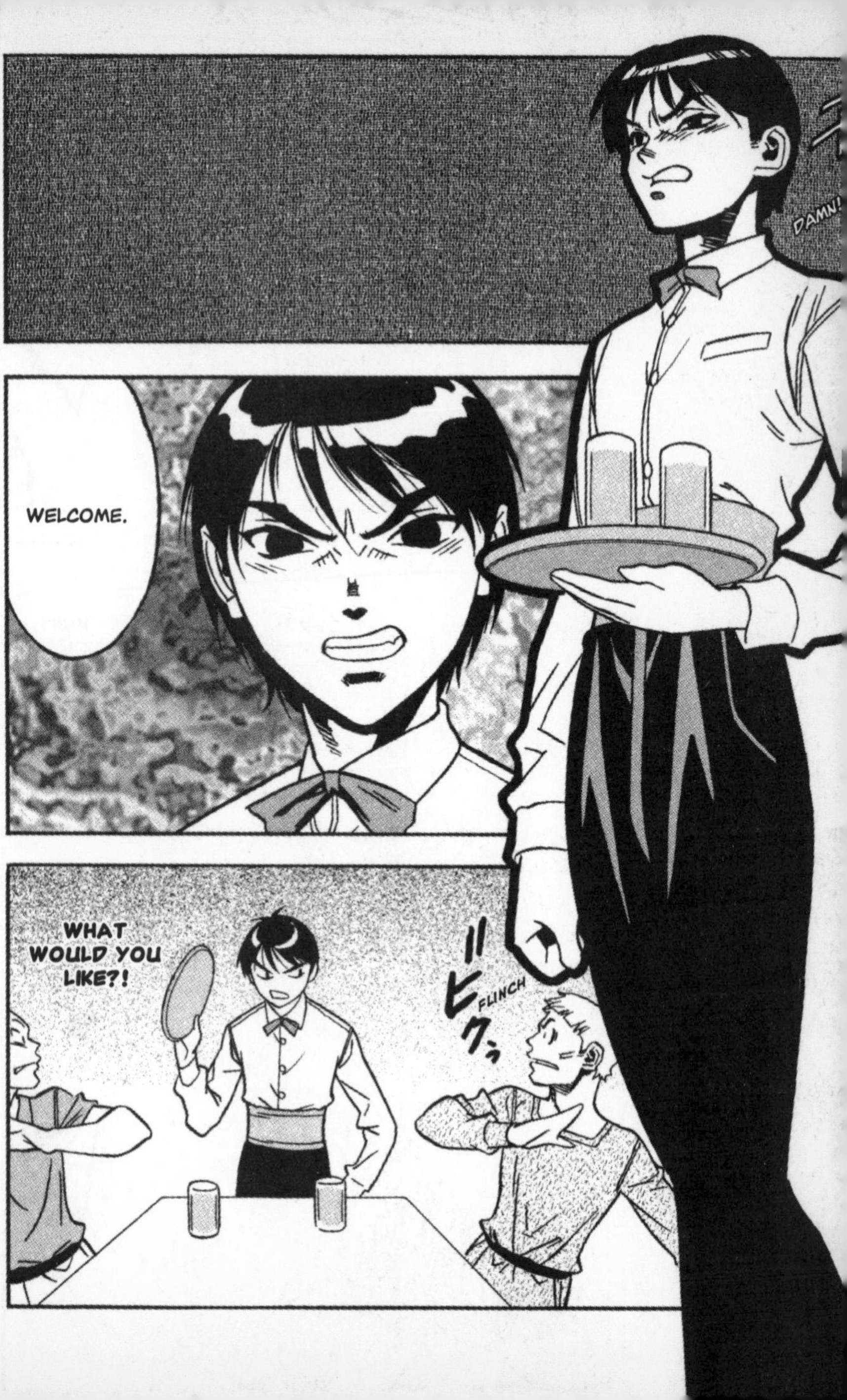
DAMN!
WELCOME.
WHAT WOULD YOU LIKE?!
FLINCH

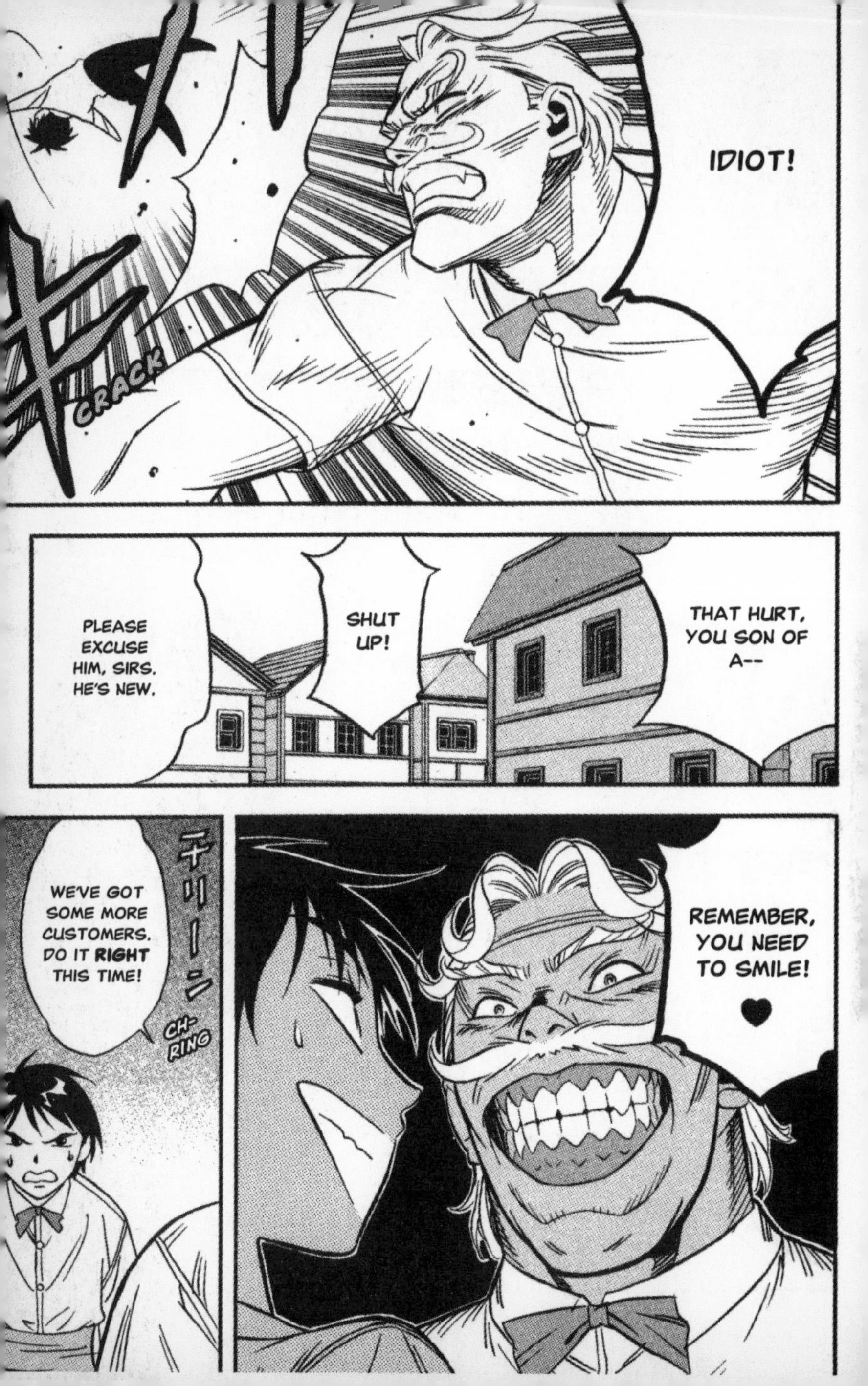
IDIOT!
CRACK
THAT HURT, YOU SON OF A--
SHUT UP!
PLEASE EXCUSE HIM, SIRS. HE'S NEW.
REMEMBER, YOU NEED TO SMILE! ♥
チリーン
CH-RING
WE'VE GOT SOME MORE CUSTOMERS. DO IT **RIGHT** THIS TIME!

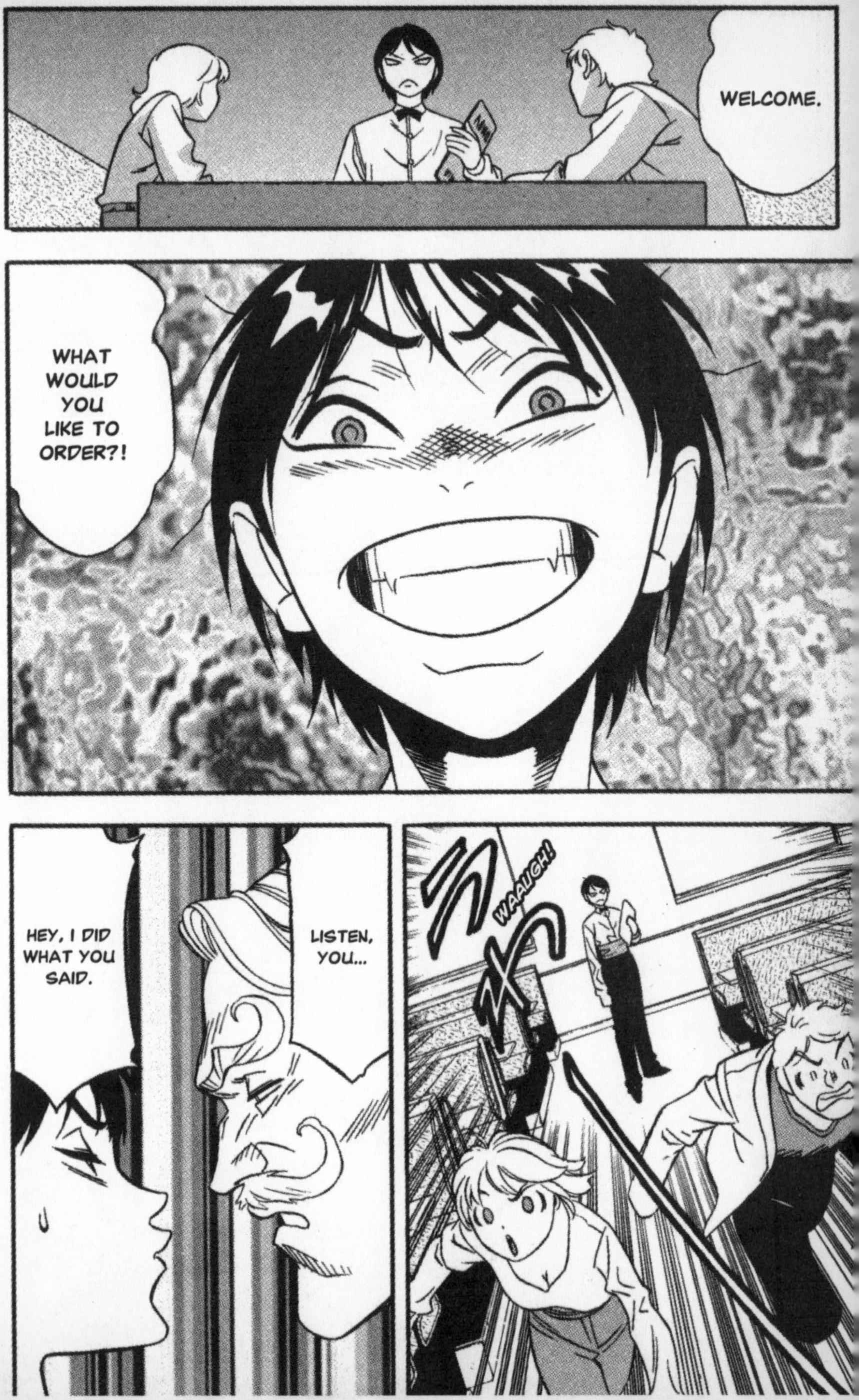
WELCOME.
WHAT WOULD YOU LIKE TO ORDER?!
WAAUGH!
LISTEN, YOU...
HEY, I DID WHAT YOU SAID.

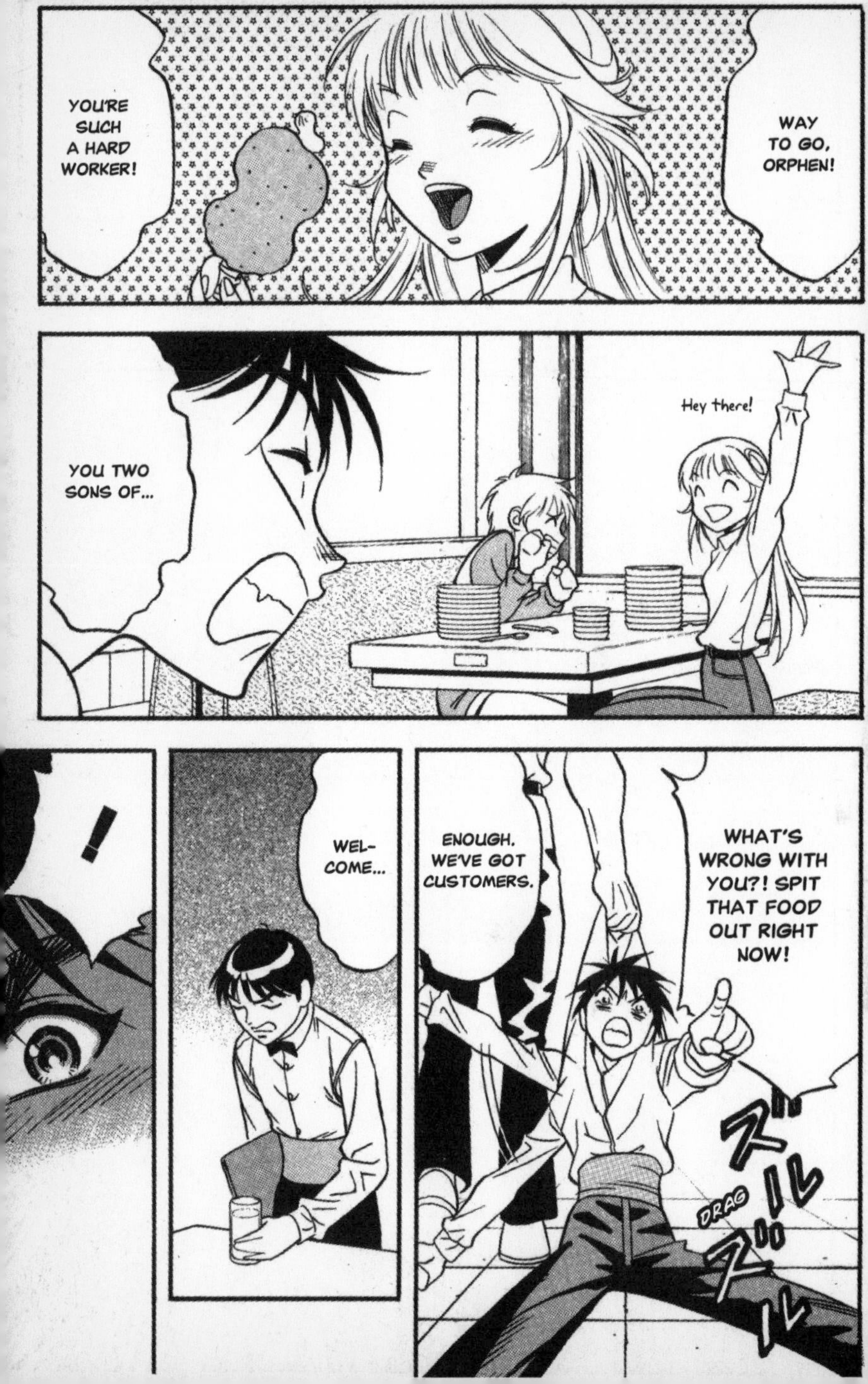
WAY TO GO, ORPHEN!
YOU'RE SUCH A HARD WORKER!
Hey there!
YOU TWO SONS OF...
WHAT'S WRONG WITH YOU?! SPIT THAT FOOD OUT RIGHT NOW!
ENOUGH. WE'VE GOT CUSTOMERS.
ズルズル
DRAG
WEL- COME...
!

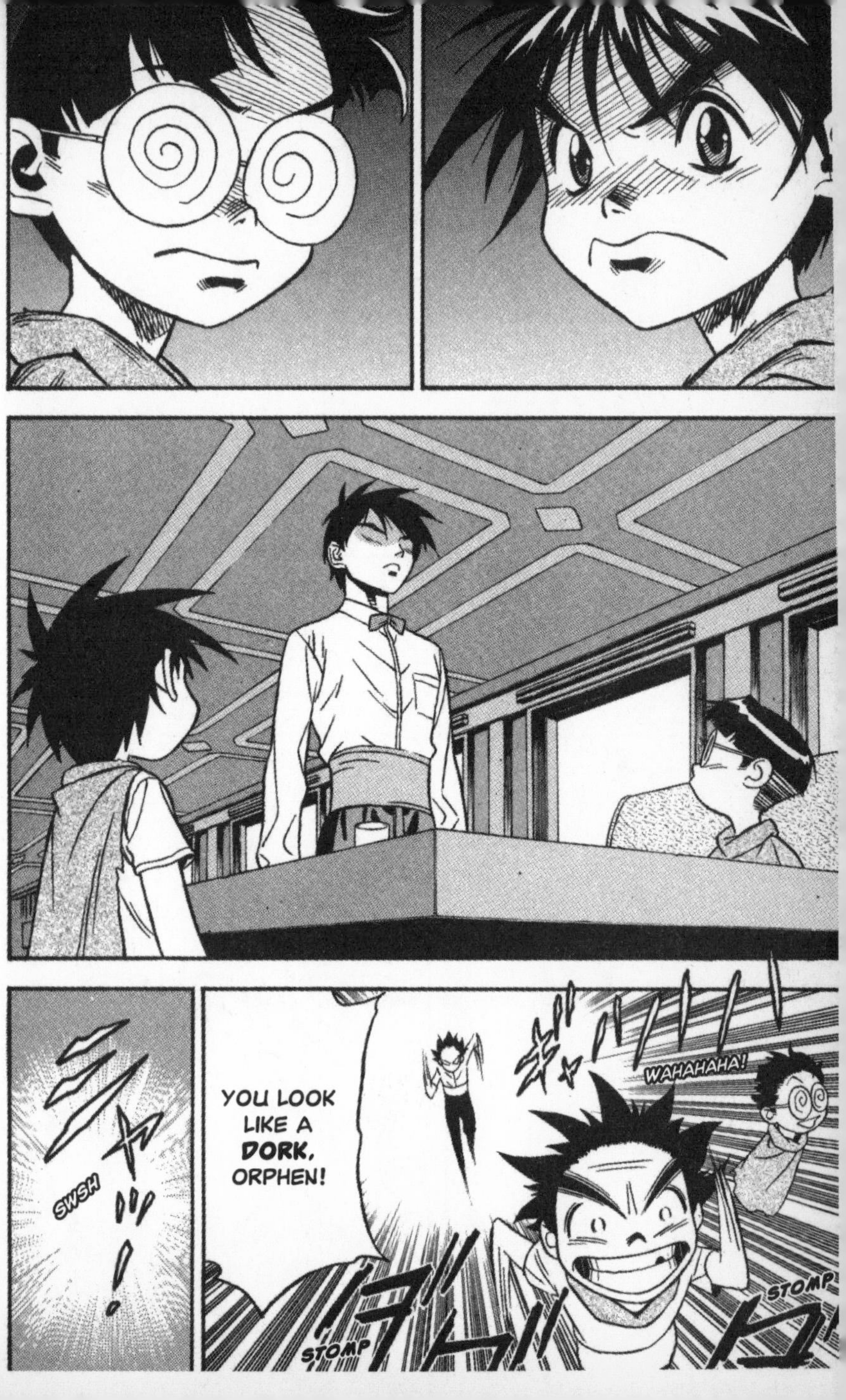

SWSH
WAHAHAHA!
YOU LOOK LIKE A **DORK,** ORPHEN!
STOMP
STOMP

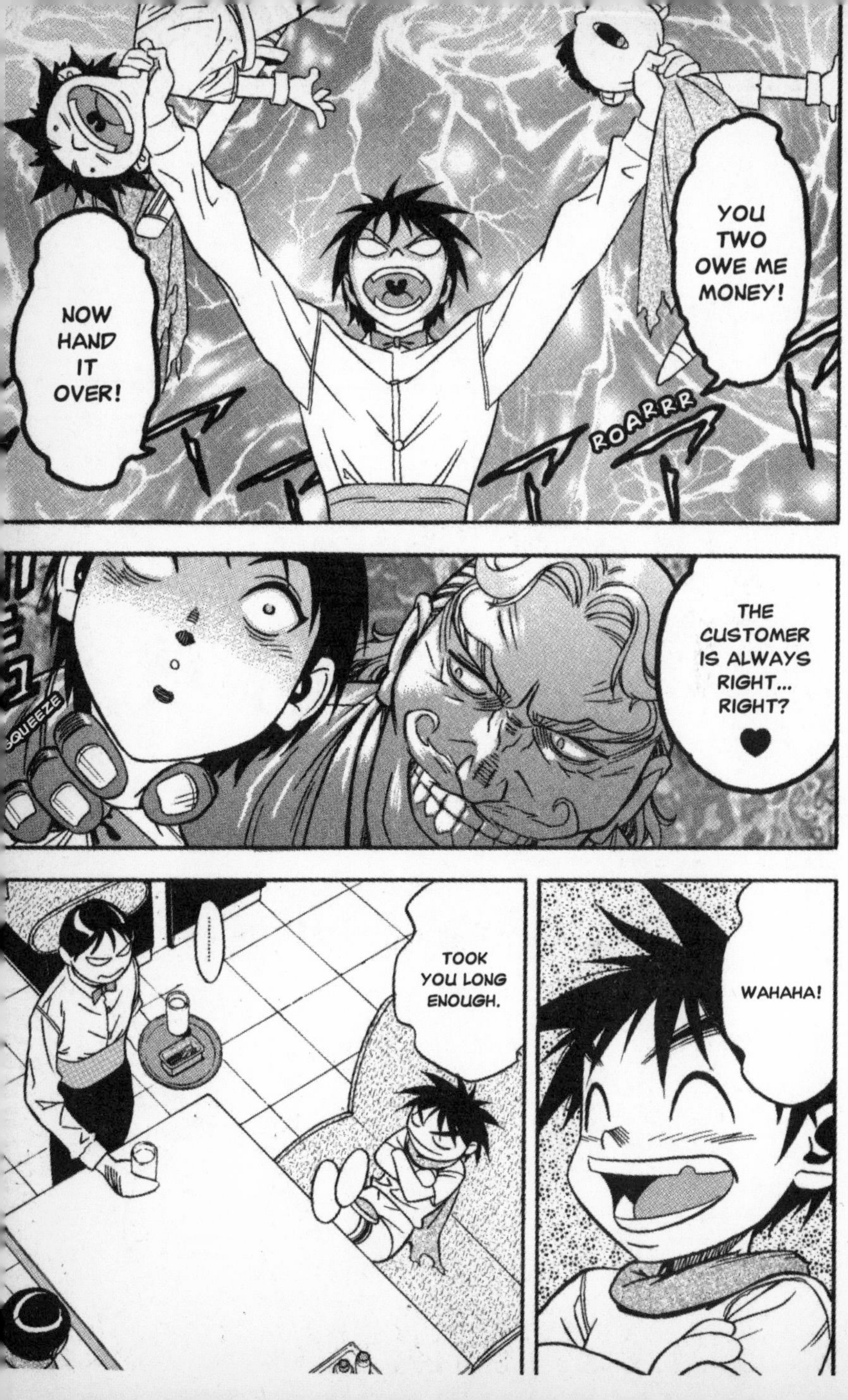

YOU TWO OWE ME MONEY!
NOW HAND IT OVER!
ROARRR
SQUEEZE
THE CUSTOMER IS ALWAYS RIGHT... RIGHT? ♥
TOOK YOU LONG ENOUGH.
WAHAHA!

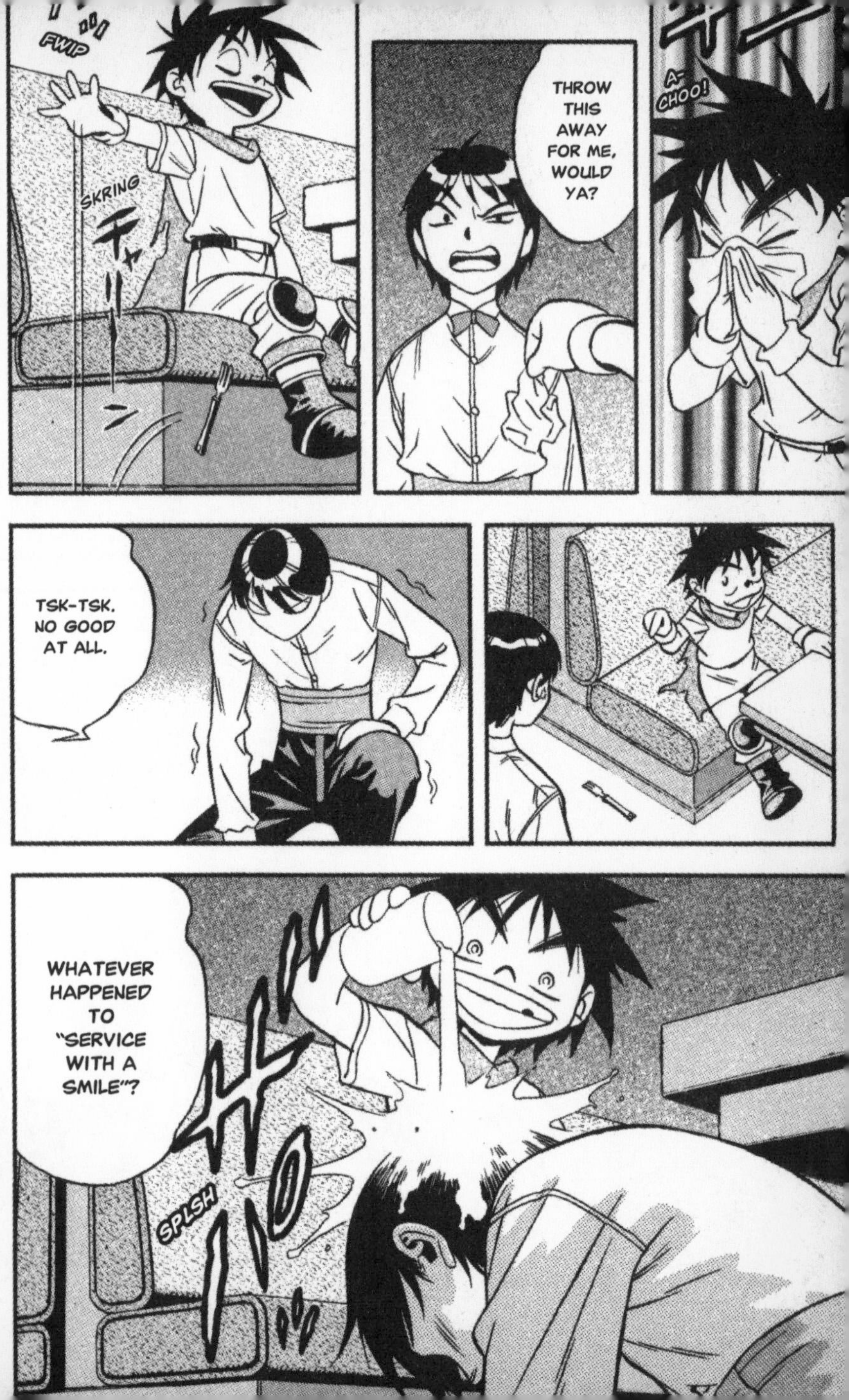
A-CHOO!
THROW THIS AWAY FOR ME, WOULD YA?
FWIP
SKRING
TSK-TSK. NO GOOD AT ALL.
WHATEVER HAPPENED TO "SERVICE WITH A SMILE"?
SPLSH

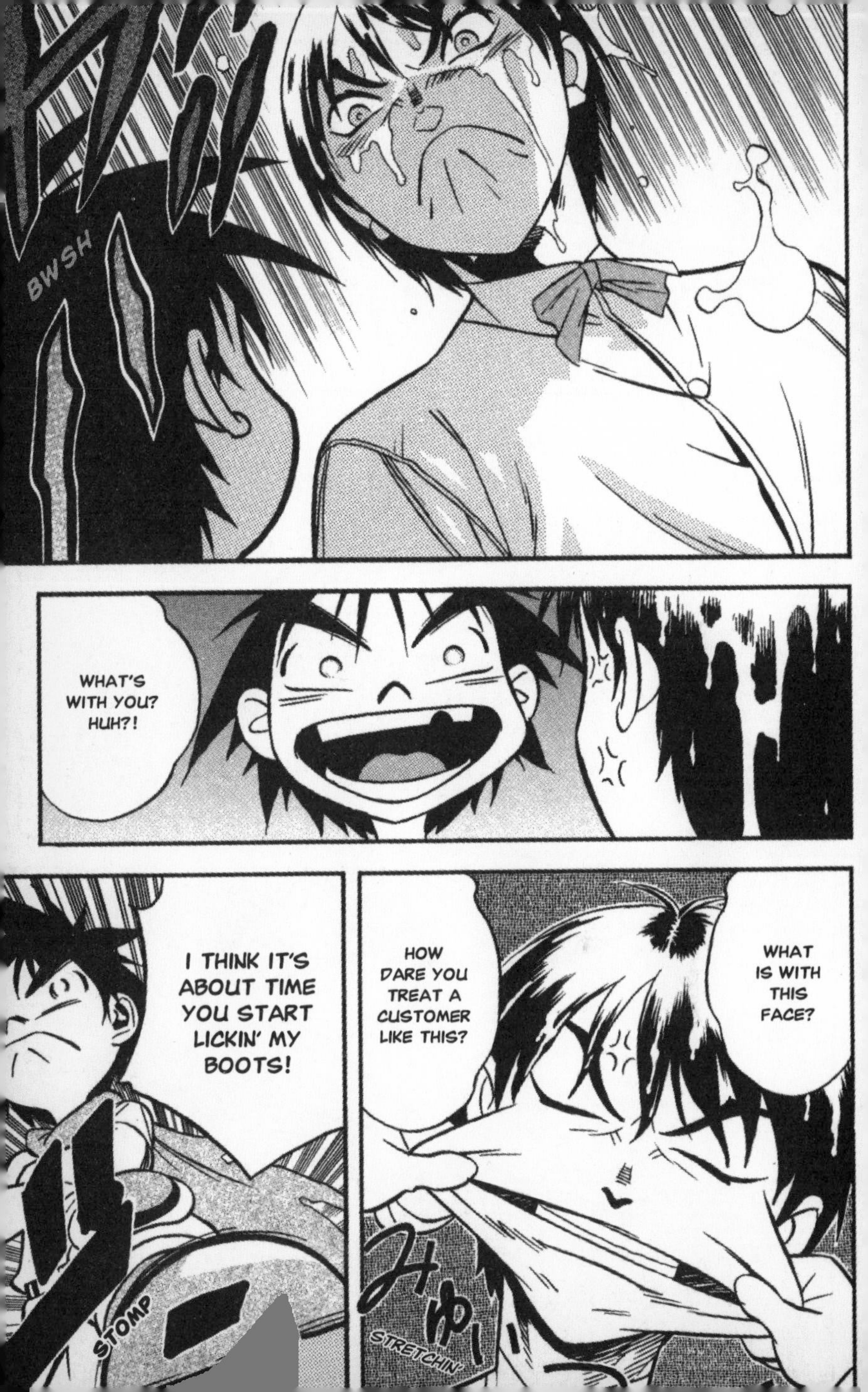
BWSH
WHAT'S WITH YOU? HUH?!
WHAT IS WITH THIS FACE?
HOW DARE YOU TREAT A CUSTOMER LIKE THIS?
みゅ
STRETCHIN'
I THINK IT'S ABOUT TIME YOU START LICKIN' MY BOOTS!
STOMP

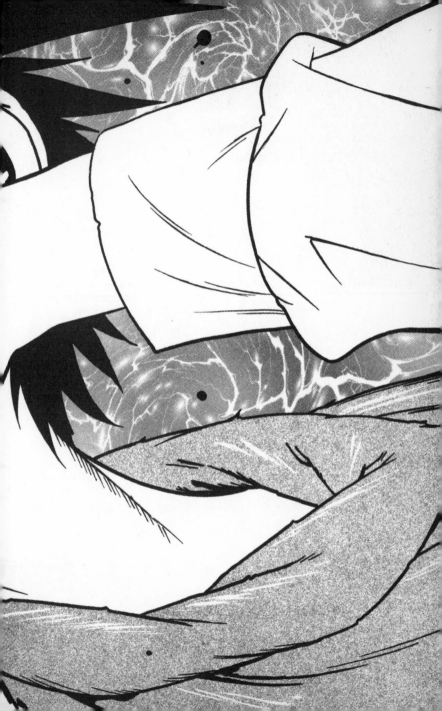

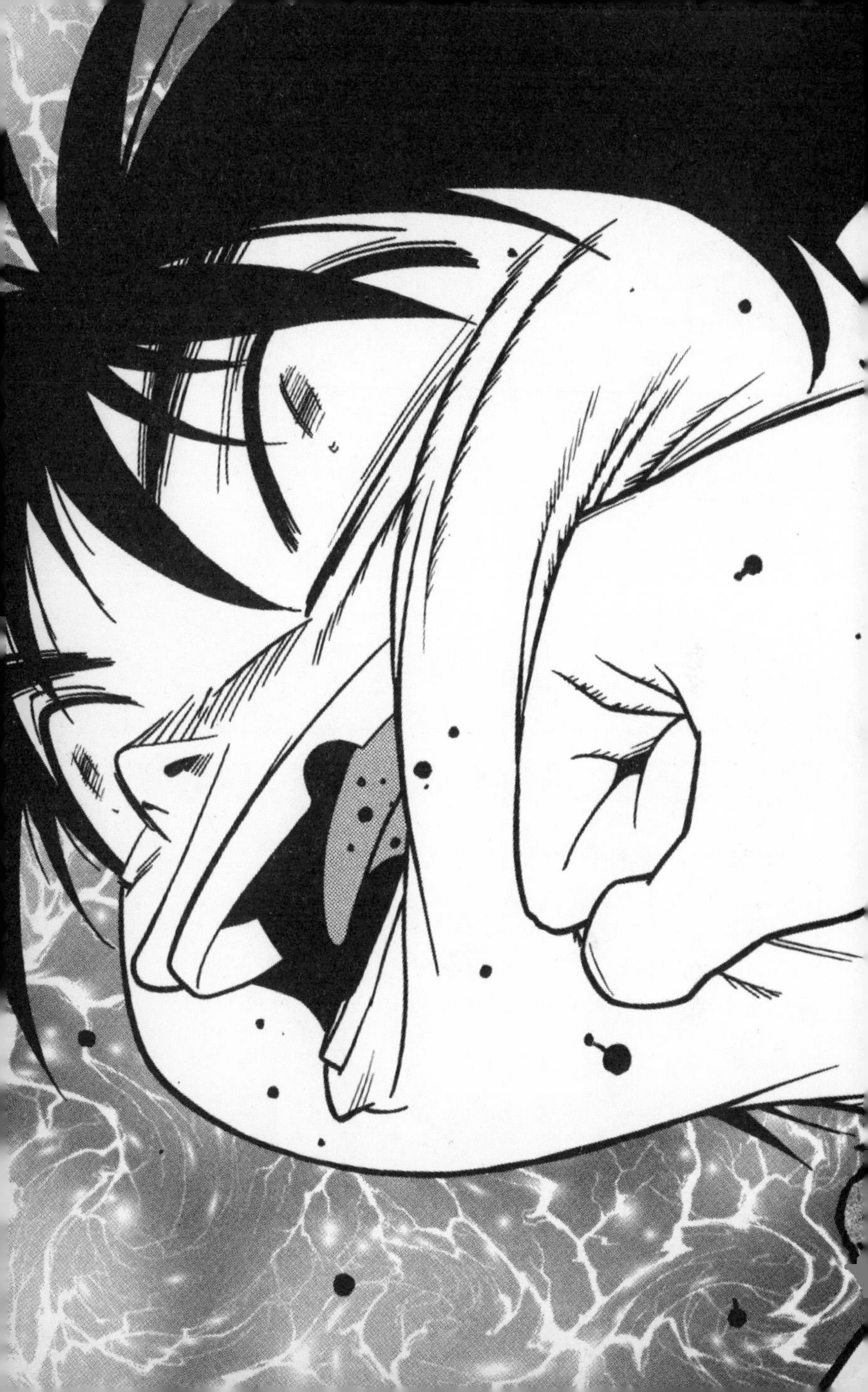

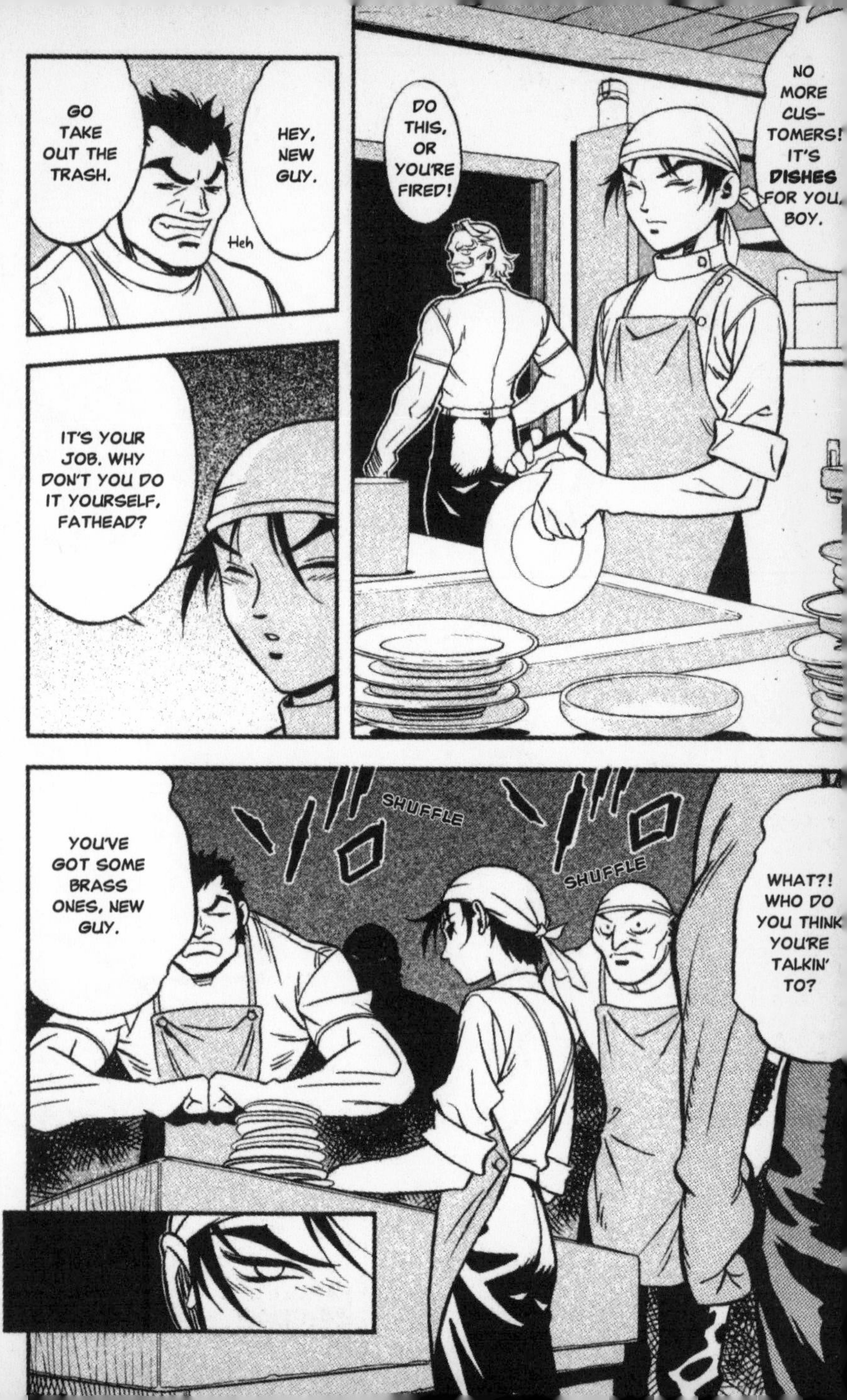
NO MORE CUS-TOMERS! IT'S **DISHES** FOR YOU, BOY.
DO THIS, OR YOU'RE FIRED!
HEY, NEW GUY.
GO TAKE OUT THE TRASH.
Heh
IT'S YOUR JOB. WHY DON'T YOU DO IT YOURSELF, FATHEAD?
WHAT?! WHO DO YOU THINK YOU'RE TALKIN' TO?
SHUFFLE
SHUFFLE
YOU'VE GOT SOME BRASS ONES, NEW GUY.

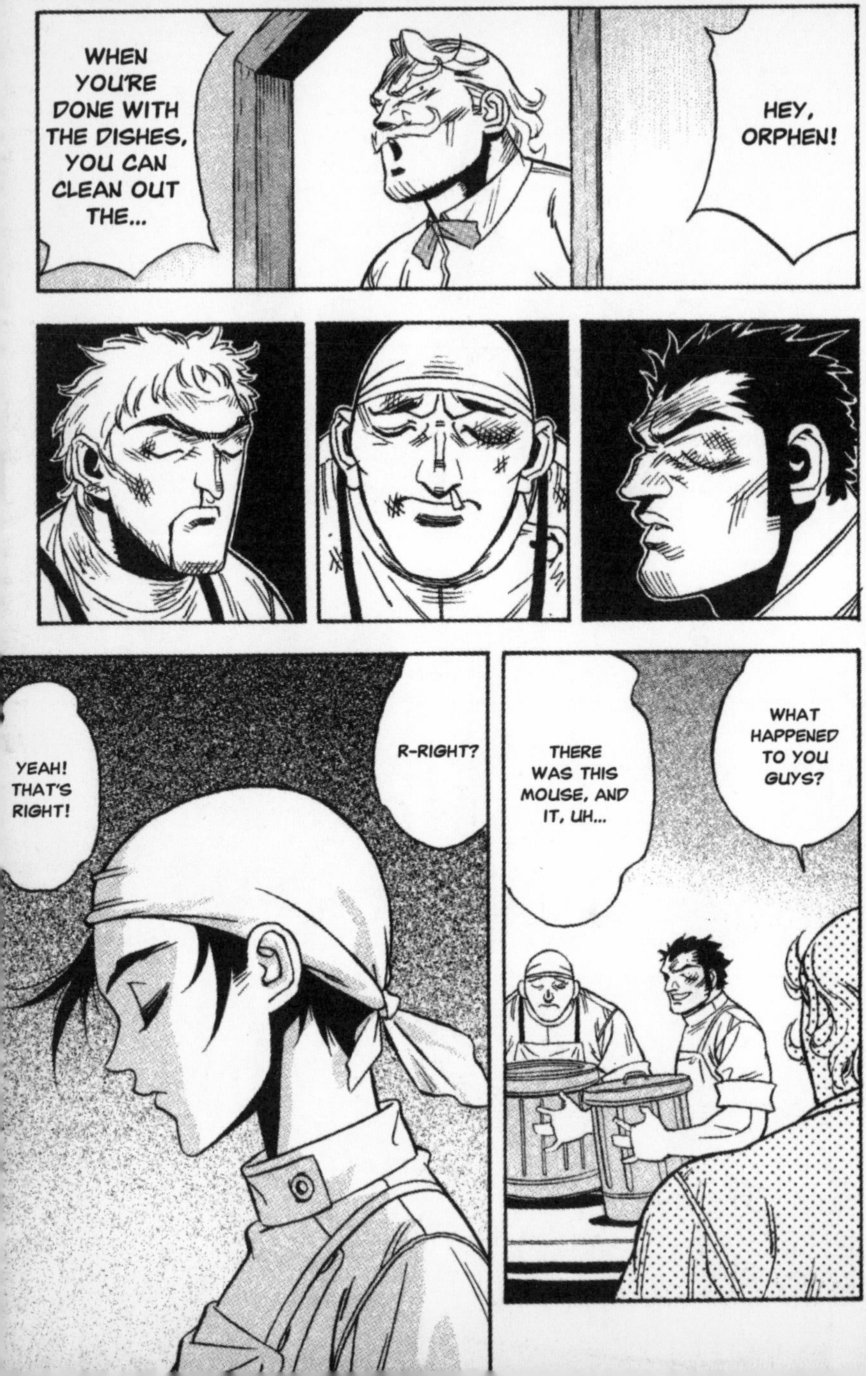
HEY, ORPHEN!
WHEN YOU'RE DONE WITH THE DISHES, YOU CAN CLEAN OUT THE...
WHAT HAPPENED TO YOU GUYS?
THERE WAS THIS MOUSE, AND IT, UH...
R-RIGHT?
YEAH! THAT'S RIGHT!

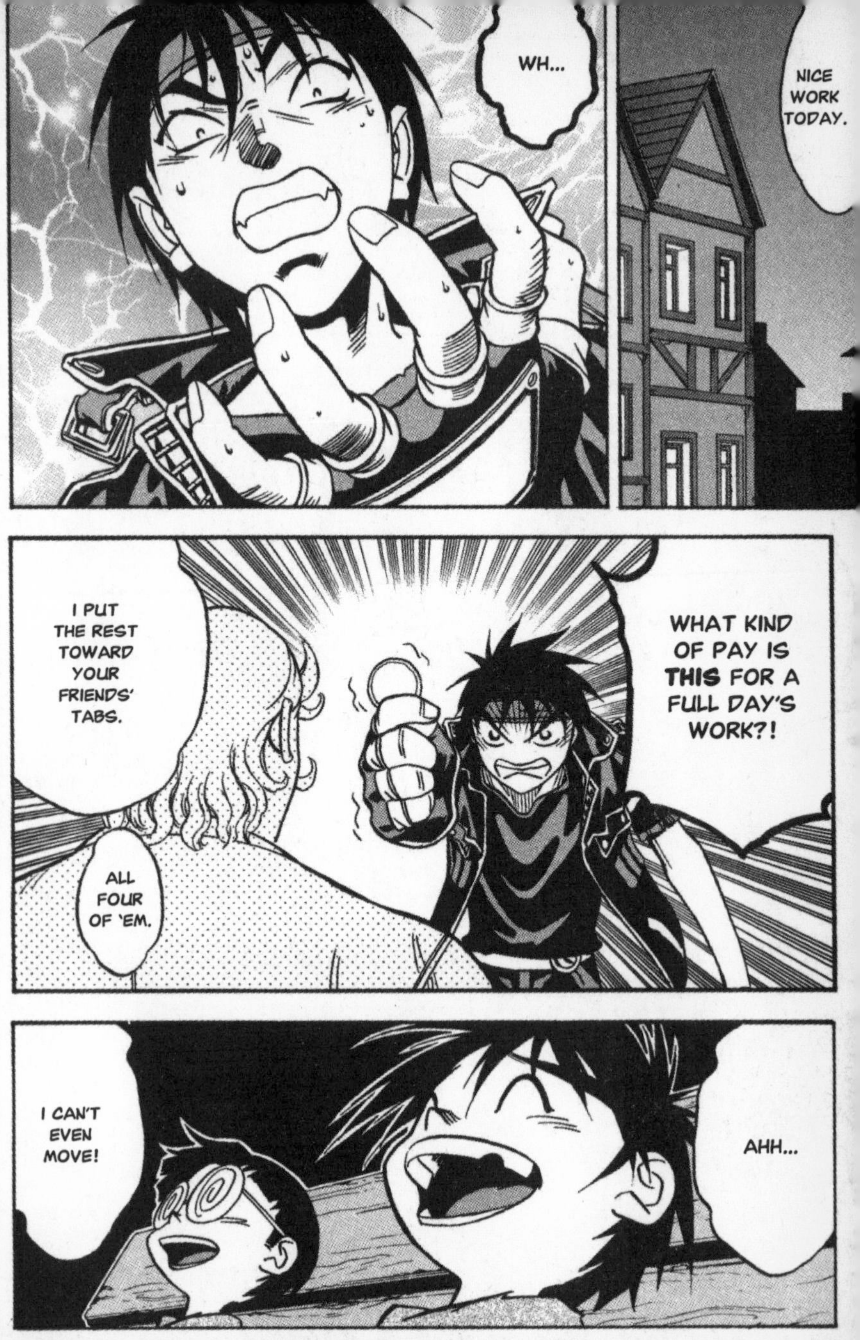
NICE WORK TODAY.
WH...
WHAT KIND OF PAY IS **THIS** FOR A FULL DAY'S WORK?!
I PUT THE REST TOWARD YOUR FRIENDS' TABS.
ALL FOUR OF 'EM.
AHH...
I CAN'T EVEN MOVE!

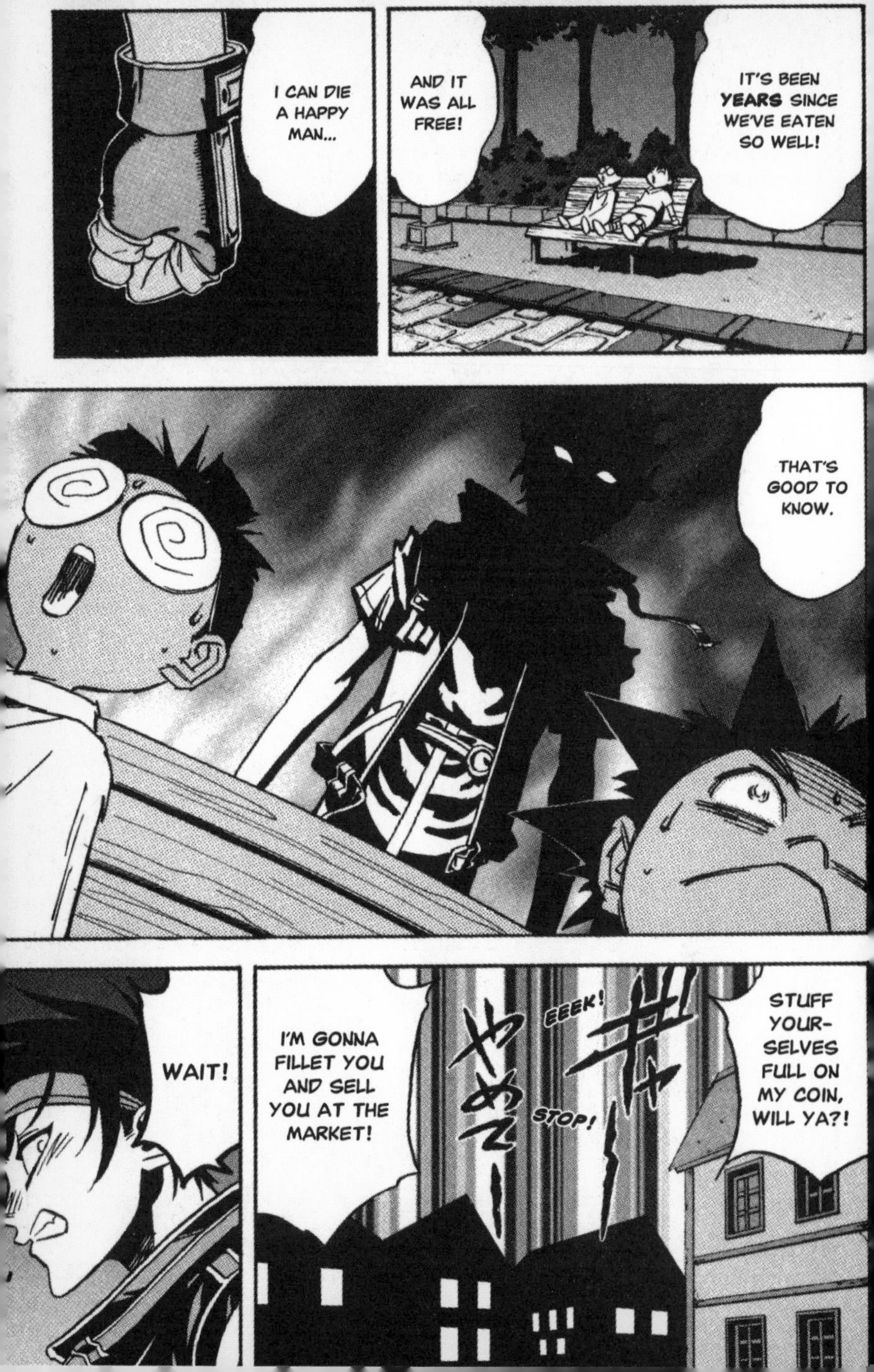
IT'S BEEN YEARS SINCE WE'VE EATEN SO WELL!
AND IT WAS ALL FREE!
I CAN DIE A HAPPY MAN...
THAT'S GOOD TO KNOW.
STUFF YOUR-SELVES FULL ON MY COIN, WILL YA?!
EEEK!
STOP!
I'M GONNA FILLET YOU AND SELL YOU AT THE MARKET!
WAIT!

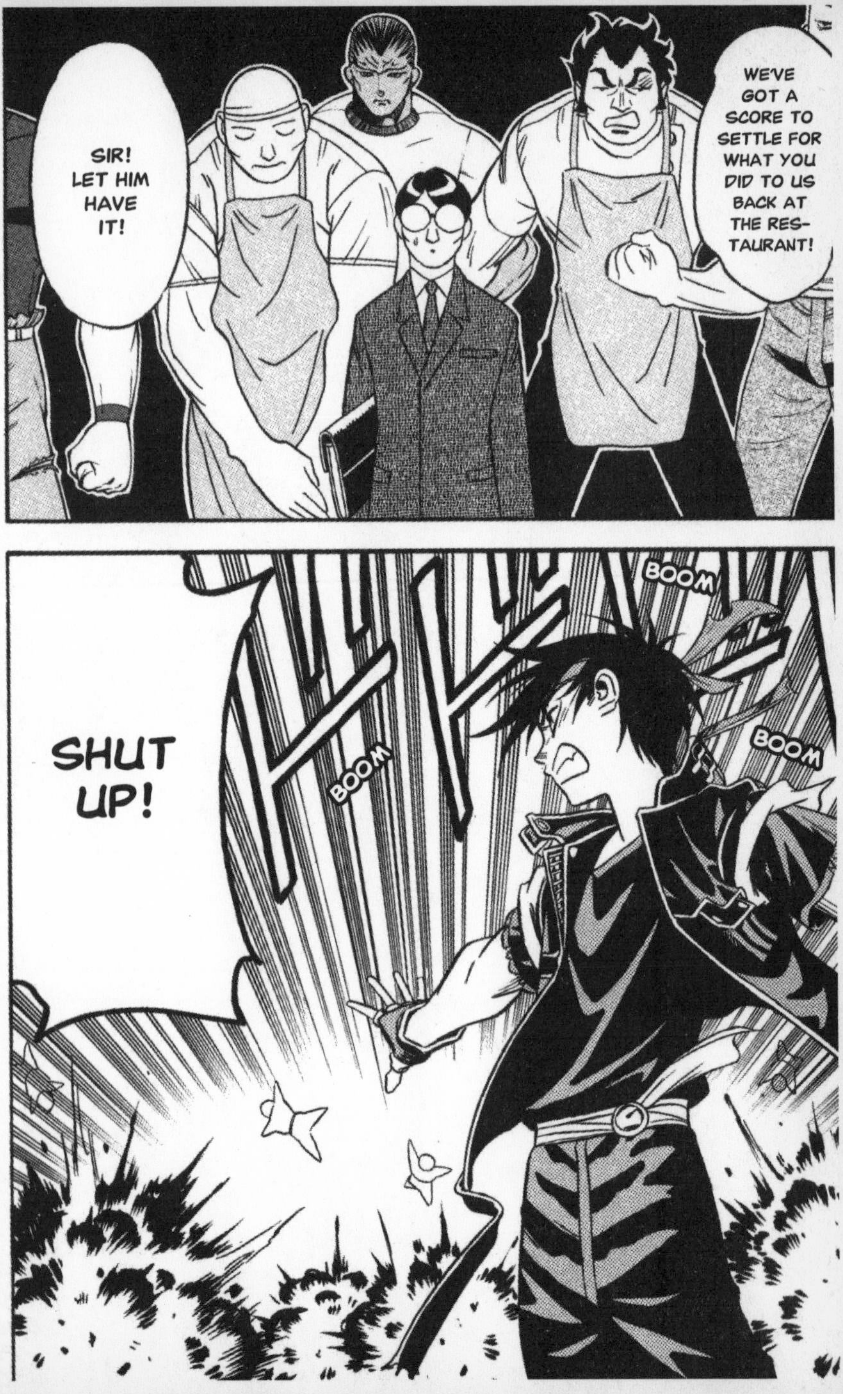
WE'VE GOT A SCORE TO SETTLE FOR WHAT YOU DID TO US BACK AT THE RES-TAURANT!
SIR! LET HIM HAVE IT!
BOOM
BOOM
BOOM
SHUT UP!

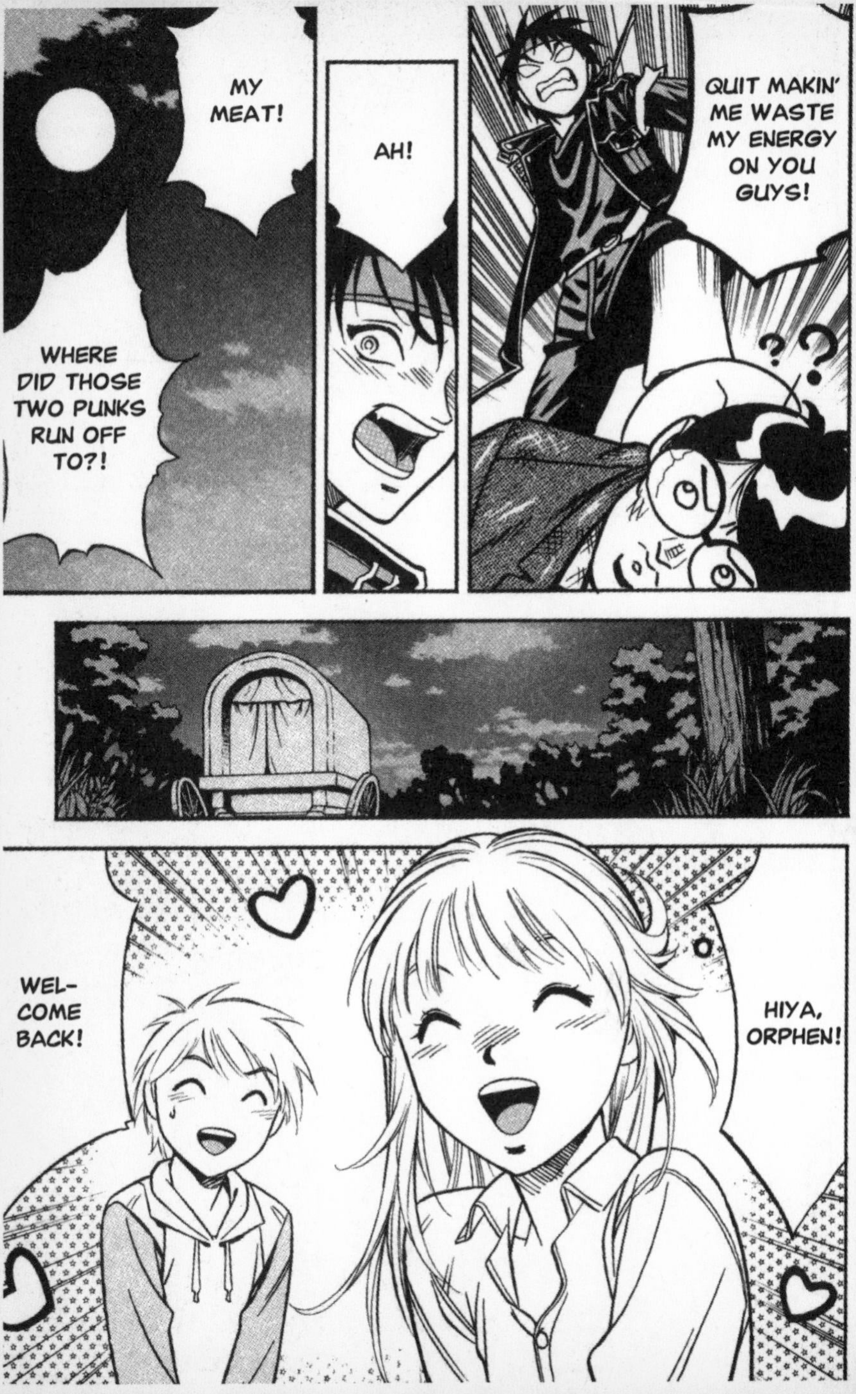
MY MEAT!
WHERE DID THOSE TWO PUNKS RUN OFF TO?!
AH!
QUIT MAKIN' ME WASTE MY ENERGY ON YOU GUYS!
??
WEL-COME BACK!
HIYA, ORPHEN!

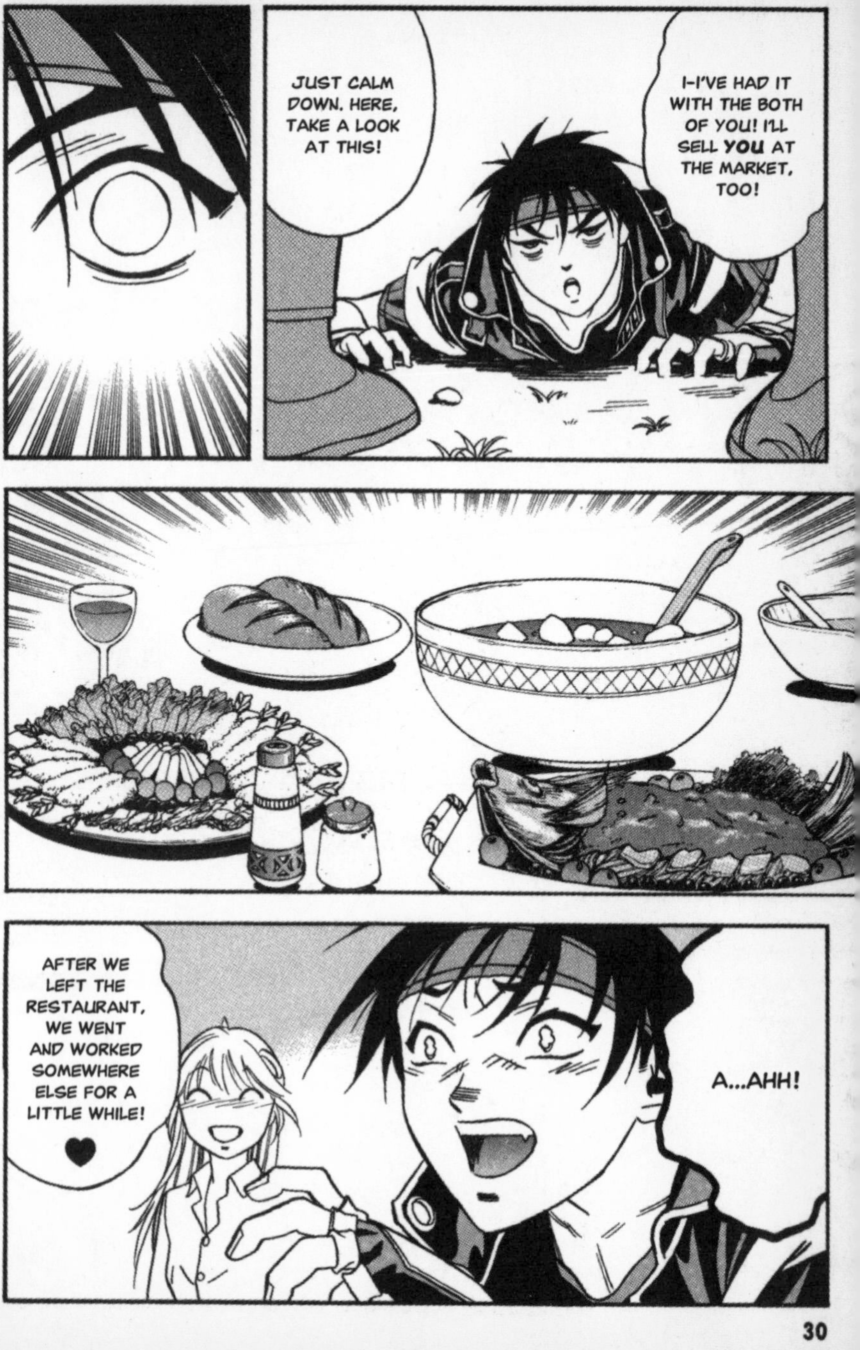
I-I'VE HAD IT WITH THE BOTH OF YOU! I'LL SELL YOU AT THE MARKET, TOO!
JUST CALM DOWN. HERE, TAKE A LOOK AT THIS!
A...AHH!
AFTER WE LEFT THE RESTAURANT, WE WENT AND WORKED SOMEWHERE ELSE FOR A LITTLE WHILE! ♥

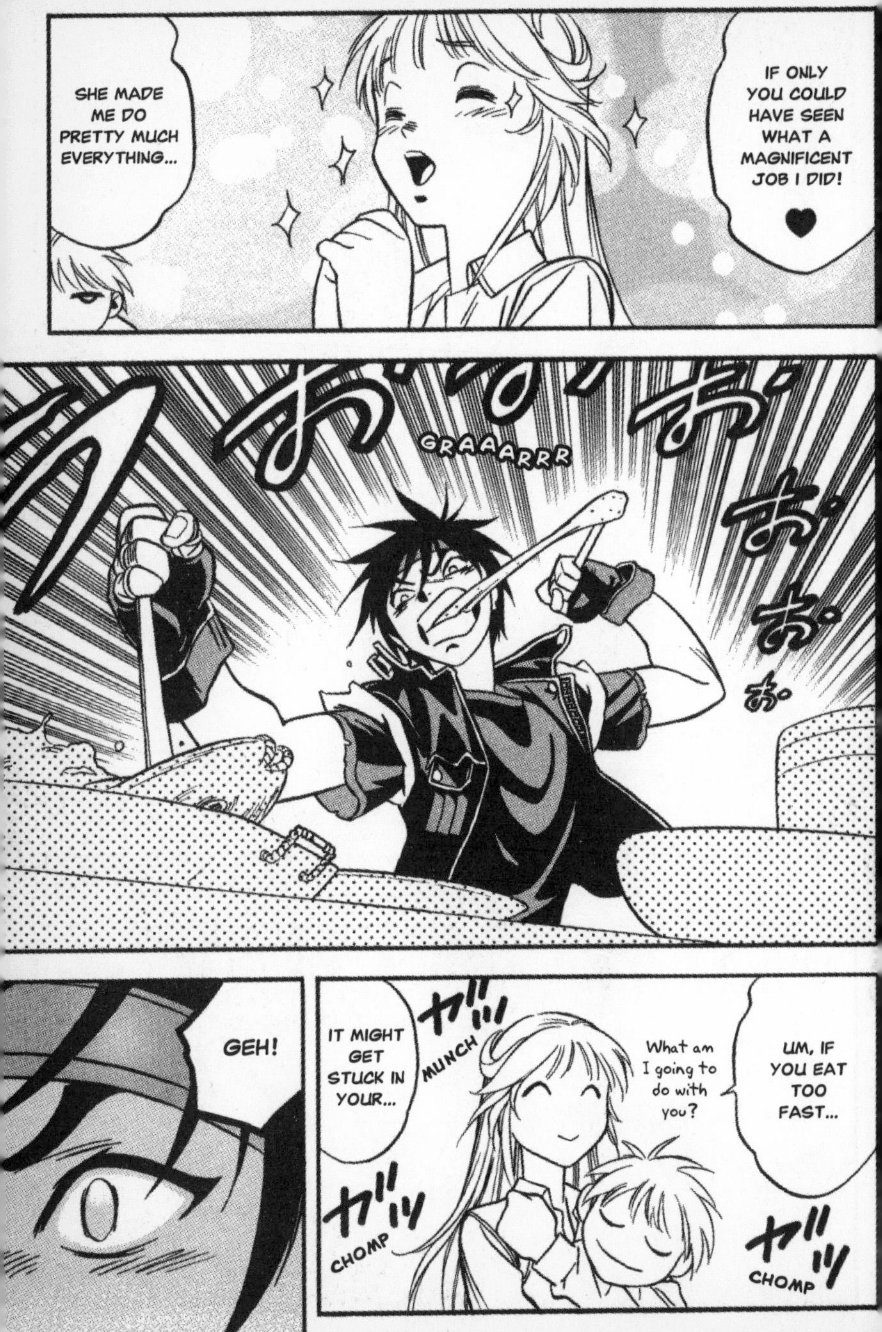
IF ONLY YOU COULD HAVE SEEN WHAT A MAGNIFICENT JOB I DID! ♥
SHE MADE ME DO PRETTY MUCH EVERYTHING...
GRAAAARRR
UM, IF YOU EAT TOO FAST...
ガツ
CHOMP
What am I going to do with you?
ガツ
MUNCH
IT MIGHT GET STUCK IN YOUR...
ガツ
CHOMP
GEH!

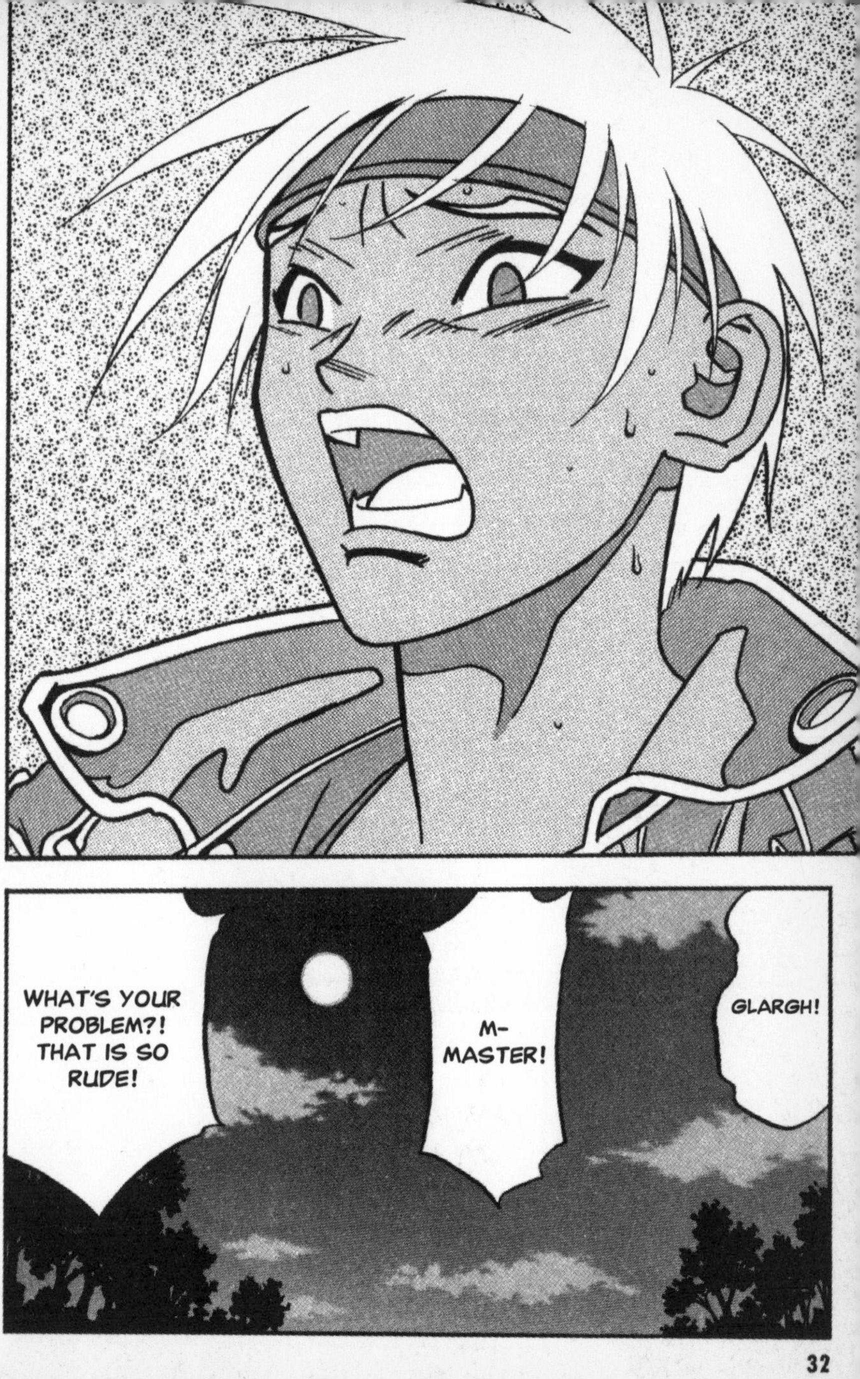
GLARGH!
M-MASTER!
WHAT'S YOUR PROBLEM?! THAT IS SO RUDE!

Chapter 20: Orphen and the Path of the Animal (Part 1)

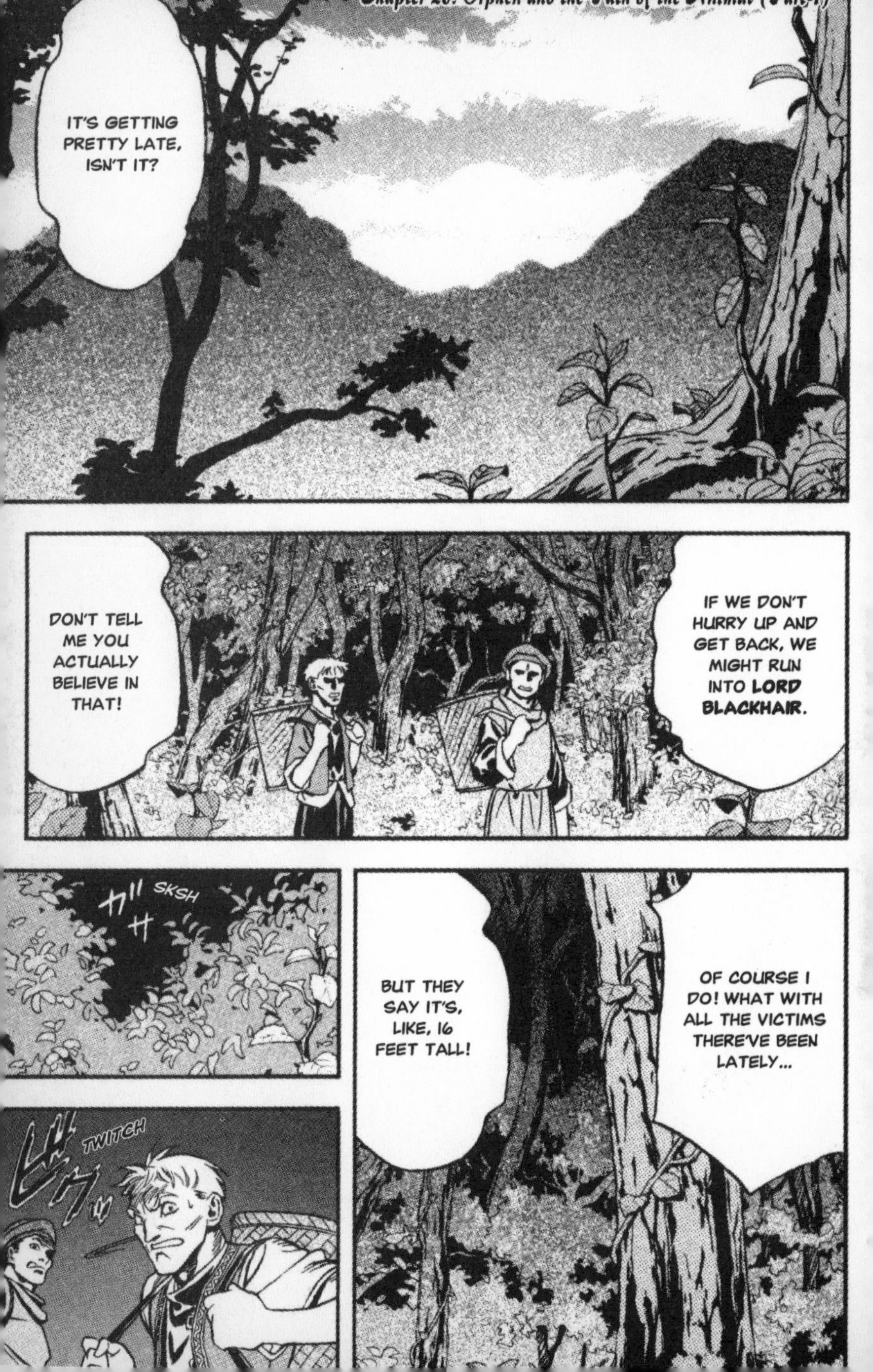
IT'S GETTING PRETTY LATE, ISN'T IT?
IF WE DON'T HURRY UP AND GET BACK, WE MIGHT RUN INTO **LORD BLACKHAIR**.
DON'T TELL ME YOU ACTUALLY BELIEVE IN THAT!
OF COURSE I DO! WHAT WITH ALL THE VICTIMS THERE'VE BEEN LATELY...
BUT THEY SAY IT'S, LIKE, 16 FEET TALL!
SKSH
TWITCH

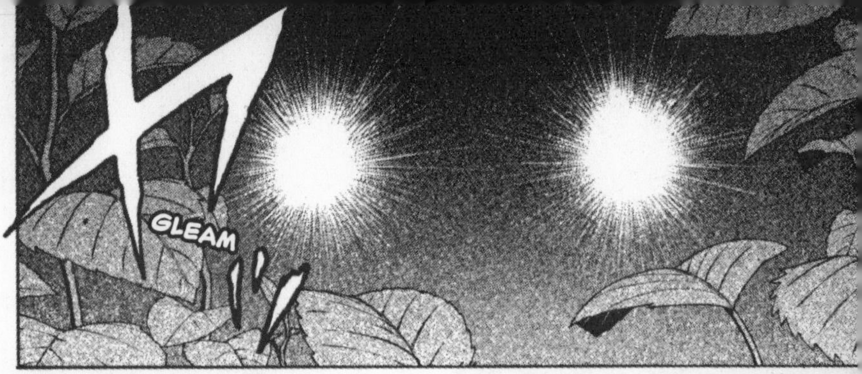
GLEAM
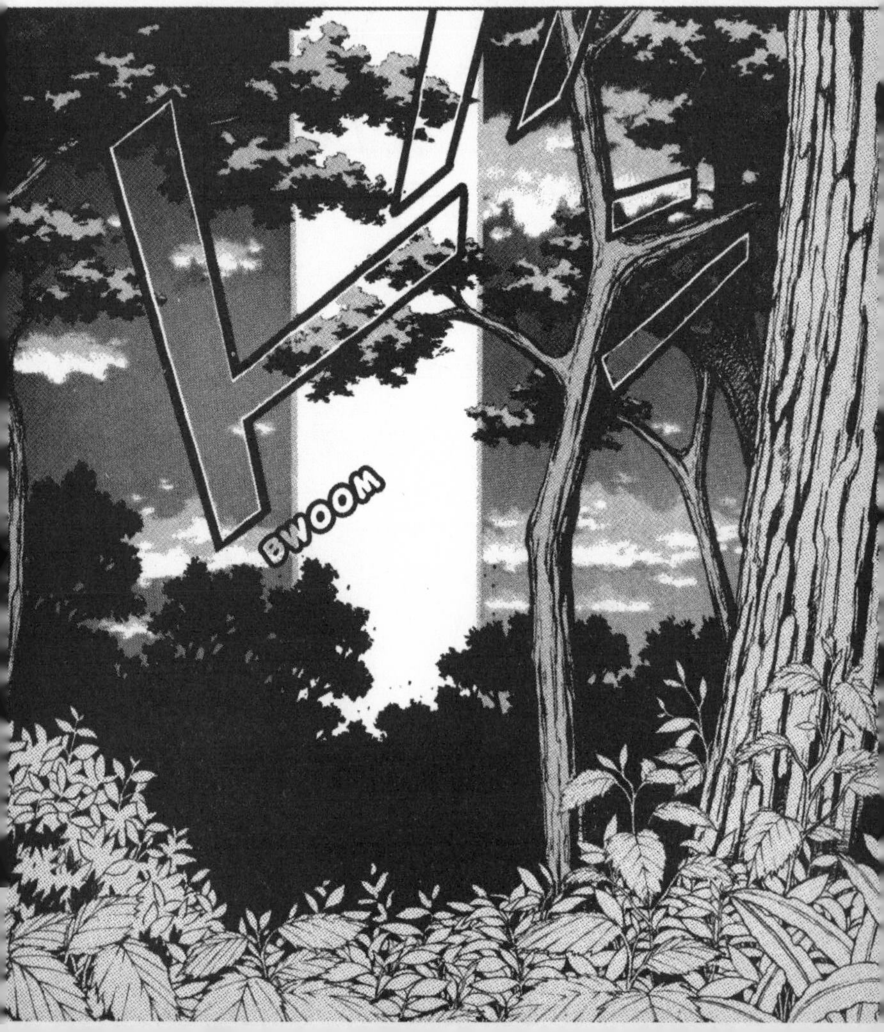
BWOOM

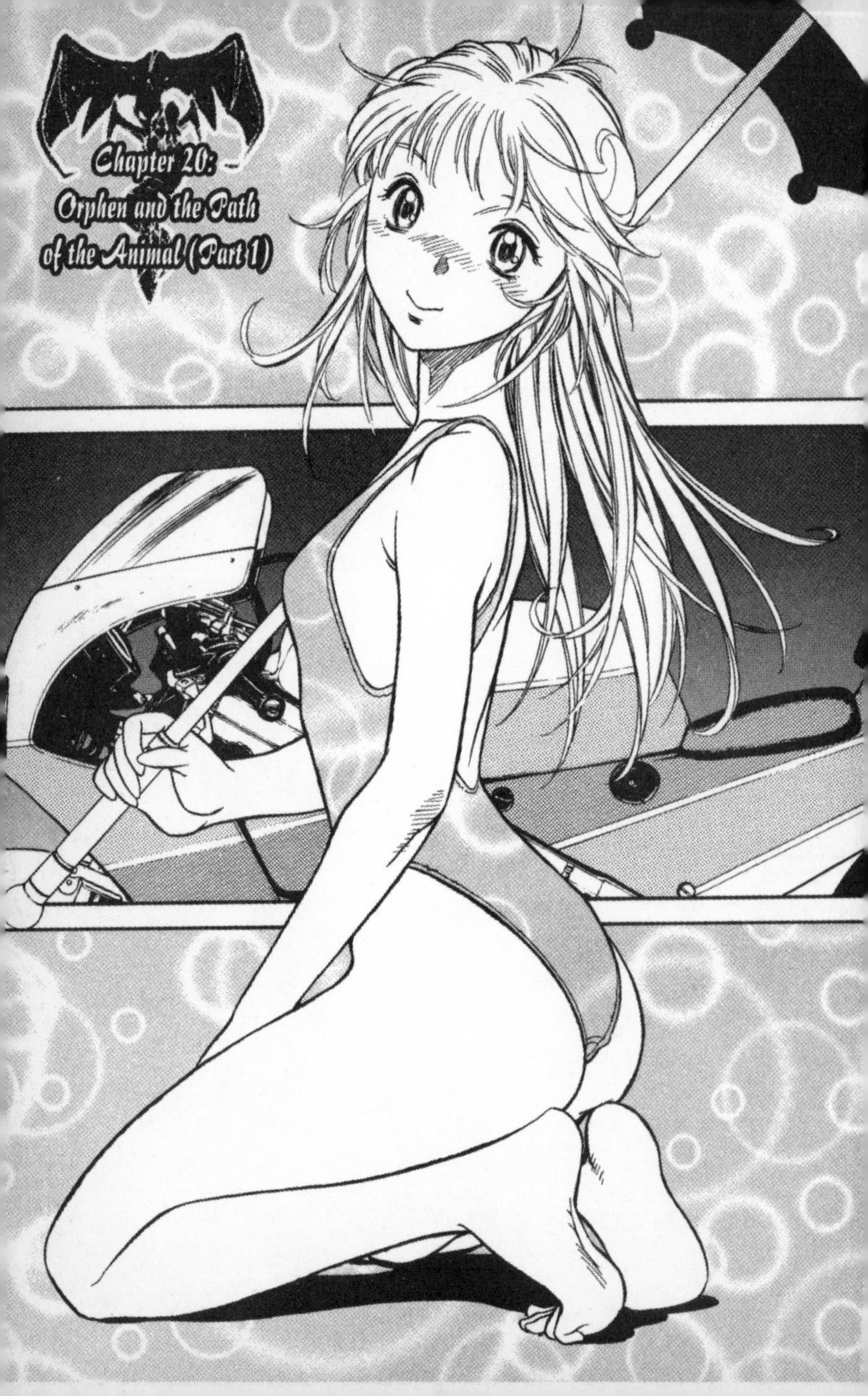
Chapter 20:
Orphen and the Path of the Animal (Part 1)

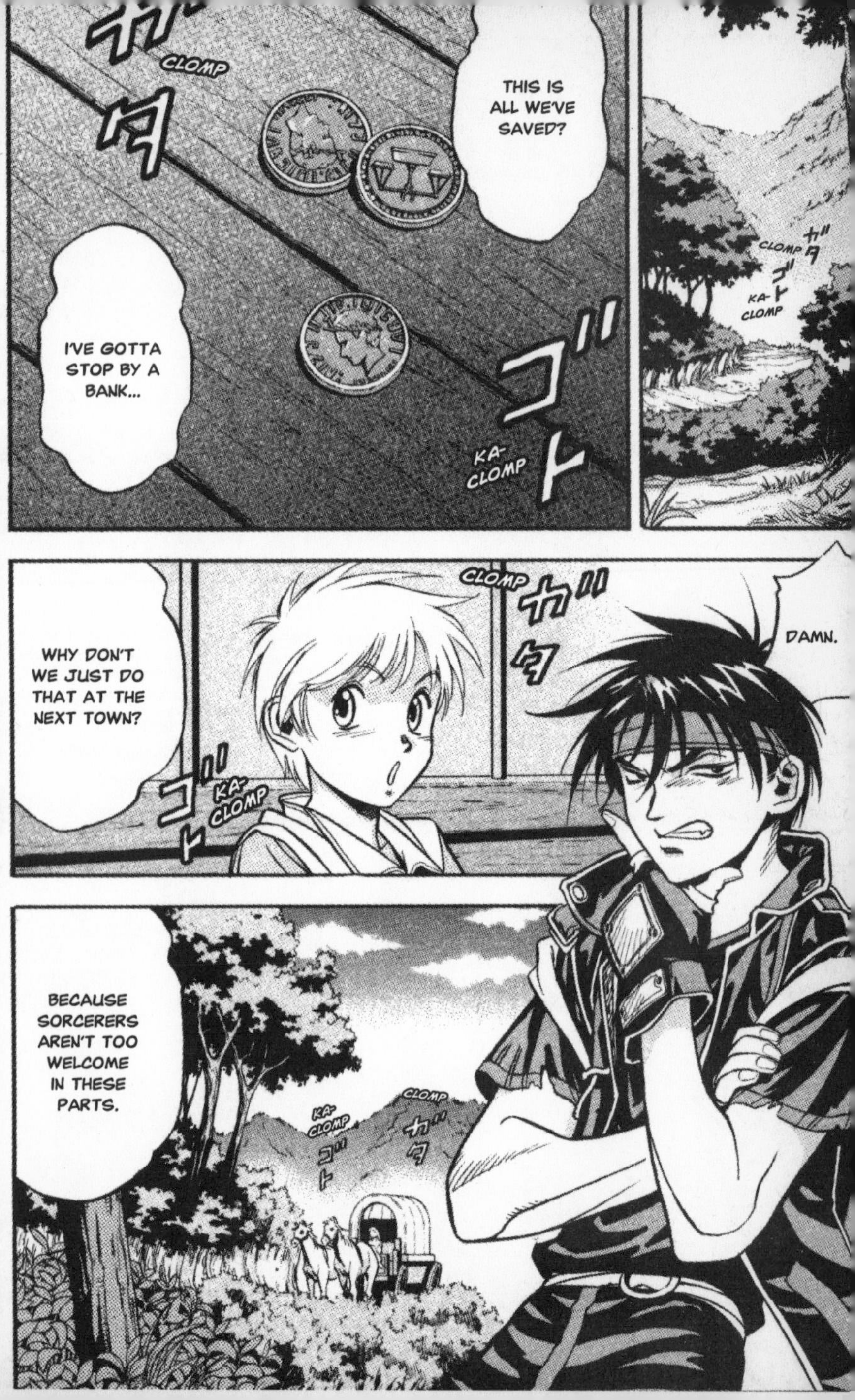
CLOMP
KA-CLOMP
CLOMP
THIS IS ALL WE'VE SAVED?
I'VE GOTTA STOP BY A BANK...
KA-CLOMP
DAMN.
CLOMP
WHY DON'T WE JUST DO THAT AT THE NEXT TOWN?
KA-CLOMP
BECAUSE SORCERERS AREN'T TOO WELCOME IN THESE PARTS.
CLOMP
KA-CLOMP

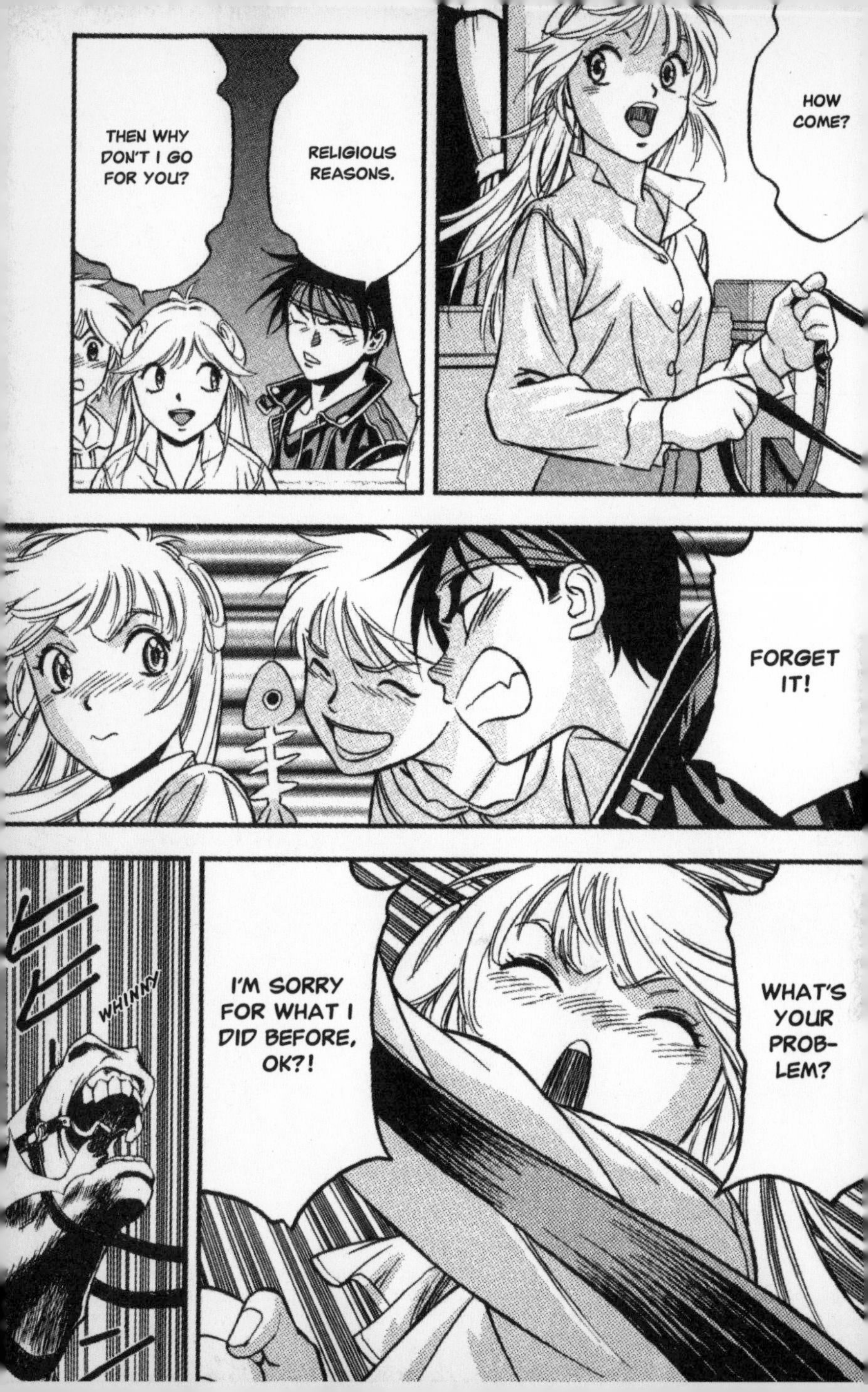
HOW COME?
THEN WHY DON'T I GO FOR YOU?
RELIGIOUS REASONS.
FORGET IT!
WHAT'S YOUR PROB-LEM?
I'M SORRY FOR WHAT I DID BEFORE, OK?!
WHINNY

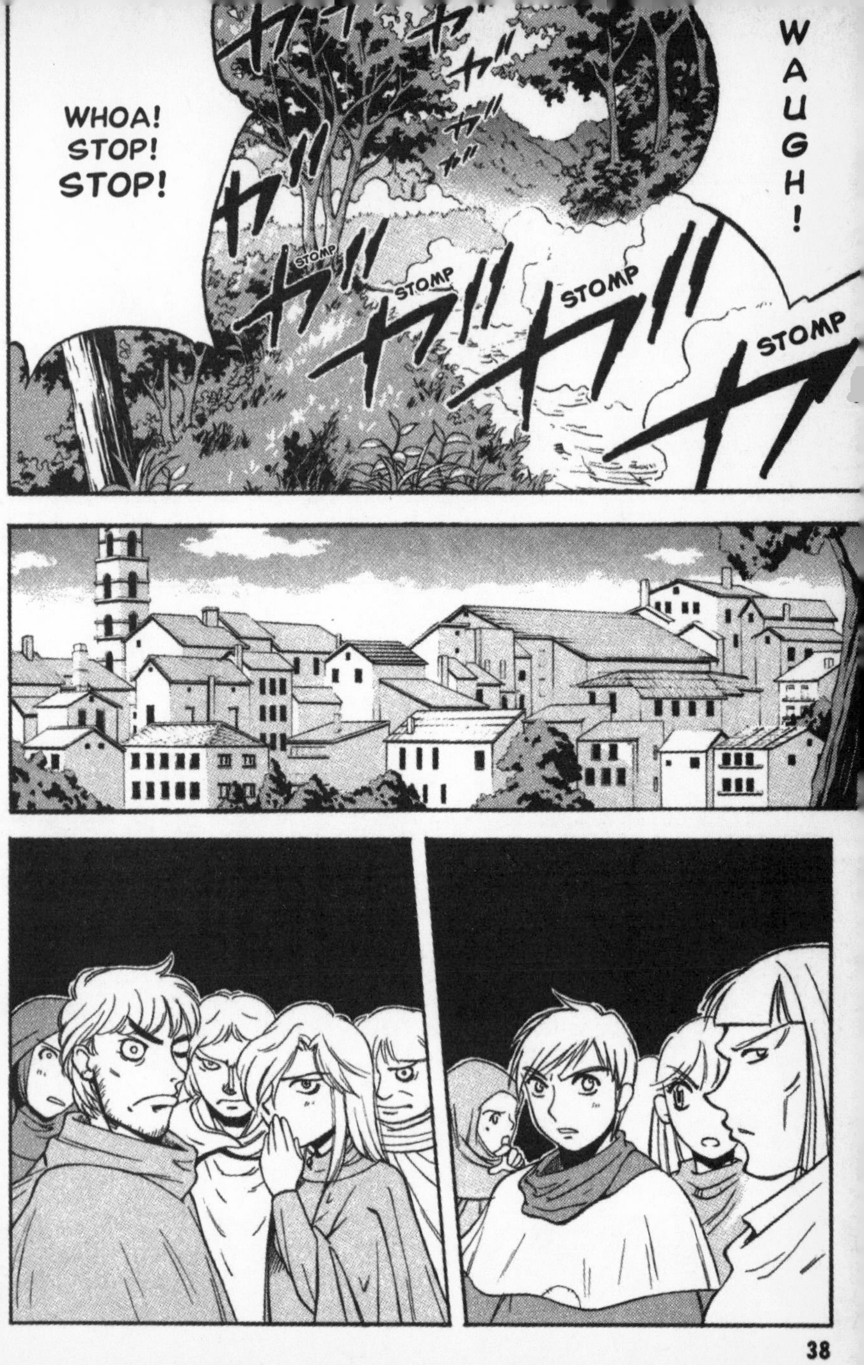
WAUGH!
WHOA! STOP! STOP!
STOMP
STOMP
STOMP
STOMP

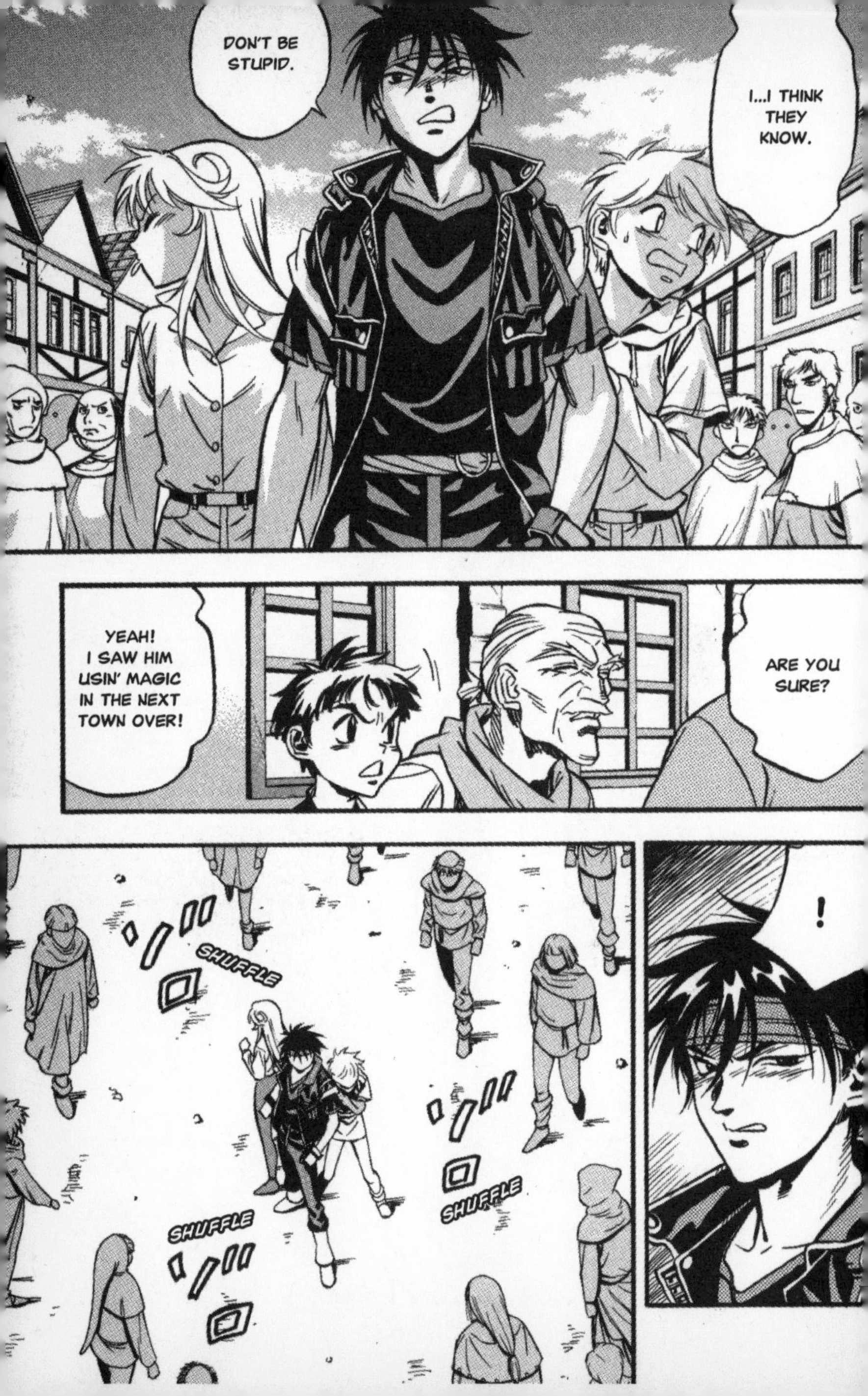
DON'T BE STUPID.
I...I THINK THEY KNOW.
YEAH! I SAW HIM USIN' MAGIC IN THE NEXT TOWN OVER!
ARE YOU SURE?
SHUFFLE
SHUFFLE
SHUFFLE
!

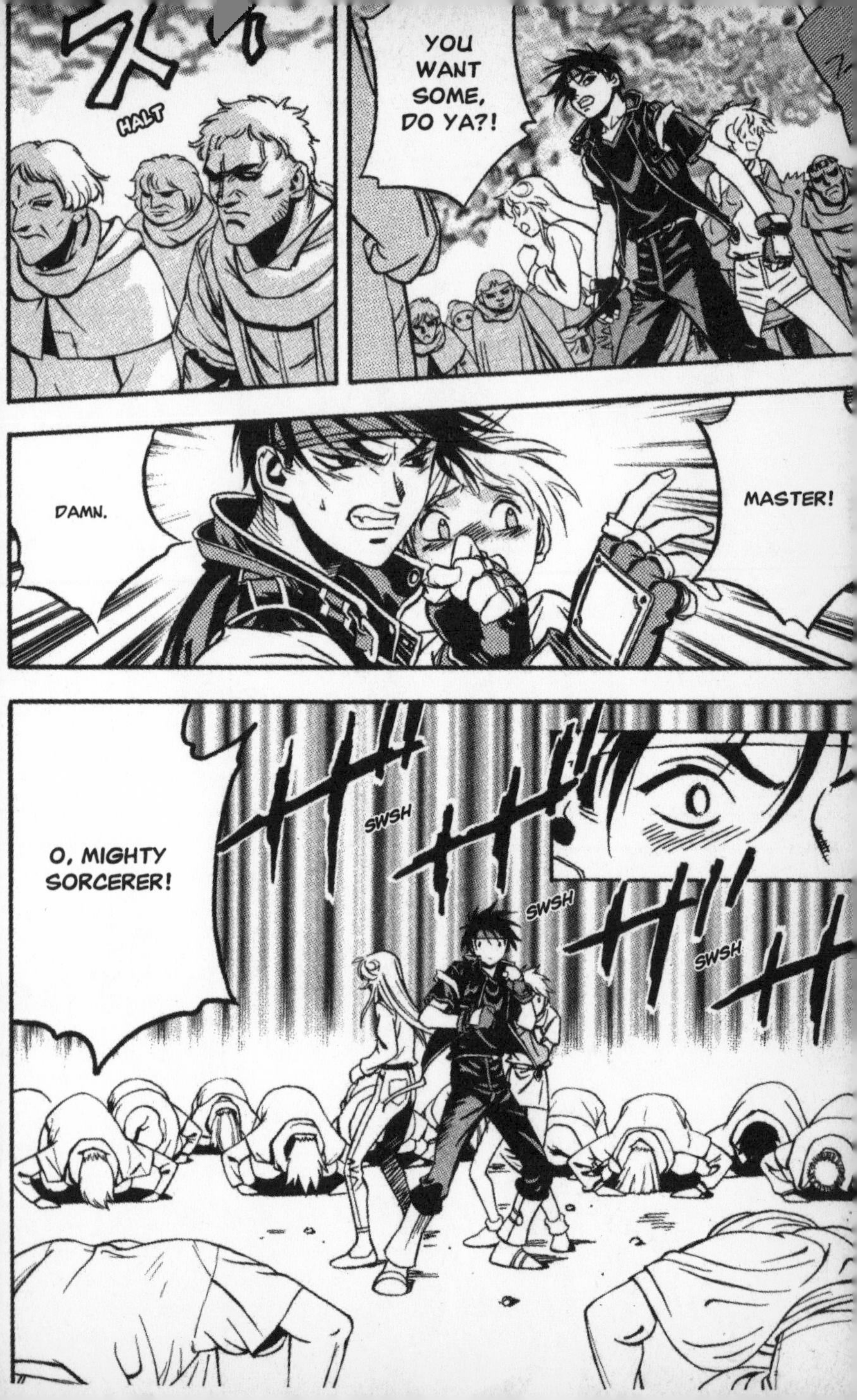
YOU WANT SOME, DO YA?!
HALT
MASTER!
DAMN.
O, MIGHTY SORCERER!
SWSH
SWSH
SWSH

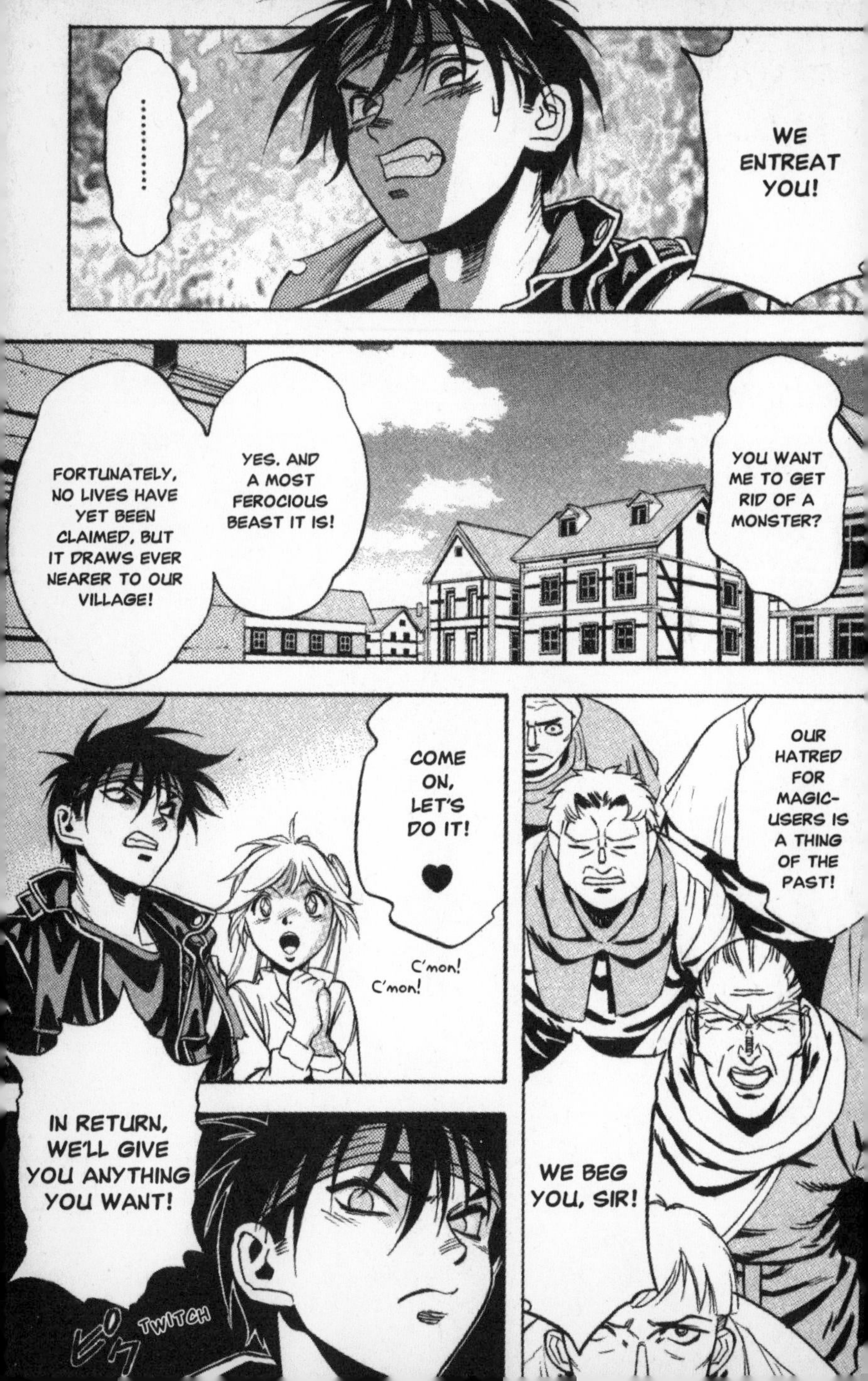
WE ENTREAT YOU!
......
YOU WANT ME TO GET RID OF A MONSTER?
YES. AND A MOST FEROCIOUS BEAST IT IS!
FORTUNATELY, NO LIVES HAVE YET BEEN CLAIMED, BUT IT DRAWS EVER NEARER TO OUR VILLAGE!
OUR HATRED FOR MAGIC-USERS IS A THING OF THE PAST!
WE BEG YOU, SIR!
COME ON, LET'S DO IT! ♥
C'mon! C'mon!
IN RETURN, WE'LL GIVE YOU ANYTHING YOU WANT!
TWITCH

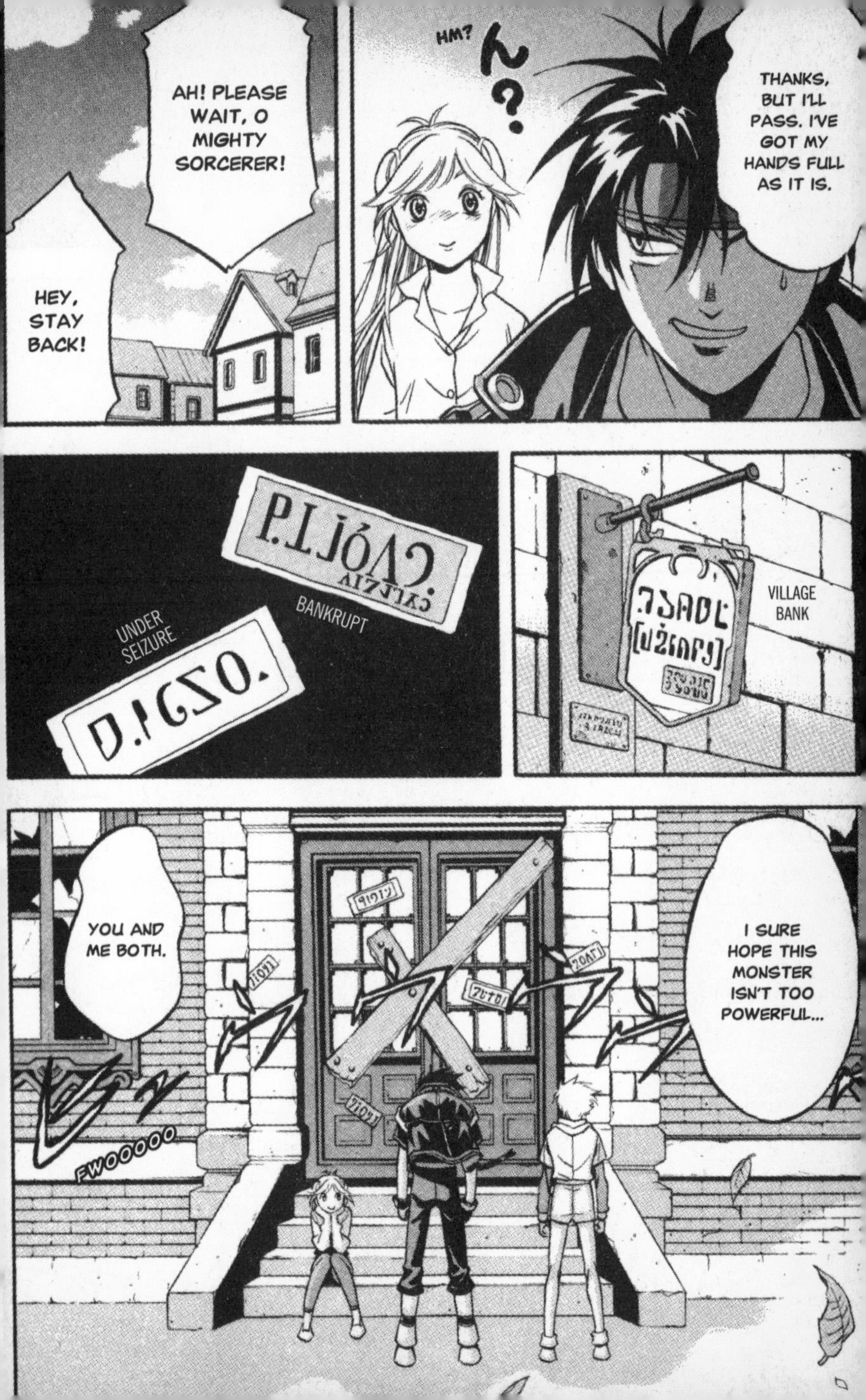
THANKS, BUT I'LL PASS. I'VE GOT MY HANDS FULL AS IT IS.
HM?
AH! PLEASE WAIT, O MIGHTY SORCERER!
HEY, STAY BACK!
VILLAGE BANK
BANKRUPT
UNDER SEIZURE
I SURE HOPE THIS MONSTER ISN'T TOO POWERFUL...
YOU AND ME BOTH.
FWOOOOO

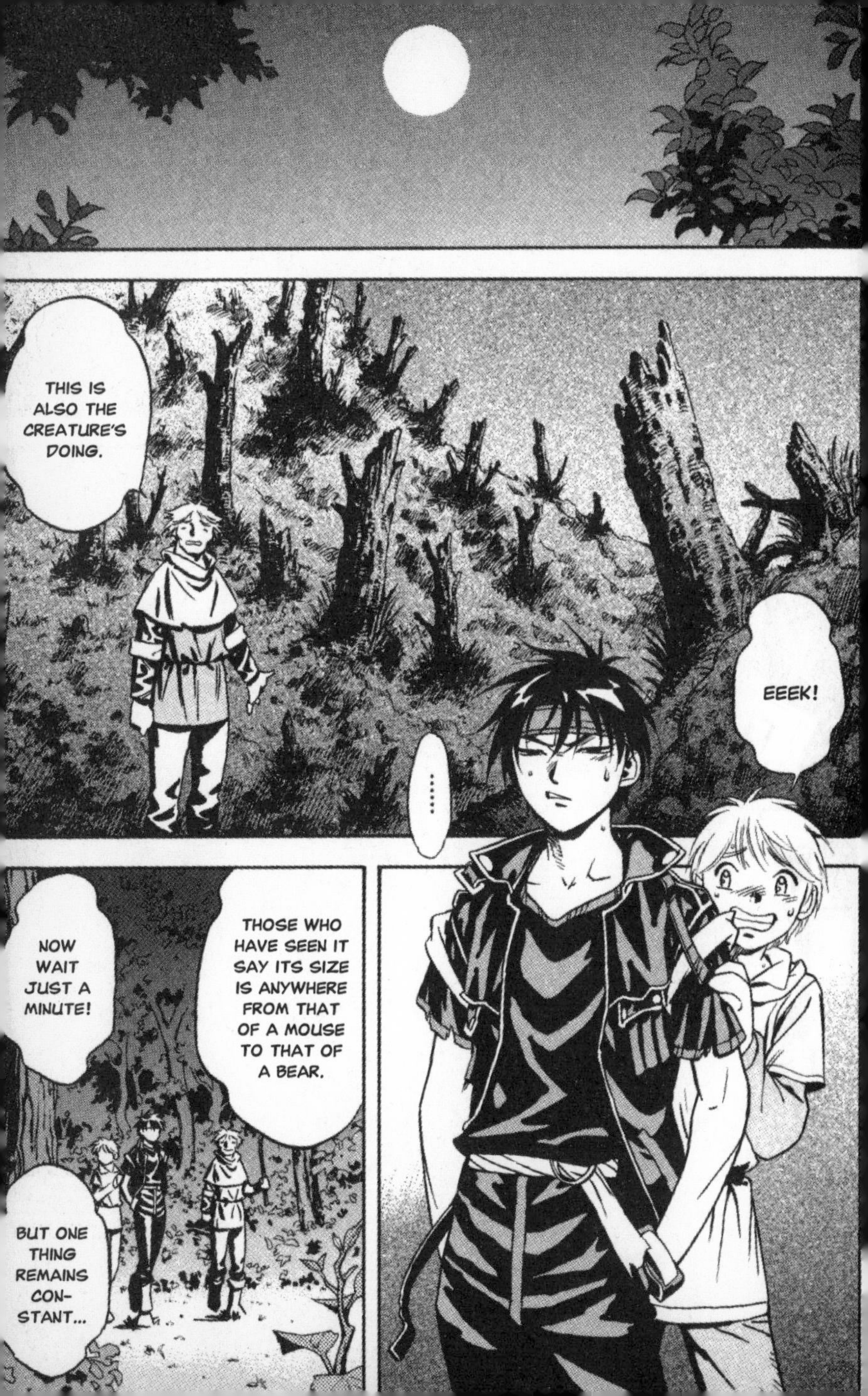
THIS IS ALSO THE CREATURE'S DOING.
EEEK!
......
THOSE WHO HAVE SEEN IT SAY ITS SIZE IS ANYWHERE FROM THAT OF A MOUSE TO THAT OF A BEAR.
NOW WAIT JUST A MINUTE!
BUT ONE THING REMAINS CON-STANT...

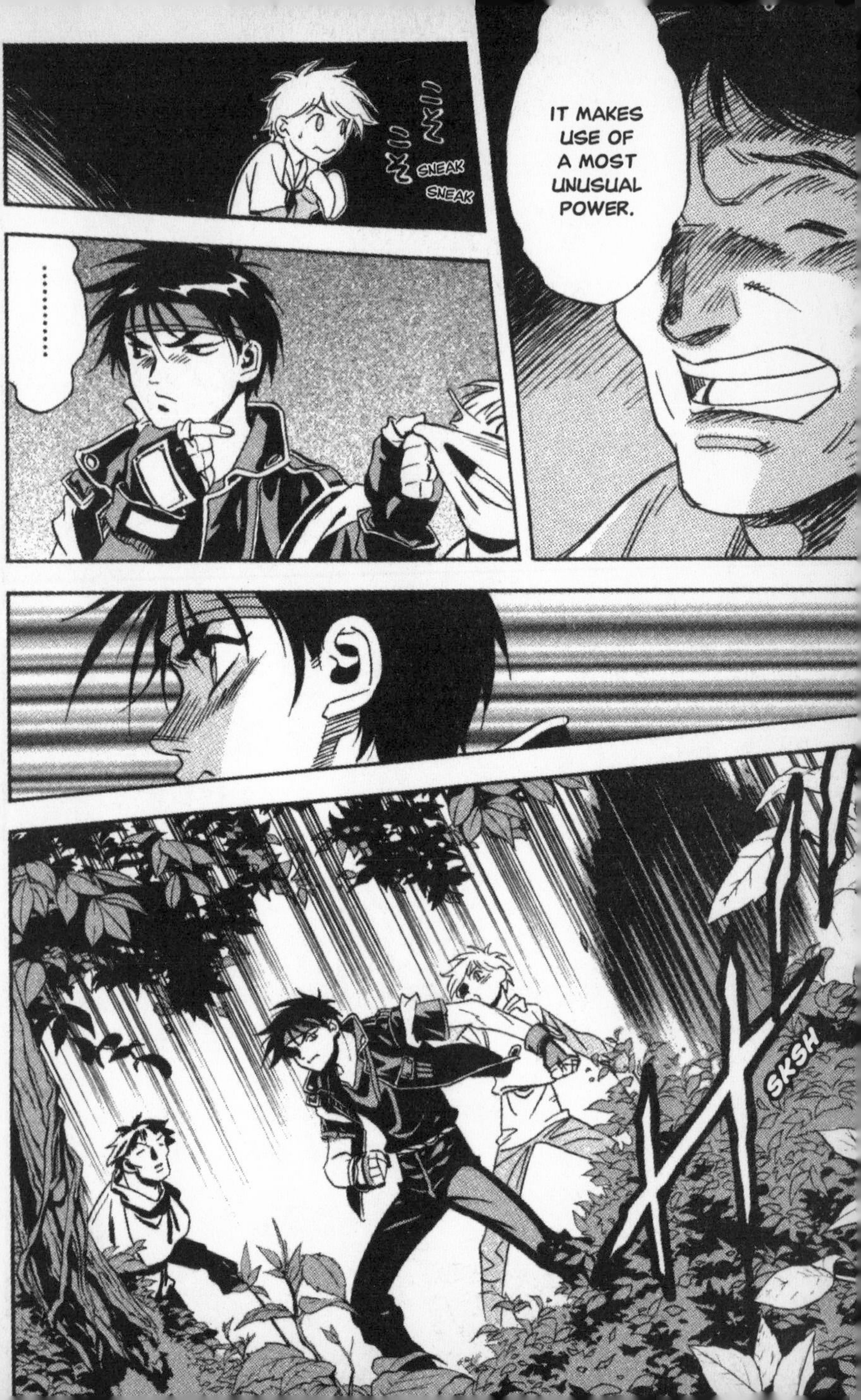
IT MAKES USE OF A MOST UNUSUAL POWER.
SNEAK
SNEAK
....
SKSH

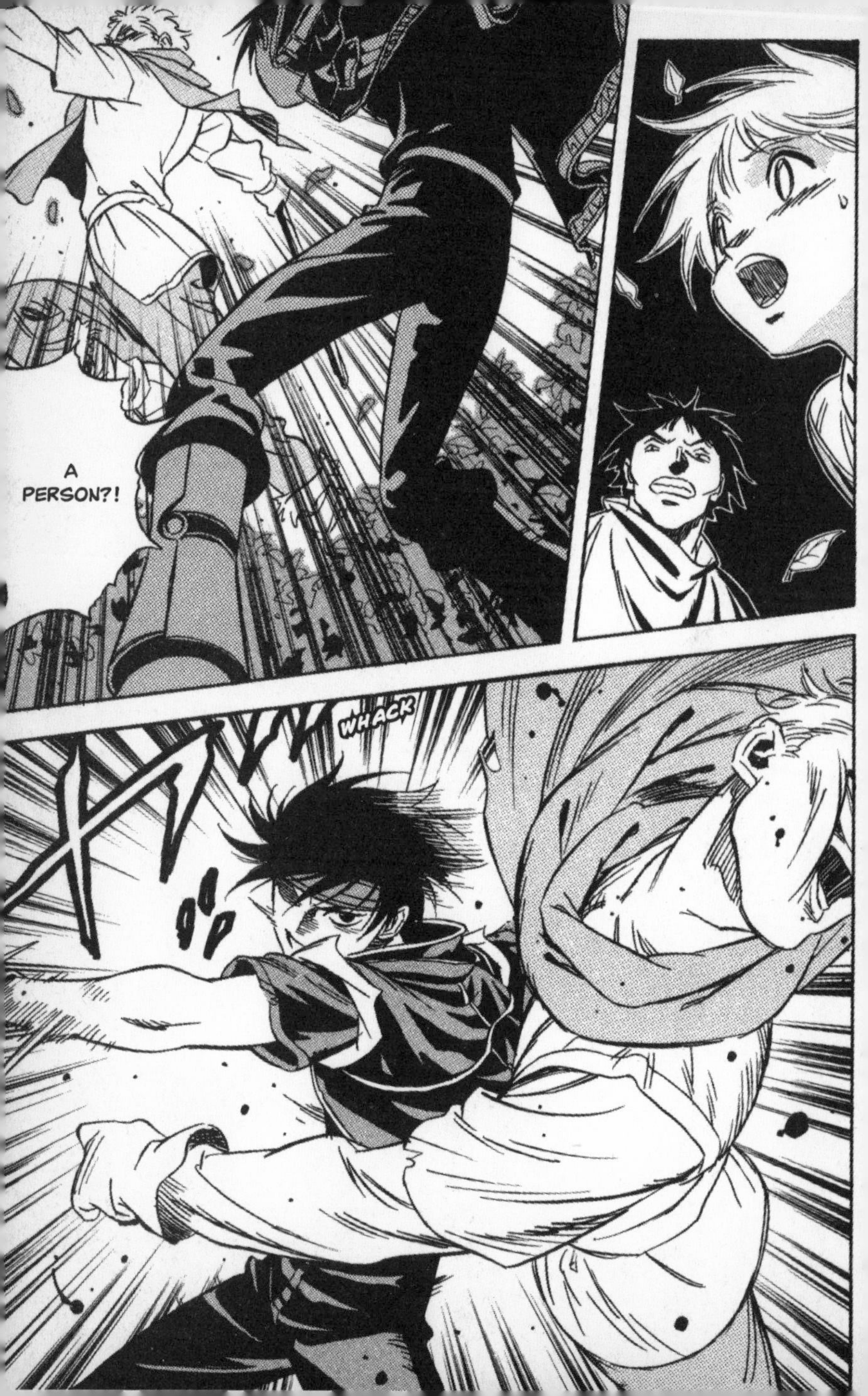

A PERSON?!
WHACK

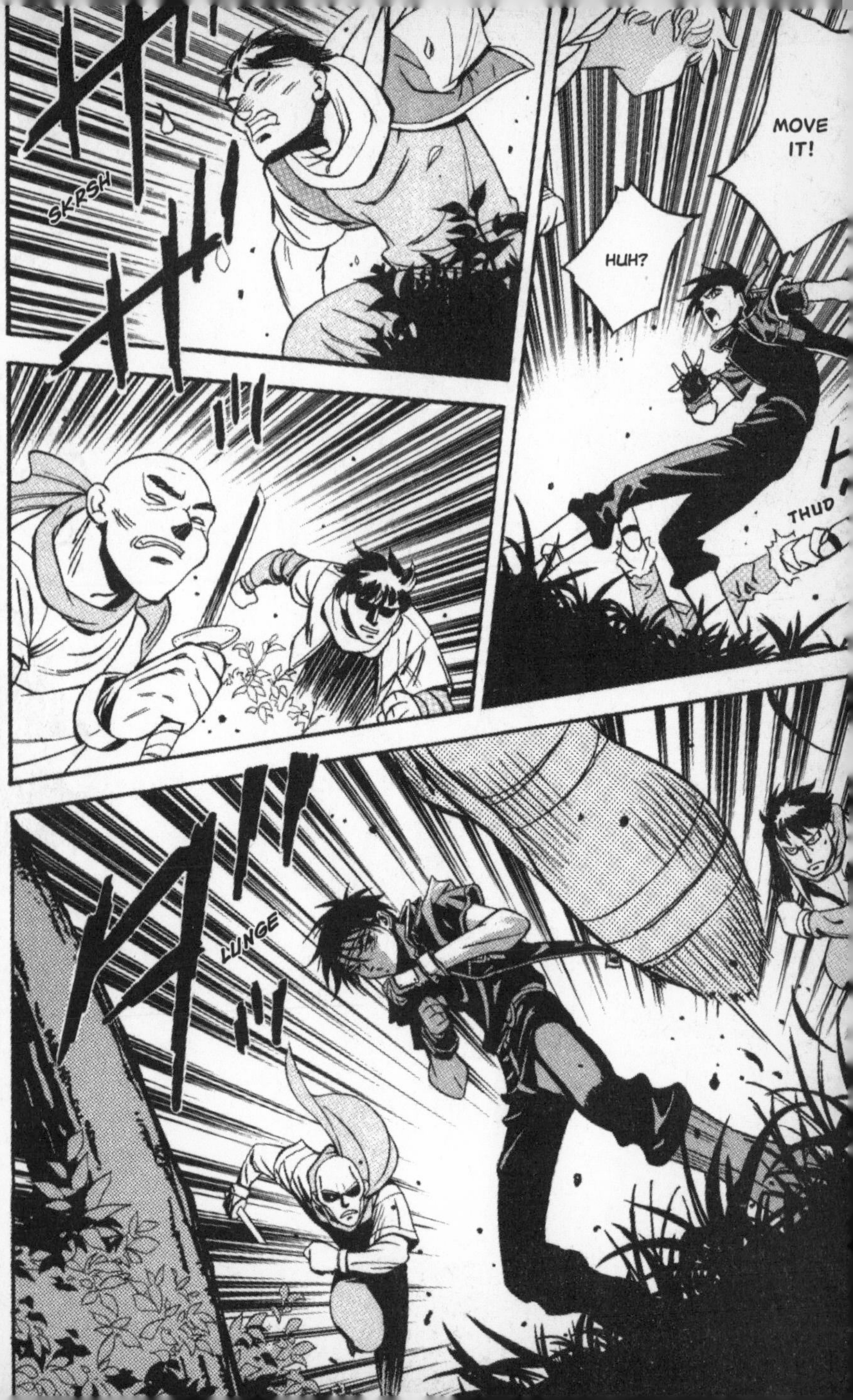
MOVE IT!
HUH?
THUD
SKRSH
LUNGE

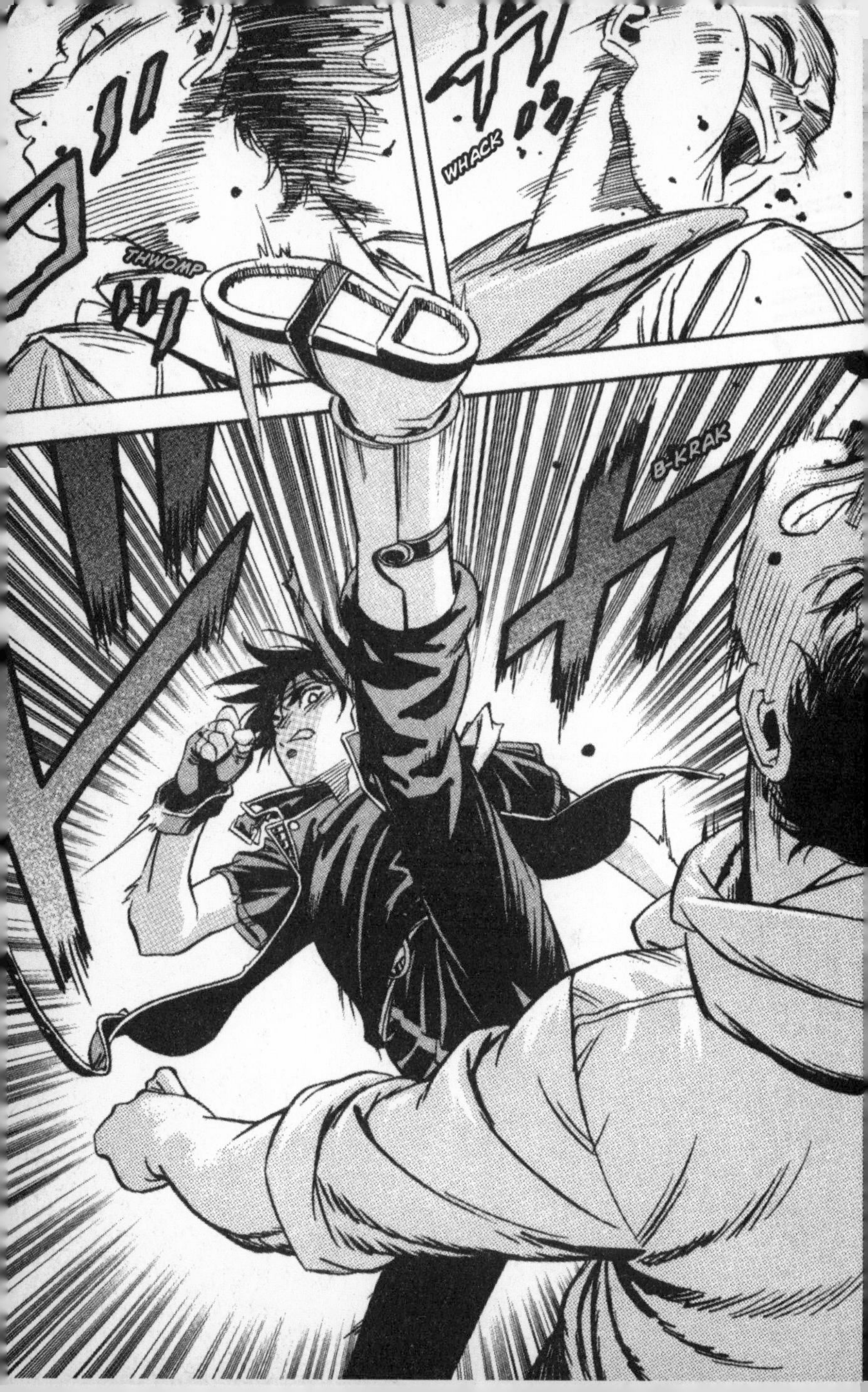
WHACK
THWOMP
B-KRAK

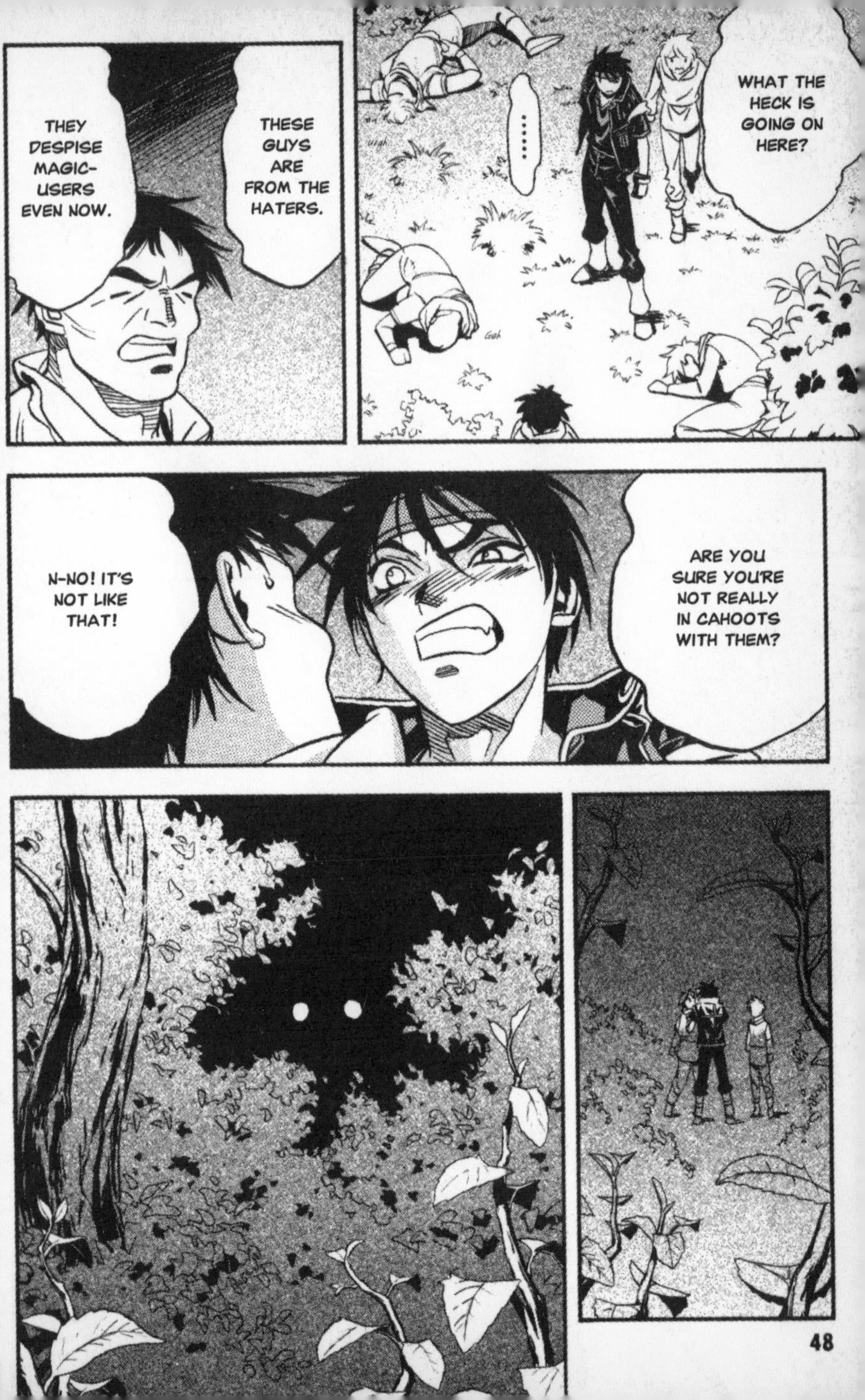
WHAT THE HECK IS GOING ON HERE?
......
THESE GUYS ARE FROM THE HATERS.
THEY DESPISE MAGIC-USERS EVEN NOW.
ARE YOU SURE YOU'RE NOT REALLY IN CAHOOTS WITH THEM?
N-NO! IT'S NOT LIKE THAT!

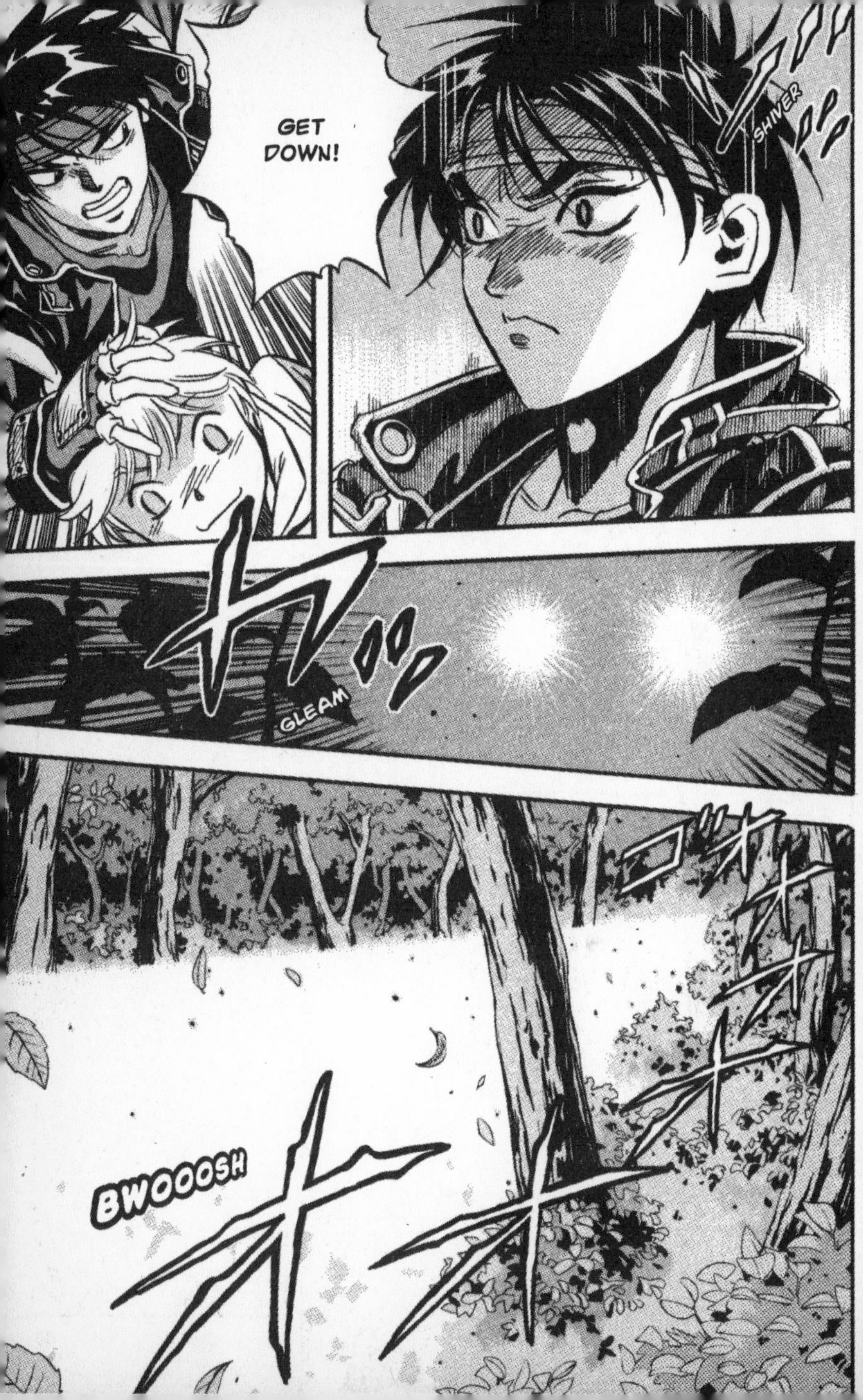
SHIVER
GET DOWN!
GLEAM
BWOOOSH

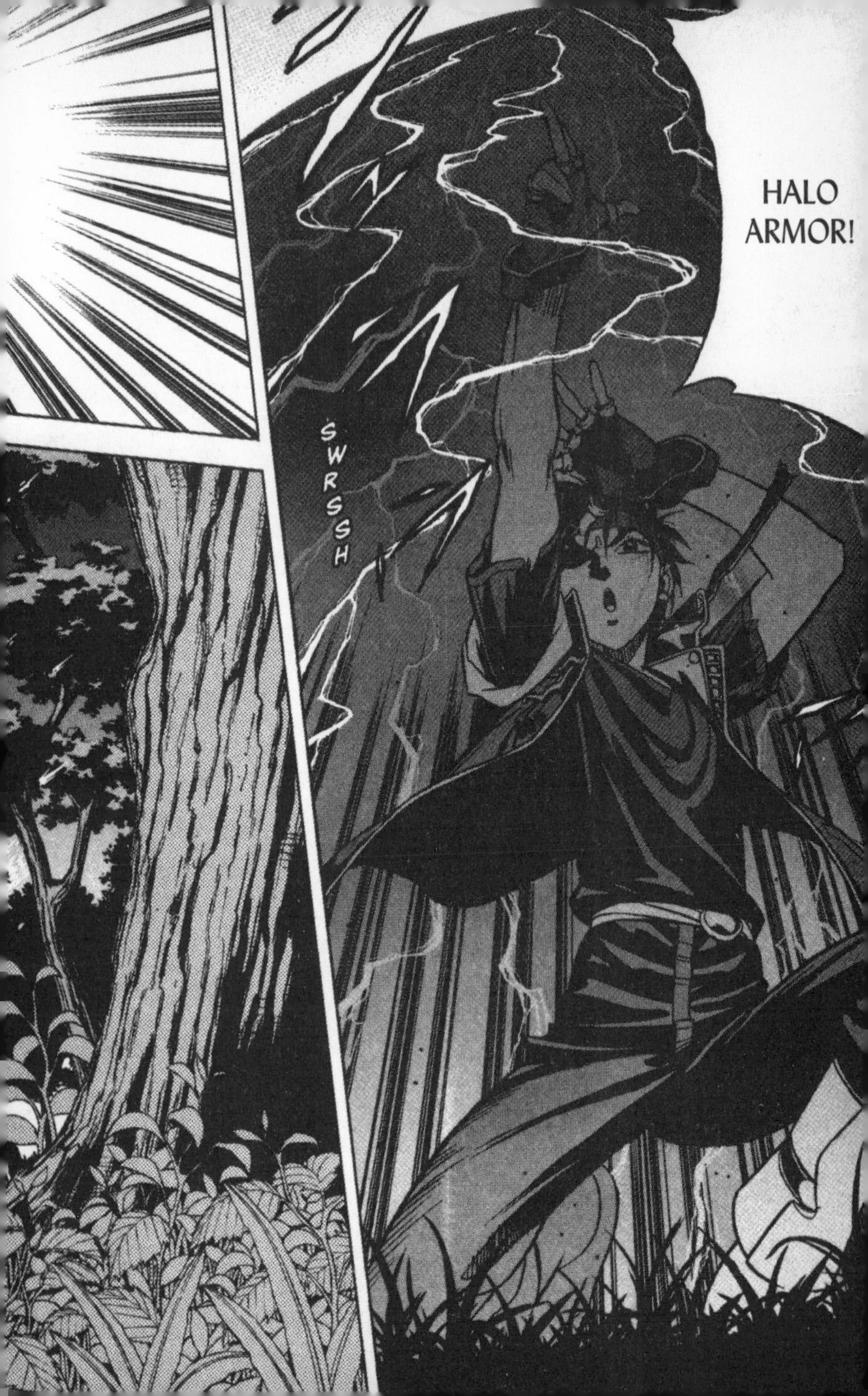
HALO
ARMOR!
SWRSSH

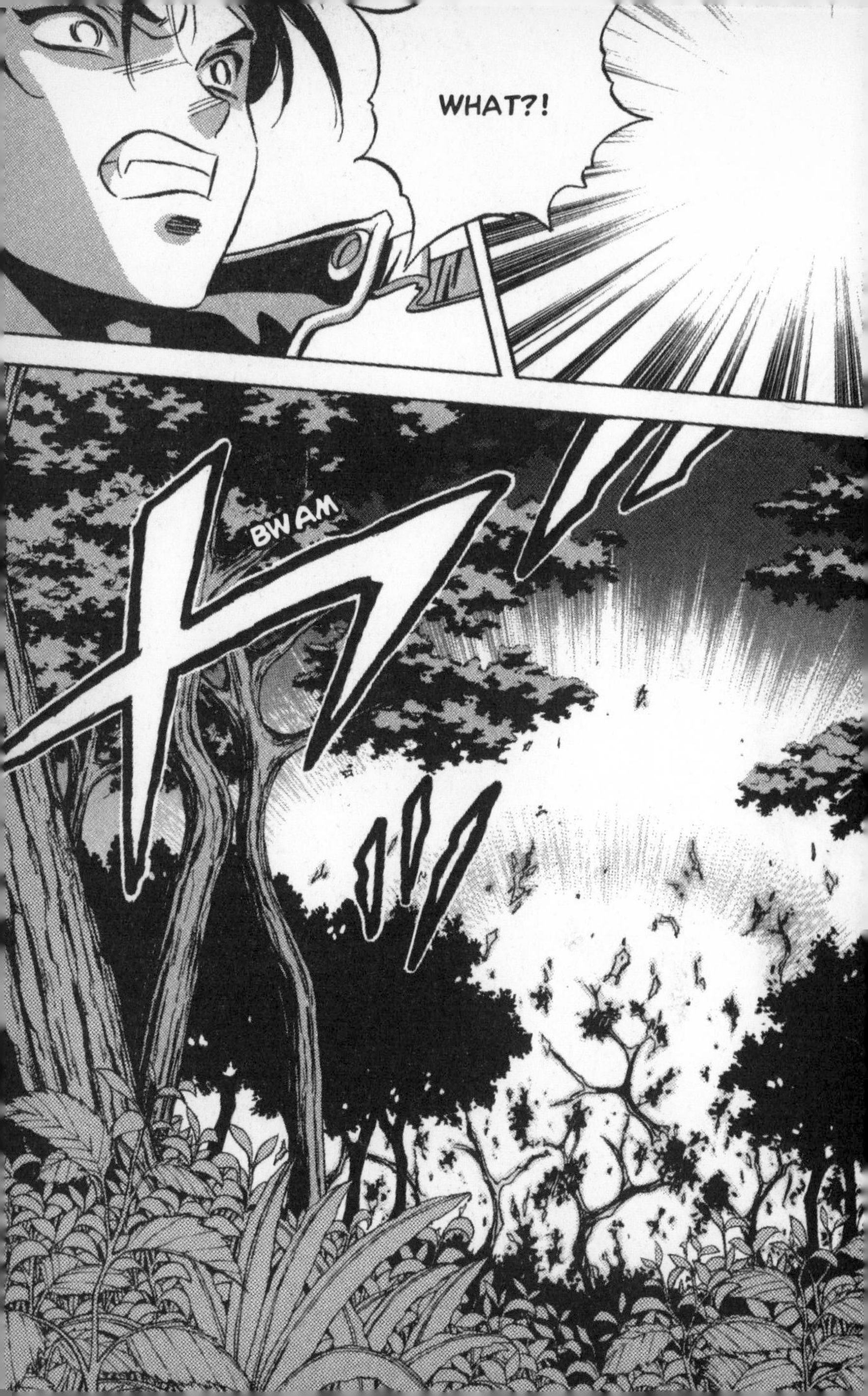
WHAT?!
BWAM

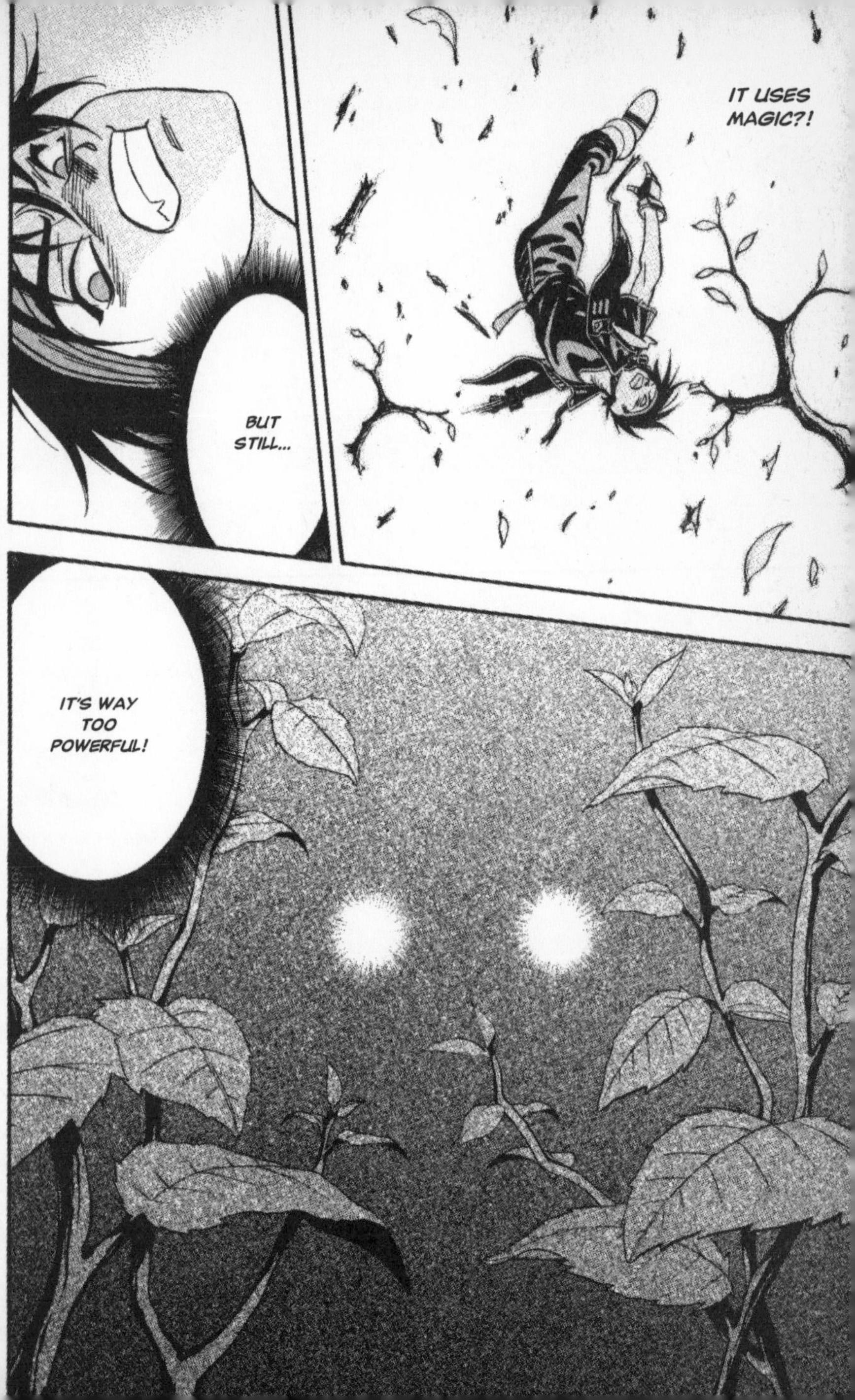
IT USES MAGIC?!
BUT STILL...
IT'S WAY TOO POWERFUL!

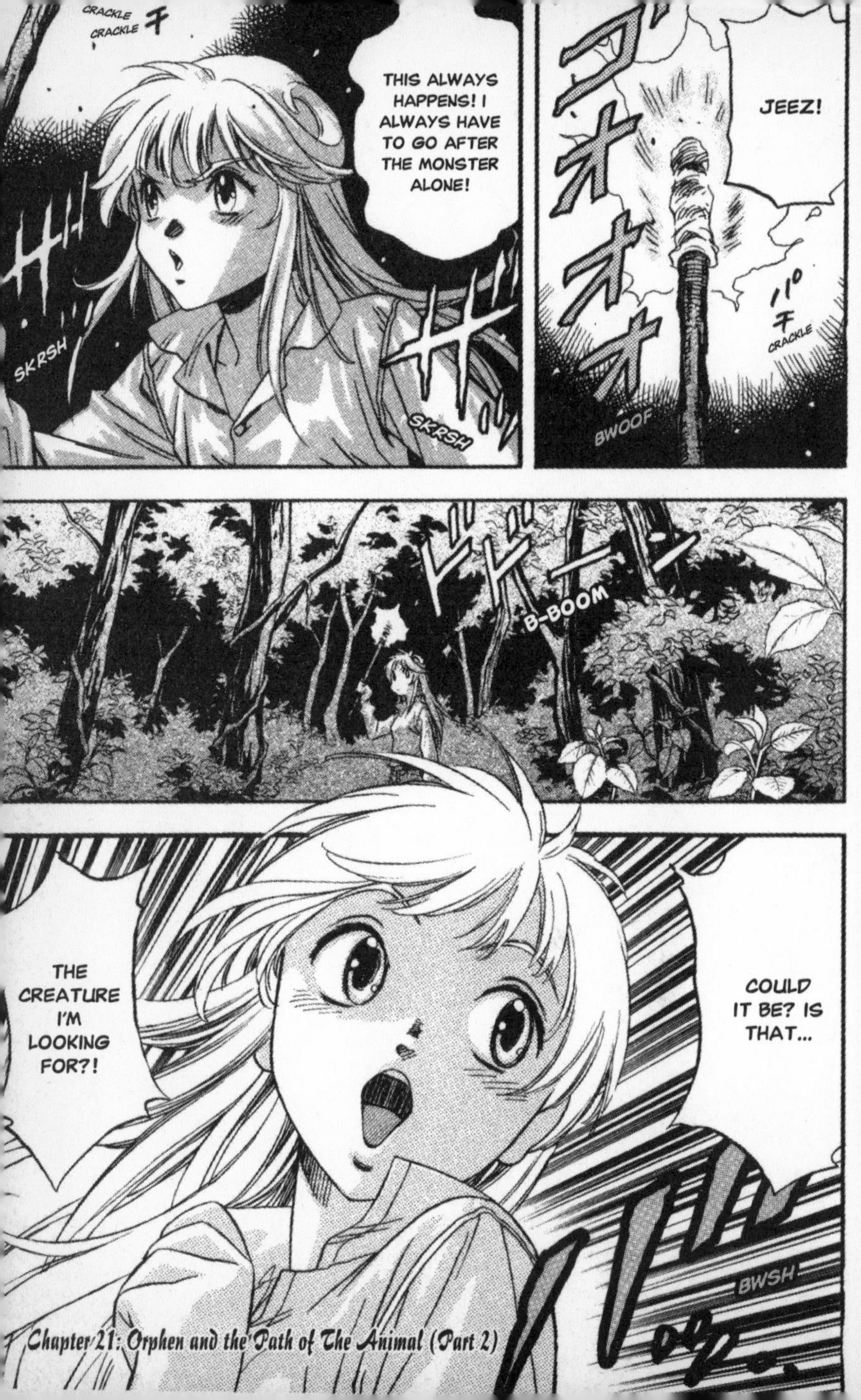
JEEZ!
CRACKLE
BWOOF
CRACKLE CRACKLE
THIS ALWAYS HAPPENS! I ALWAYS HAVE TO GO AFTER THE MONSTER ALONE!
SKRSH
SKRSH
B-BOOM
COULD IT BE? IS THAT...
THE CREATURE I'M LOOKING FOR?!
BWSH

Chapter 21: Orphen and the Path of The Animal (Part 2)

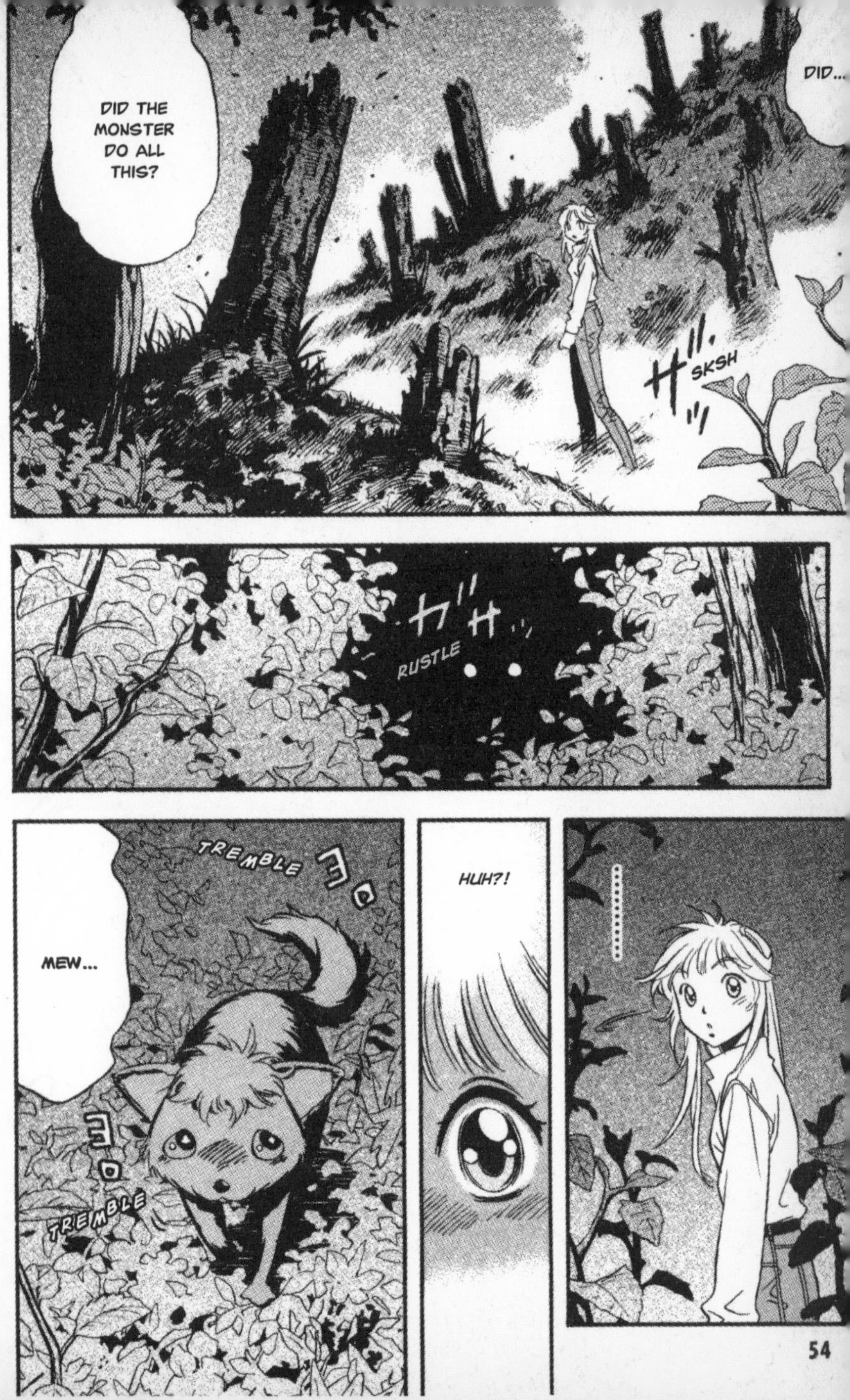
DID...
DID THE MONSTER DO ALL THIS?
SKSH
RUSTLE
....
HUH?!
TREMBLE
MEW...
TREMBLE

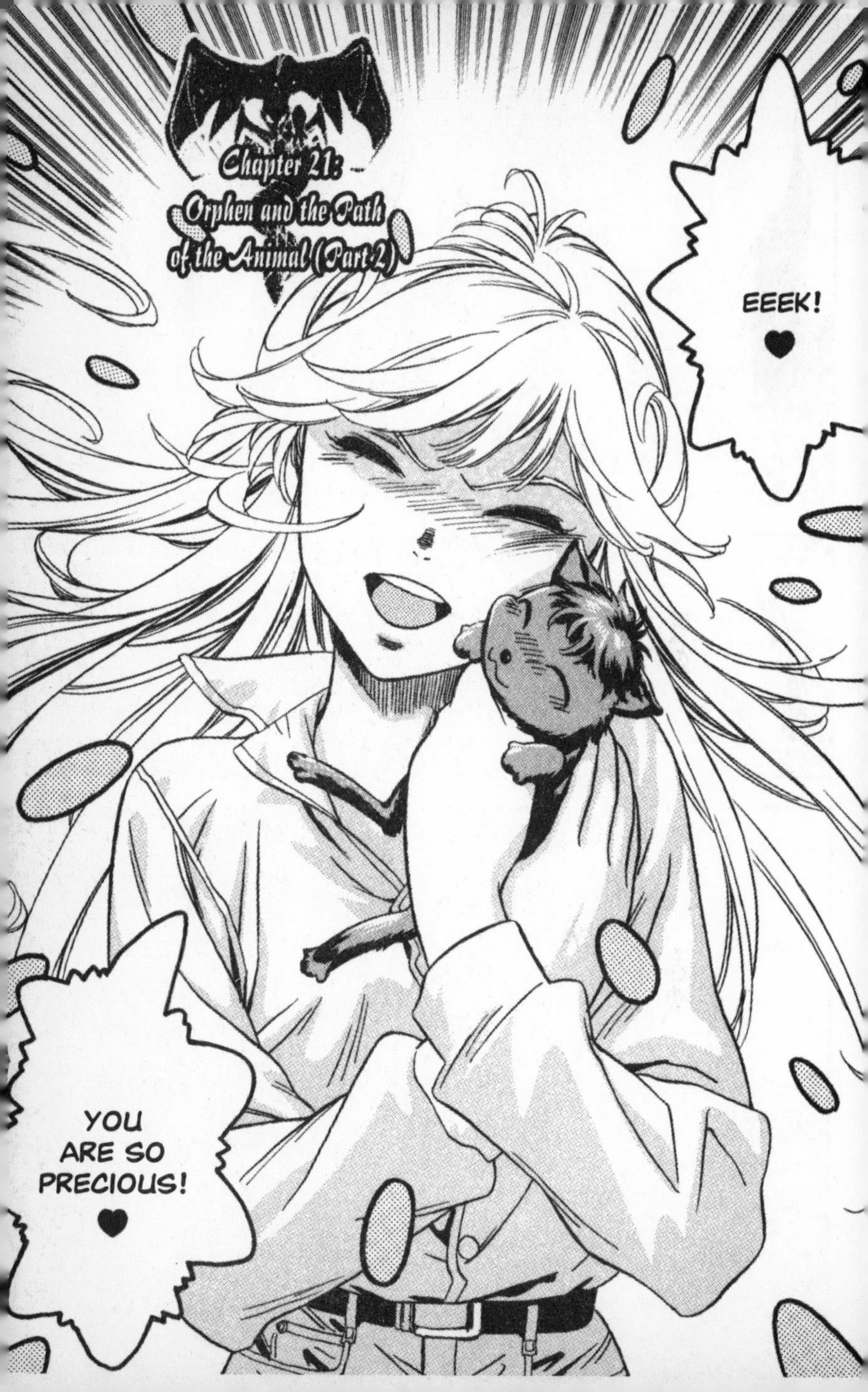
Chapter 21: Orphen and the Path of the Animal (Part 2)
EEEK! ♥
YOU ARE SO PRECIOUS! ♥

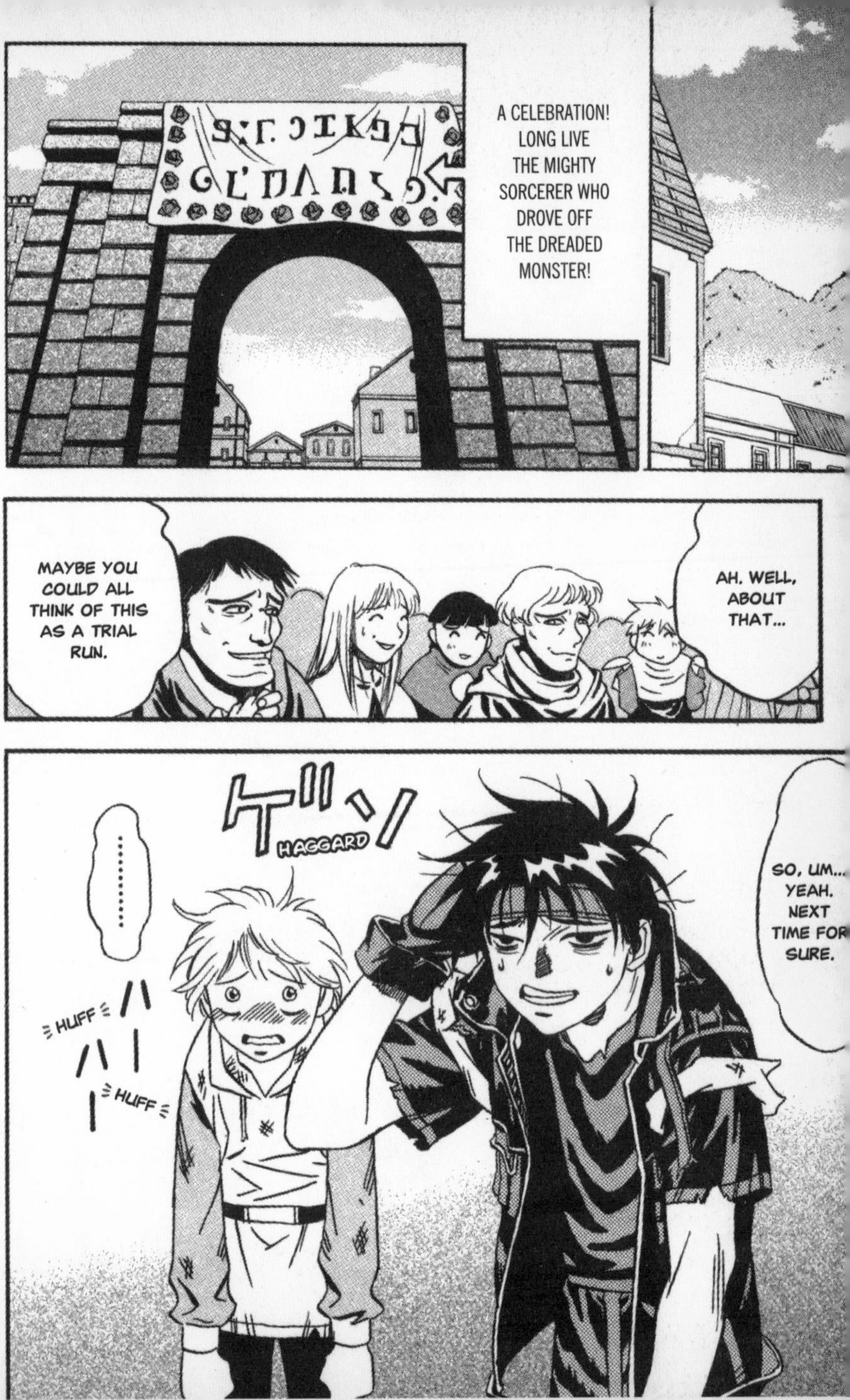
A CELEBRATION! LONG LIVE THE MIGHTY SORCERER WHO DROVE OFF THE DREADED MONSTER!
AH. WELL, ABOUT THAT...
MAYBE YOU COULD ALL THINK OF THIS AS A TRIAL RUN.
SO, UM... YEAH. NEXT TIME FOR SURE.
HAGGARD
......
HUFF
HUFF

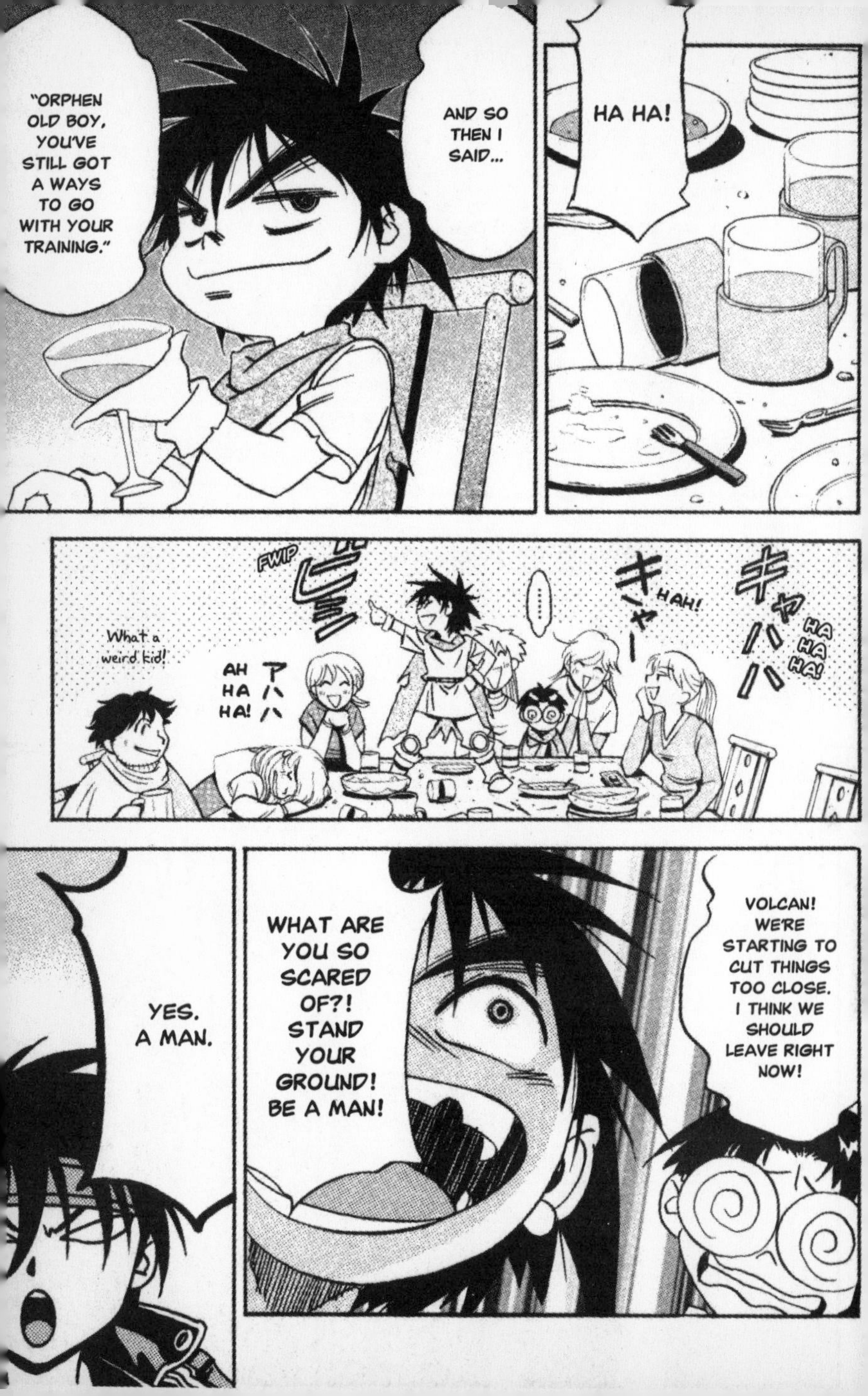
AND SO THEN I SAID...
"ORPHEN OLD BOY, YOU'VE STILL GOT A WAYS TO GO WITH YOUR TRAINING."
HA HA!
キャハハハ
HA HA HA!
キャー
HAH!
......
ビシ
FWIP
アハハ
AH HA HA!
What a weird kid!
VOLCAN! WE'RE STARTING TO CUT THINGS TOO CLOSE. I THINK WE SHOULD LEAVE RIGHT NOW!
WHAT ARE YOU SO SCARED OF?! STAND YOUR GROUND! BE A MAN!
YES. A MAN.

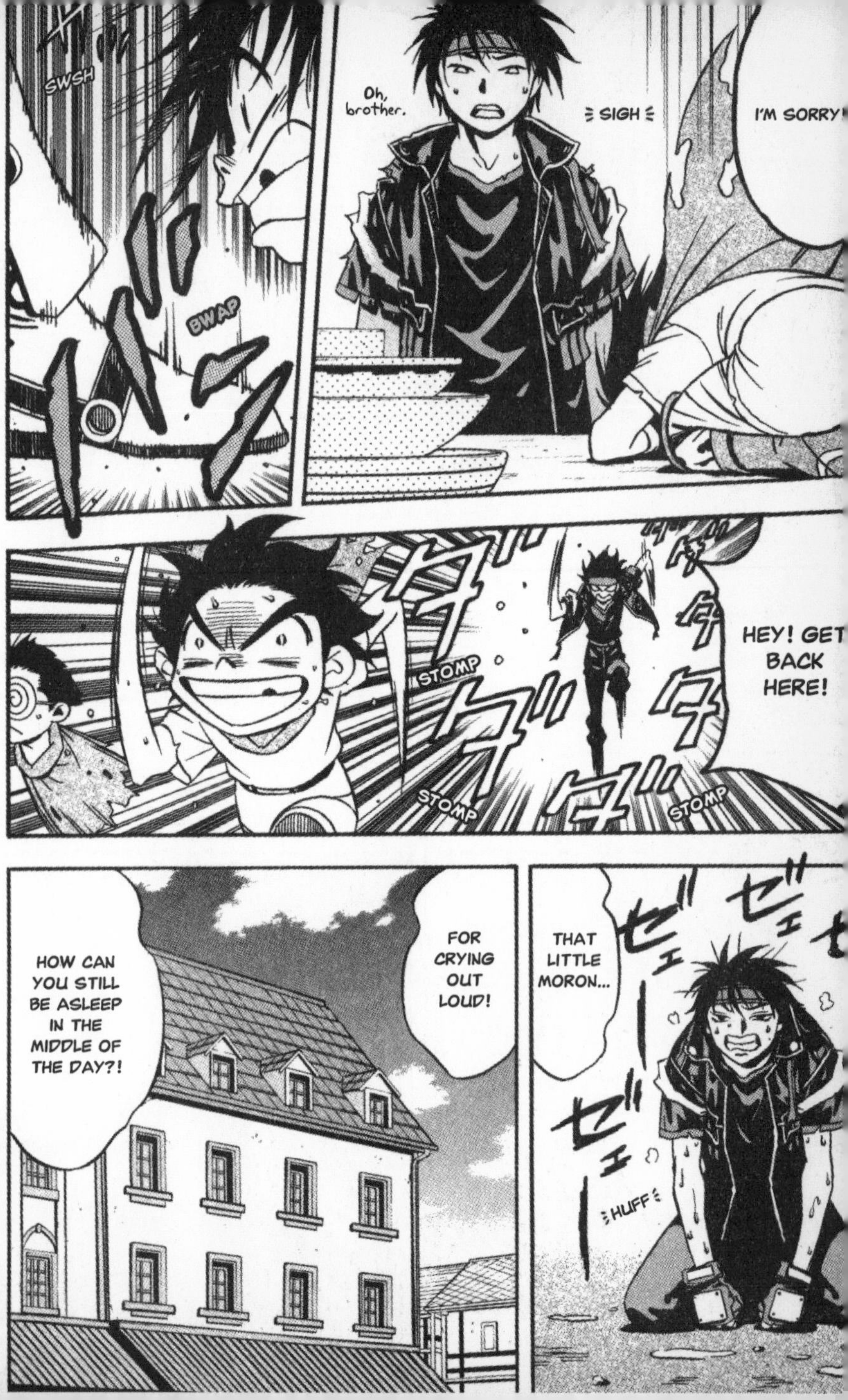
I'M SORRY!
≡ SIGH ≡
Oh, brother.
SWSH
BWAP
HEY! GET BACK HERE!
STOMP
STOMP
STOMP
THAT LITTLE MORON...
HUFF
FOR CRYING OUT LOUD!
HOW CAN YOU STILL BE ASLEEP IN THE MIDDLE OF THE DAY?!

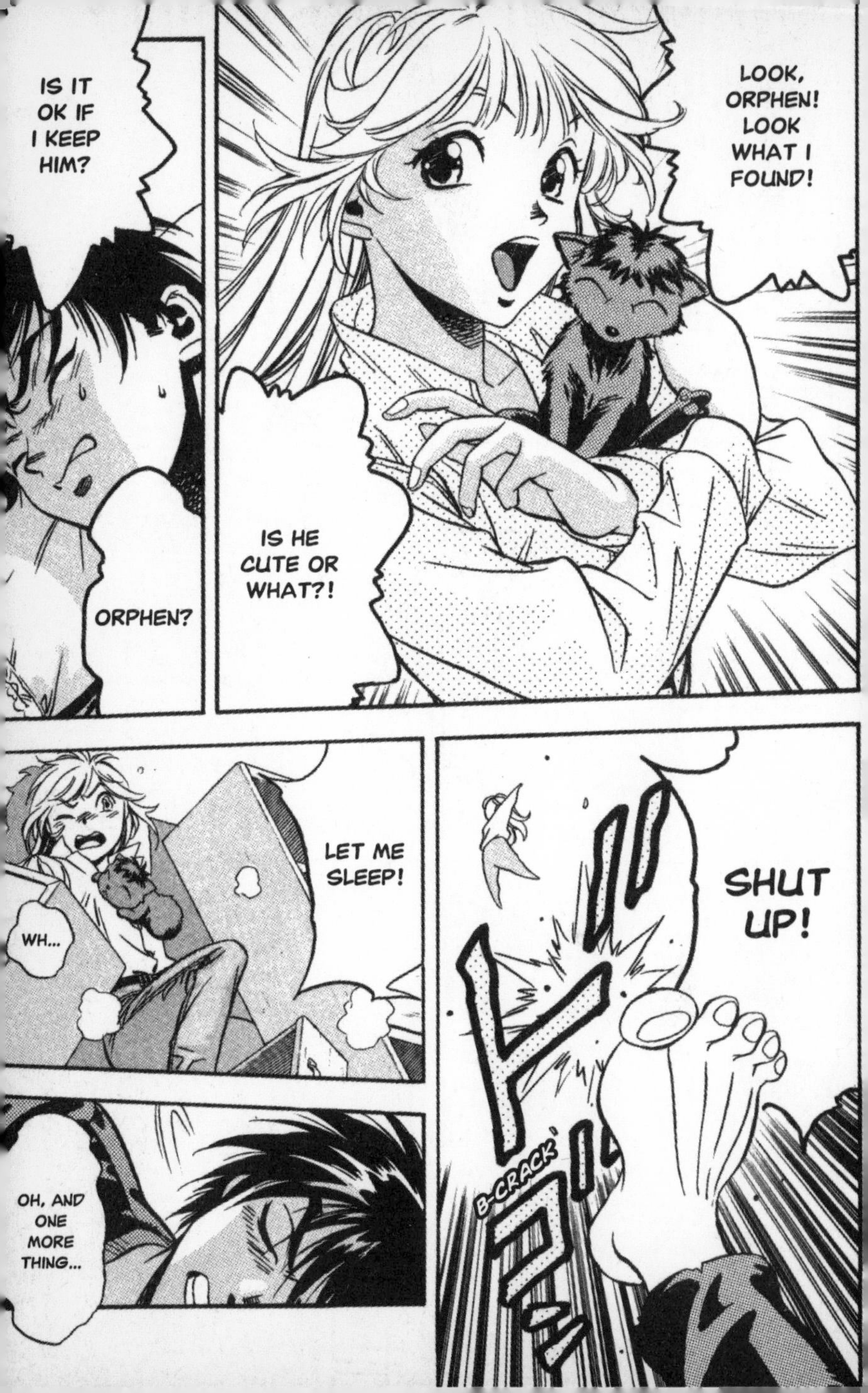
LOOK, ORPHEN! LOOK WHAT I FOUND!
IS HE CUTE OR WHAT?!
IS IT OK IF I KEEP HIM?
ORPHEN?
SHUT UP!
B-CRACK
LET ME SLEEP!
WH...
OH, AND ONE MORE THING...

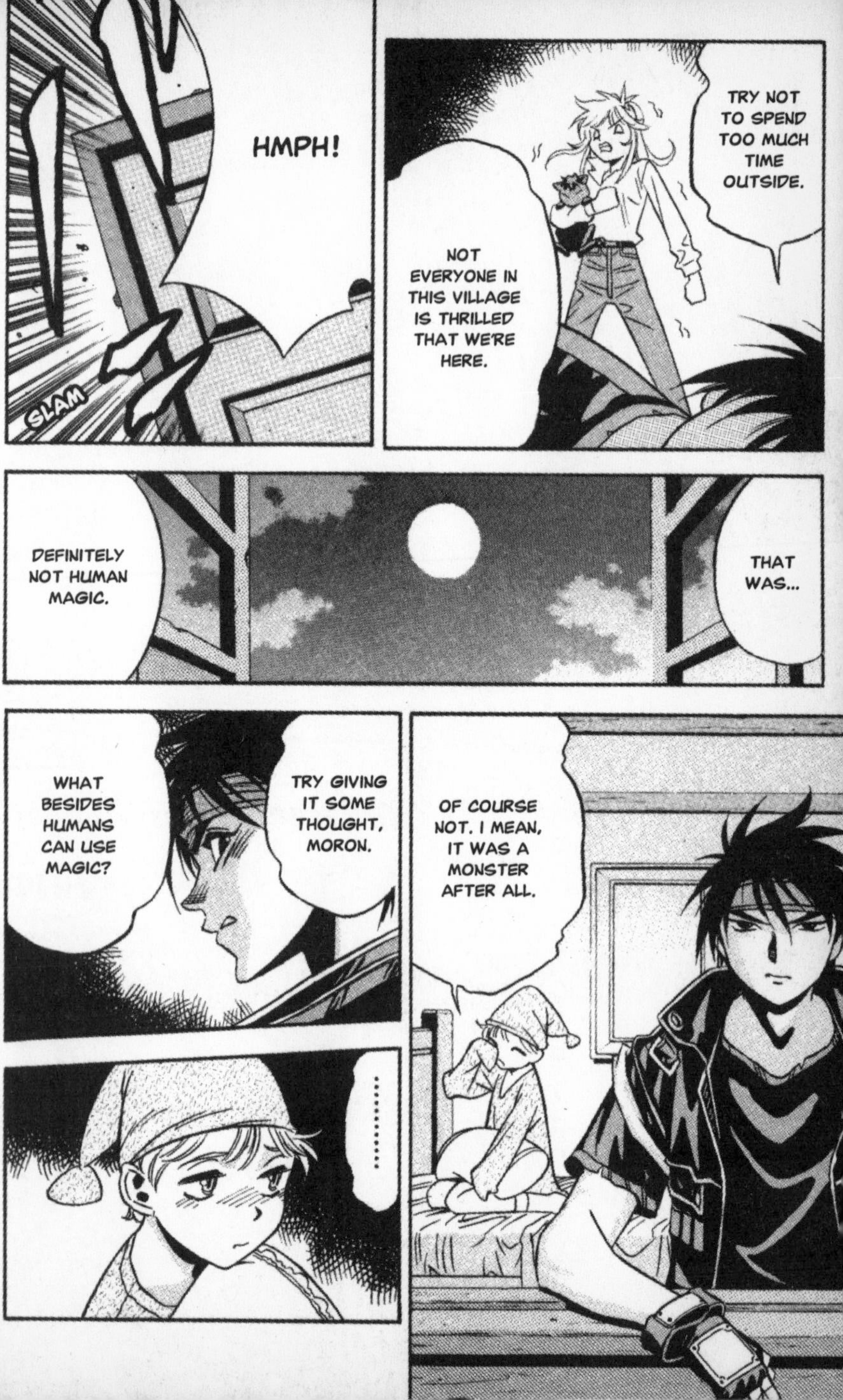
TRY NOT TO SPEND TOO MUCH TIME OUTSIDE.
NOT EVERYONE IN THIS VILLAGE IS THRILLED THAT WE'RE HERE.
HMPH!
SLAM
THAT WAS...
DEFINITELY NOT HUMAN MAGIC.
OF COURSE NOT. I MEAN, IT WAS A MONSTER AFTER ALL.
TRY GIVING IT SOME THOUGHT, MORON.
WHAT BESIDES HUMANS CAN USE MAGIC?
....

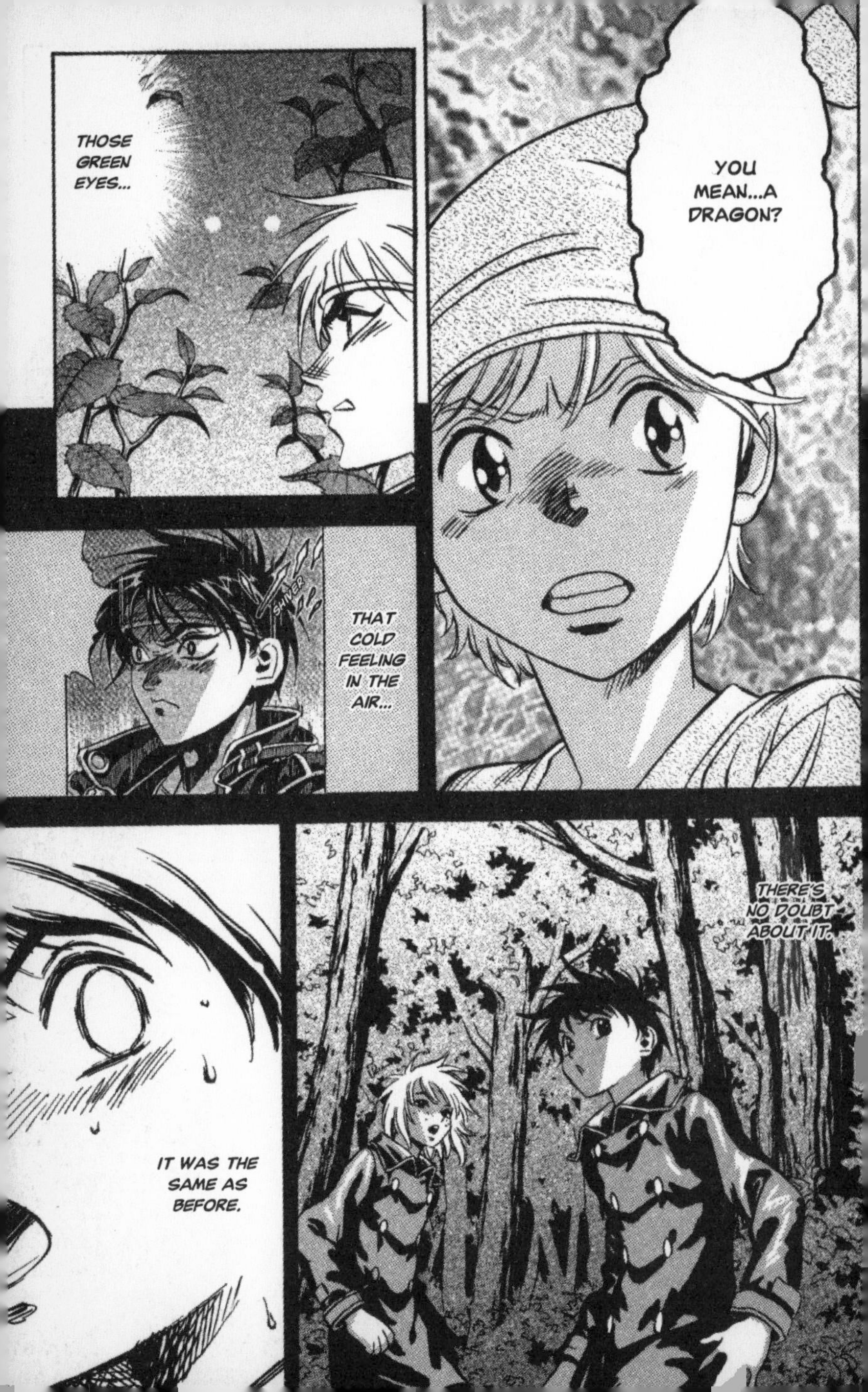
YOU MEAN...A DRAGON?
THOSE GREEN EYES...
SHIVER
THAT COLD FEELING IN THE AIR...
THERE'S NO DOUBT ABOUT IT.
IT WAS THE SAME AS BEFORE.

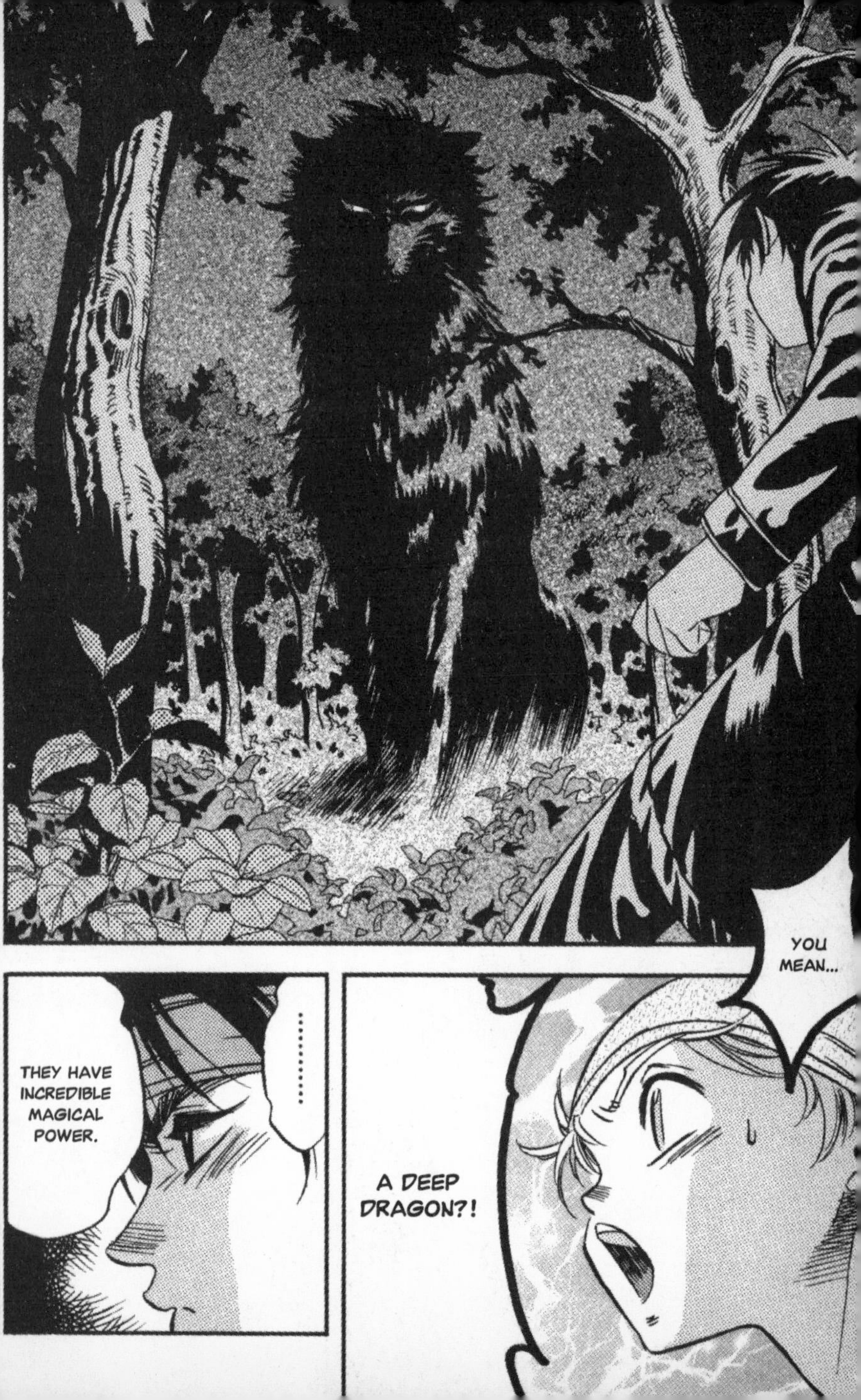
YOU MEAN...
A DEEP DRAGON?!
....
THEY HAVE INCREDIBLE MAGICAL POWER.

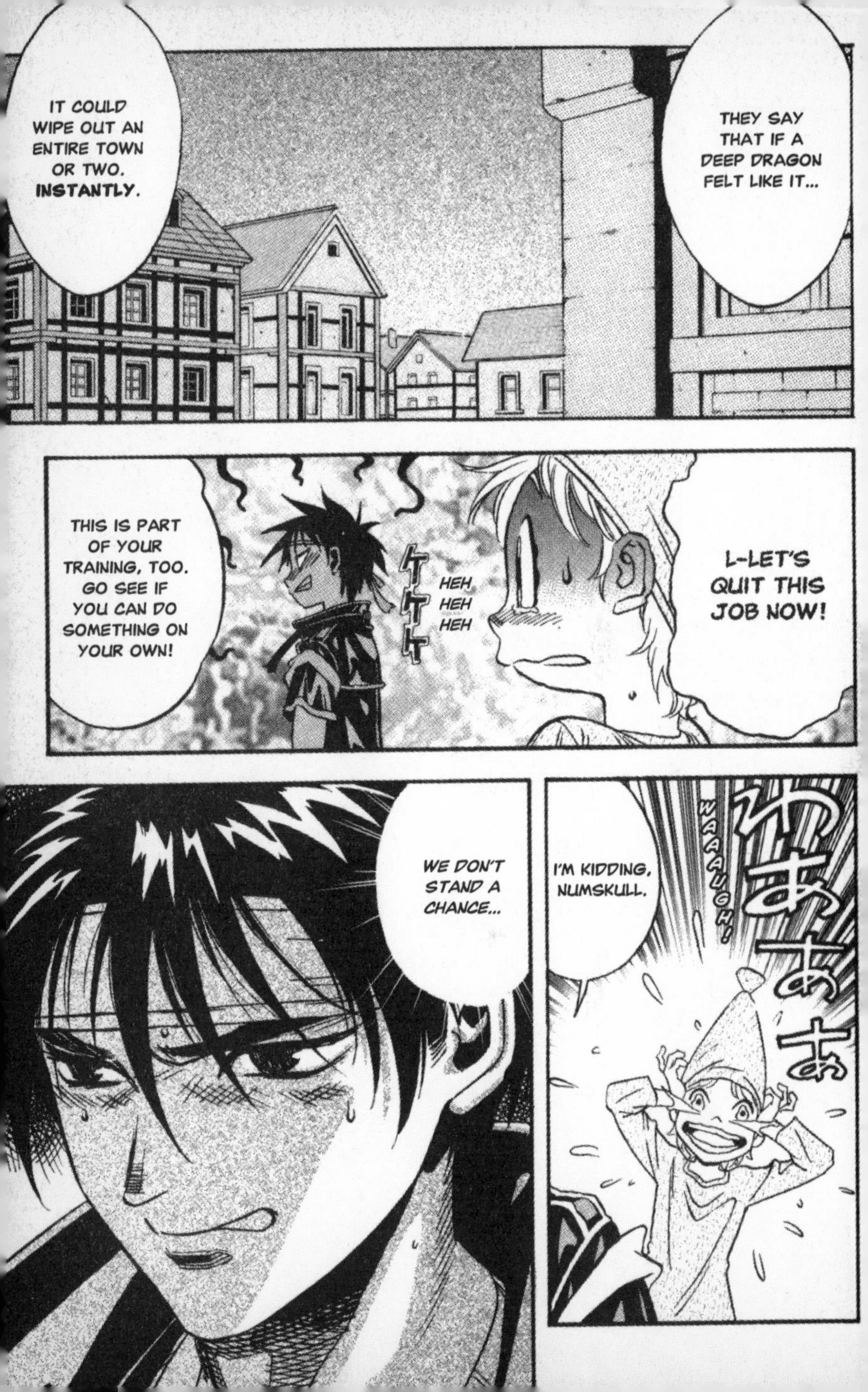
THEY SAY THAT IF A DEEP DRAGON FELT LIKE IT...
IT COULD WIPE OUT AN ENTIRE TOWN OR TWO. **INSTANTLY.**
L-LET'S QUIT THIS JOB NOW!
HEH HEH HEH
THIS IS PART OF YOUR TRAINING, TOO. GO SEE IF YOU CAN DO SOMETHING ON YOUR OWN!
WAAAAUGH!
I'M KIDDING, NUMSKULL.
WE DON'T STAND A CHANCE...

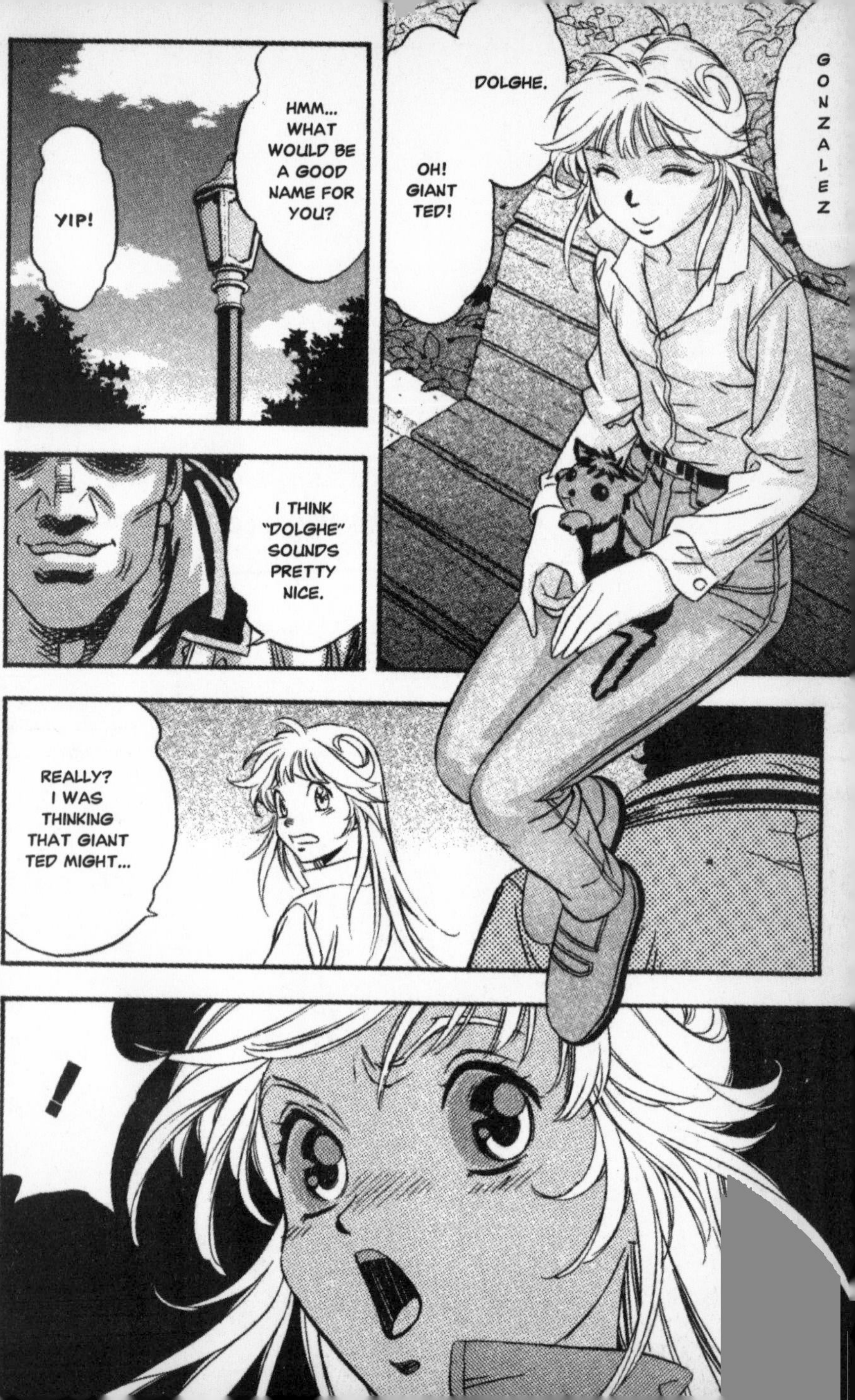
GONZALEZ
DOLGHE.
OH! GIANT TED!
HMM... WHAT WOULD BE A GOOD NAME FOR YOU?
YIP!
I THINK "DOLGHE" SOUNDS PRETTY NICE.
REALLY? I WAS THINKING THAT GIANT TED MIGHT...
!

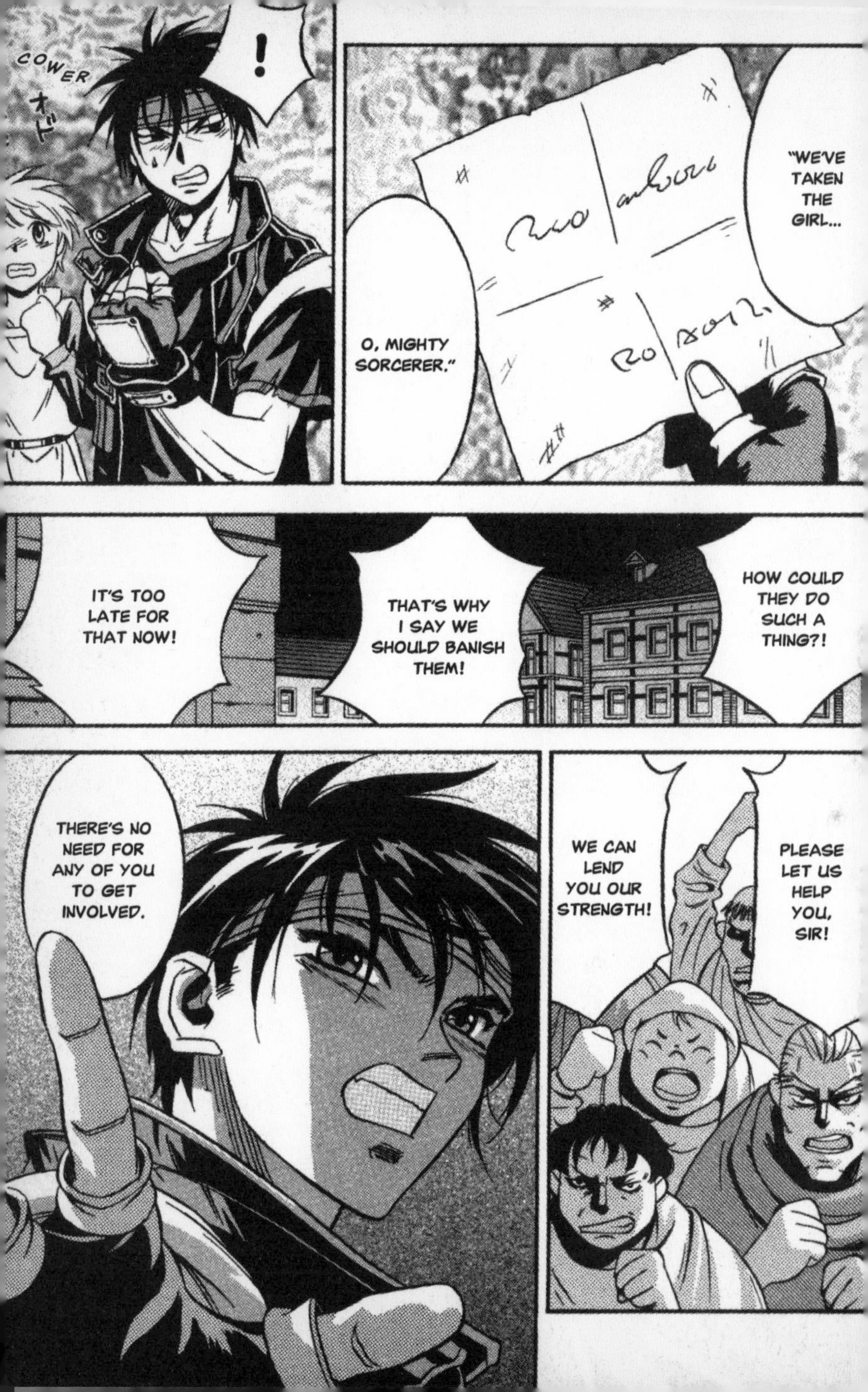
"WE'VE TAKEN THE GIRL...
O, MIGHTY SORCERER."
!
COWER
オド
HOW COULD THEY DO SUCH A THING?!
THAT'S WHY I SAY WE SHOULD BANISH THEM!
IT'S TOO LATE FOR THAT NOW!
PLEASE LET US HELP YOU, SIR!
WE CAN LEND YOU OUR STRENGTH!
THERE'S NO NEED FOR ANY OF YOU TO GET INVOLVED.

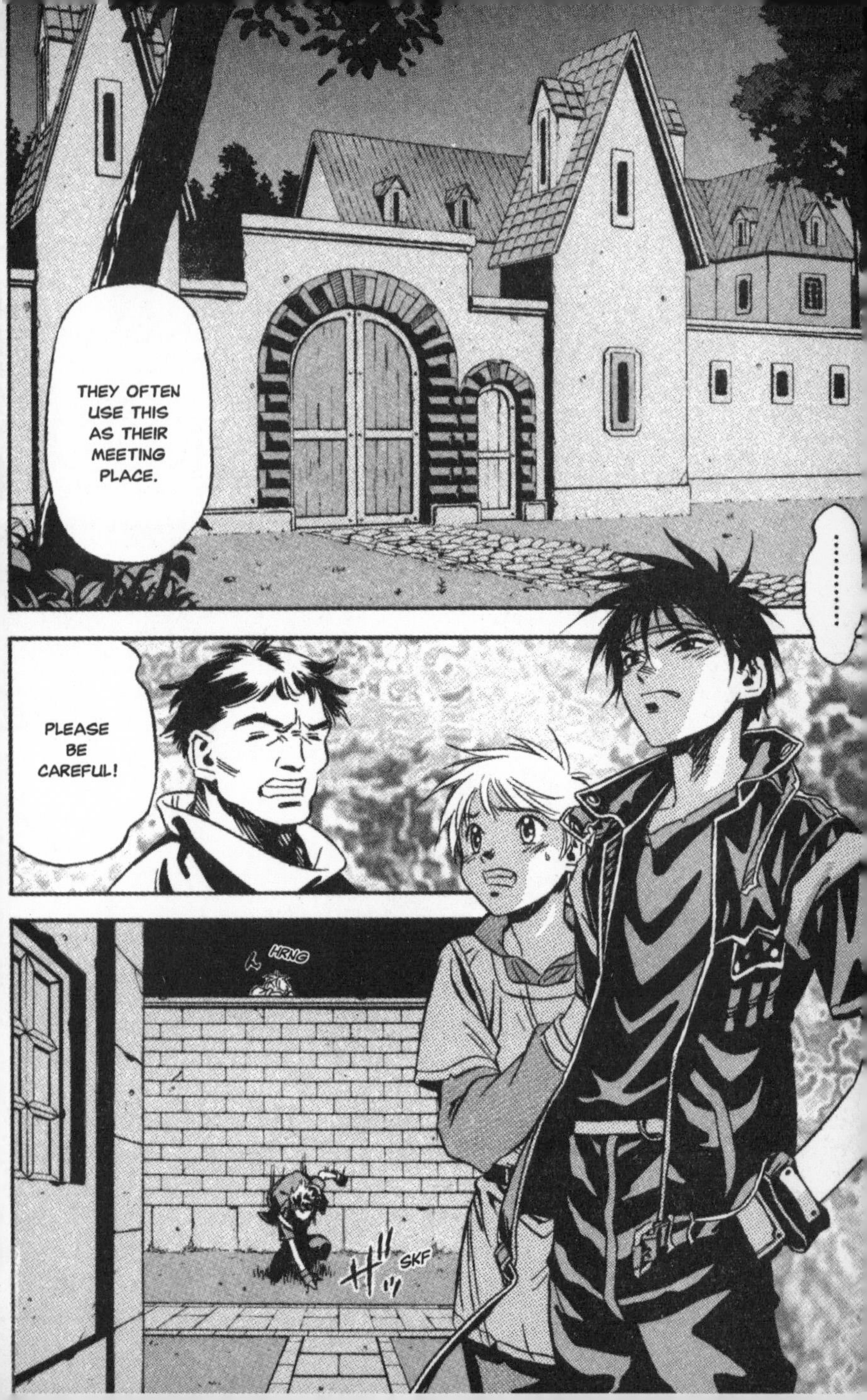
......
THEY OFTEN USE THIS AS THEIR MEETING PLACE.
PLEASE BE CAREFUL!
HRNG
SKF

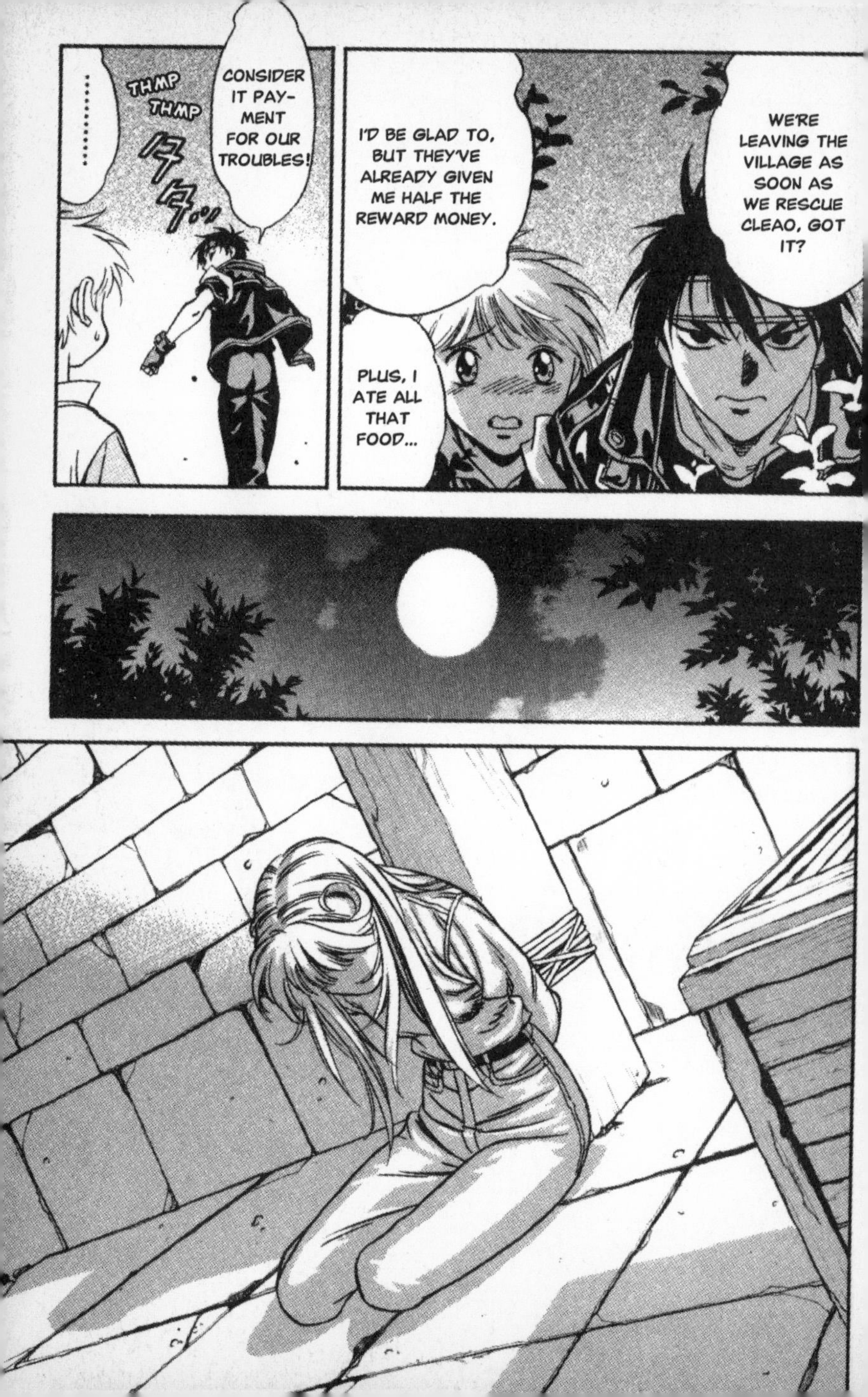
WE'RE LEAVING THE VILLAGE AS SOON AS WE RESCUE CLEAO, GOT IT?
I'D BE GLAD TO, BUT THEY'VE ALREADY GIVEN ME HALF THE REWARD MONEY.
PLUS, I ATE ALL THAT FOOD...
CONSIDER IT PAY-MENT FOR OUR TROUBLES!
THMP THMP
....

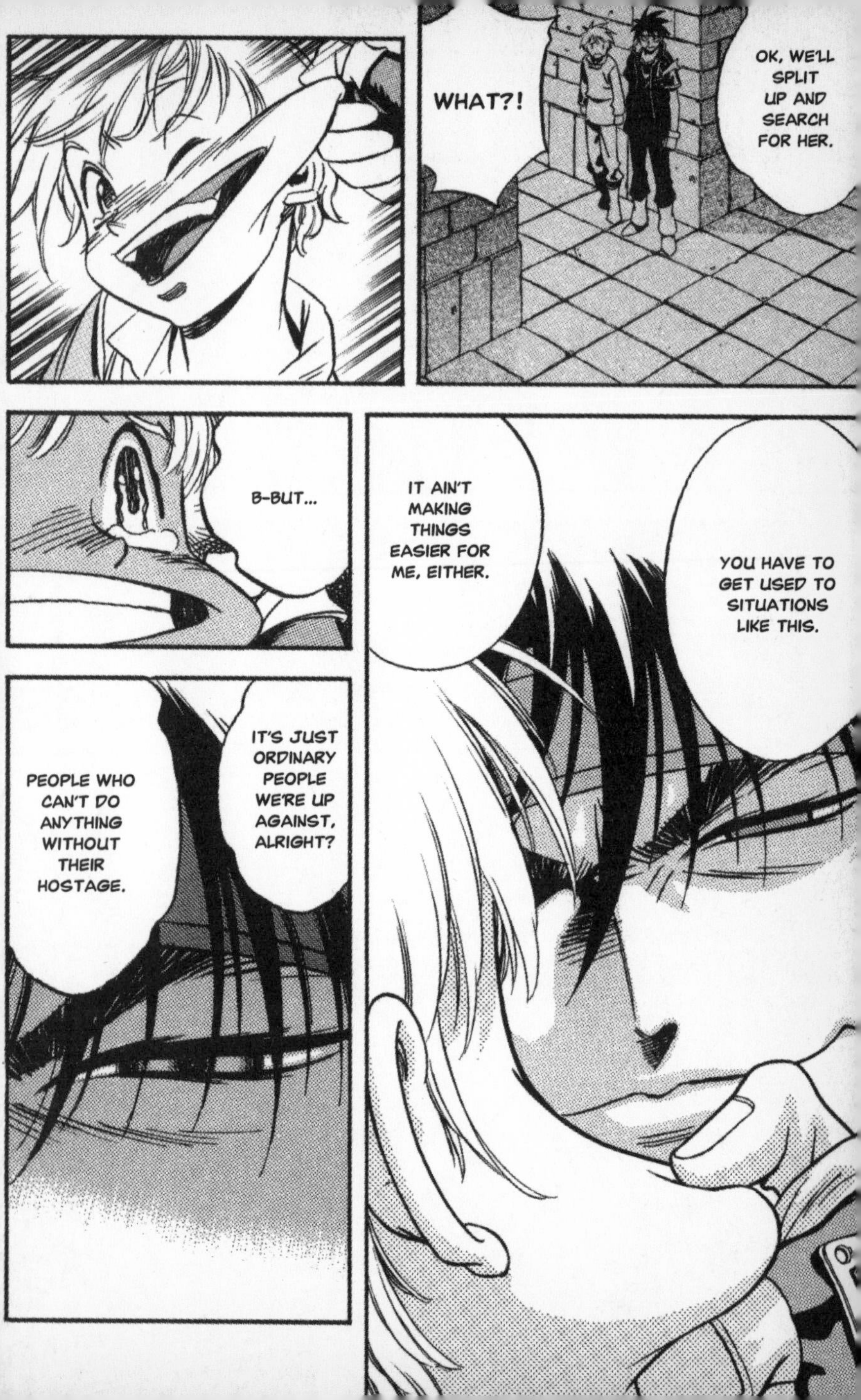
OK, WE'LL SPLIT UP AND SEARCH FOR HER.
WHAT?!
YOU HAVE TO GET USED TO SITUATIONS LIKE THIS.
IT AIN'T MAKING THINGS EASIER FOR ME, EITHER.
B-BUT...
IT'S JUST ORDINARY PEOPLE WE'RE UP AGAINST, ALRIGHT?
PEOPLE WHO CAN'T DO ANYTHING WITHOUT THEIR HOSTAGE.

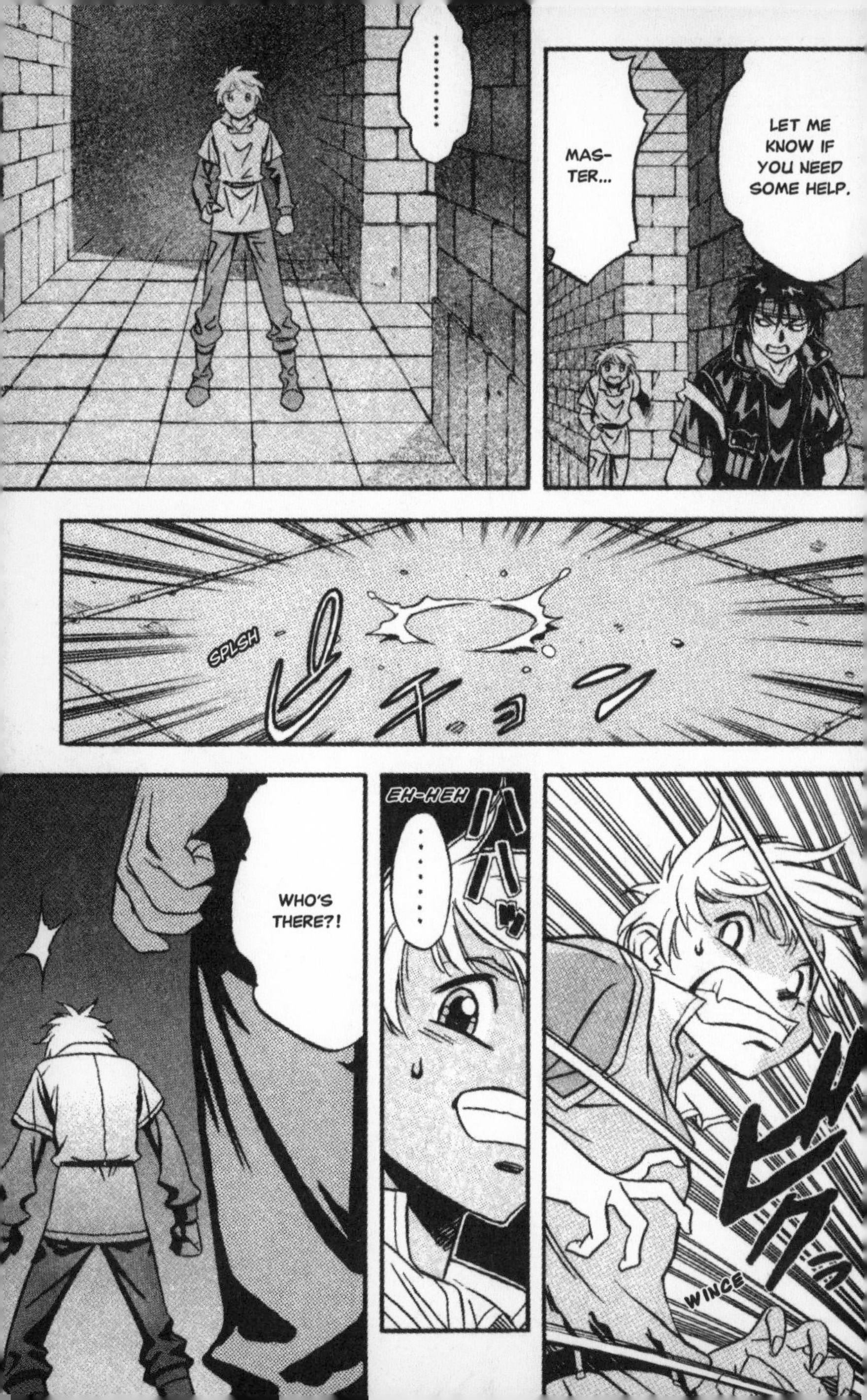
LET ME KNOW IF YOU NEED SOME HELP.
MAS-TER...
......
SPLSH
WINCE
EH-HEH
......
WHO'S THERE?!

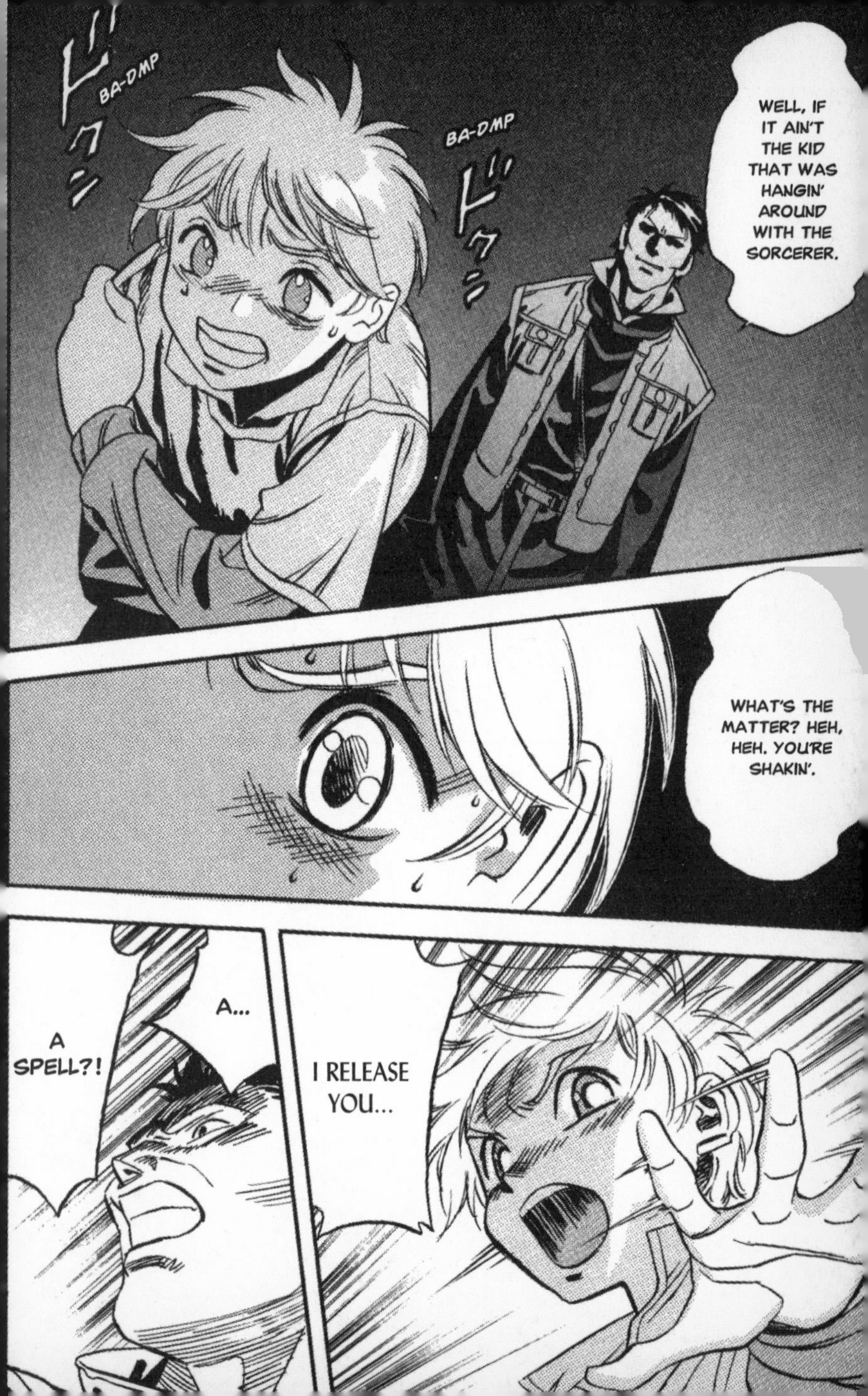
WELL, IF IT AIN'T THE KID THAT WAS HANGIN' AROUND WITH THE SORCERER.
BA-DMP
BA-DMP
WHAT'S THE MATTER? HEH, HEH. YOU'RE SHAKIN'.
I RELEASE YOU...
A...
A SPELL?!

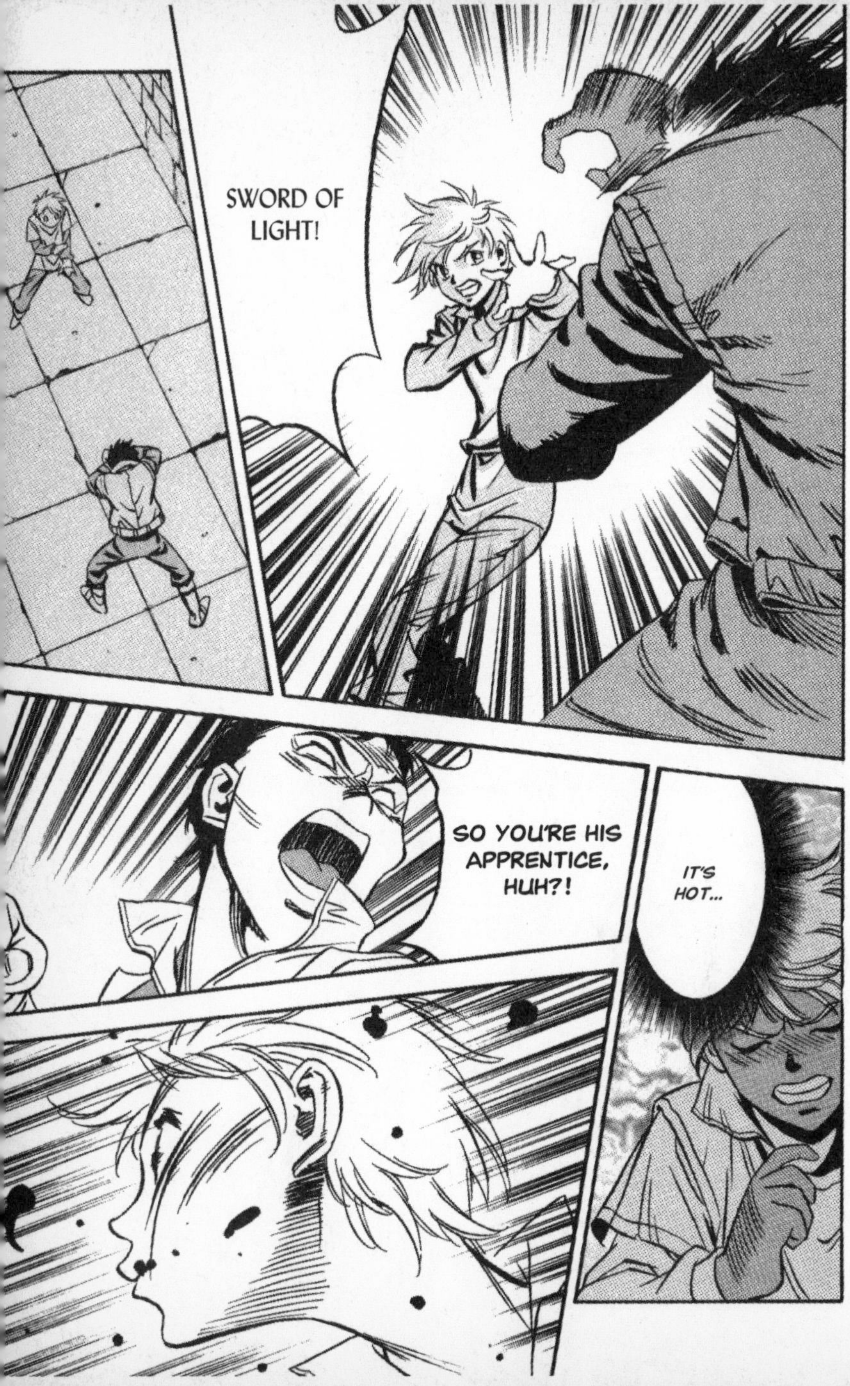
SWORD OF LIGHT!
SO YOU'RE HIS APPRENTICE, HUH?!
IT'S HOT...

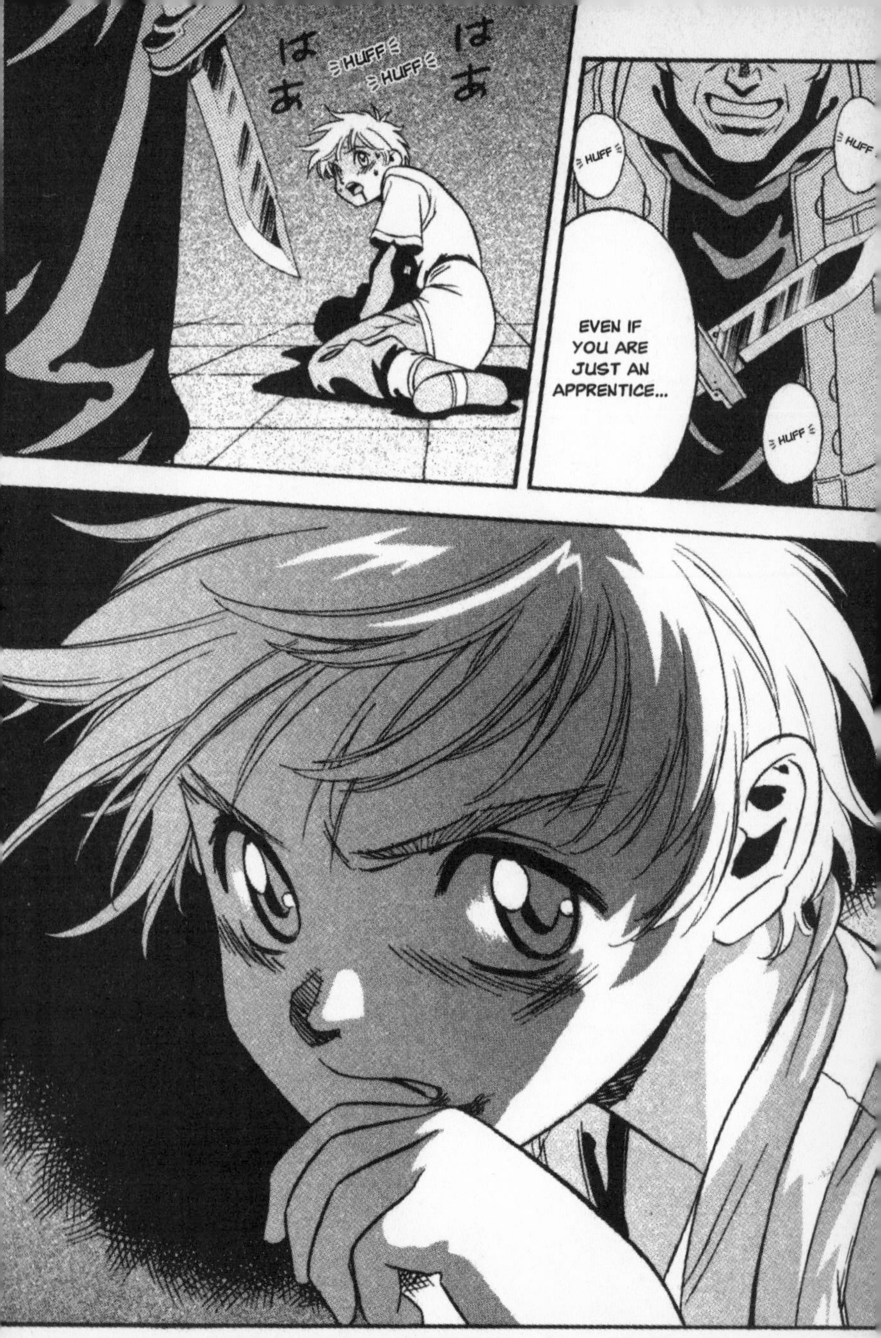

HUFF
HUFF
EVEN IF YOU ARE JUST AN APPRENTICE...
HUFF
はあ
HUFF
HUFF
はあ

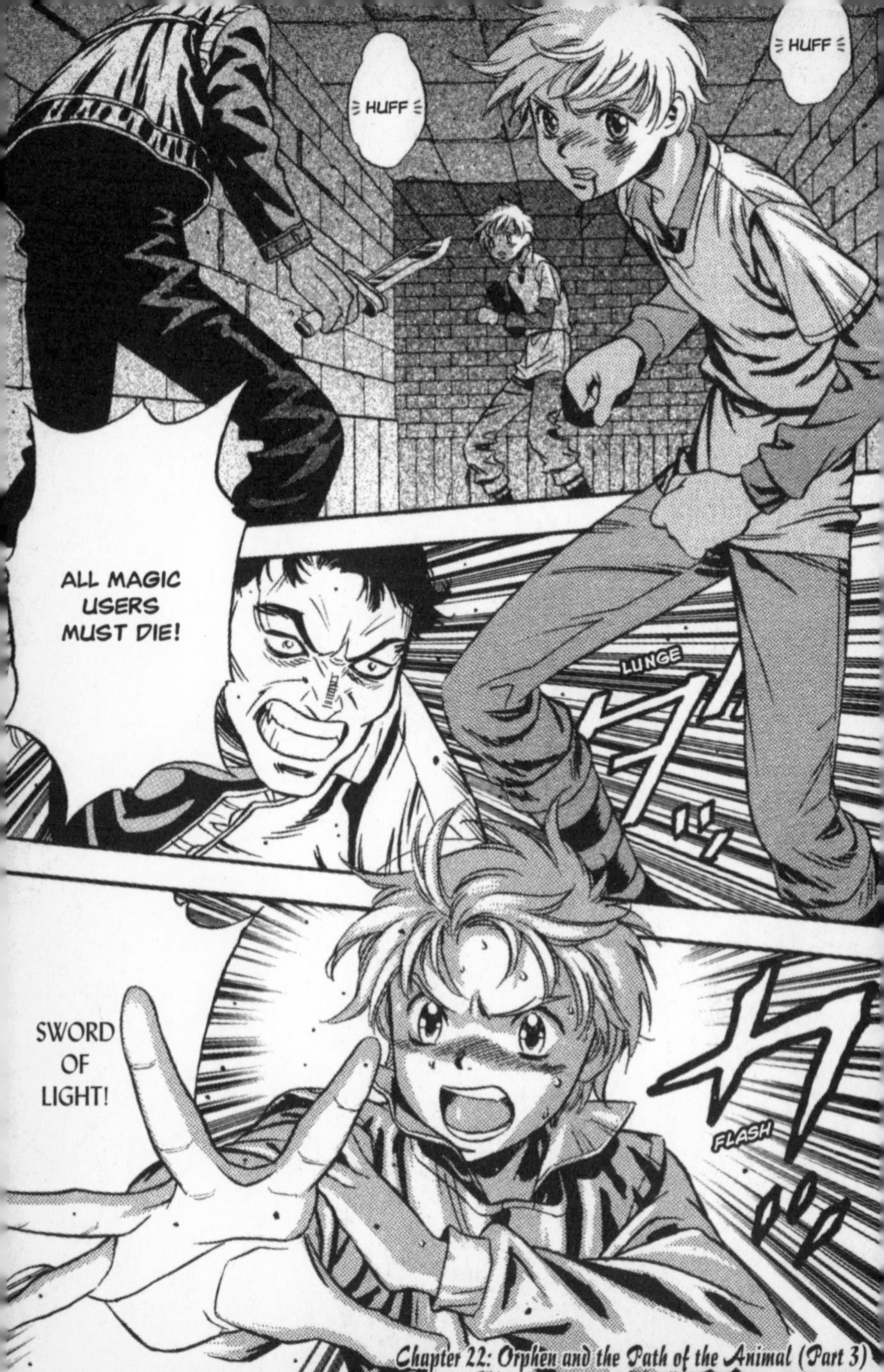
HUFF
HUFF
ALL MAGIC USERS MUST DIE!
LUNGE
SWORD OF LIGHT!
FLASH

Chapter 22: Orphen and the Path of the Animal (Part 3)

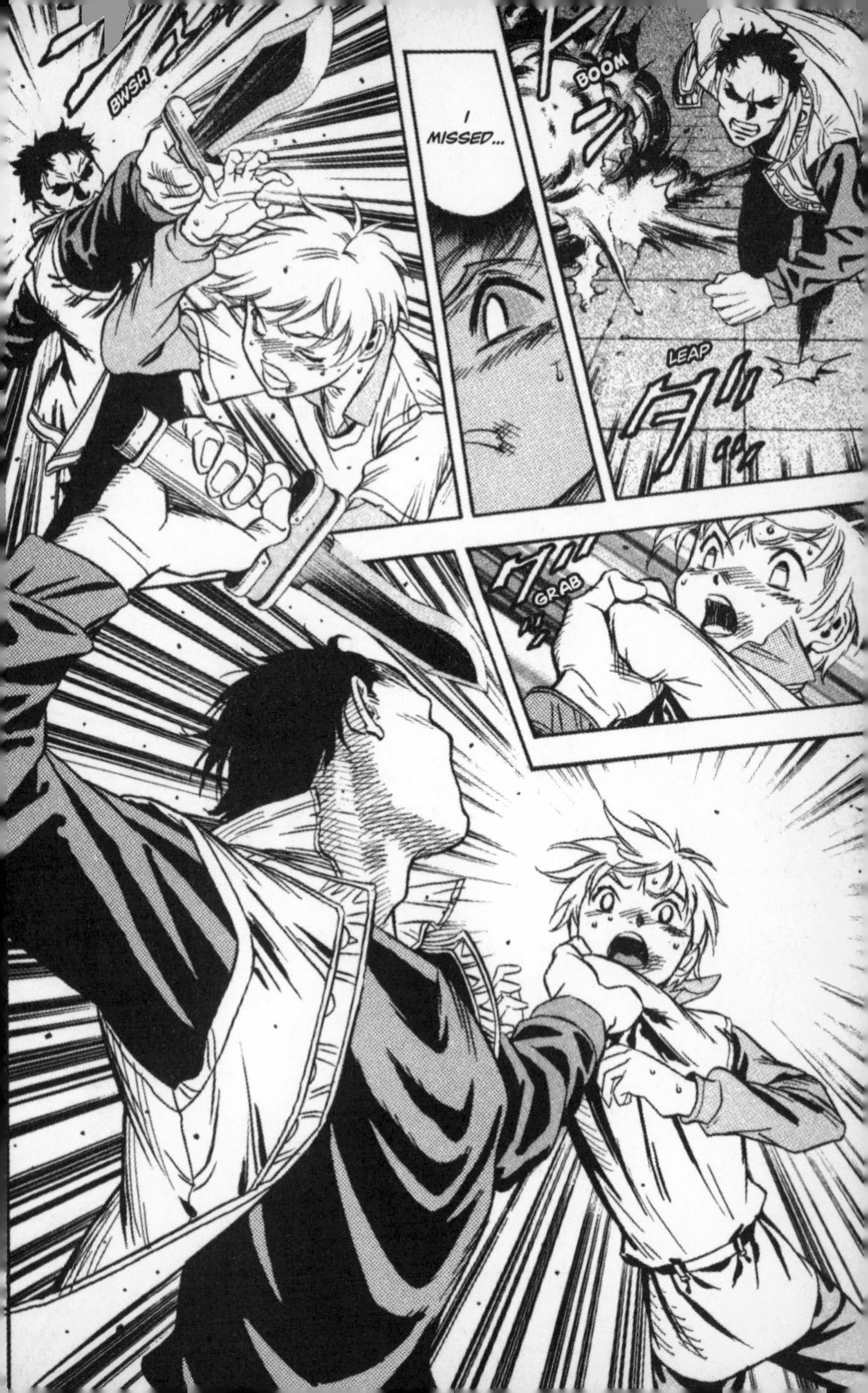
BOOM
I MISSED...
BWSH
LEAP
GRAB

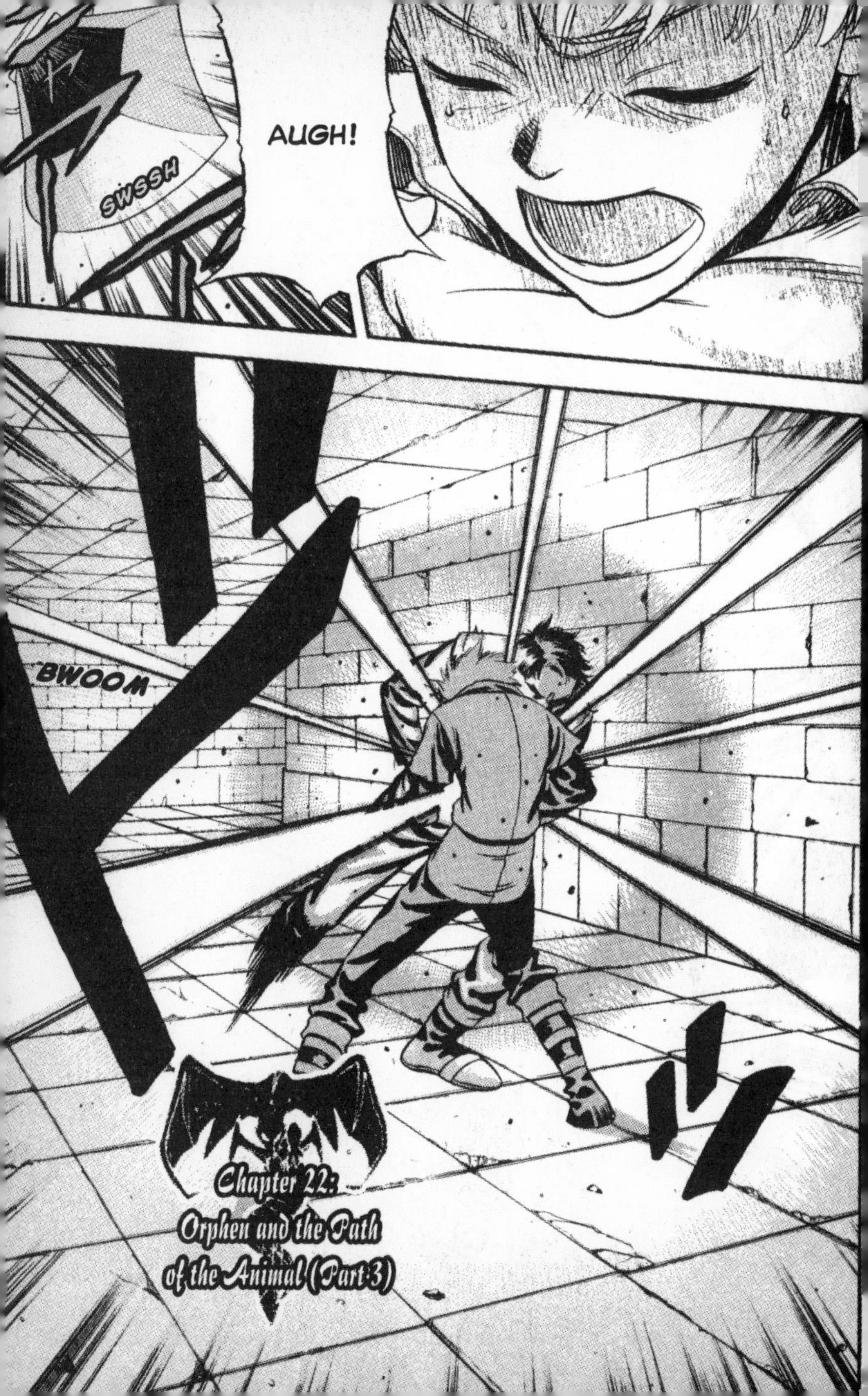
AUGH!
SWSSH
BWOOM
Chapter 22:
Orphen and the Path of the Animal (Part 3)

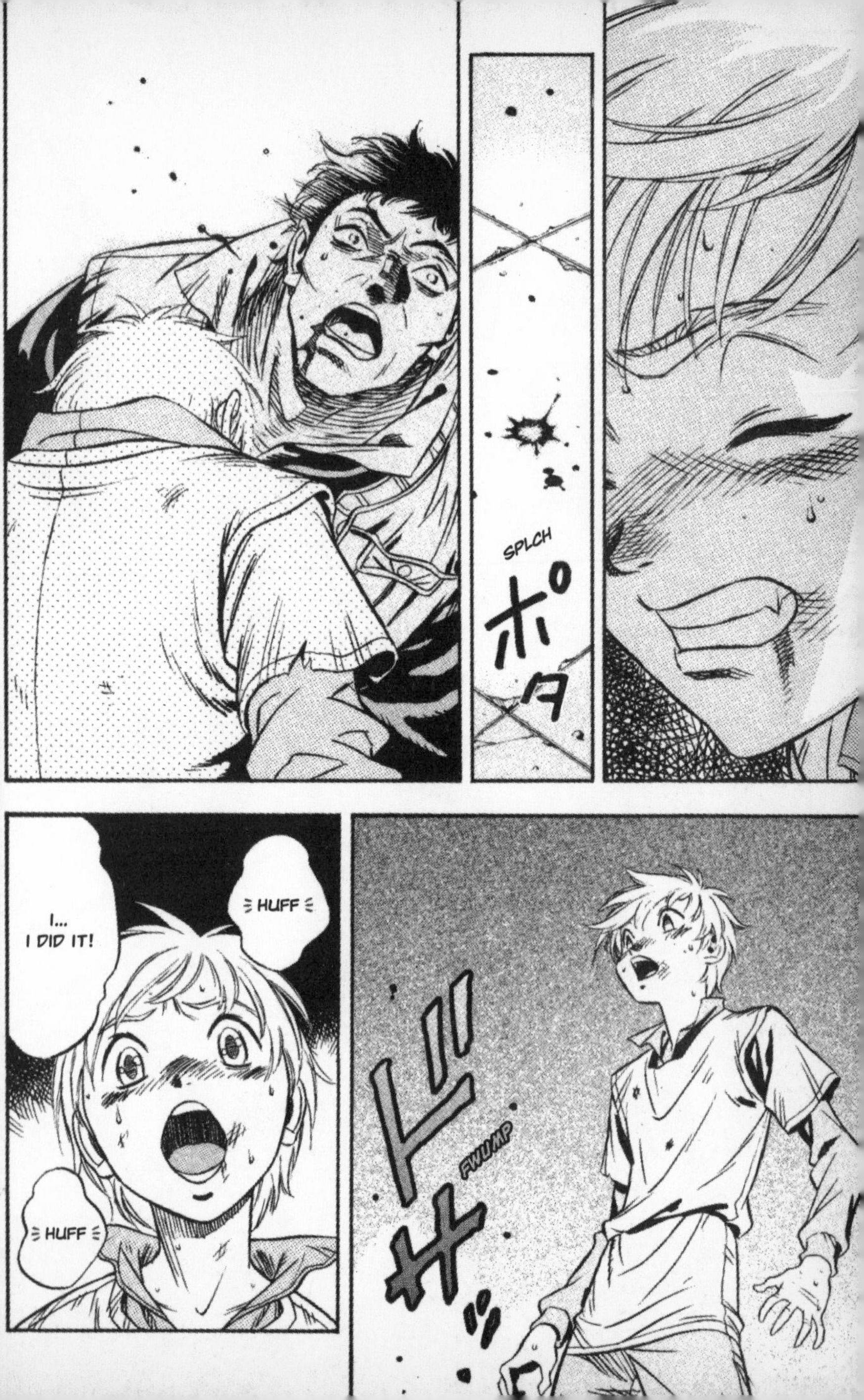
SPLCH
ポタ
FWUMP
ドサッ
HUFF
I...
I DID IT!
HUFF

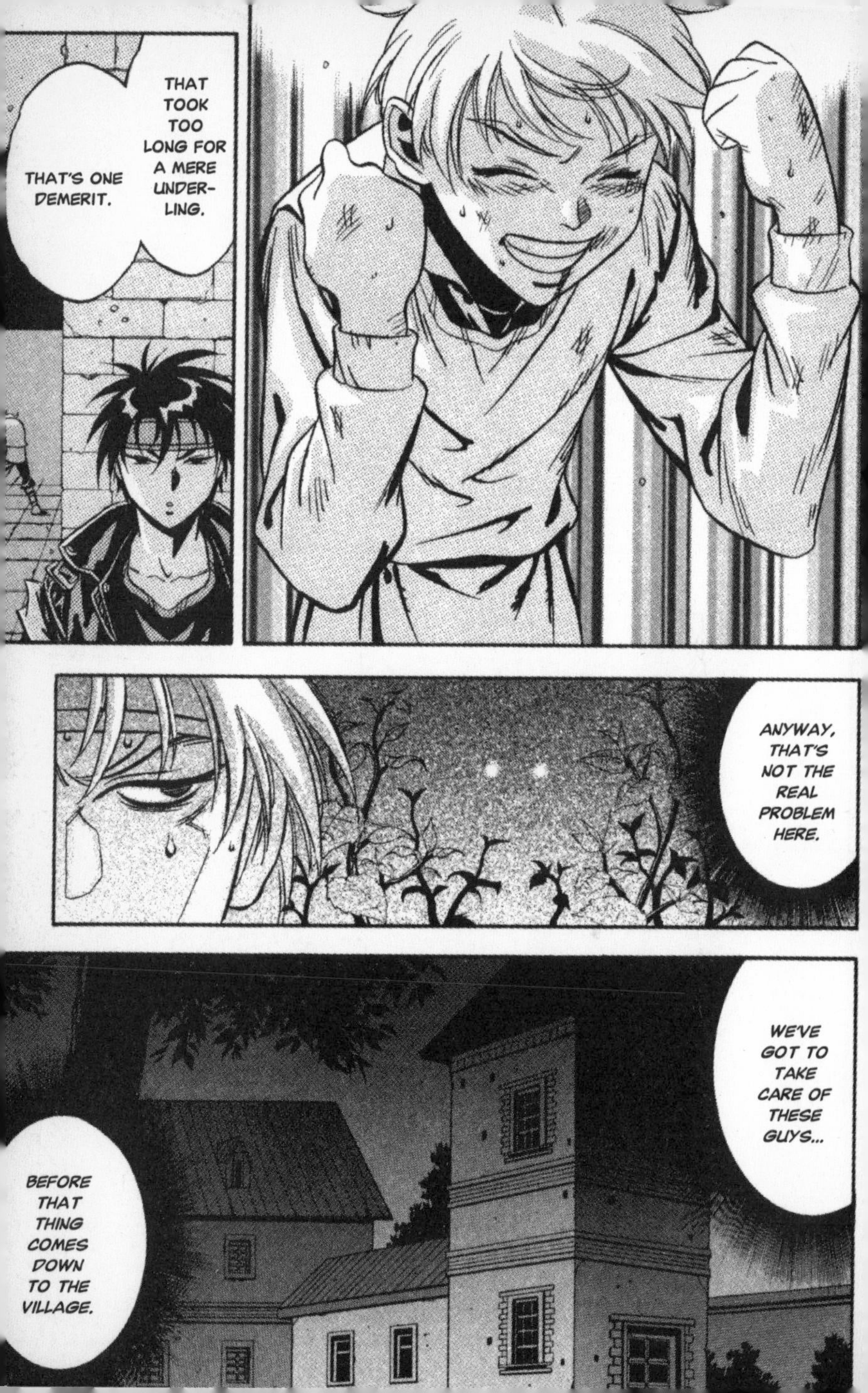
THAT TOOK TOO LONG FOR A MERE UNDER-LING.
THAT'S ONE DEMERIT.
ANYWAY, THAT'S NOT THE REAL PROBLEM HERE.
WE'VE GOT TO TAKE CARE OF THESE GUYS...
BEFORE THAT THING COMES DOWN TO THE VILLAGE.

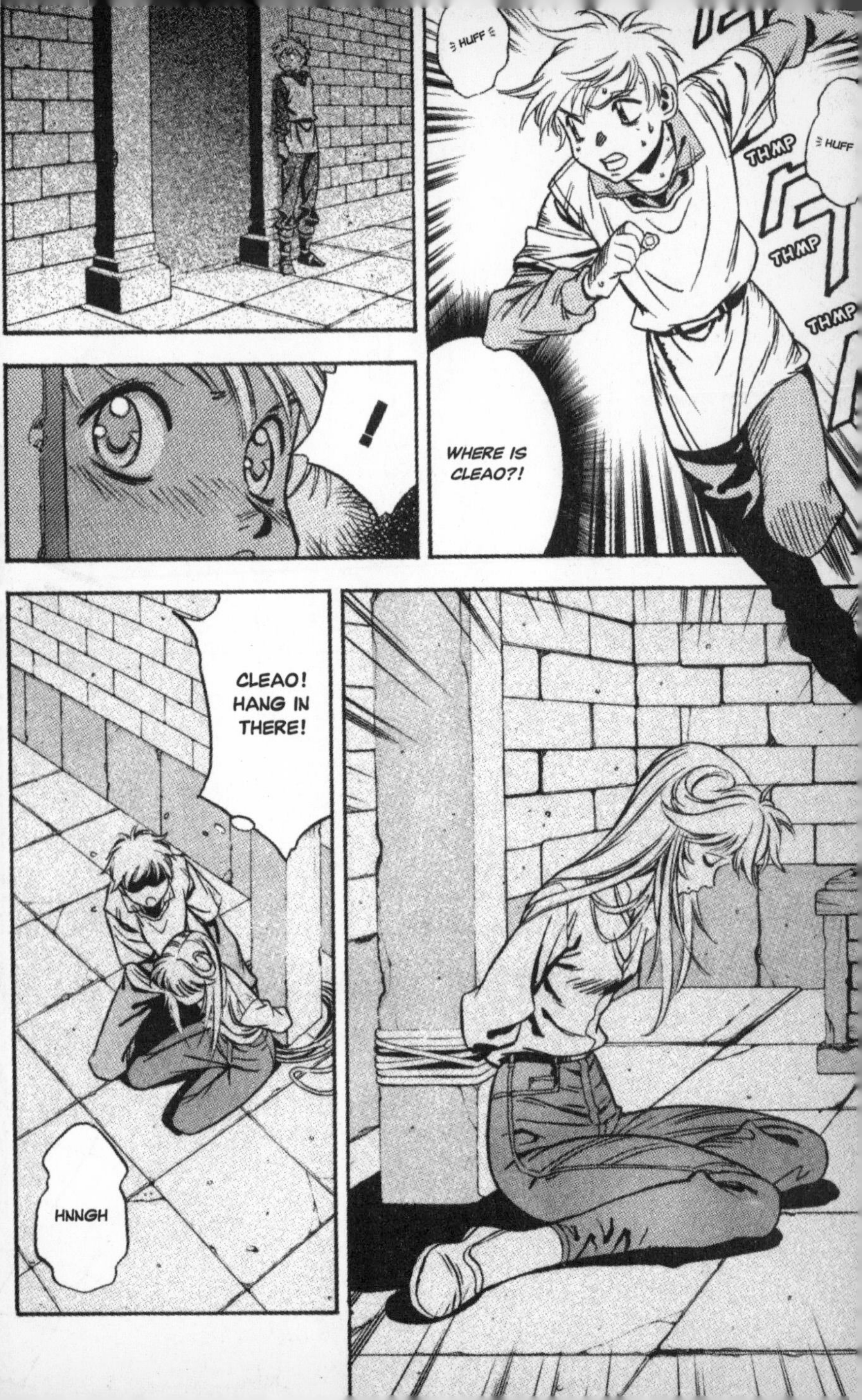

HUFF
HUFF
THMP
THMP
THMP
WHERE IS CLEAO?!
!
CLEAO! HANG IN THERE!
HNNGH

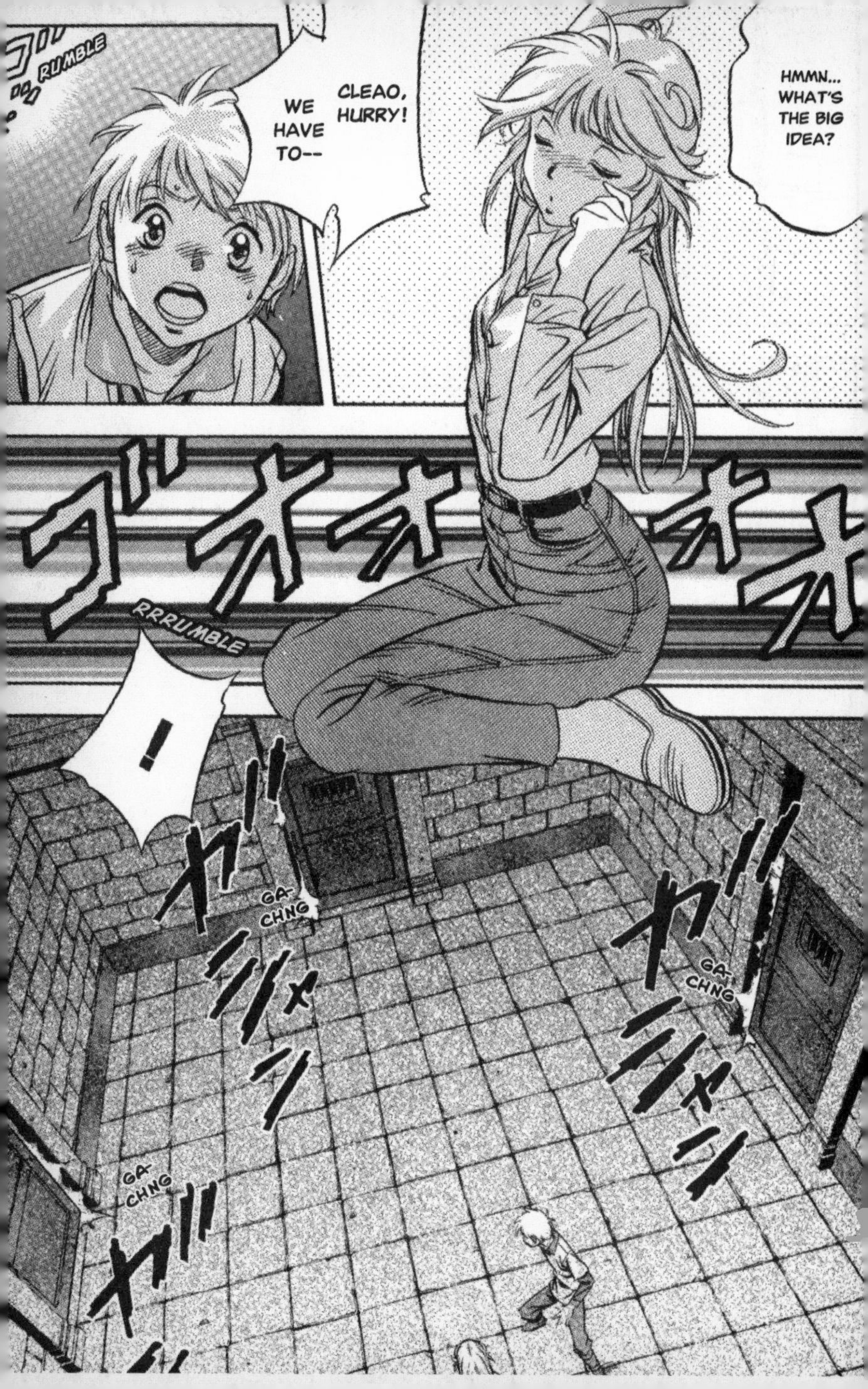

HMMN... WHAT'S THE BIG IDEA?
RUMBLE
CLEAO, HURRY!
WE HAVE TO--
RRRUMBLE
!
GA-CHNG
GA-CHNG
GA-CHNG

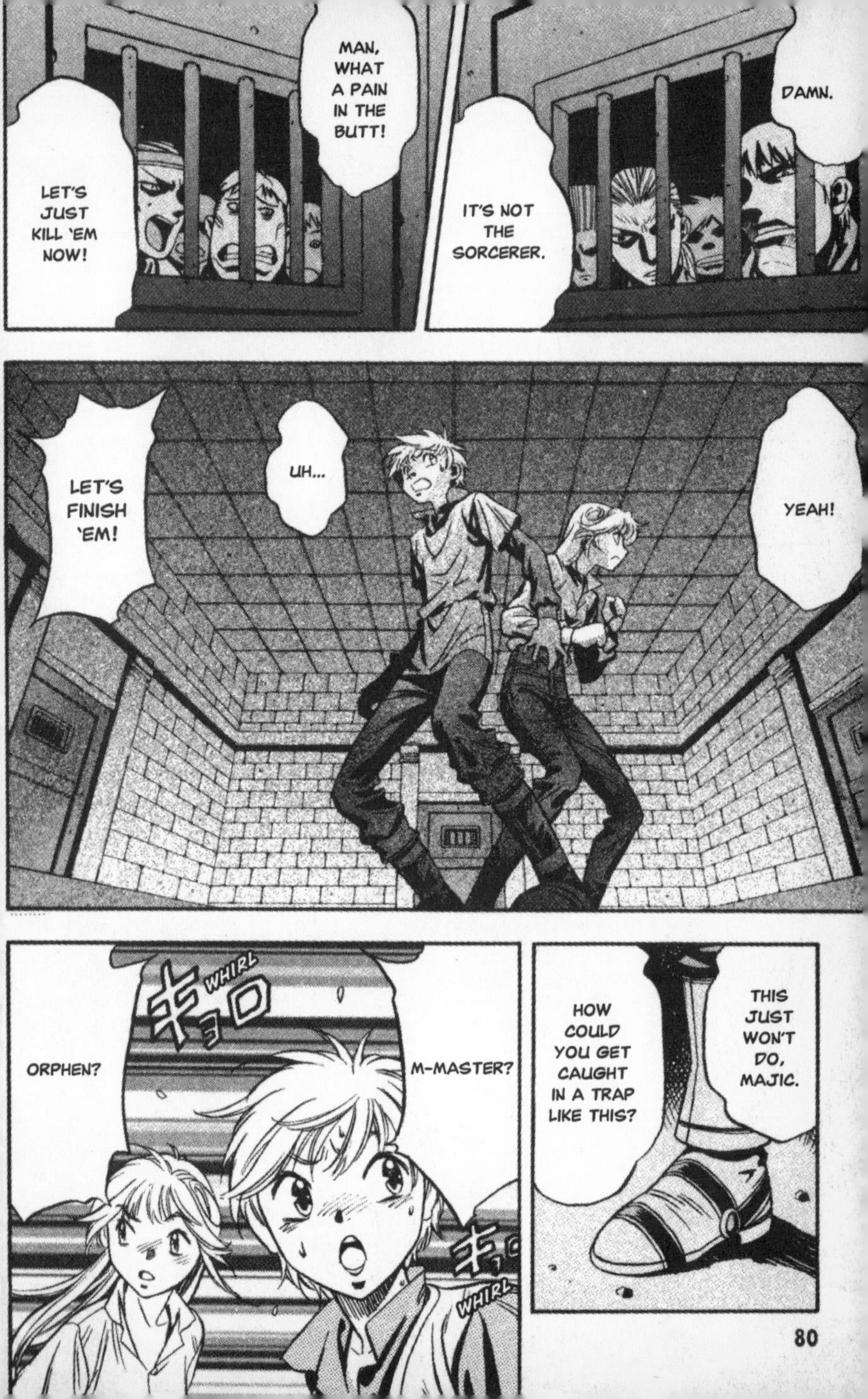
DAMN.
IT'S NOT THE SORCERER.
MAN, WHAT A PAIN IN THE BUTT!
LET'S JUST KILL 'EM NOW!
YEAH!
UH...
LET'S FINISH 'EM!
THIS JUST WON'T DO, MAJIC.
HOW COULD YOU GET CAUGHT IN A TRAP LIKE THIS?
M-MASTER?
キョロ WHIRL
キョロ WHIRL
ORPHEN?

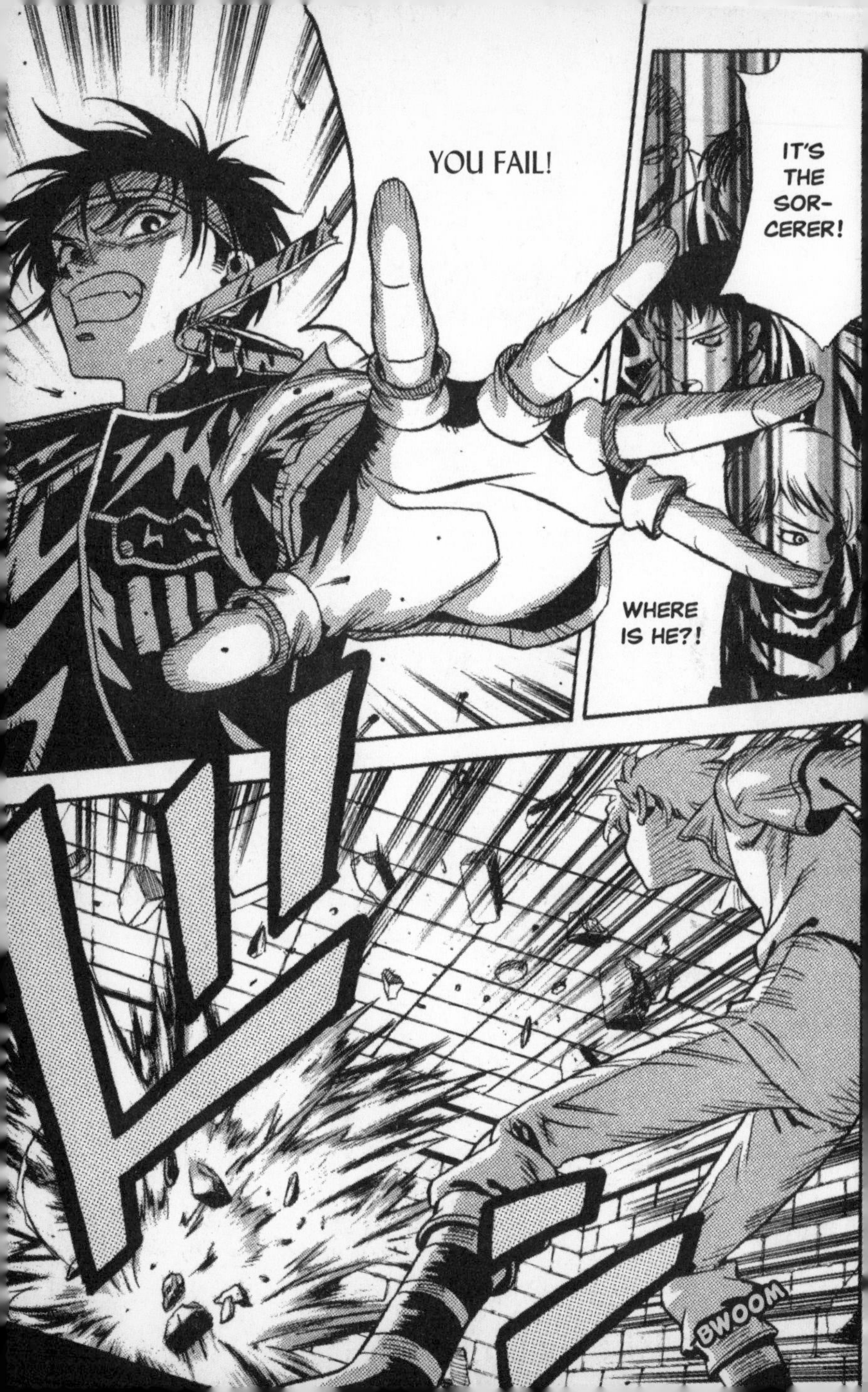
IT'S THE SORCERER!
WHERE IS HE?!
YOU FAIL!
BWOOM

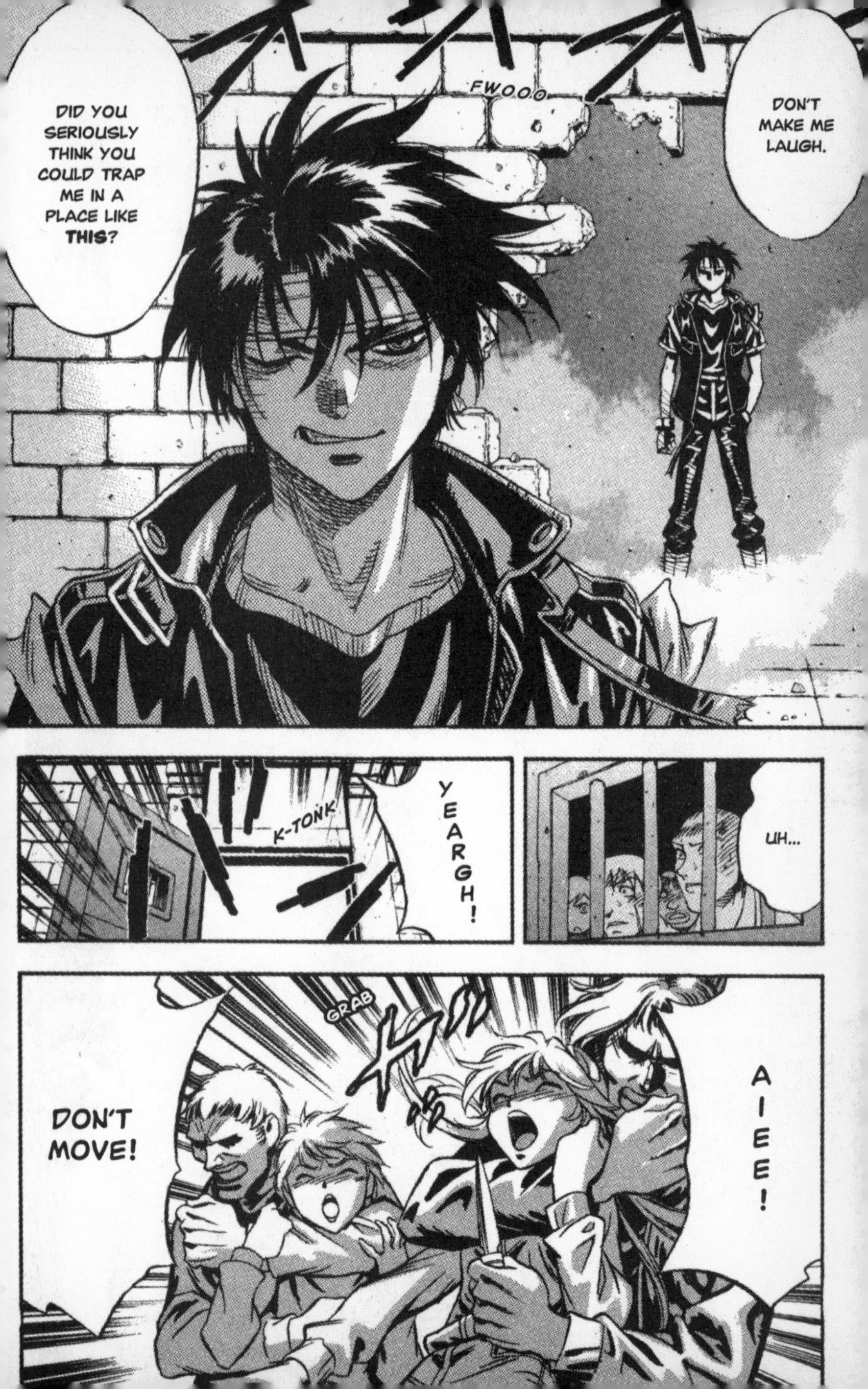
DON'T MAKE ME LAUGH.
FWOOO
DID YOU SERIOUSLY THINK YOU COULD TRAP ME IN A PLACE LIKE **THIS**?
UH...
YEARGH!
K-TONK
AIEE!
GRAB
DON'T MOVE!

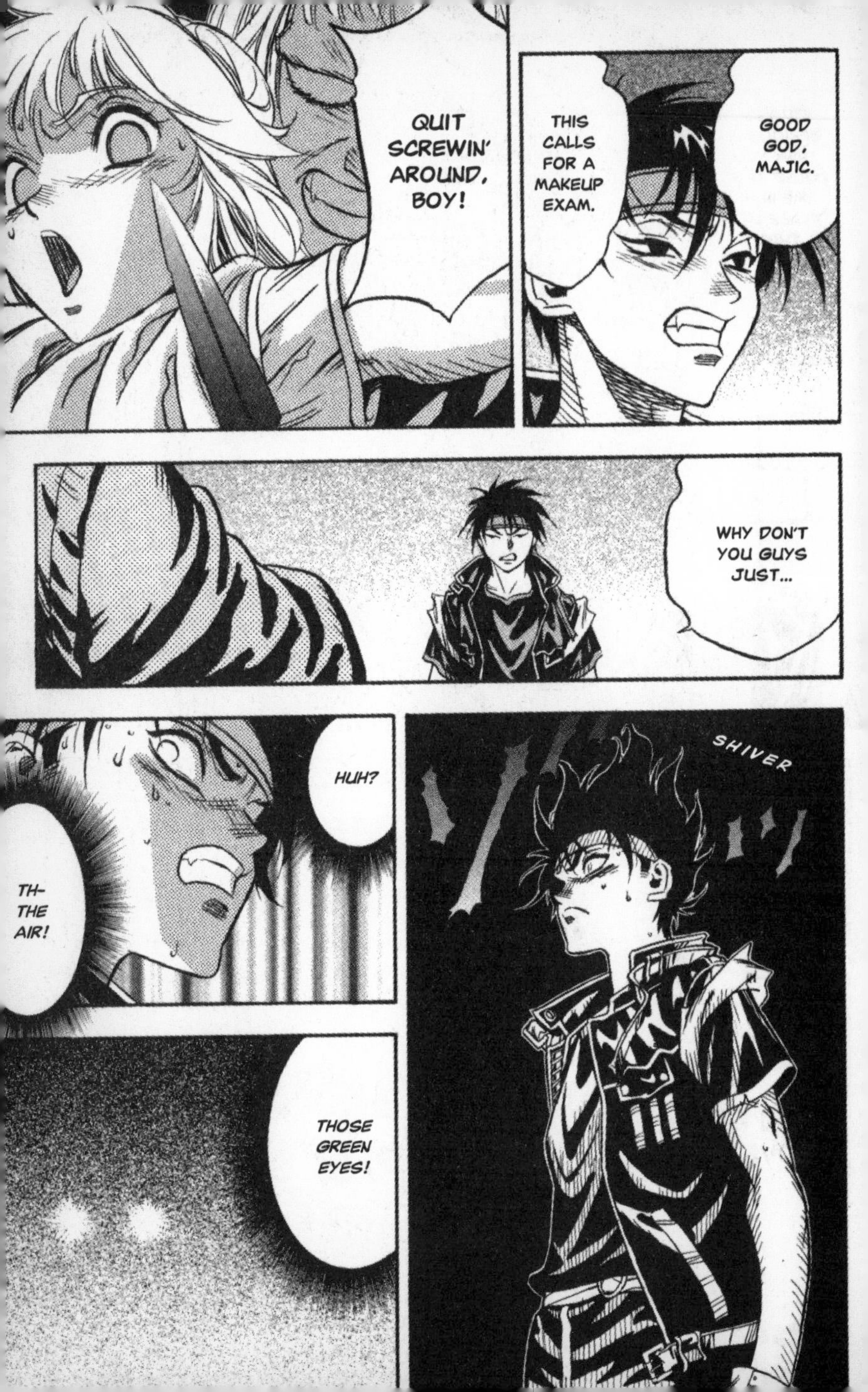
GOOD GOD, MAJIC.
THIS CALLS FOR A MAKEUP EXAM.
QUIT SCREWIN' AROUND, BOY!
WHY DON'T YOU GUYS JUST...
SHIVER
HUH?
TH- THE AIR!
THOSE GREEN EYES!

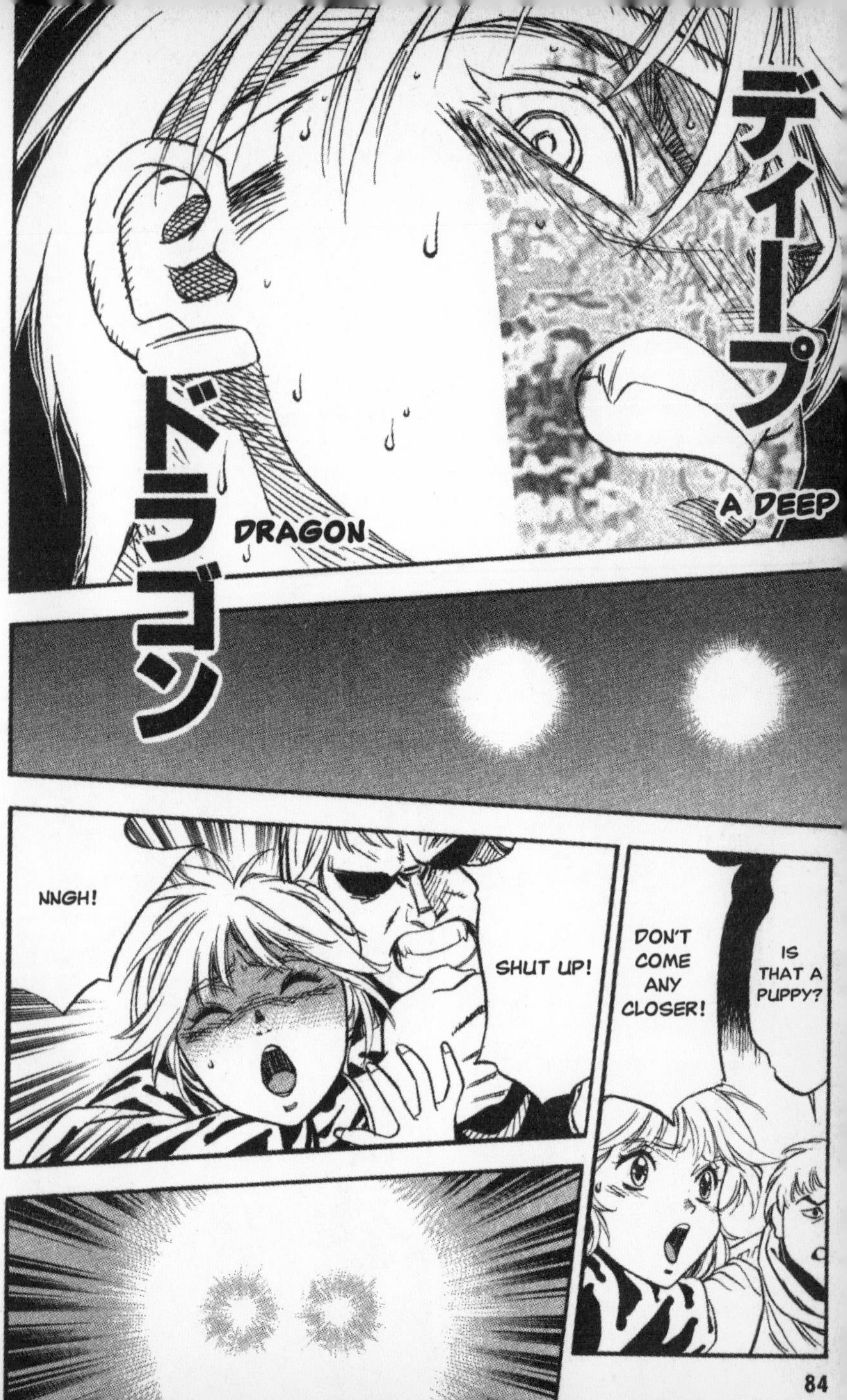

デイープ
A DEEP
ドラゴン
DRAGON
IS THAT A PUPPY?
DON'T COME ANY CLOSER!
SHUT UP!
NNGH!

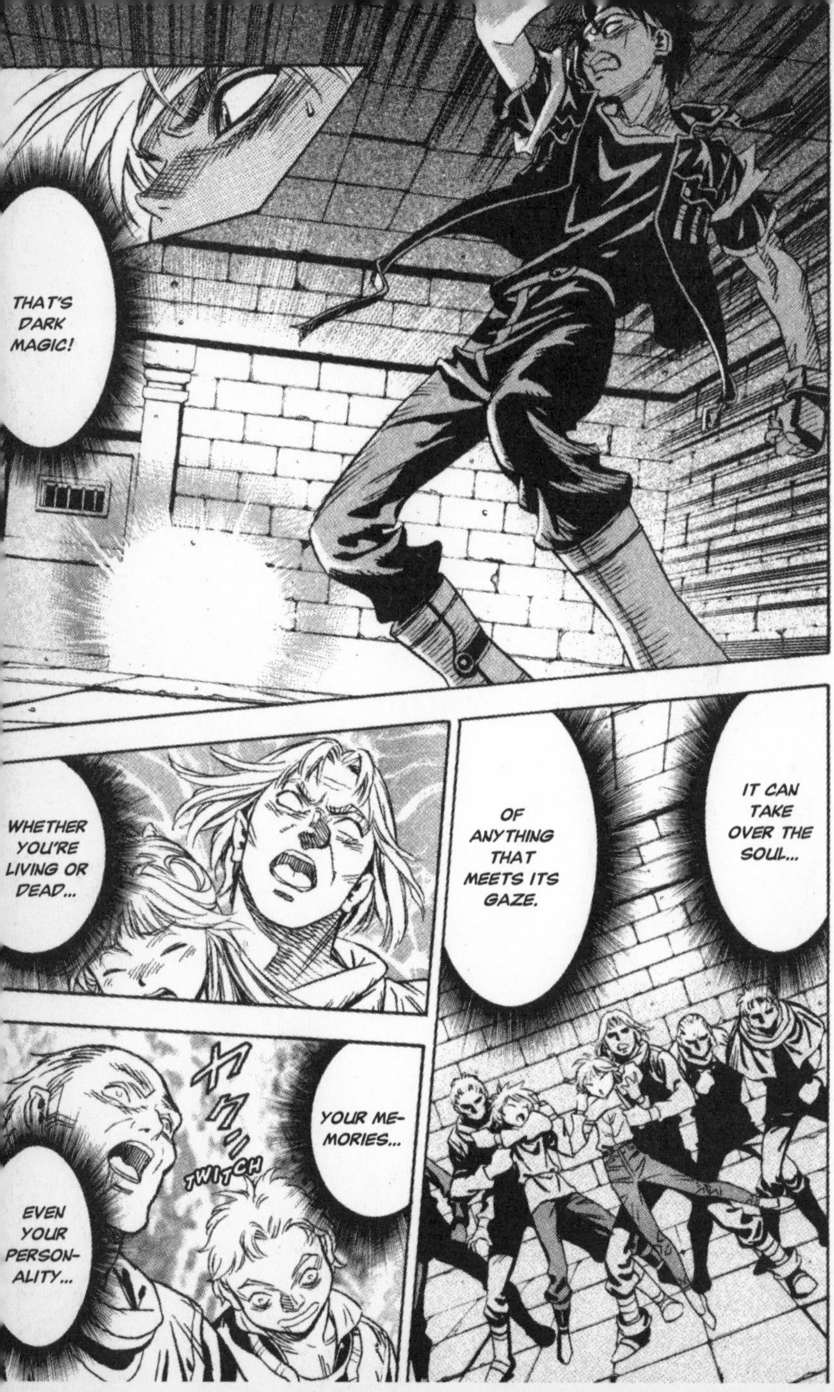
THAT'S DARK MAGIC!
IT CAN TAKE OVER THE SOUL...
OF ANYTHING THAT MEETS ITS GAZE.
WHETHER YOU'RE LIVING OR DEAD...
YOUR MEMORIES...
TWITCH
EVEN YOUR PERSONALITY...

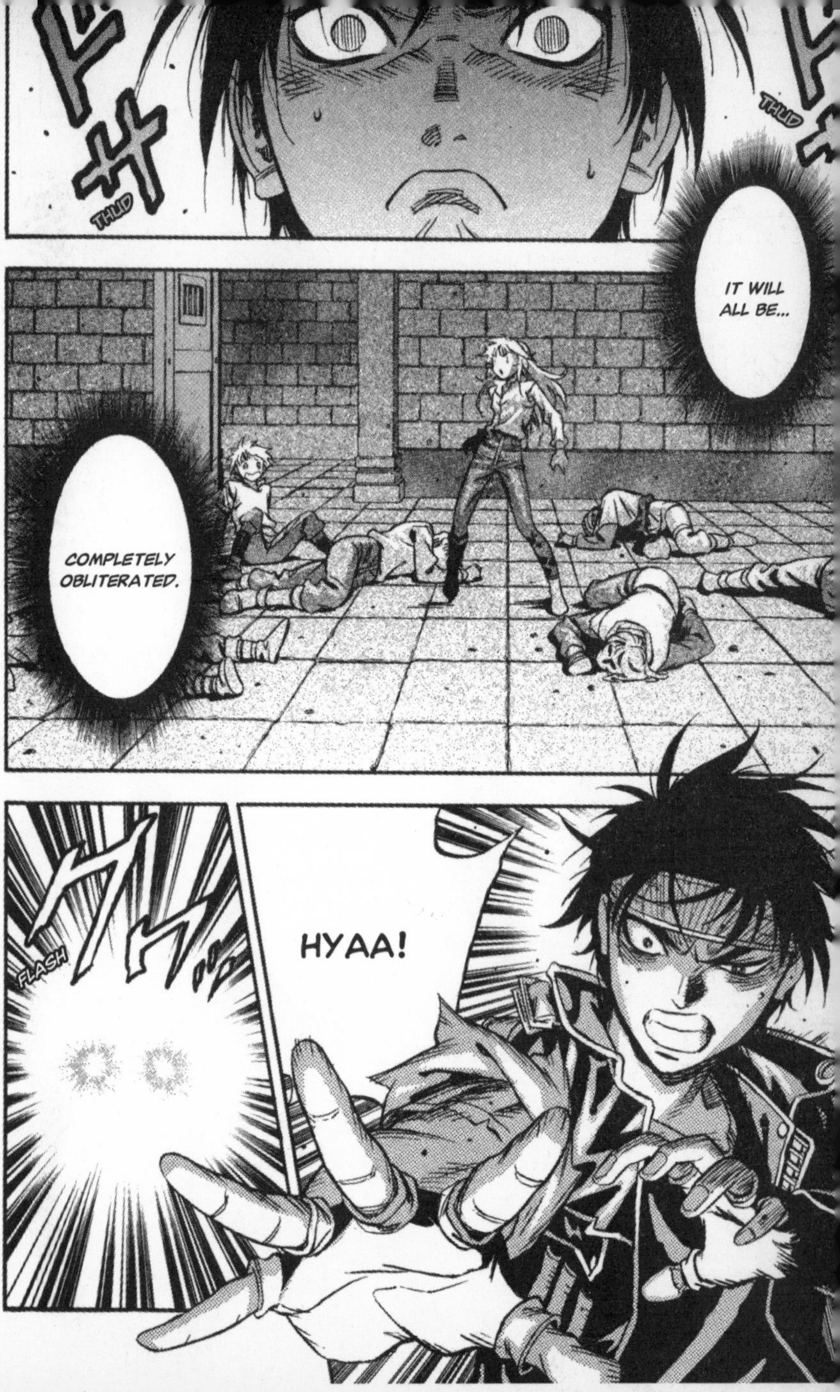
THUD
THUD
IT WILL ALL BE...
COMPLETELY OBLITERATED.
HYAA!
FLASH

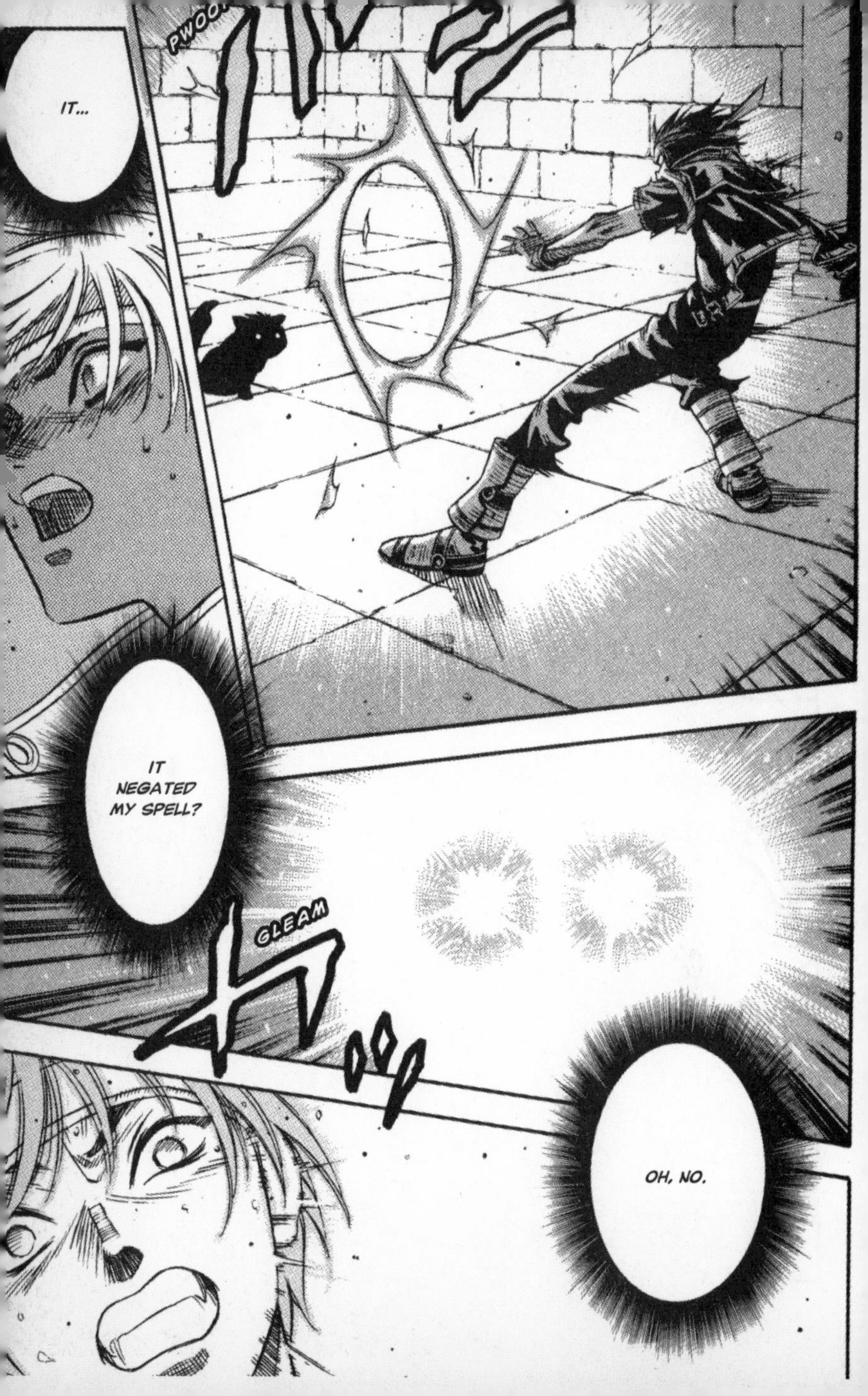
PWOOF
IT...
IT NEGATED MY SPELL?
GLEAM
OH, NO.

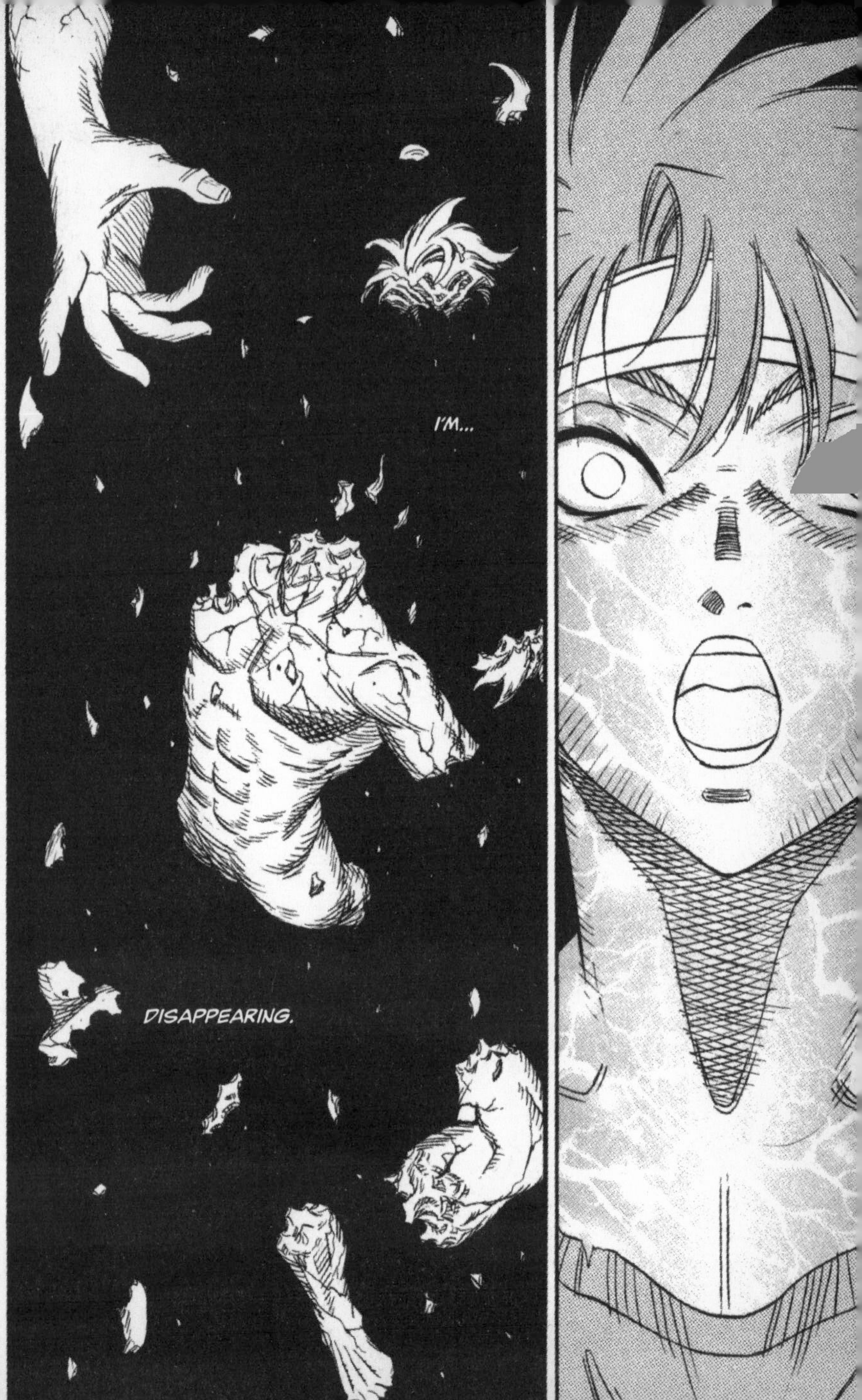
I'M...
DISAPPEARING.

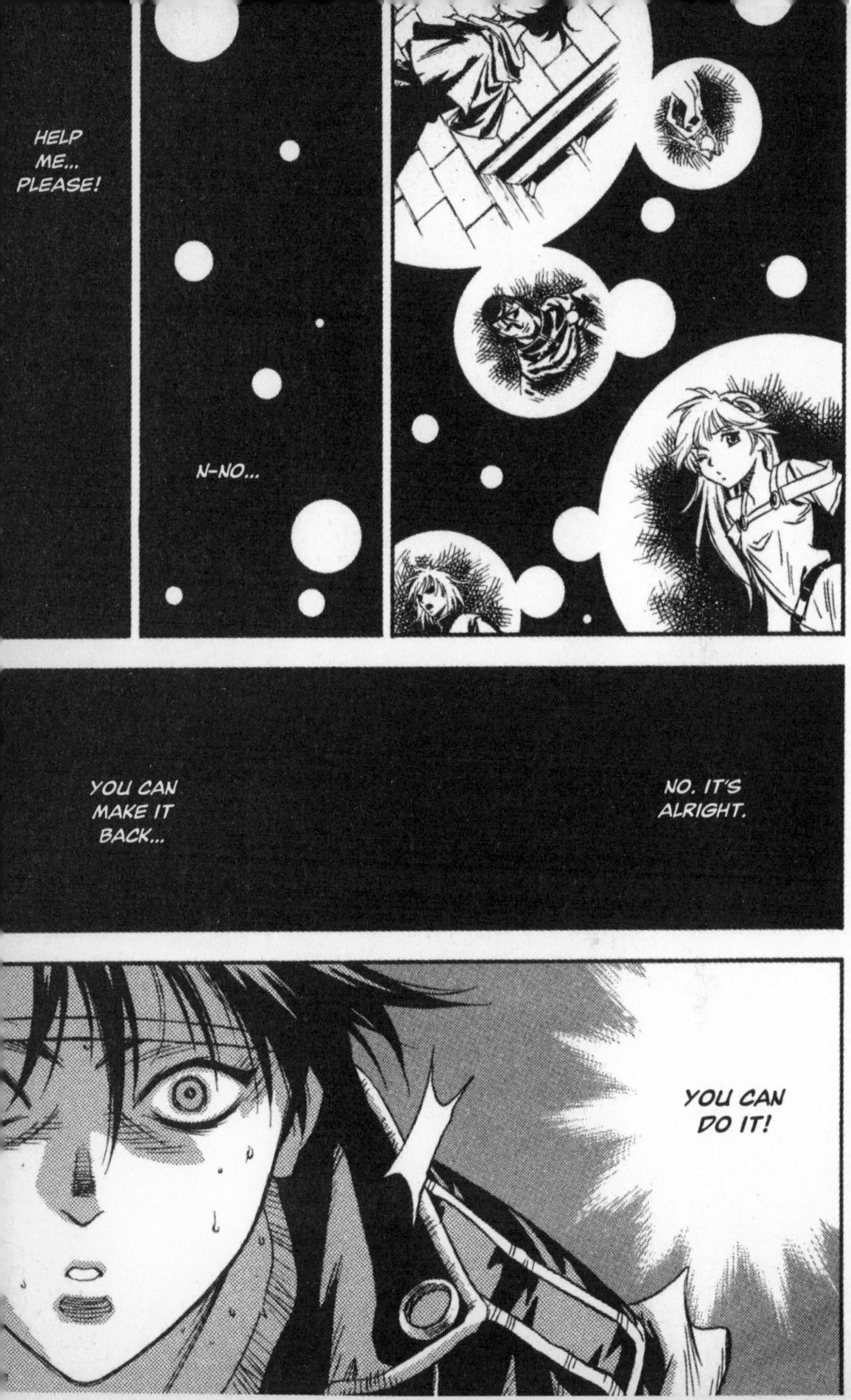

HELP ME... PLEASE!
N-NO...
NO. IT'S ALRIGHT.
YOU CAN MAKE IT BACK...
YOU CAN DO IT!

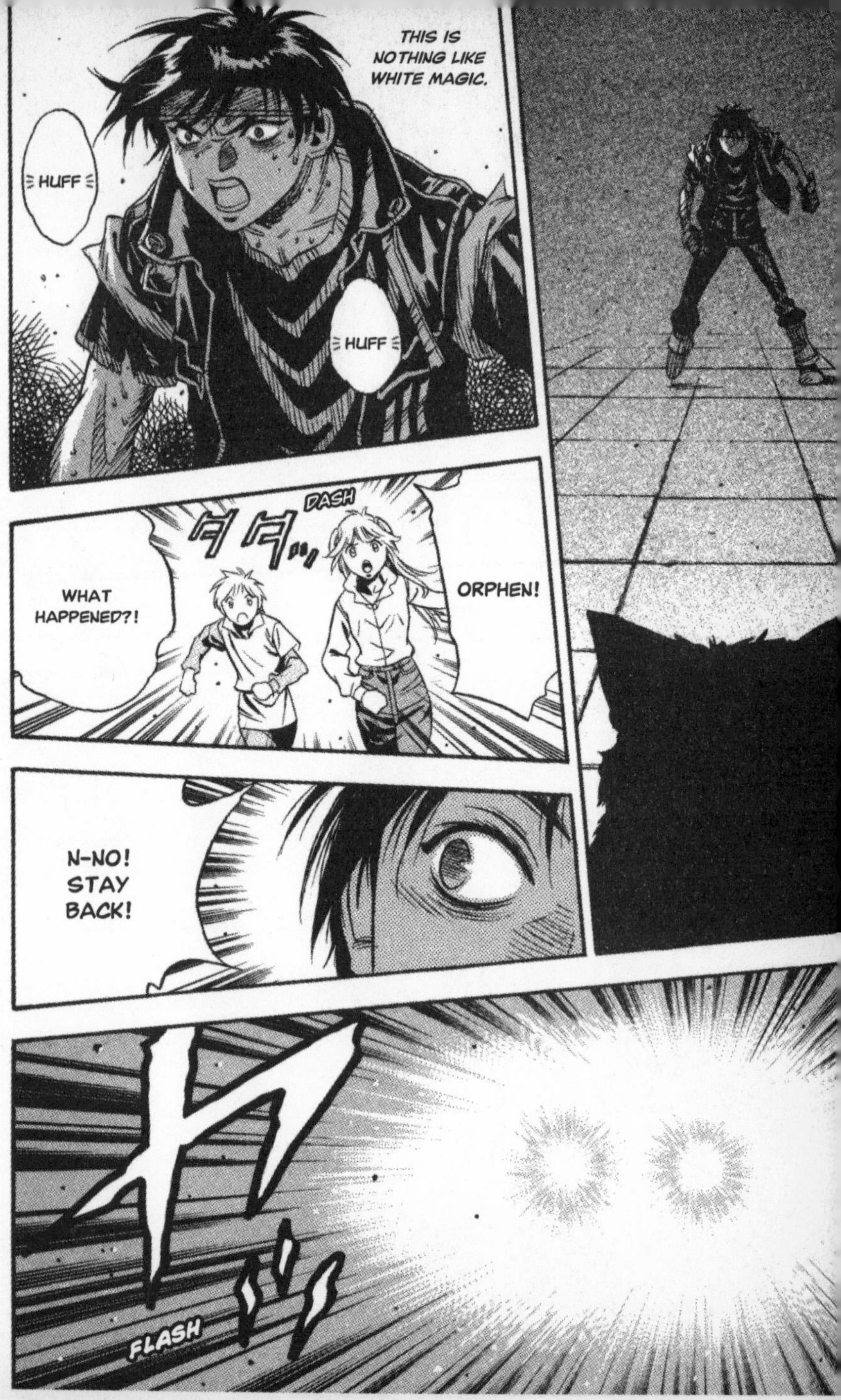
THIS IS NOTHING LIKE WHITE MAGIC.
HUFF
HUFF
ORPHEN!
DASH
WHAT HAPPENED?!
N-NO! STAY BACK!
FLASH

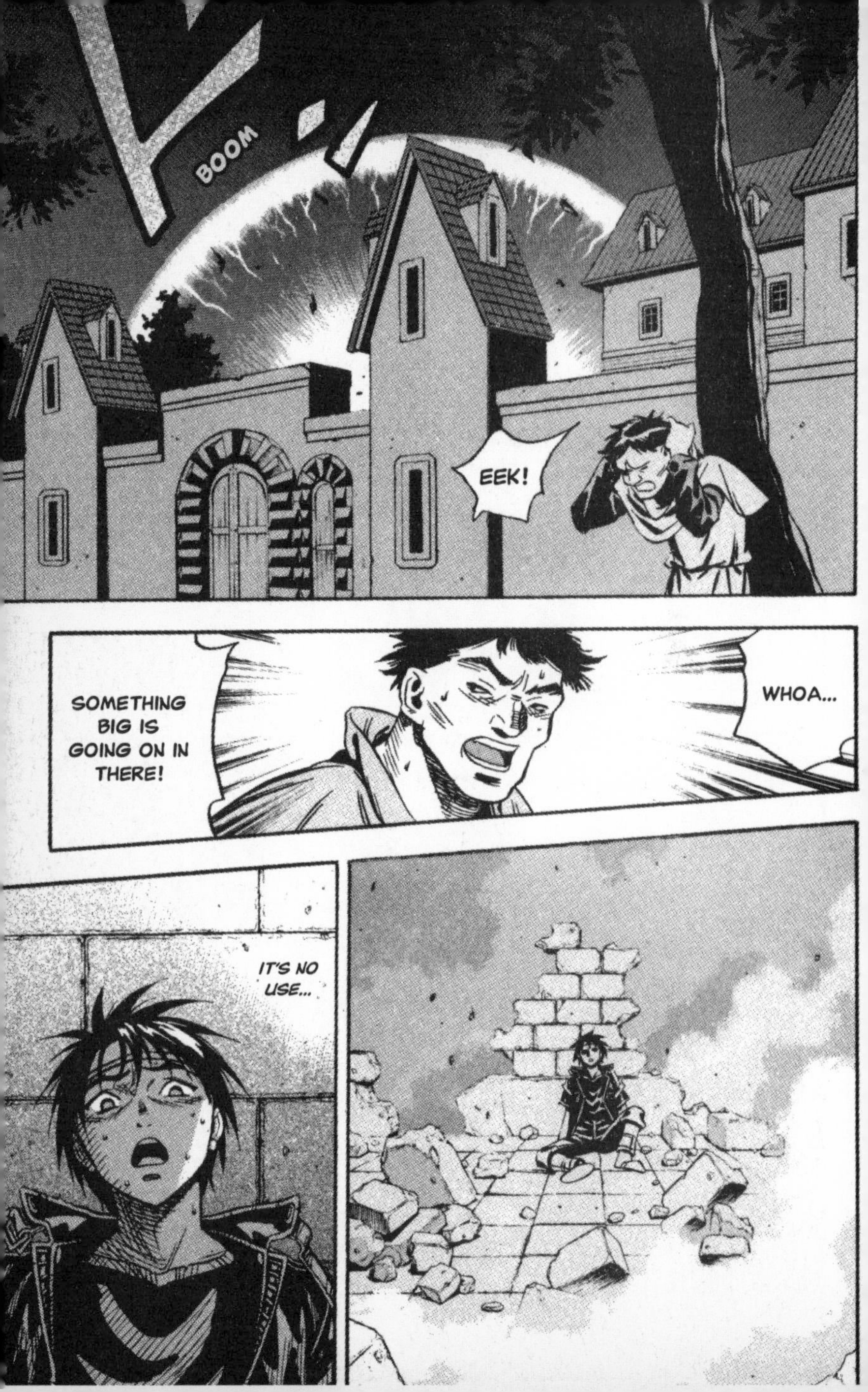
BOOM
EEK!
WHOA...
SOMETHING BIG IS GOING ON IN THERE!
IT'S NO USE...

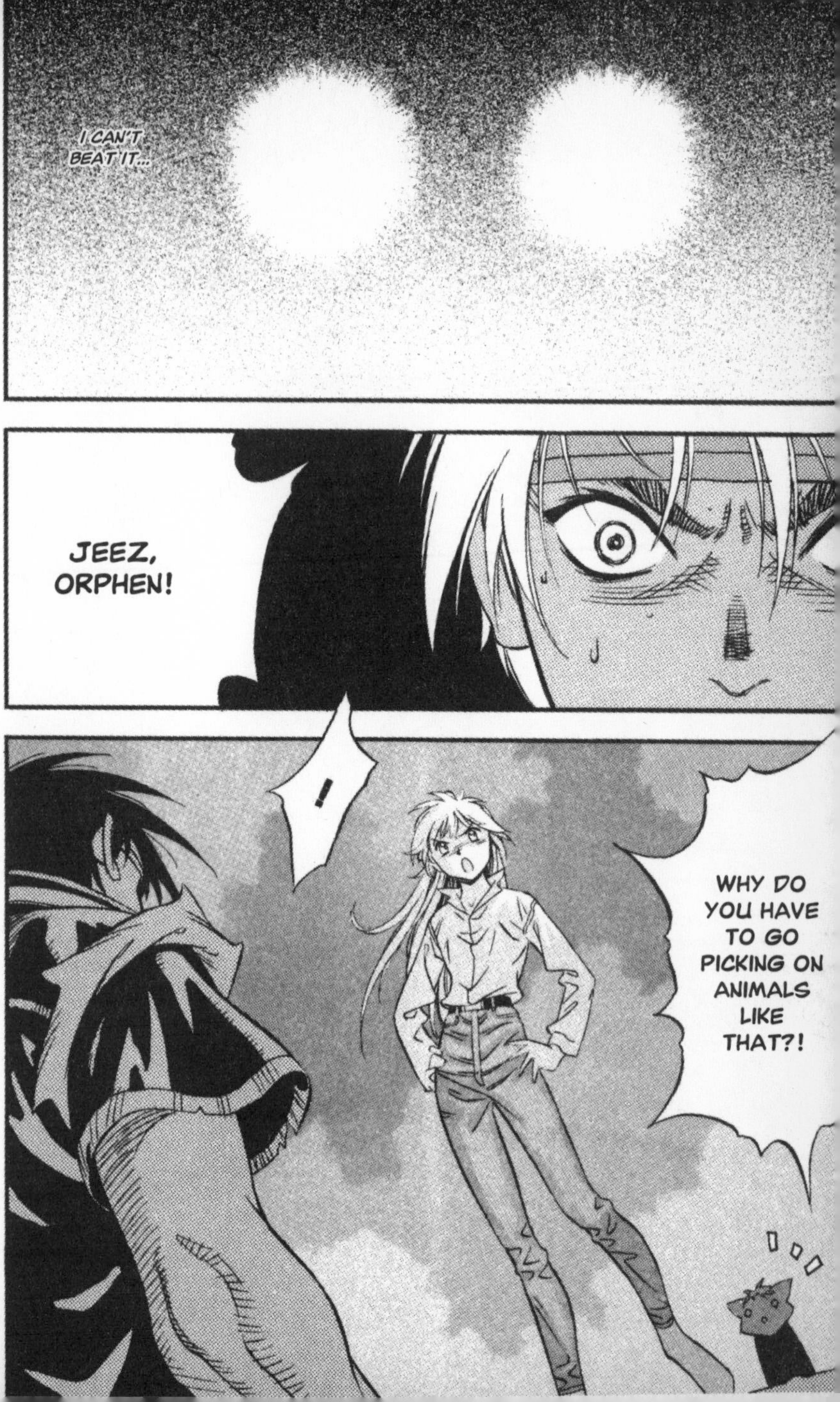
I CAN'T BEAT IT...
JEEZ, ORPHEN!
!
WHY DO YOU HAVE TO GO PICKING ON ANIMALS LIKE THAT?!

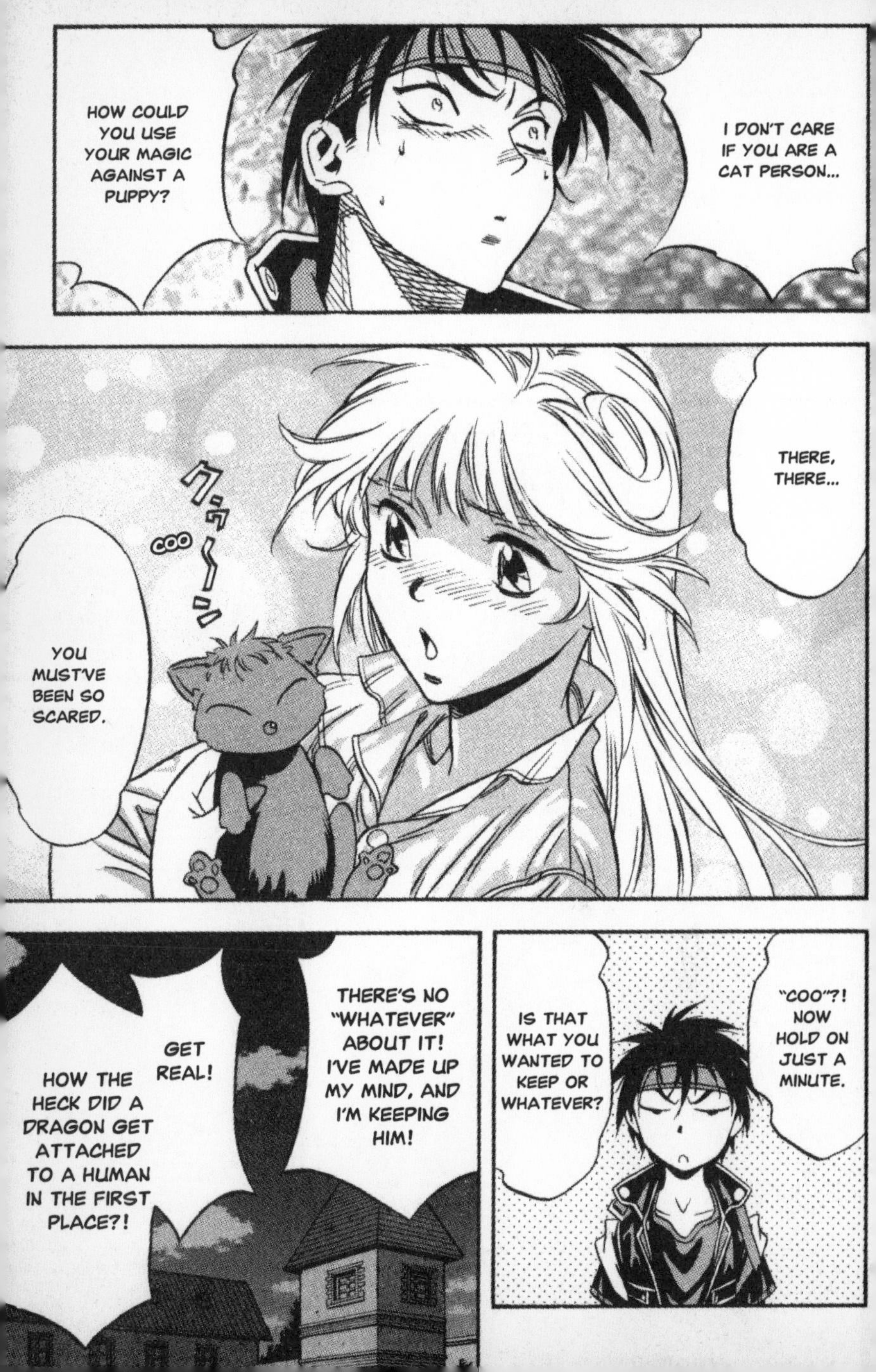
I DON'T CARE IF YOU ARE A CAT PERSON...
HOW COULD YOU USE YOUR MAGIC AGAINST A PUPPY?
THERE, THERE...
COO
YOU MUST'VE BEEN SO SCARED.
"COO"?! NOW HOLD ON JUST A MINUTE.
IS THAT WHAT YOU WANTED TO KEEP OR WHATEVER?
THERE'S NO "WHATEVER" ABOUT IT! I'VE MADE UP MY MIND, AND I'M KEEPING HIM!
GET REAL!
HOW THE HECK DID A DRAGON GET ATTACHED TO A HUMAN IN THE FIRST PLACE?!

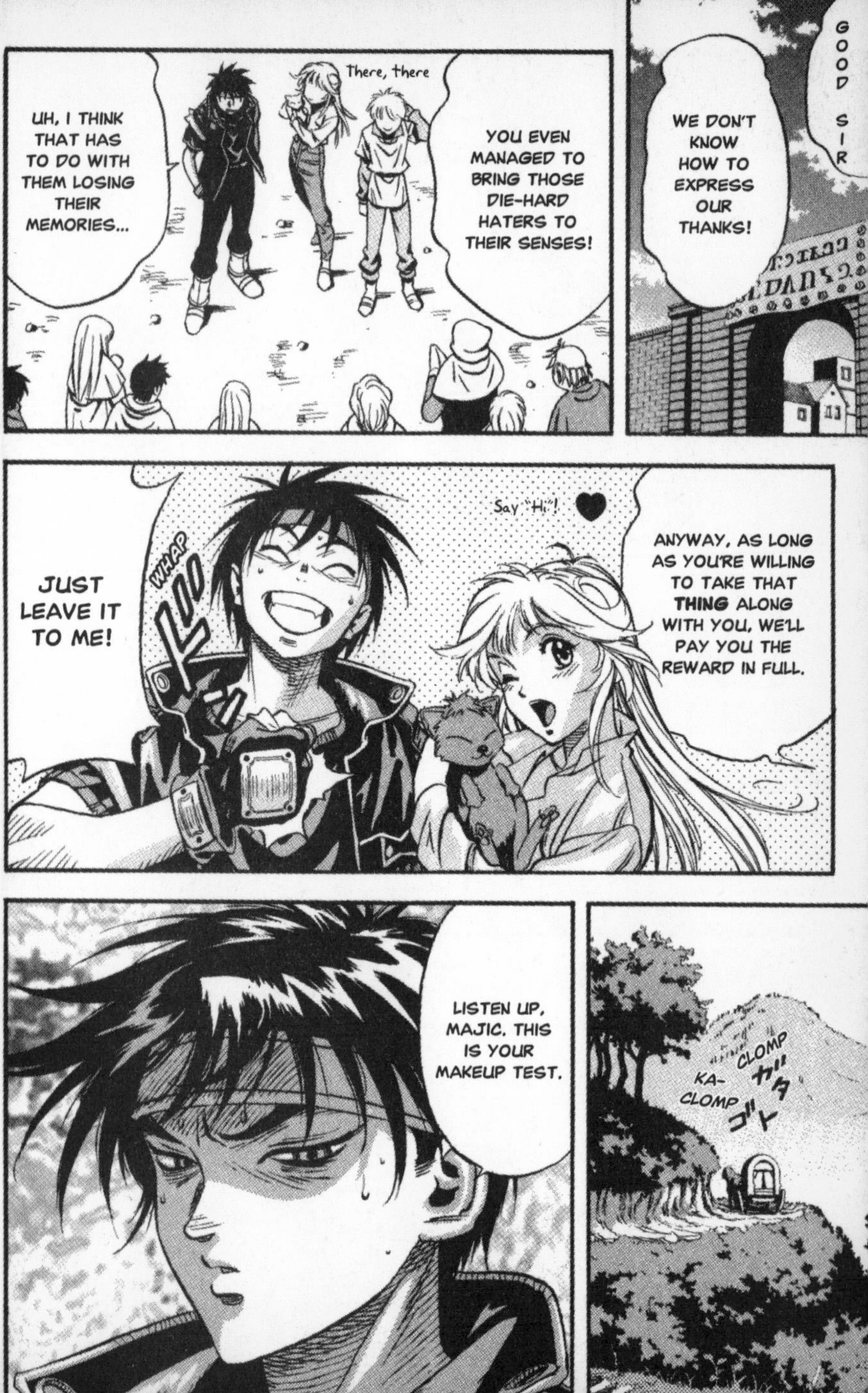
GOOD SIR
WE DON'T KNOW HOW TO EXPRESS OUR THANKS!
YOU EVEN MANAGED TO BRING THOSE DIE-HARD HATERS TO THEIR SENSES!
There, there
UH, I THINK THAT HAS TO DO WITH THEM LOSING THEIR MEMORIES...
ANYWAY, AS LONG AS YOU'RE WILLING TO TAKE THAT THING ALONG WITH YOU, WE'LL PAY YOU THE REWARD IN FULL.
Say "Hi"!
WHAP
JUST LEAVE IT TO ME!
KA-CLOMP
CLOMP
LISTEN UP, MAJIC. THIS IS YOUR MAKEUP TEST.

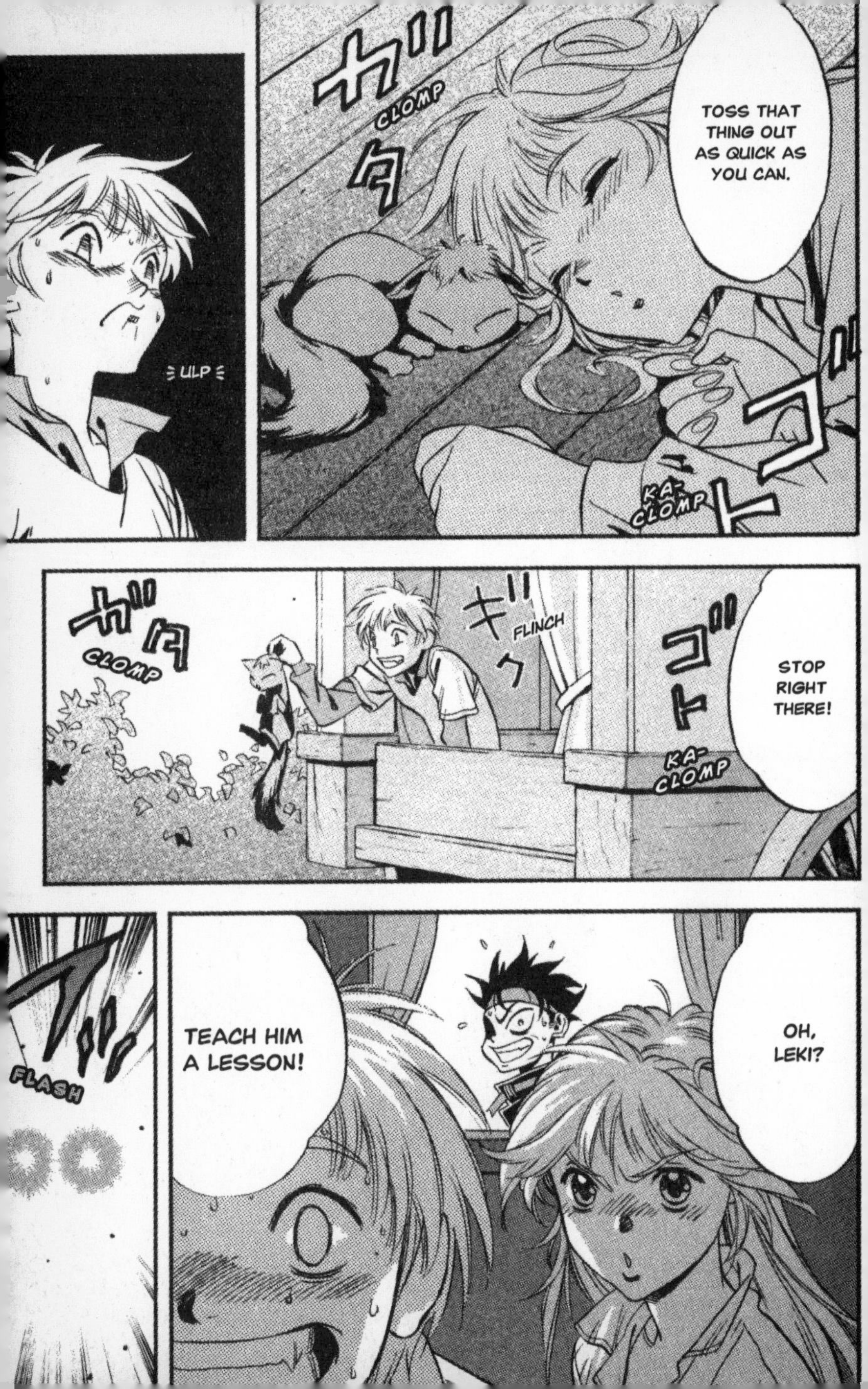

TOSS THAT THING OUT AS QUICK AS YOU CAN.
CLOMP
KA-CLOMP
ULP
STOP RIGHT THERE!
KA-CLOMP
FLINCH
CLOMP
OH, LEKI?
TEACH HIM A LESSON!
FLASH

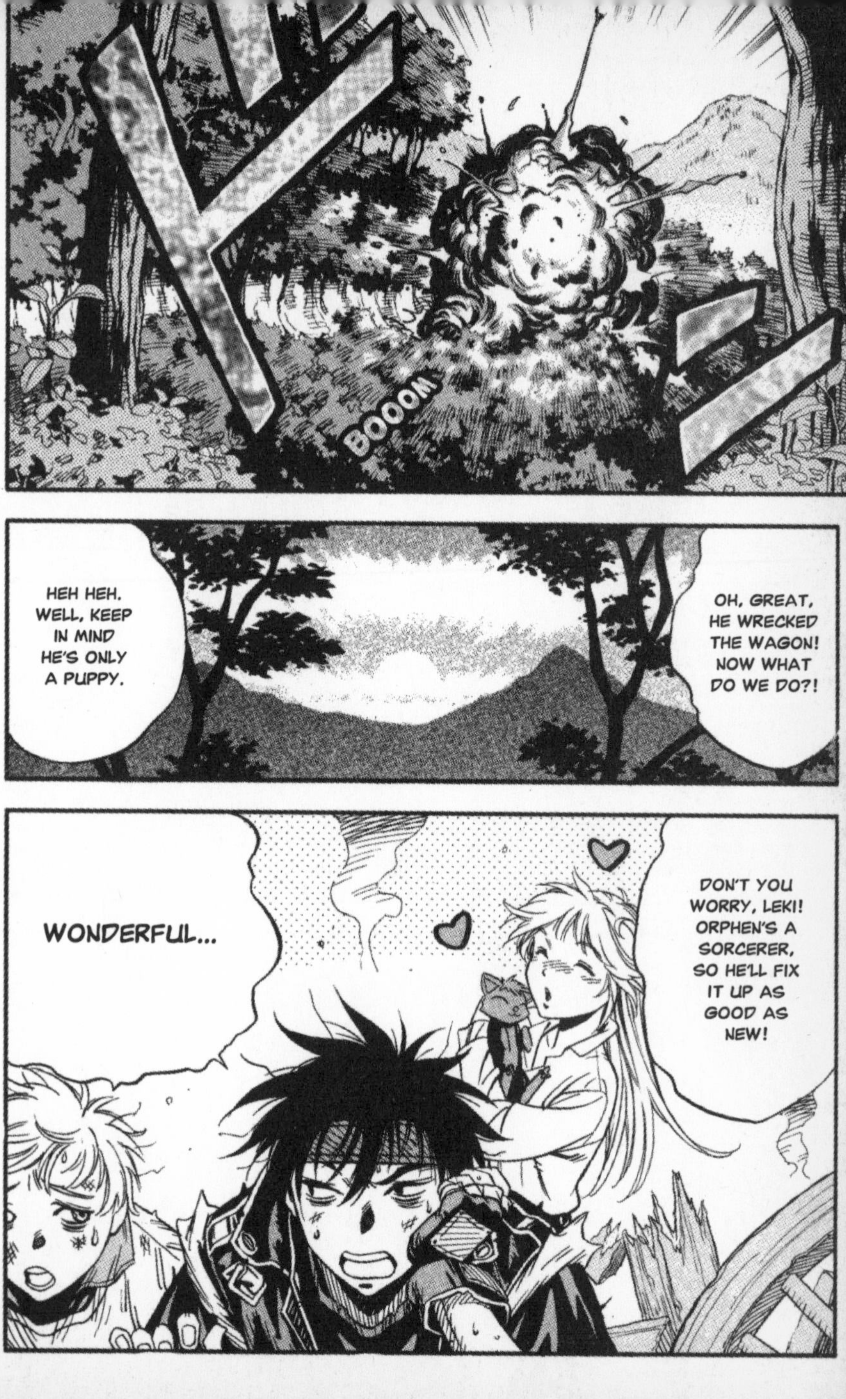
BOOOM
OH, GREAT, HE WRECKED THE WAGON! NOW WHAT DO WE DO?!
HEH HEH. WELL, KEEP IN MIND HE'S ONLY A PUPPY.
DON'T YOU WORRY, LEKI! ORPHEN'S A SORCERER, SO HE'LL FIX IT UP AS GOOD AS NEW!
WONDERFUL...

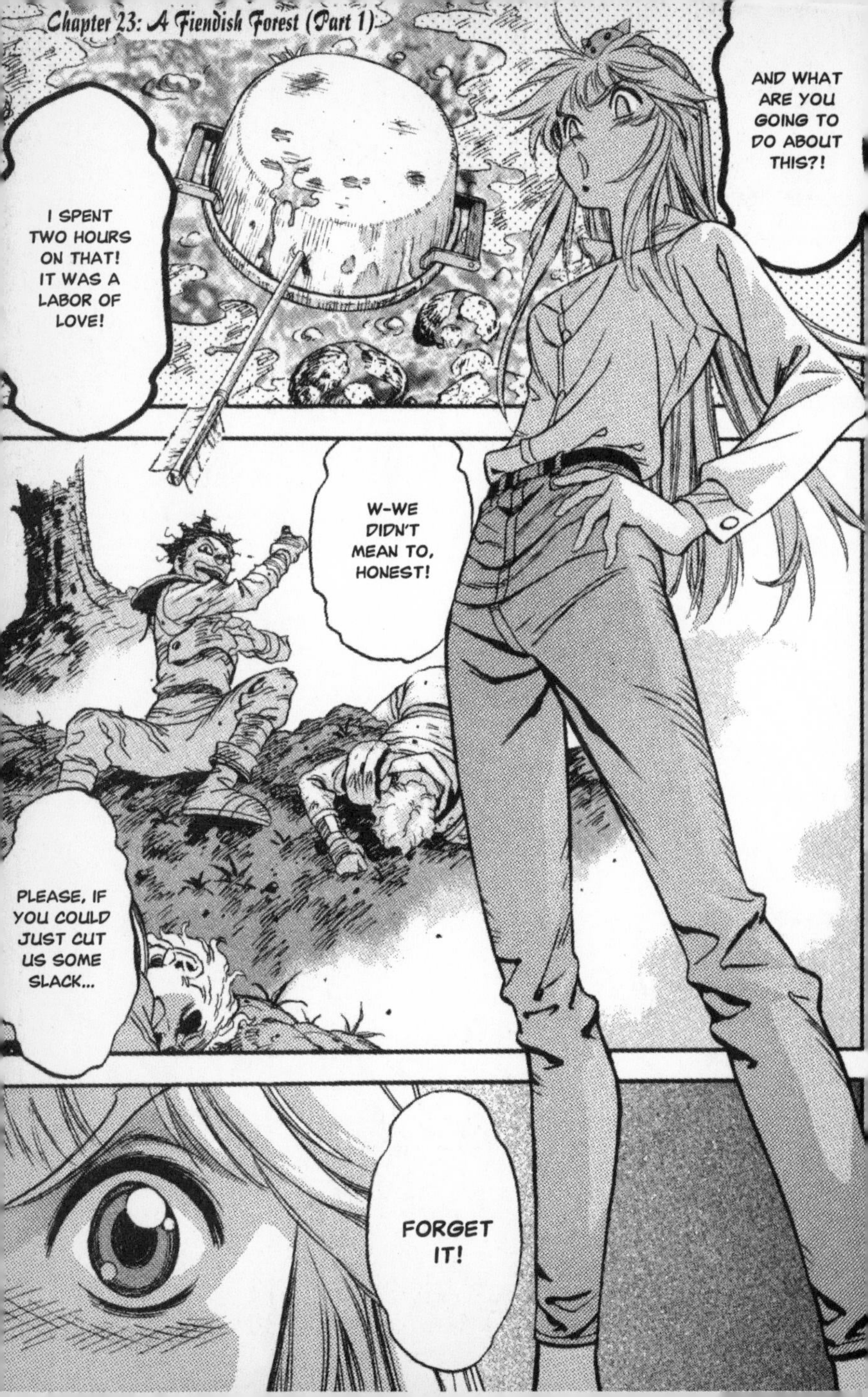
Chapter 23: A Fiendish Forest (Part 1)
AND WHAT ARE YOU GOING TO DO ABOUT THIS?!
I SPENT TWO HOURS ON THAT! IT WAS A LABOR OF LOVE!
W-WE DIDN'T MEAN TO, HONEST!
PLEASE, IF YOU COULD JUST CUT US SOME SLACK...
FORGET IT!

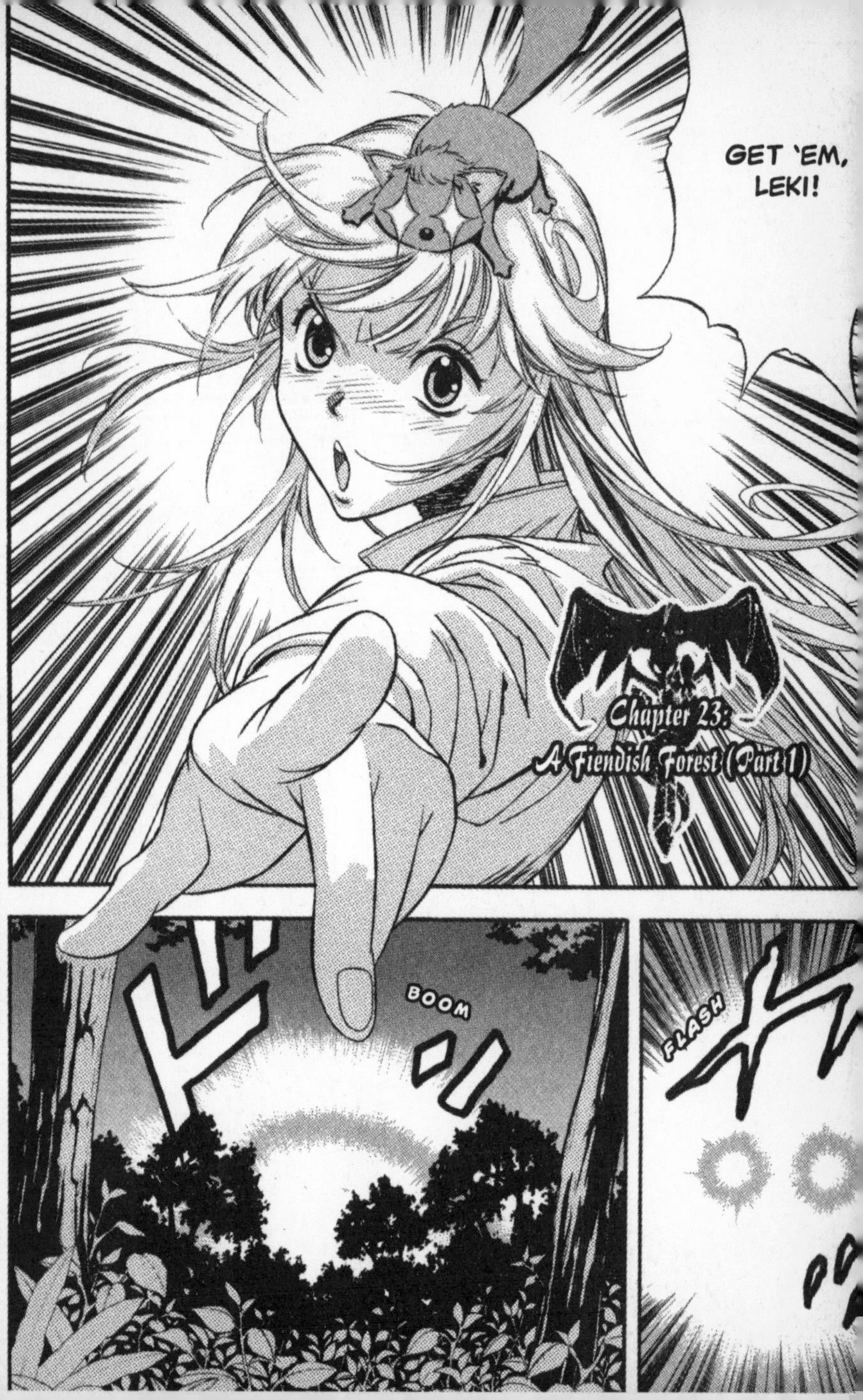
GET 'EM, LEKI!
Chapter 23:
A Fiendish Forest (Part 1)
BOOM
FLASH

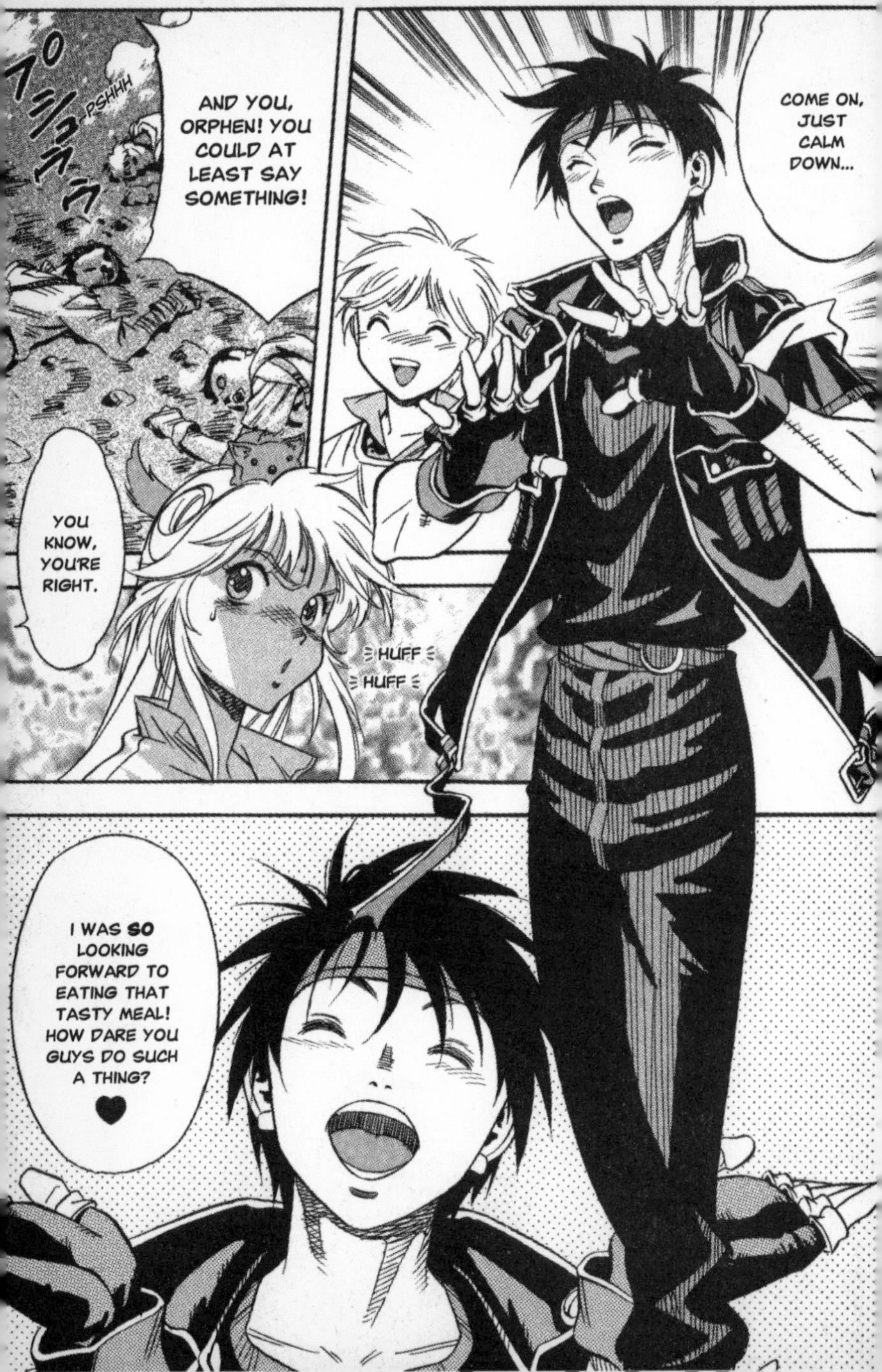
COME ON, JUST CALM DOWN...
AND YOU, ORPHEN! YOU COULD AT LEAST SAY SOMETHING!
PSHHH
YOU KNOW, YOU'RE RIGHT.
HUFF
HUFF
I WAS **SO** LOOKING FORWARD TO EATING THAT TASTY MEAL! HOW DARE YOU GUYS DO SUCH A THING? ♥

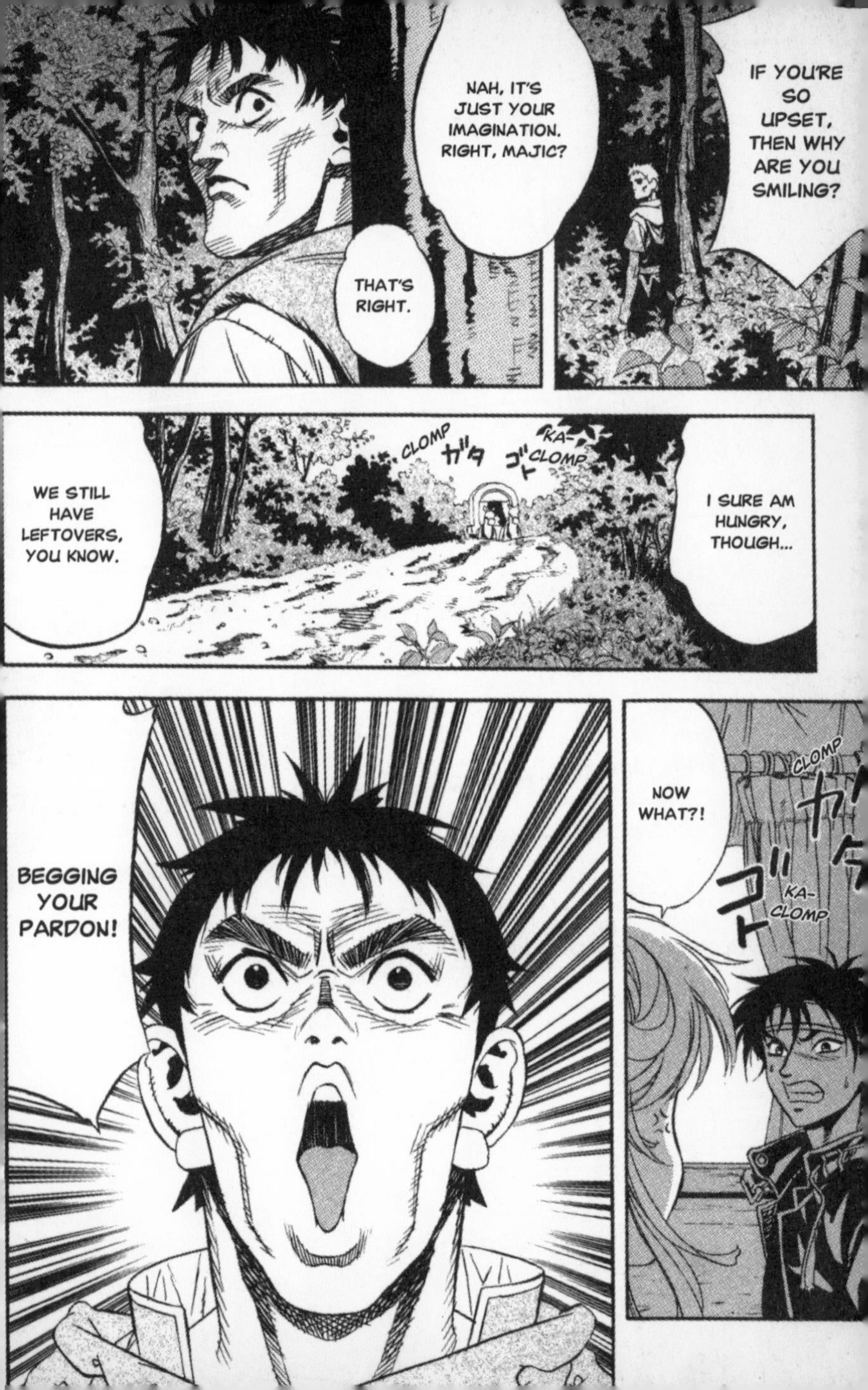
IF YOU'RE SO UPSET, THEN WHY ARE YOU SMILING?
NAH, IT'S JUST YOUR IMAGINATION. RIGHT, MAJIC?
THAT'S RIGHT.
KA-CLOMP
ゴト
ガタ
CLOMP
I SURE AM HUNGRY, THOUGH...
WE STILL HAVE LEFTOVERS, YOU KNOW.
CLOMP
KA-CLOMP
NOW WHAT?!
BEGGING YOUR PARDON!

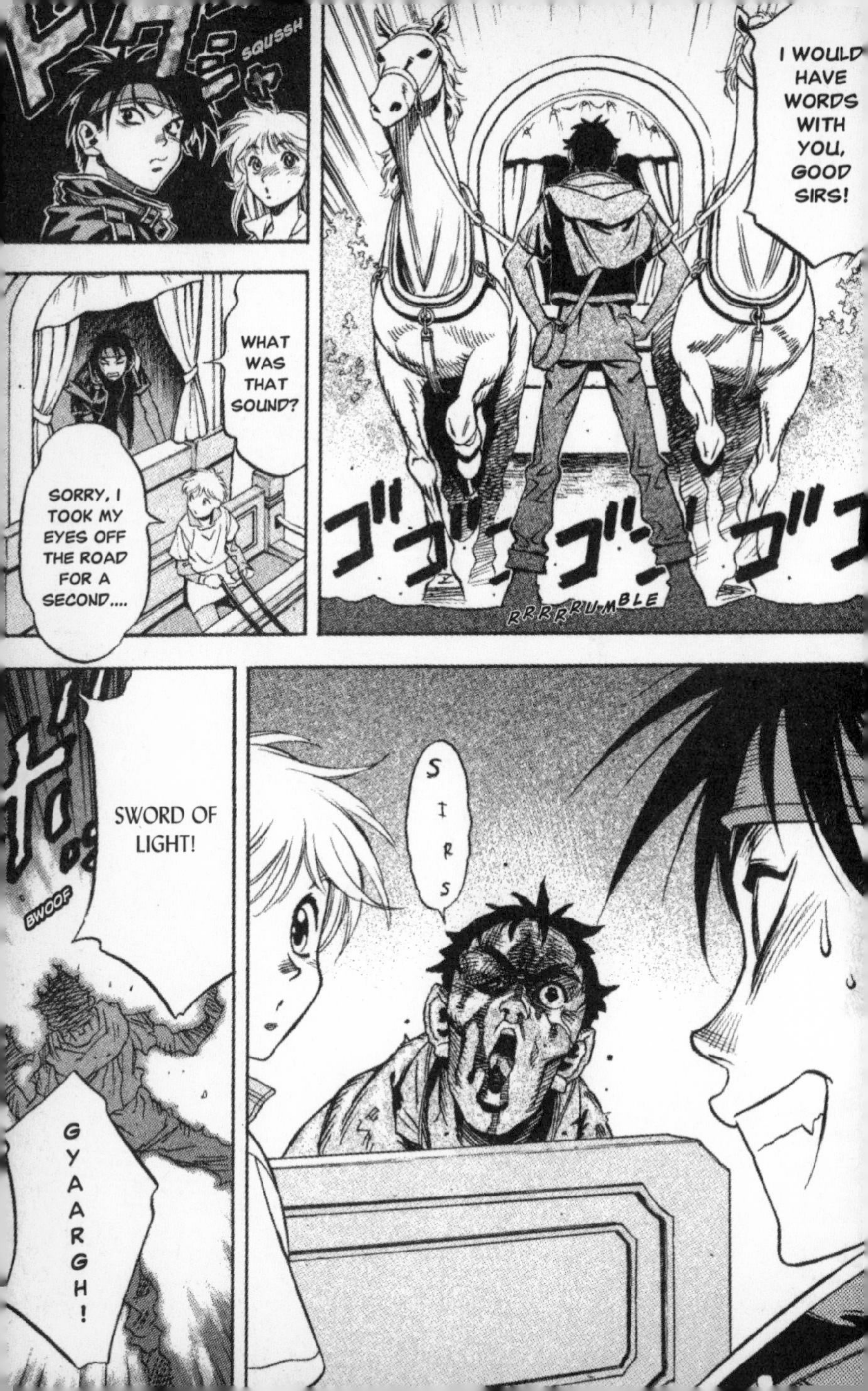
I WOULD HAVE WORDS WITH YOU, GOOD SIRS!
SQUSSH
WHAT WAS THAT SOUND?
SORRY, I TOOK MY EYES OFF THE ROAD FOR A SECOND....
RRRRRUMBLE
SIRS
SWORD OF LIGHT!
BWOOF
GYAARGH!

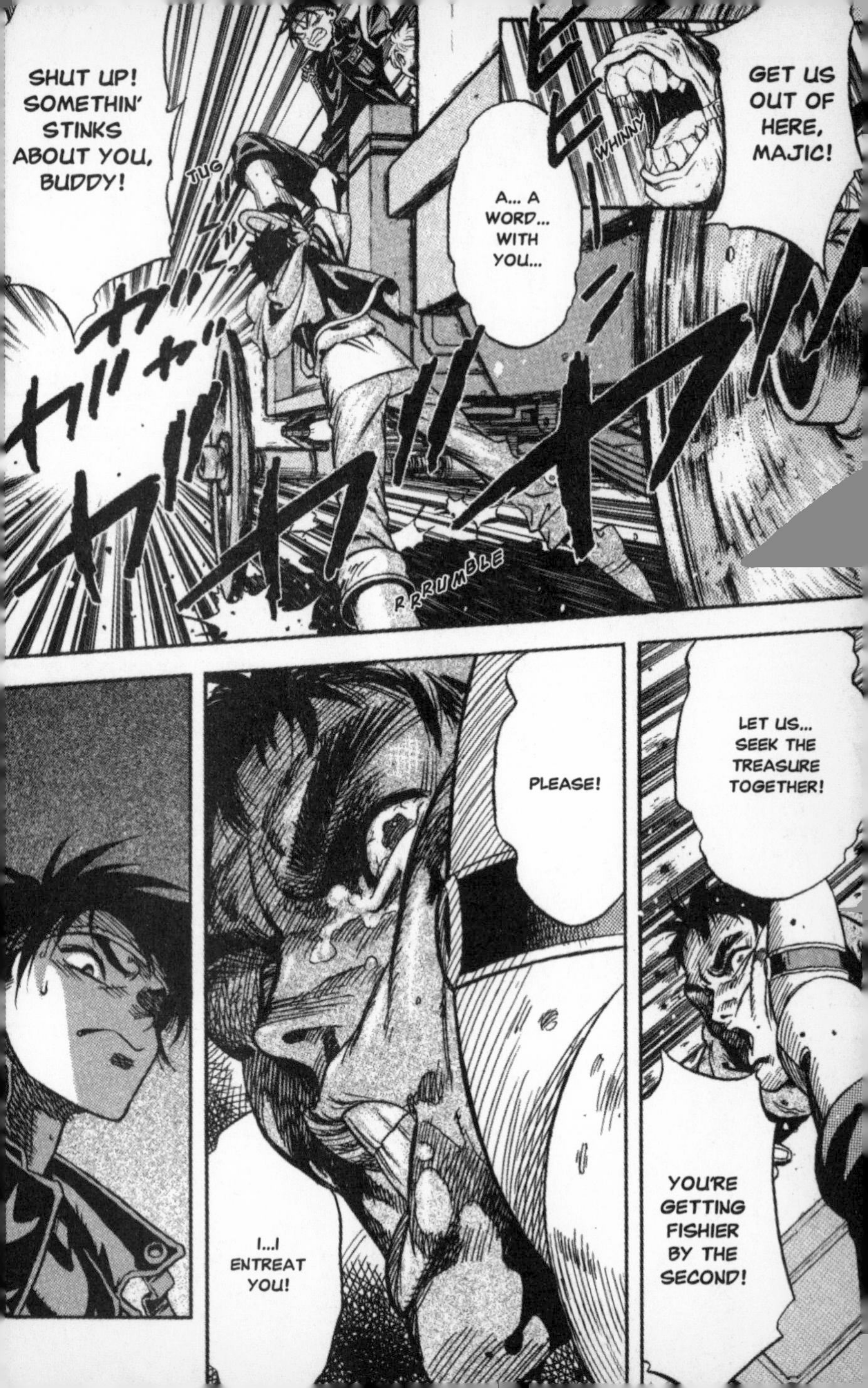
GET US OUT OF HERE, MAJIC!
WHINNY
A... A WORD... WITH YOU...
TUG
SHUT UP! SOMETHIN' STINKS ABOUT YOU, BUDDY!
RRRUMBLE
LET US... SEEK THE TREASURE TOGETHER!
YOU'RE GETTING FISHIER BY THE SECOND!
PLEASE!
I...I ENTREAT YOU!

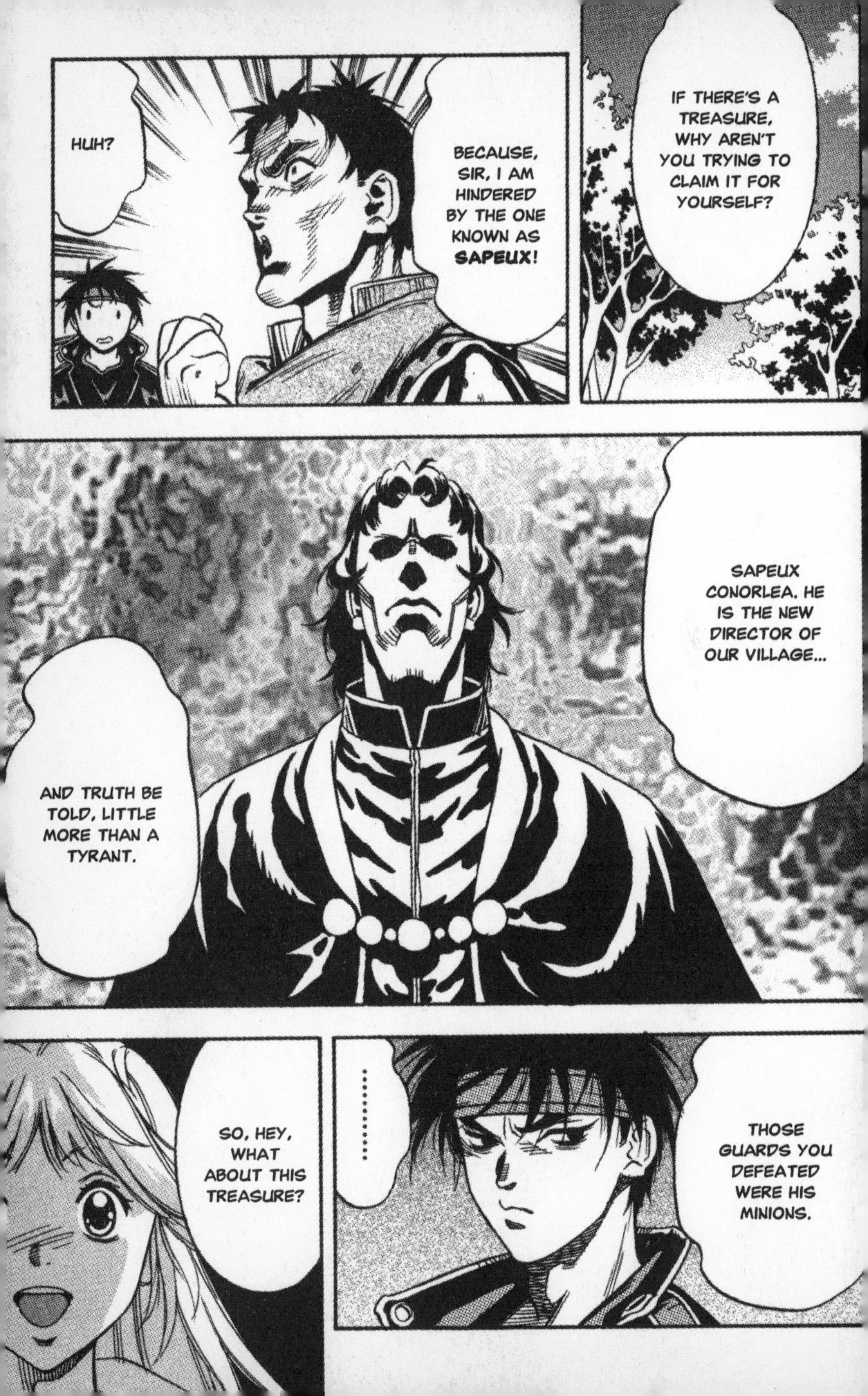
IF THERE'S A TREASURE, WHY AREN'T YOU TRYING TO CLAIM IT FOR YOURSELF?
BECAUSE, SIR, I AM HINDERED BY THE ONE KNOWN AS **SAPEUX!**
HUH?
SAPEUX CONORLEA. HE IS THE NEW DIRECTOR OF OUR VILLAGE...
AND TRUTH BE TOLD, LITTLE MORE THAN A TYRANT.
THOSE GUARDS YOU DEFEATED WERE HIS MINIONS.
......
SO, HEY, WHAT ABOUT THIS TREASURE?

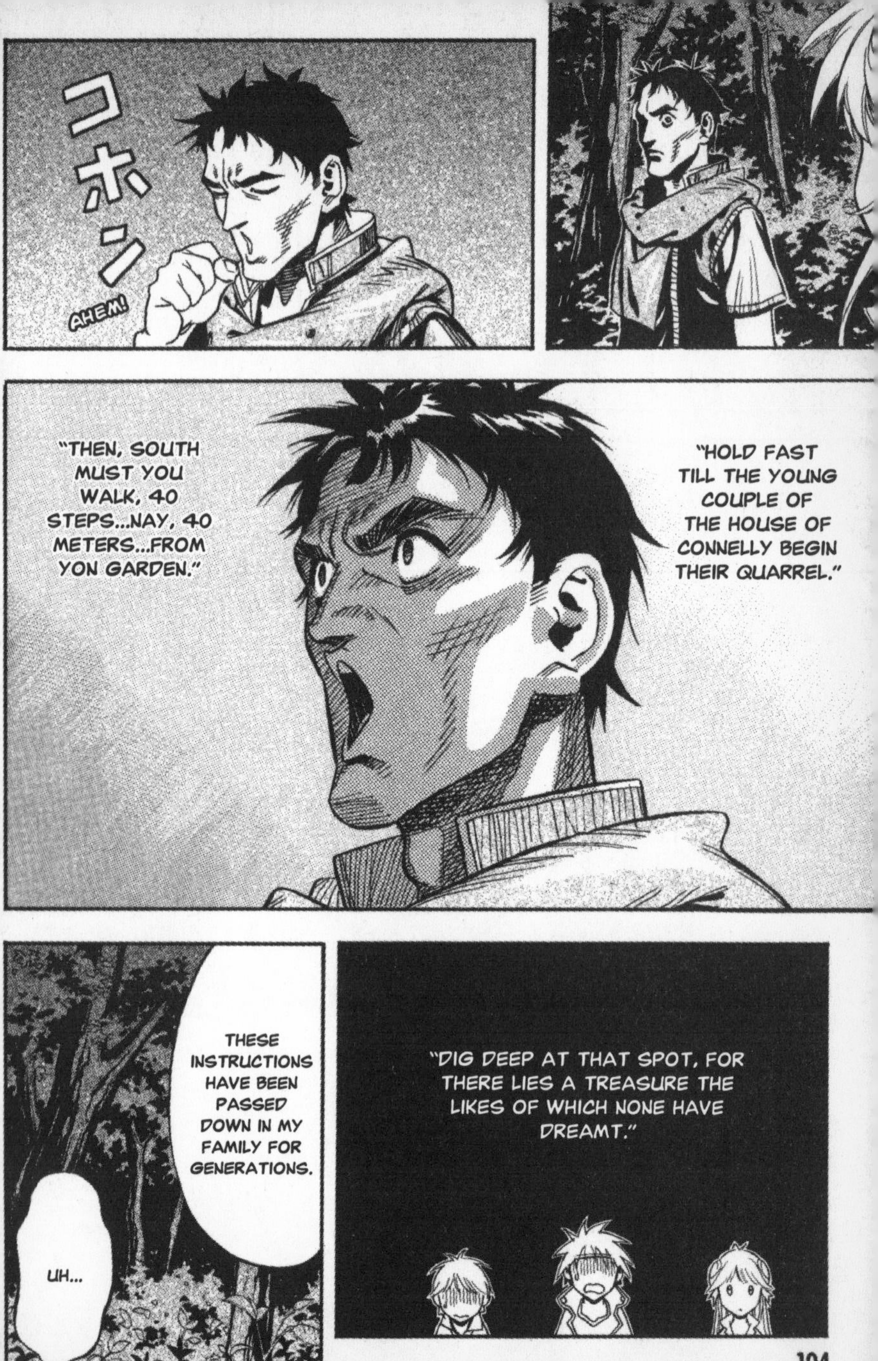
コホン
AHEM!
"HOLD FAST TILL THE YOUNG COUPLE OF THE HOUSE OF CONNELLY BEGIN THEIR QUARREL."
"THEN, SOUTH MUST YOU WALK, 40 STEPS...NAY, 40 METERS...FROM YON GARDEN."
"DIG DEEP AT THAT SPOT, FOR THERE LIES A TREASURE THE LIKES OF WHICH NONE HAVE DREAMT."
THESE INSTRUCTIONS HAVE BEEN PASSED DOWN IN MY FAMILY FOR GENERATIONS.
UH...

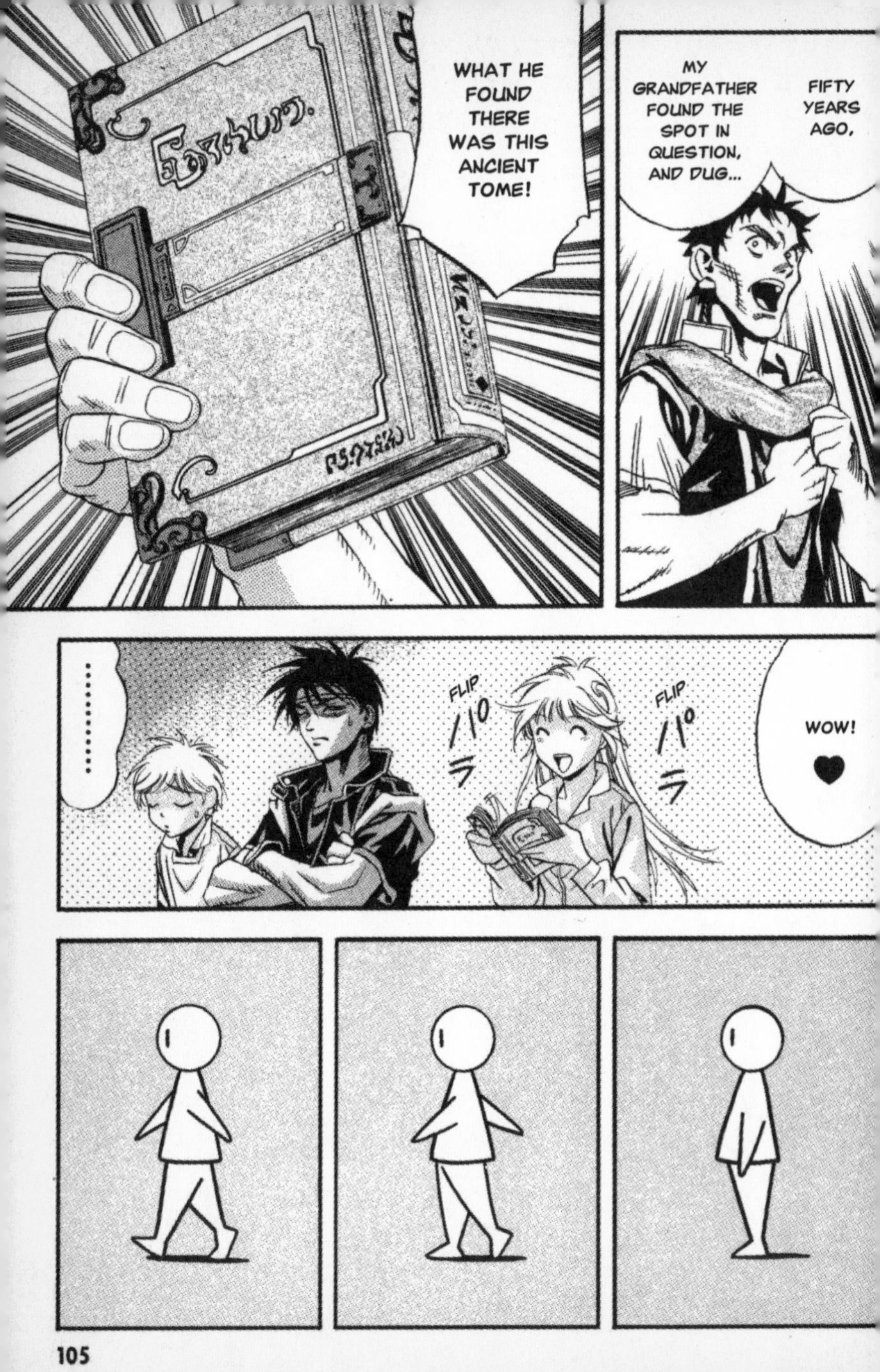
FIFTY YEARS AGO,
MY GRANDFATHER FOUND THE SPOT IN QUESTION, AND DUG...
WHAT HE FOUND THERE WAS THIS ANCIENT TOME!
WOW! ♥
FLIP
FLIP
......

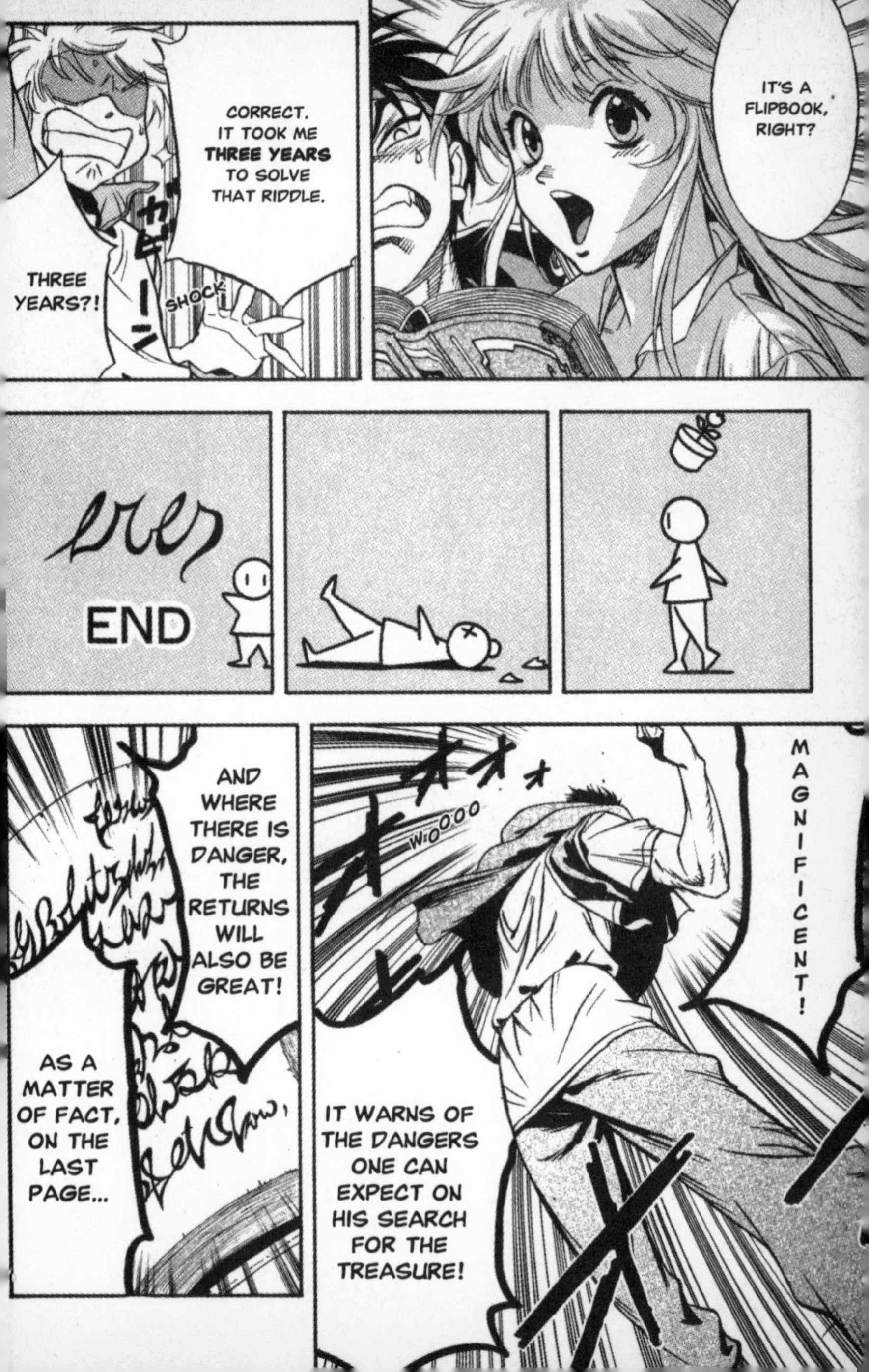
IT'S A FLIPBOOK, RIGHT?
CORRECT. IT TOOK ME THREE YEARS TO SOLVE THAT RIDDLE.
THREE YEARS?!
SHOCK
END
MAGNIFICENT!
WOOOO
IT WARNS OF THE DANGERS ONE CAN EXPECT ON HIS SEARCH FOR THE TREASURE!
AND WHERE THERE IS DANGER, THE RETURNS WILL ALSO BE GREAT!
AS A MATTER OF FACT, ON THE LAST PAGE...

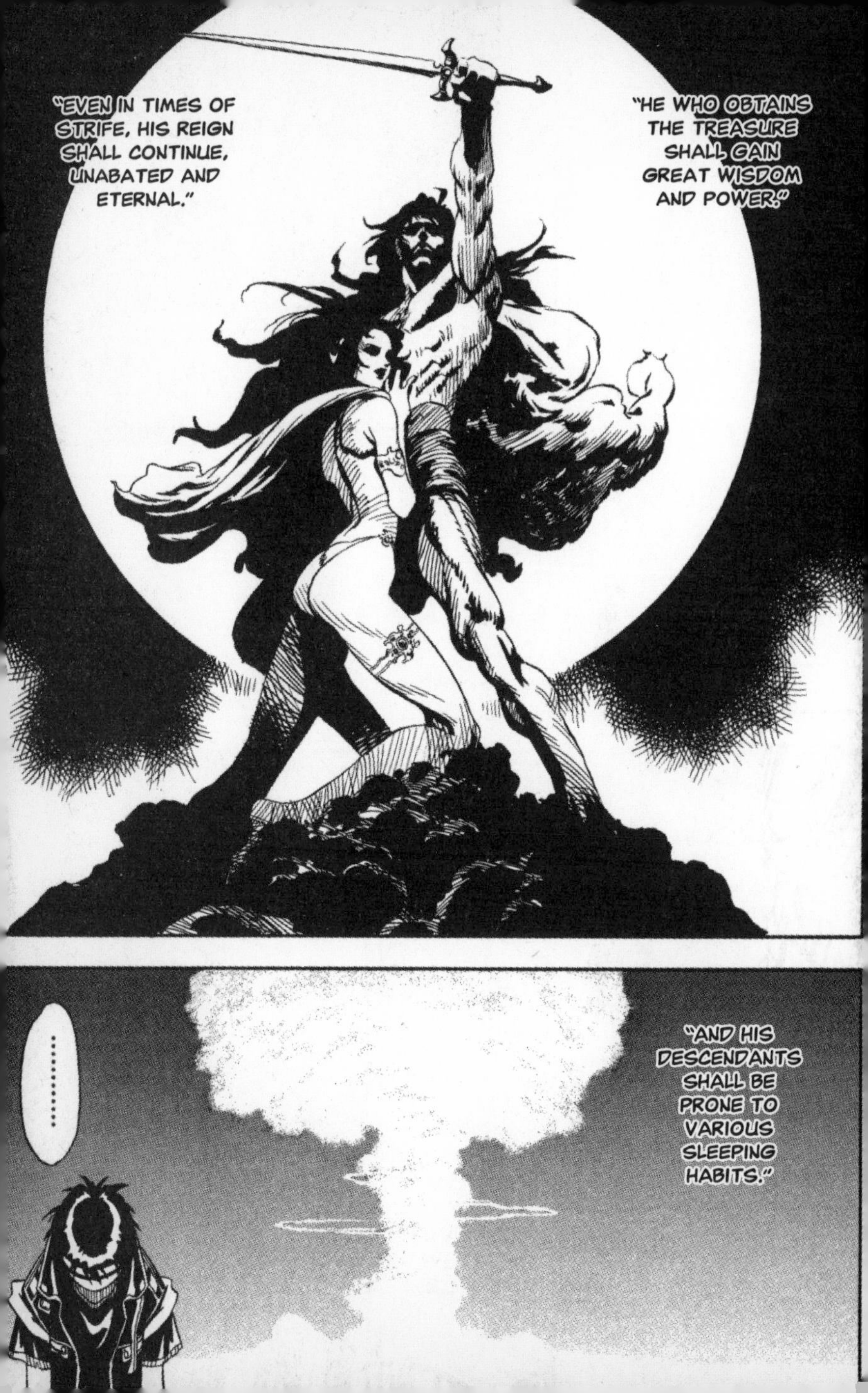
"HE WHO OBTAINS THE TREASURE SHALL GAIN GREAT WISDOM AND POWER."
"EVEN IN TIMES OF STRIFE, HIS REIGN SHALL CONTINUE, UNABATED AND ETERNAL."
"AND HIS DESCENDANTS SHALL BE PRONE TO VARIOUS SLEEPING HABITS."
....

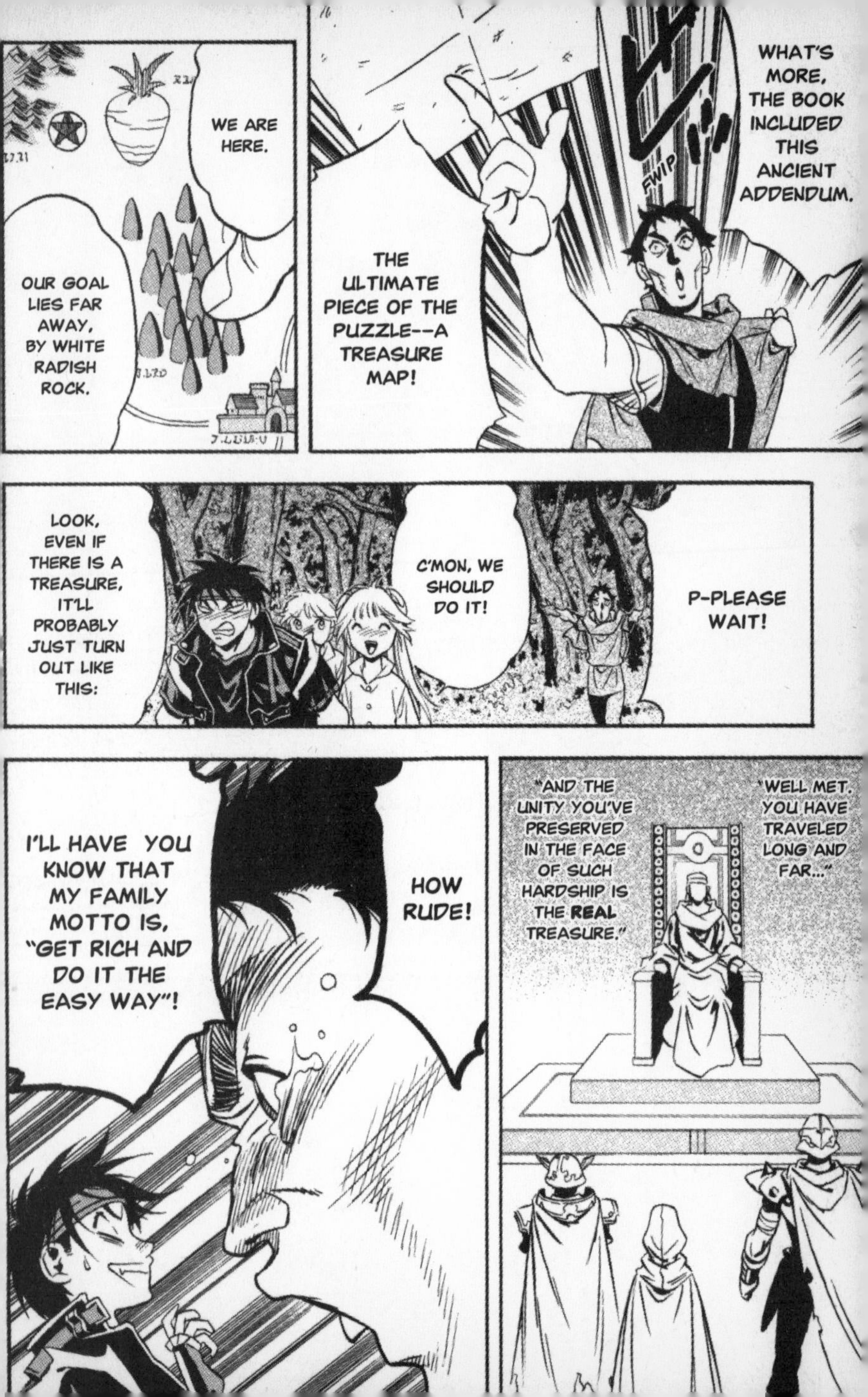
WHAT'S MORE, THE BOOK INCLUDED THIS ANCIENT ADDENDUM.
FWIP
THE ULTIMATE PIECE OF THE PUZZLE--A TREASURE MAP!
WE ARE HERE.
OUR GOAL LIES FAR AWAY, BY WHITE RADISH ROCK.
P-PLEASE WAIT!
C'MON, WE SHOULD DO IT!
LOOK, EVEN IF THERE IS A TREASURE, IT'LL PROBABLY JUST TURN OUT LIKE THIS:
"WELL MET. YOU HAVE TRAVELED LONG AND FAR..."
"AND THE UNITY YOU'VE PRESERVED IN THE FACE OF SUCH HARDSHIP IS THE **REAL** TREASURE."
HOW RUDE!
I'LL HAVE YOU KNOW THAT MY FAMILY MOTTO IS, "GET RICH AND DO IT THE EASY WAY"!

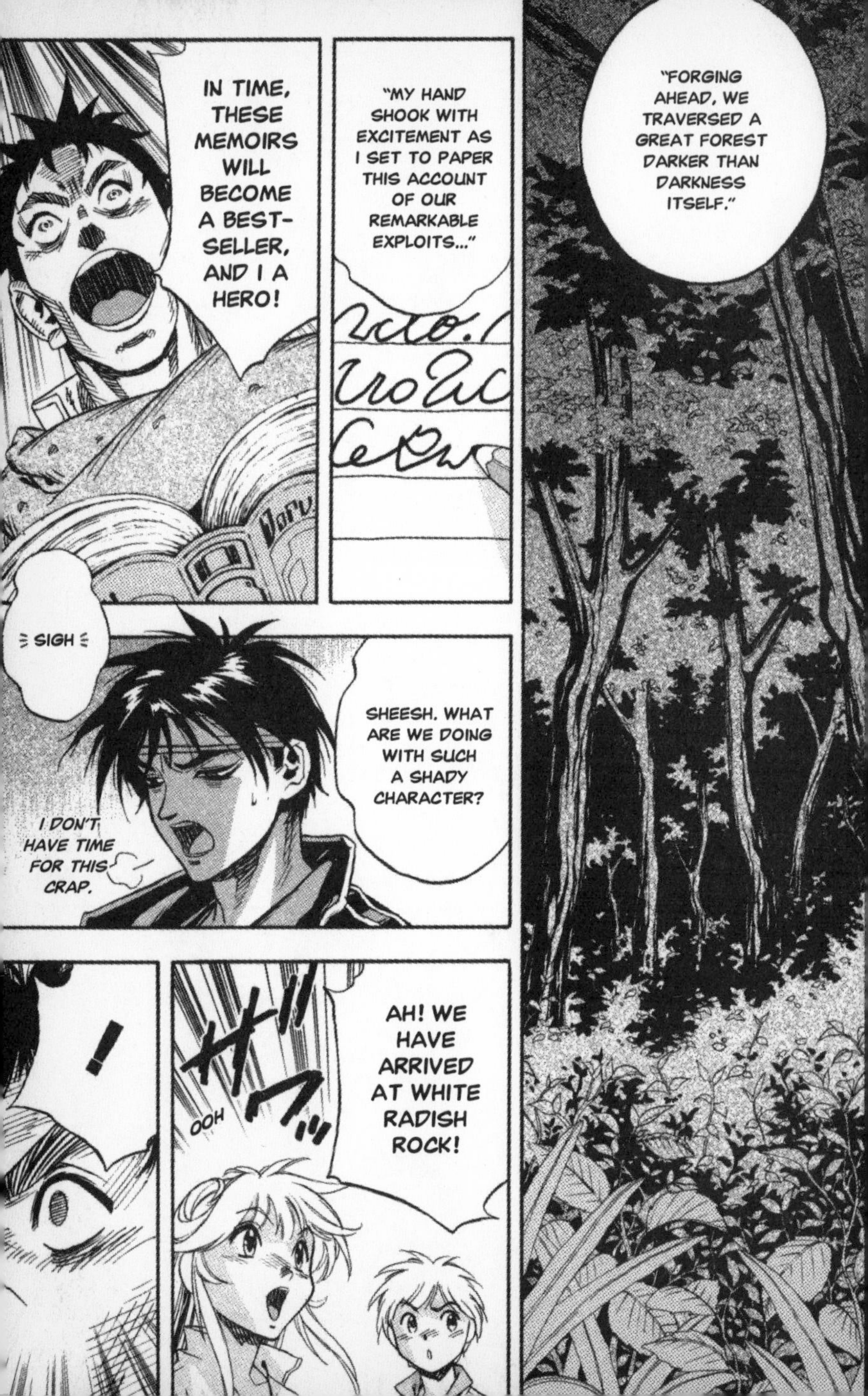
"FORGING AHEAD, WE TRAVERSED A GREAT FOREST DARKER THAN DARKNESS ITSELF."
"MY HAND SHOOK WITH EXCITEMENT AS I SET TO PAPER THIS ACCOUNT OF OUR REMARKABLE EXPLOITS..."
IN TIME, THESE MEMOIRS WILL BECOME A BEST-SELLER, AND I A HERO!
SHEESH. WHAT ARE WE DOING WITH SUCH A SHADY CHARACTER?
SIGH
I DON'T HAVE TIME FOR THIS CRAP.
AH! WE HAVE ARRIVED AT WHITE RADISH ROCK!
OOH
!

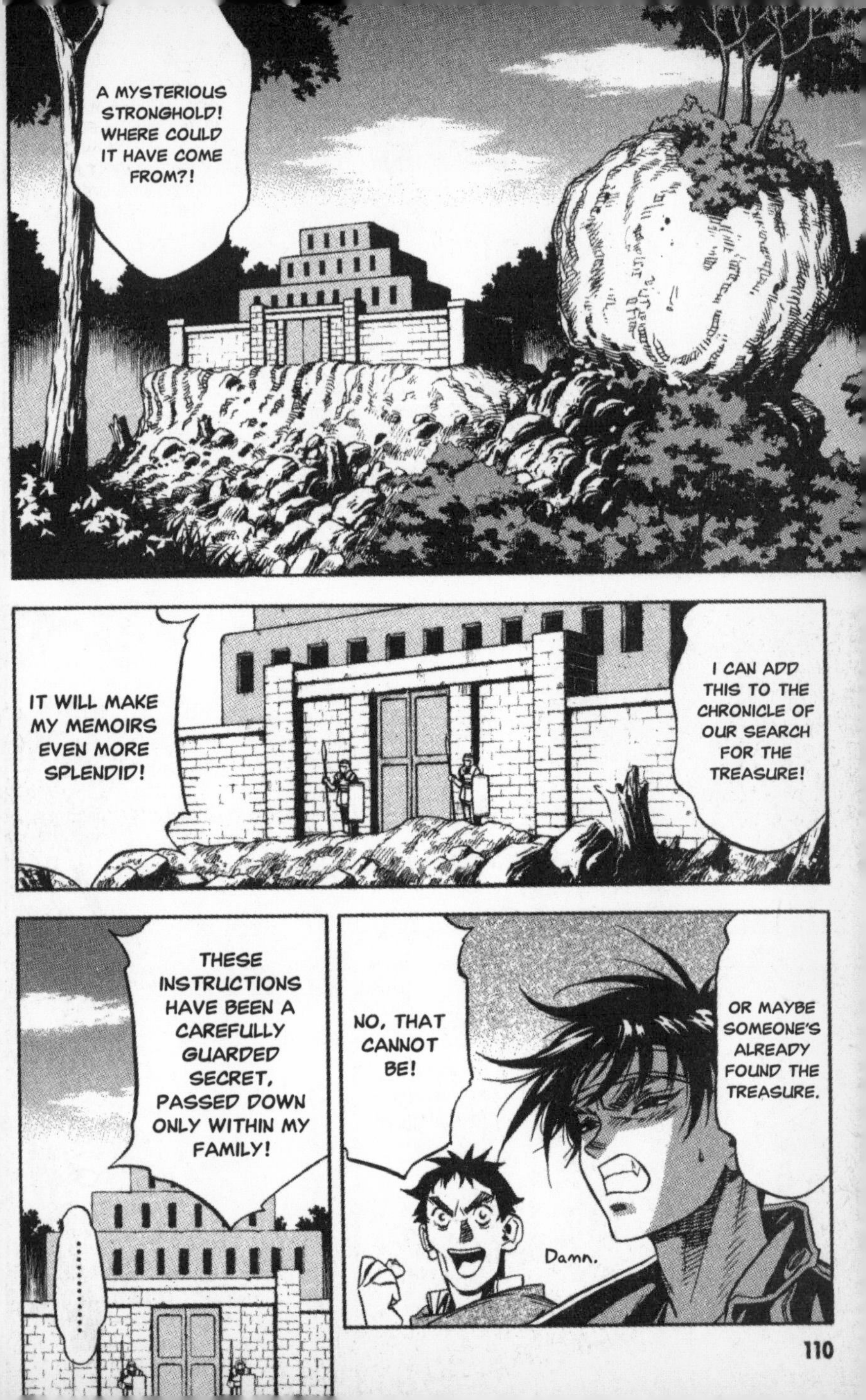
A MYSTERIOUS STRONGHOLD! WHERE COULD IT HAVE COME FROM?!
I CAN ADD THIS TO THE CHRONICLE OF OUR SEARCH FOR THE TREASURE!
IT WILL MAKE MY MEMOIRS EVEN MORE SPLENDID!
OR MAYBE SOMEONE'S ALREADY FOUND THE TREASURE.
Damn.
NO, THAT CANNOT BE!
THESE INSTRUCTIONS HAVE BEEN A CAREFULLY GUARDED SECRET, PASSED DOWN ONLY WITHIN MY FAMILY!
......

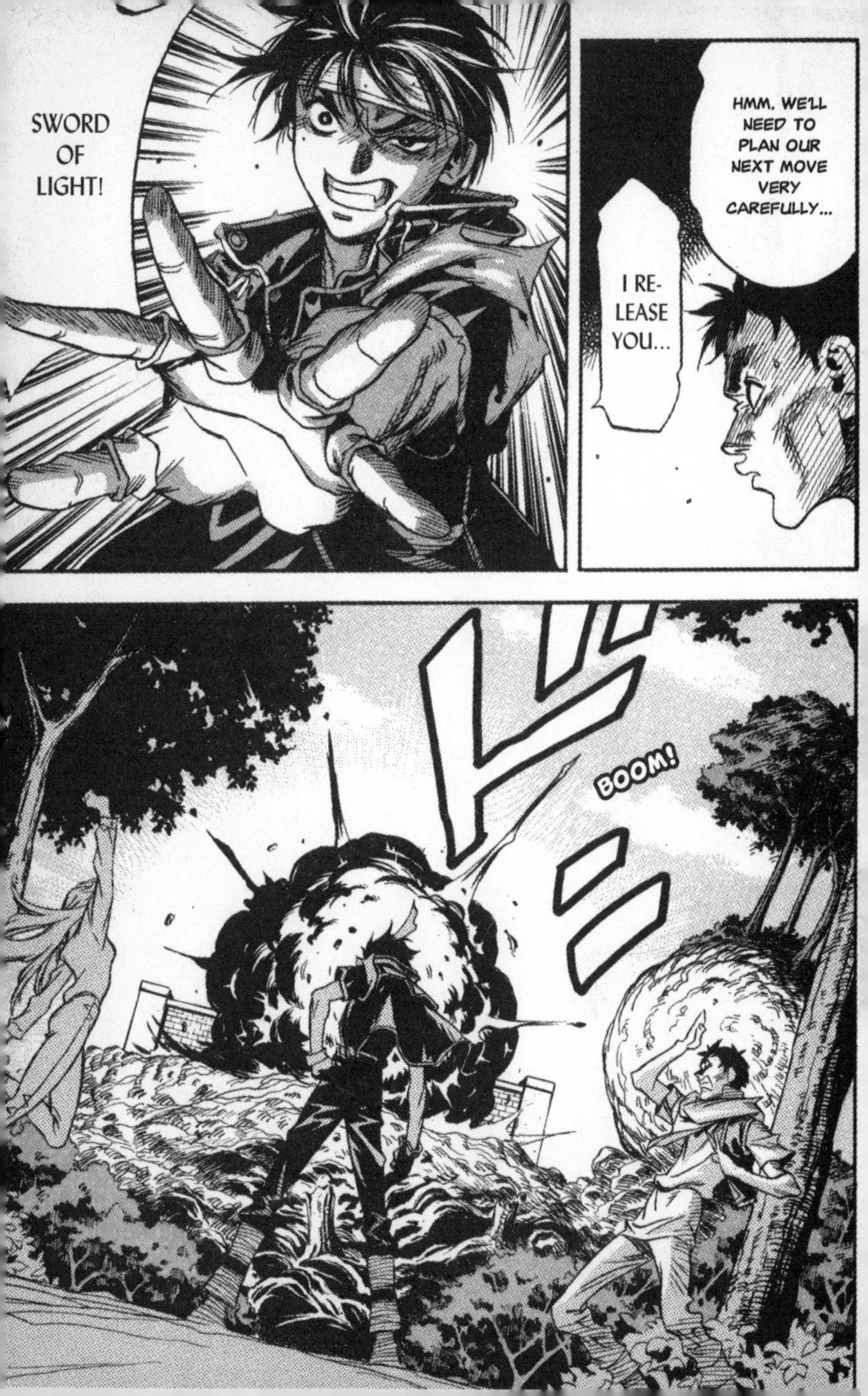
HMM. WE'LL NEED TO PLAN OUR NEXT MOVE VERY CAREFULLY...
I RE-LEASE YOU...
SWORD OF LIGHT!
BOOM!

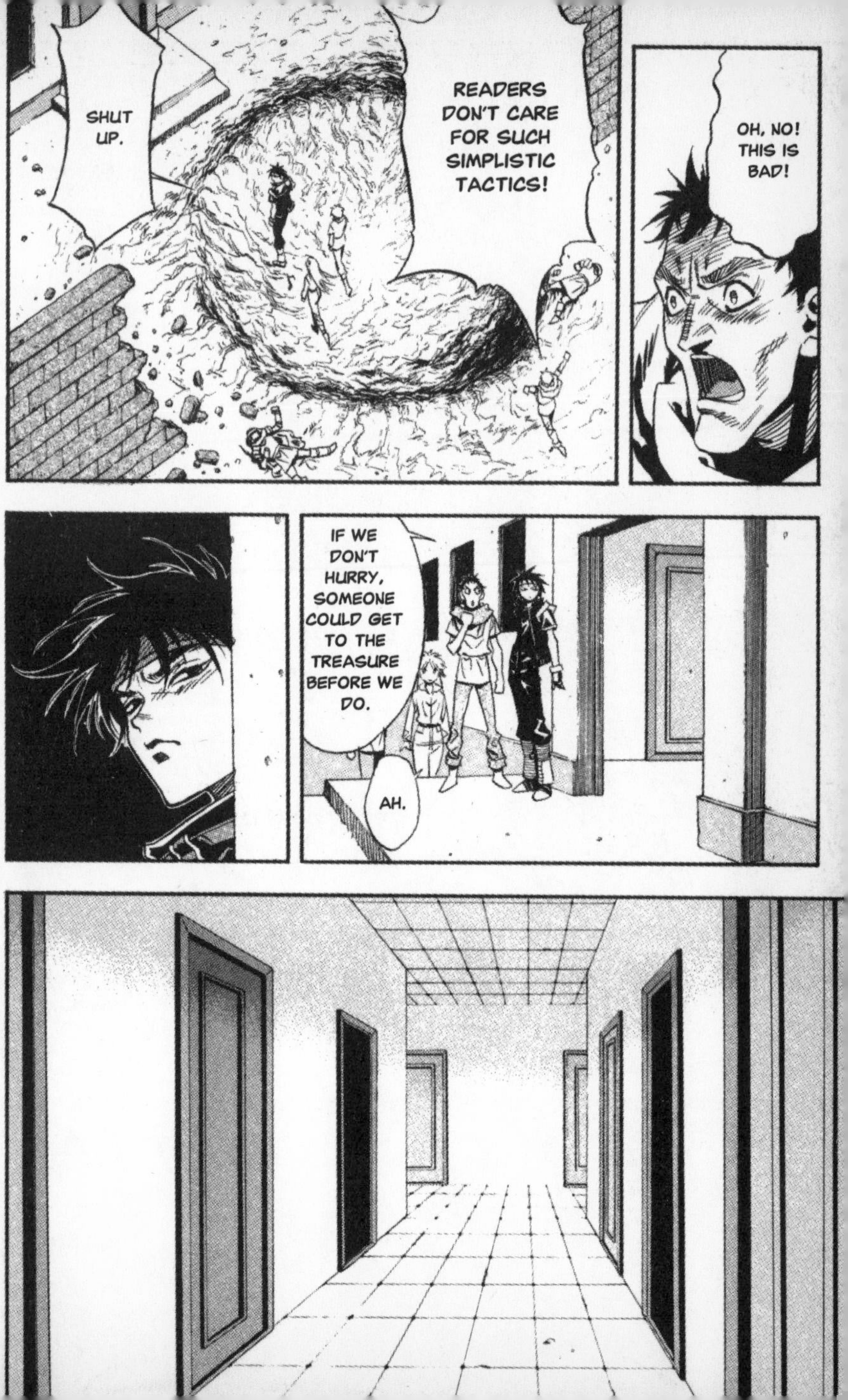
OH, NO! THIS IS BAD!
READERS DON'T CARE FOR SUCH SIMPLISTIC TACTICS!
SHUT UP.
IF WE DON'T HURRY, SOMEONE COULD GET TO THE TREASURE BEFORE WE DO.
AH.

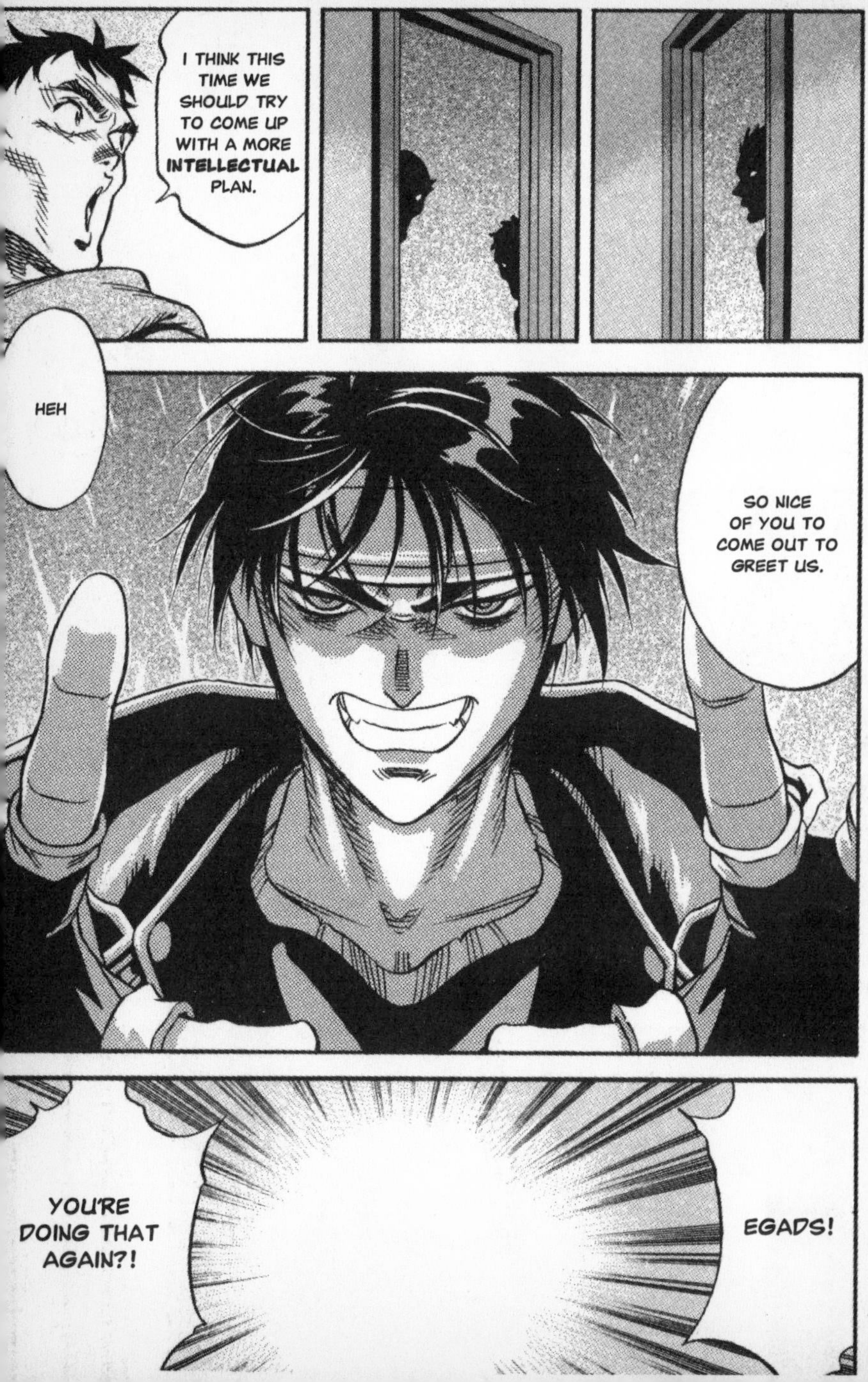
I THINK THIS TIME WE SHOULD TRY TO COME UP WITH A MORE INTELLECTUAL PLAN.
HEH
SO NICE OF YOU TO COME OUT TO GREET US.
EGADS!
YOU'RE DOING THAT AGAIN?!

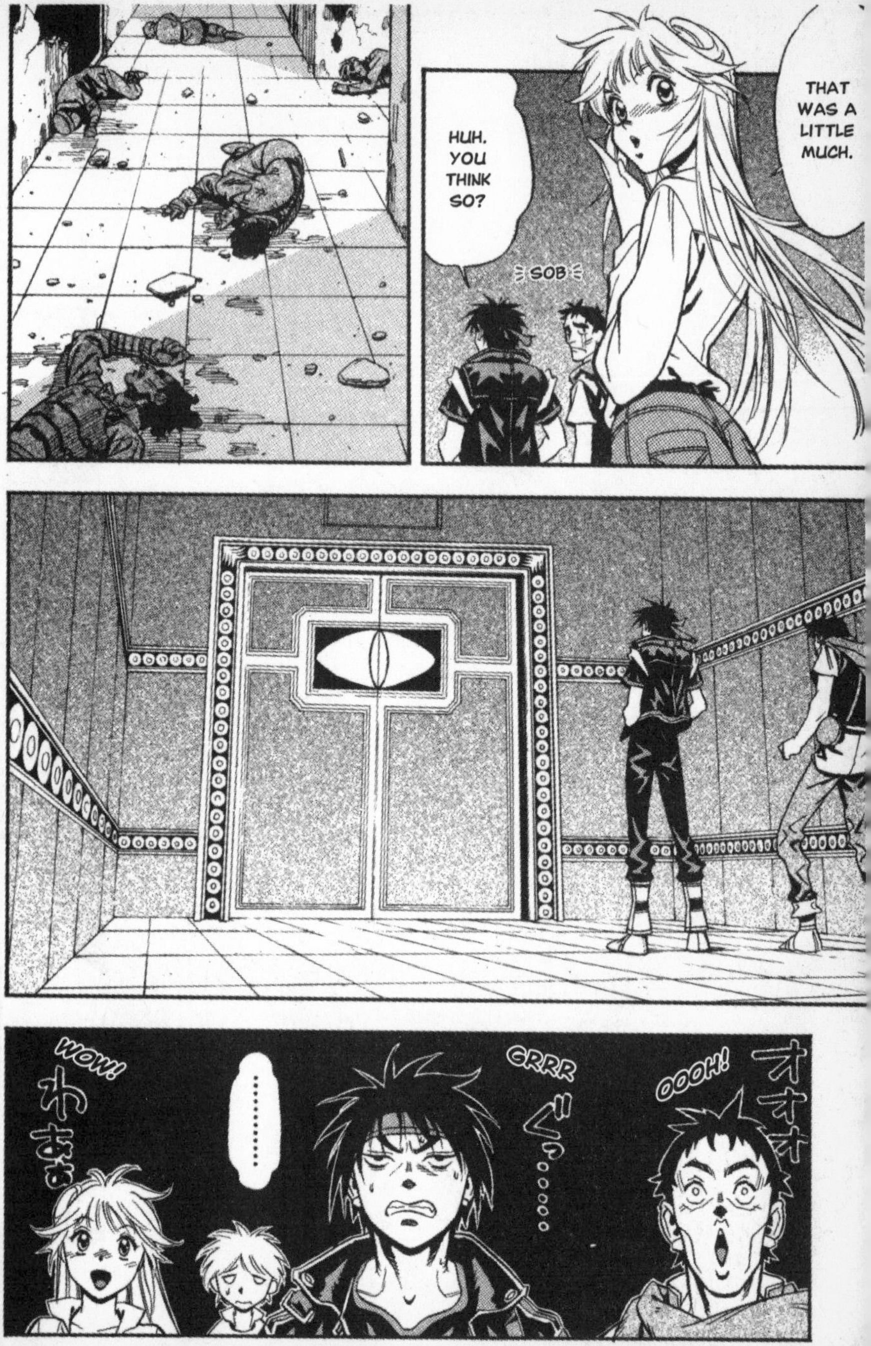
THAT WAS A LITTLE MUCH.
HUH. YOU THINK SO?
SOB
OOOH!
オオオ
GRRR
ぐ……
……
WOW!
わぁ

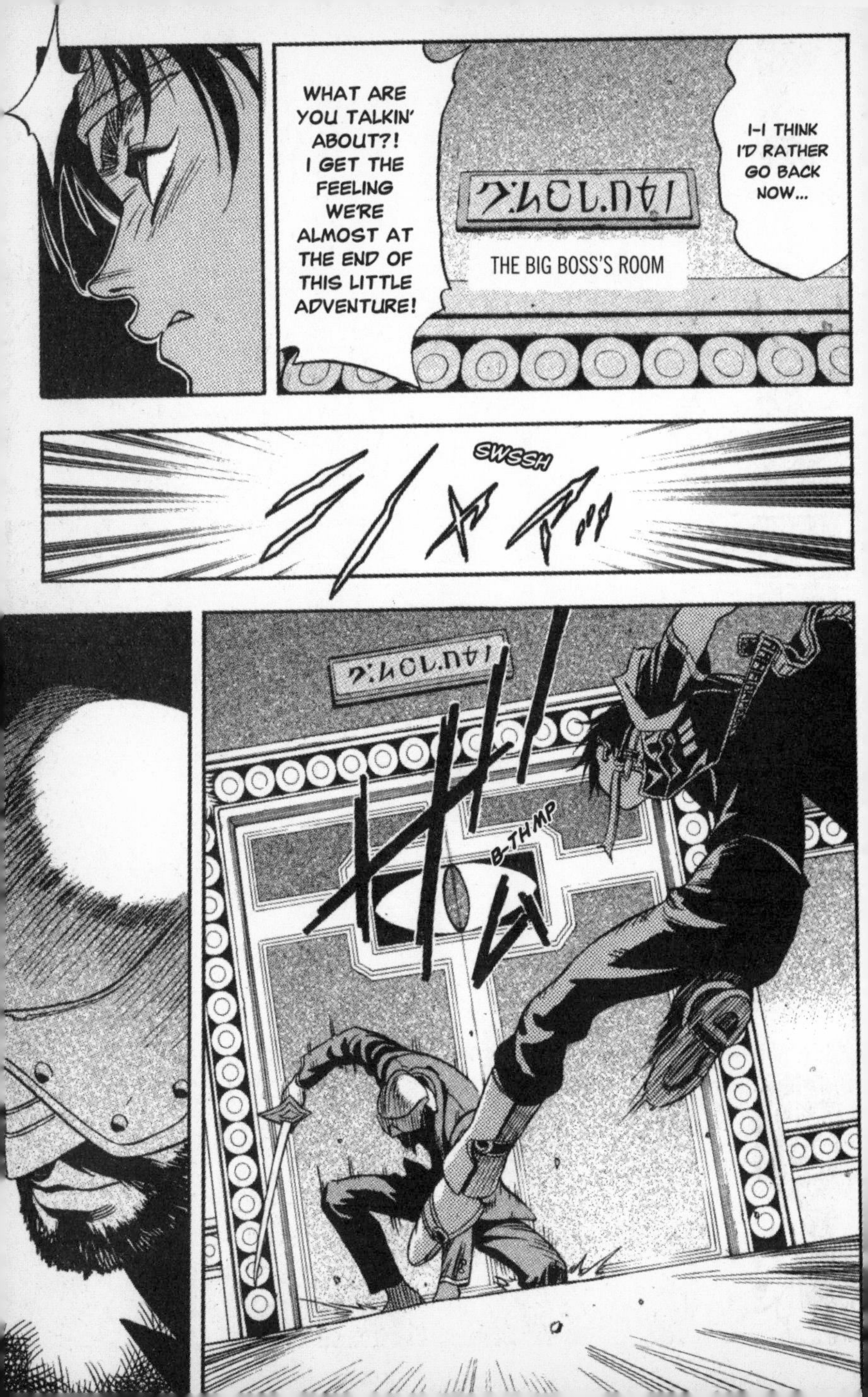
I-I THINK I'D RATHER GO BACK NOW...
WHAT ARE YOU TALKIN' ABOUT?! I GET THE FEELING WE'RE ALMOST AT THE END OF THIS LITTLE ADVENTURE!
THE BIG BOSS'S ROOM
SWSSH
B-THMP

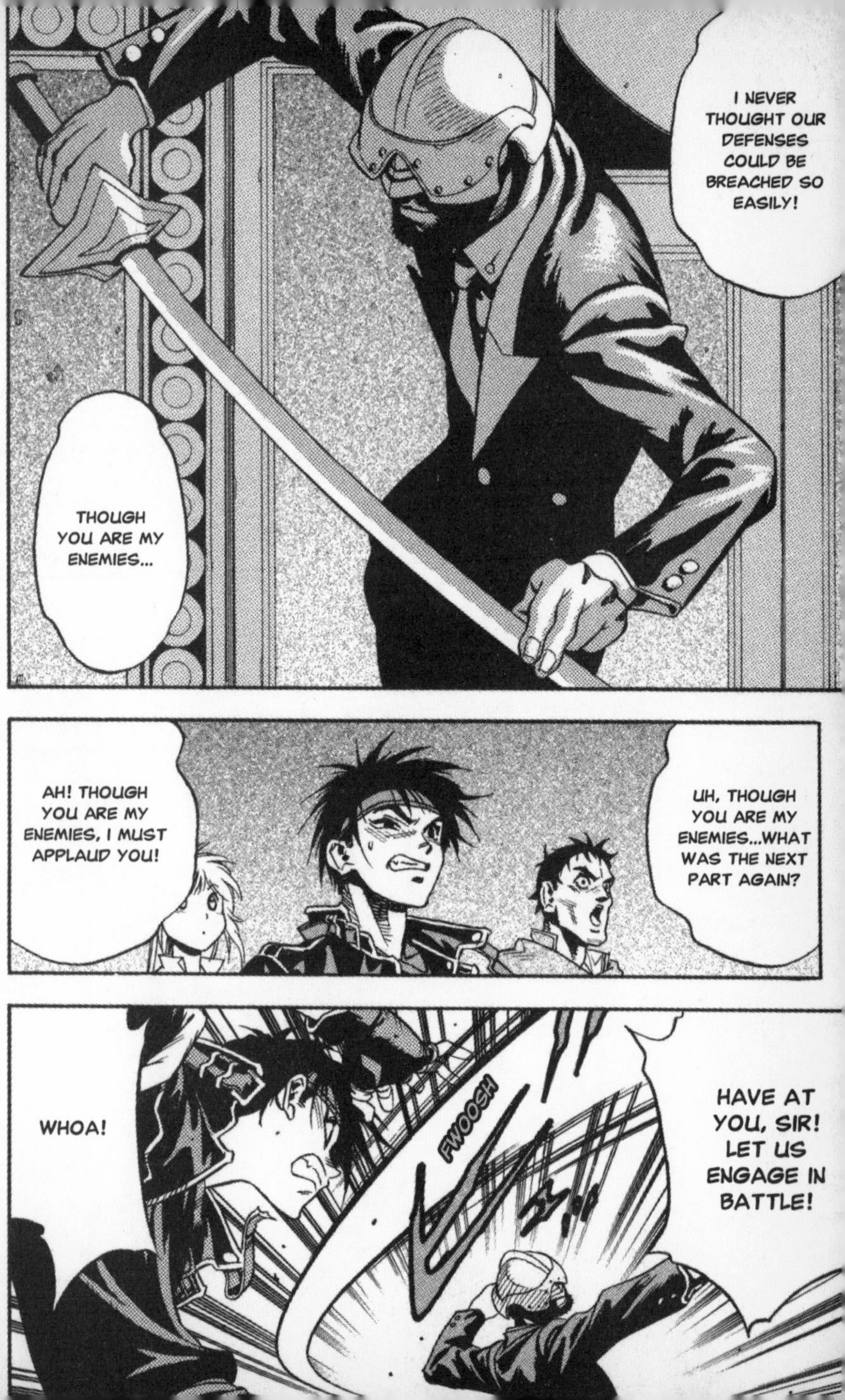
I NEVER THOUGHT OUR DEFENSES COULD BE BREACHED SO EASILY!
THOUGH YOU ARE MY ENEMIES...
UH, THOUGH YOU ARE MY ENEMIES...WHAT WAS THE NEXT PART AGAIN?
AH! THOUGH YOU ARE MY ENEMIES, I MUST APPLAUD YOU!
HAVE AT YOU, SIR! LET US ENGAGE IN BATTLE!
FWOOSH
WHOA!

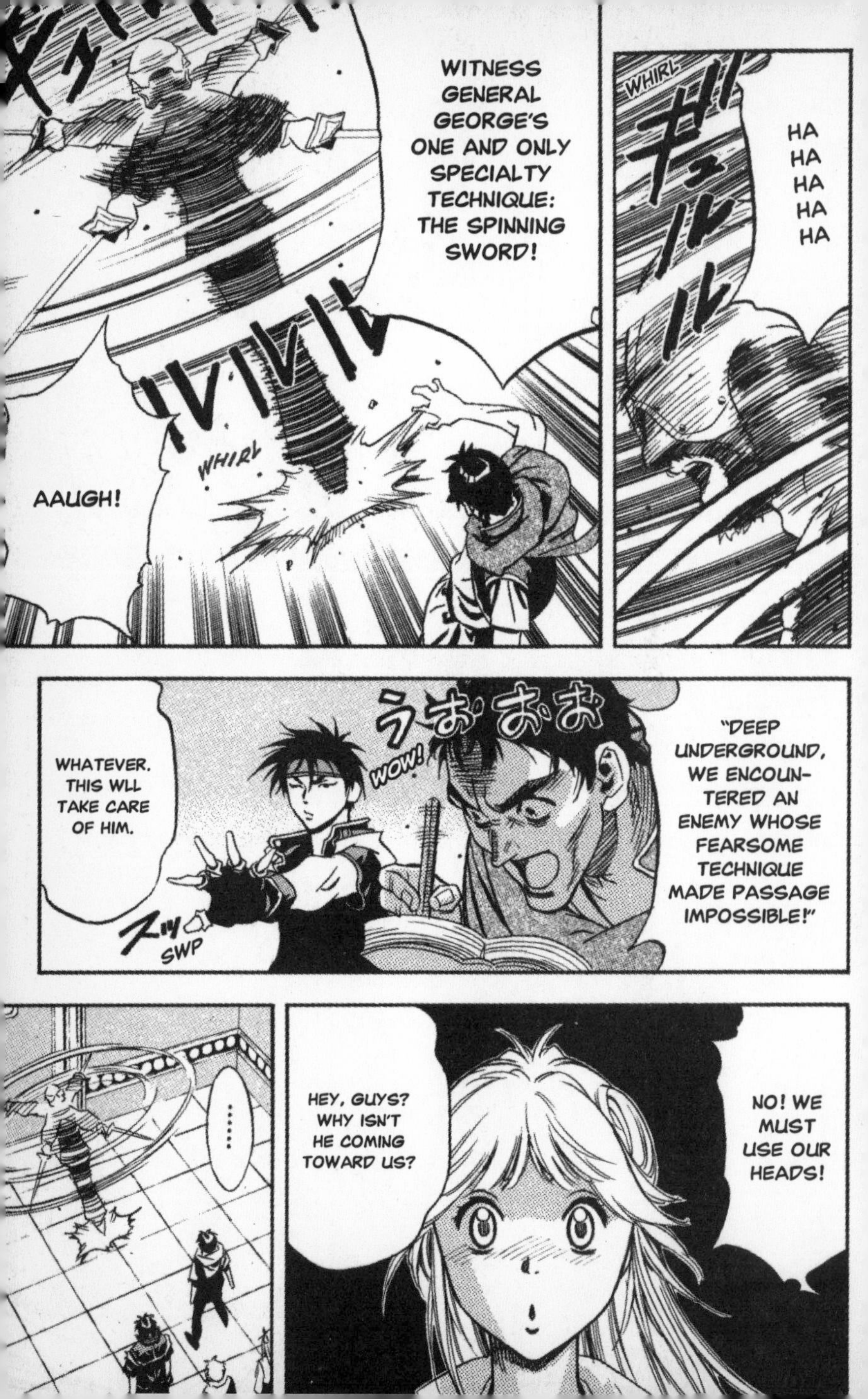

WHIRL
HA HA HA HA HA
WITNESS GENERAL GEORGE'S ONE AND ONLY SPECIALTY TECHNIQUE: THE SPINNING SWORD!
WHIRL
AAUGH!
"DEEP UNDERGROUND, WE ENCOUNTERED AN ENEMY WHOSE FEARSOME TECHNIQUE MADE PASSAGE IMPOSSIBLE!"
WOW!
WHATEVER. THIS WLL TAKE CARE OF HIM.
SWP
NO! WE MUST USE OUR HEADS!
HEY, GUYS? WHY ISN'T HE COMING TOWARD US?
......

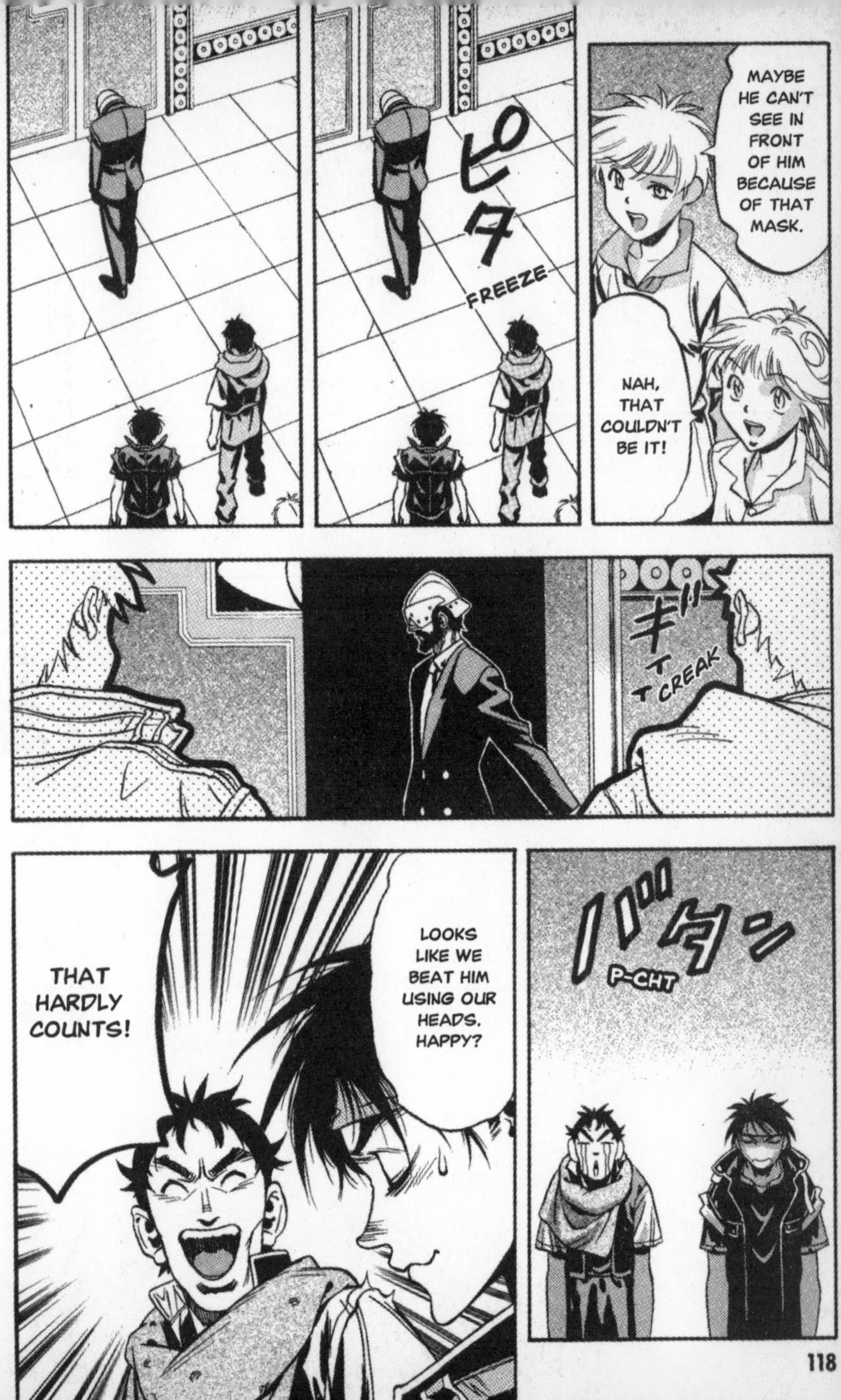
MAYBE HE CAN'T SEE IN FRONT OF HIM BECAUSE OF THAT MASK.
NAH, THAT COULDN'T BE IT!
ピタ
FREEZE
ギィ
CREAK
バタン
P-CHT
LOOKS LIKE WE BEAT HIM USING OUR HEADS. HAPPY?
THAT HARDLY COUNTS!

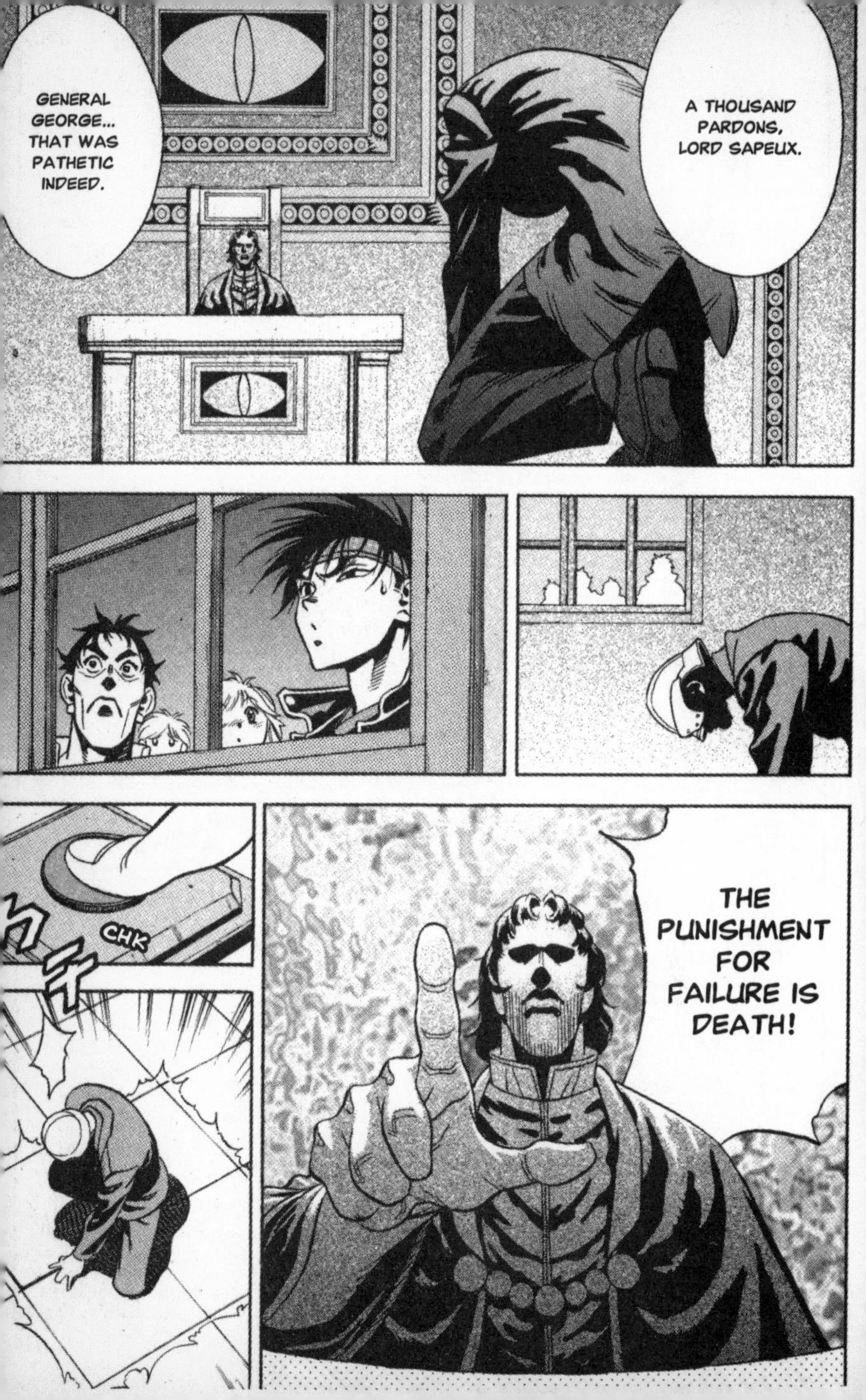
A THOUSAND PARDONS, LORD SAPEUX.
GENERAL GEORGE... THAT WAS PATHETIC INDEED.
CHK
THE PUNISHMENT FOR FAILURE IS DEATH!

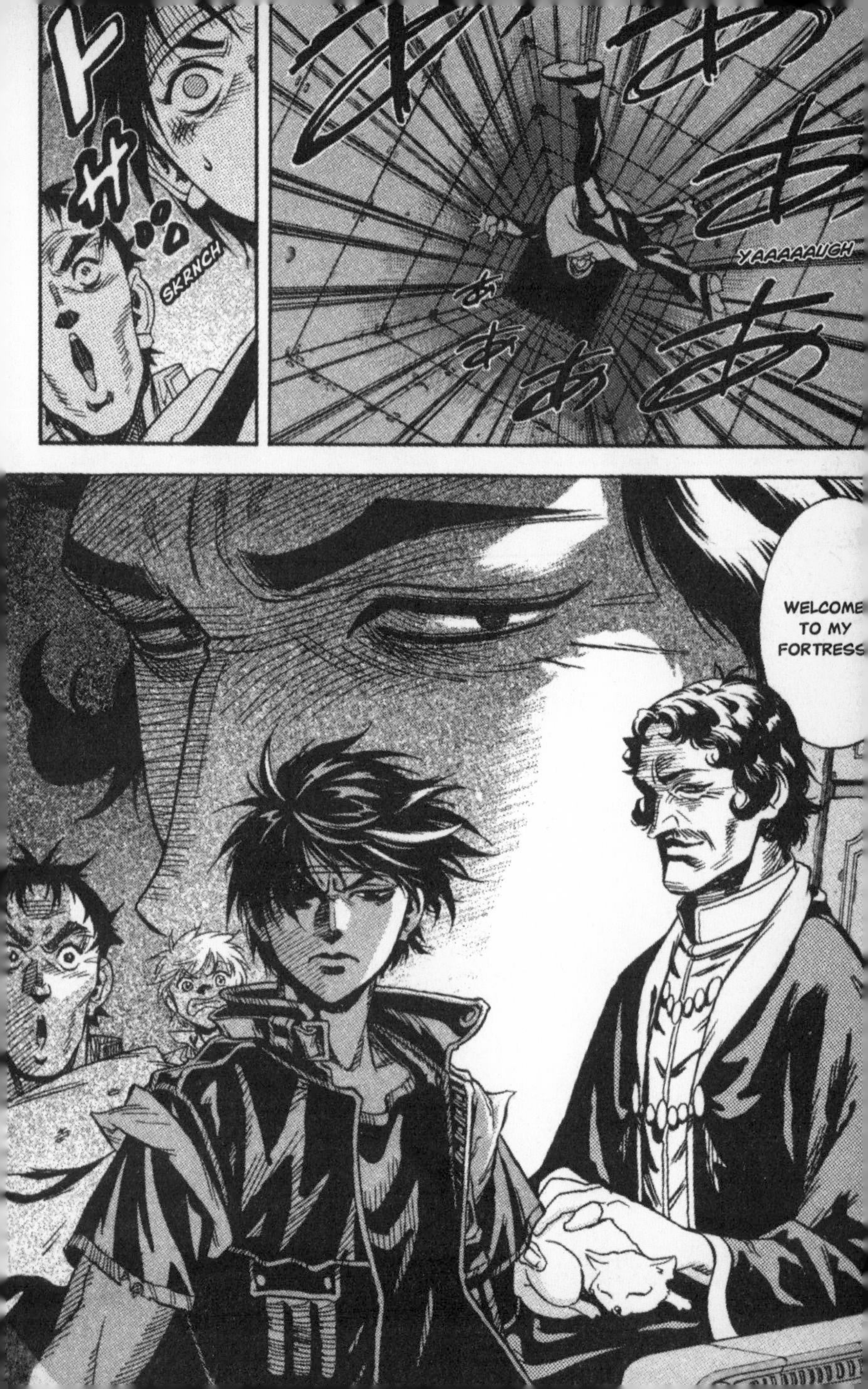
YAAAAAUGH
SKRNCH
WELCOME TO MY FORTRESS

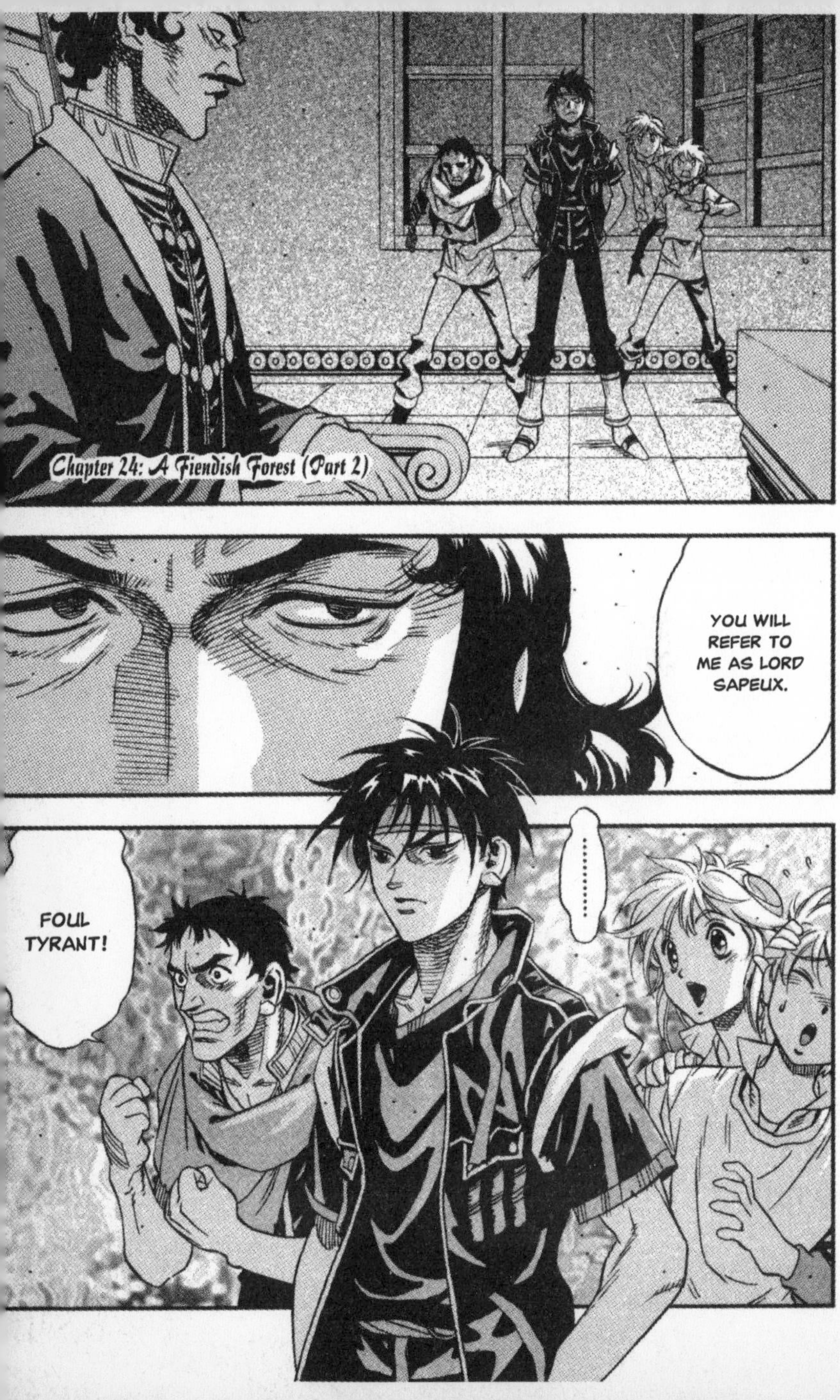
Chapter 24: A Fiendish Forest (Part 2)
YOU WILL REFER TO ME AS LORD SAPEUX.
FOUL TYRANT!
......

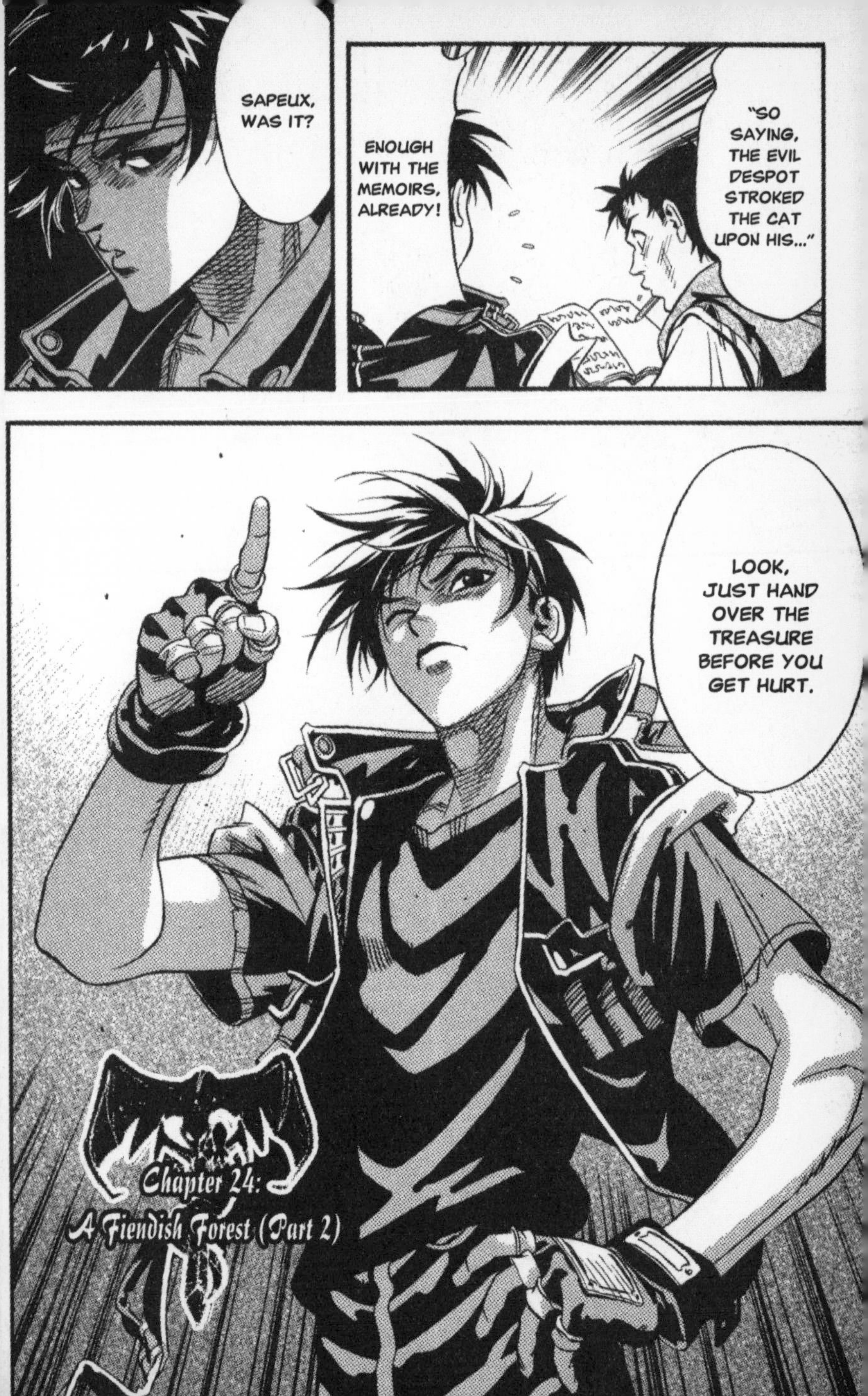
"SO SAYING, THE EVIL DESPOT STROKED THE CAT UPON HIS..."
ENOUGH WITH THE MEMOIRS, ALREADY!
SAPEUX, WAS IT?
LOOK, JUST HAND OVER THE TREASURE BEFORE YOU GET HURT.
Chapter 24:
A Fiendish Forest (Part 2)

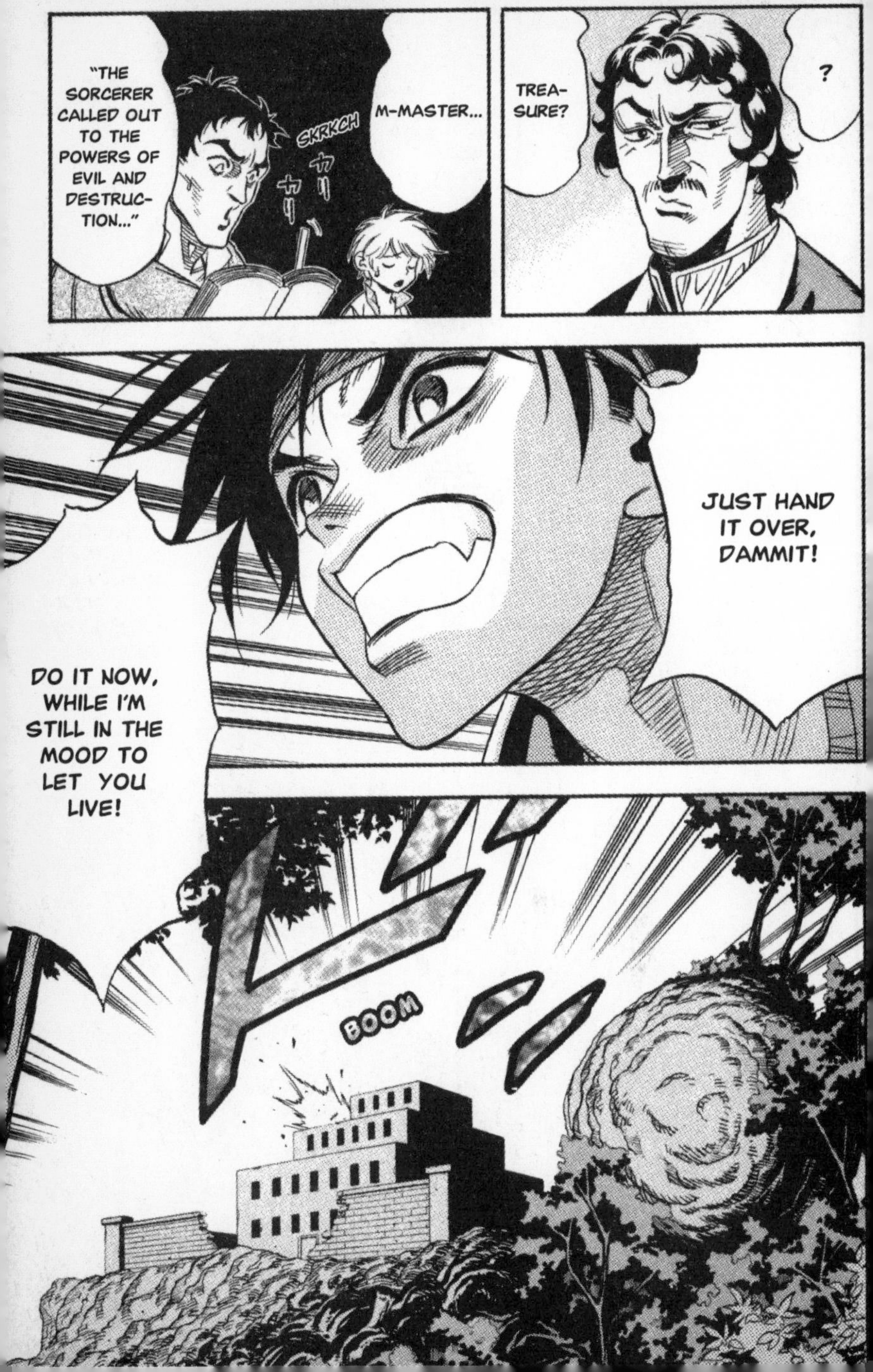
?
TREA-SURE?
M-MASTER...
SKRKCH
カリ
カリ
"THE SORCERER CALLED OUT TO THE POWERS OF EVIL AND DESTRUCTION..."
JUST HAND IT OVER, DAMMIT!
DO IT NOW, WHILE I'M STILL IN THE MOOD TO LET YOU LIVE!
BOOM

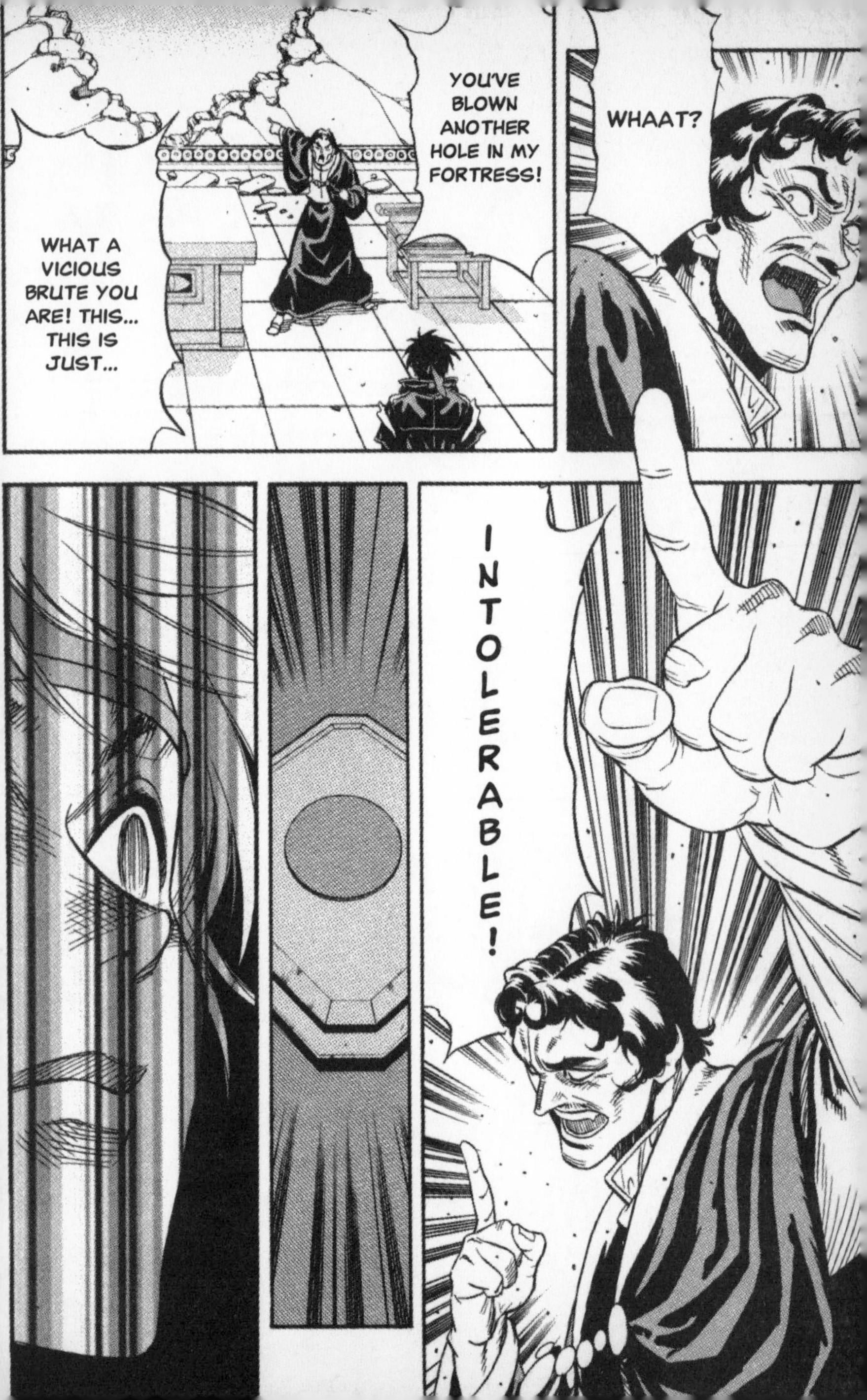

WHAAT?
YOU'VE BLOWN ANOTHER HOLE IN MY FORTRESS!
WHAT A VICIOUS BRUTE YOU ARE! THIS... THIS IS JUST...
INTOLERABLE!

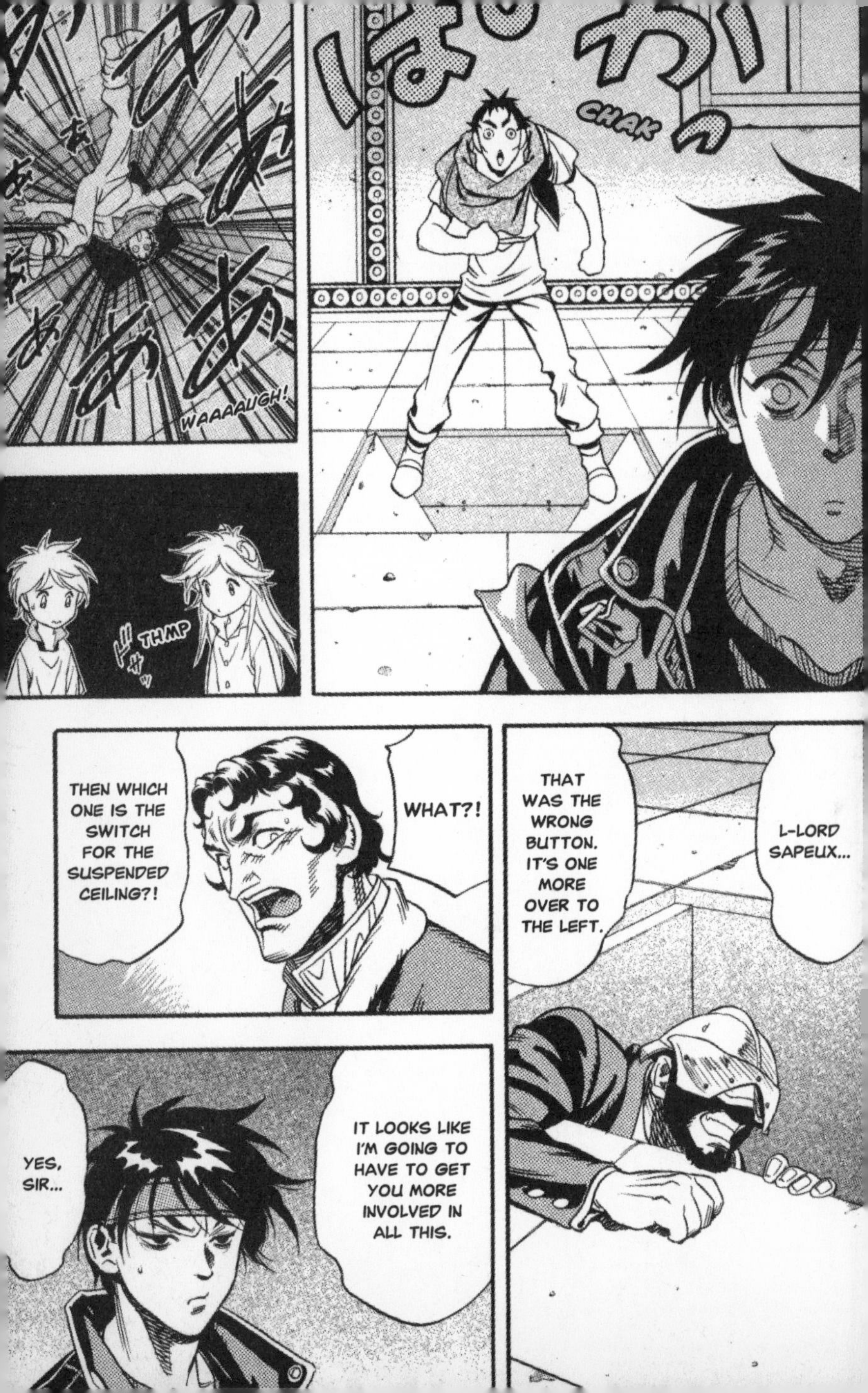
CHAK
WAAAAUGH!
THMP
L-LORD SAPEUX...
THAT WAS THE WRONG BUTTON. IT'S ONE MORE OVER TO THE LEFT.
WHAT?!
THEN WHICH ONE IS THE SWITCH FOR THE SUSPENDED CEILING?!
IT LOOKS LIKE I'M GOING TO HAVE TO GET YOU MORE INVOLVED IN ALL THIS.
YES, SIR...

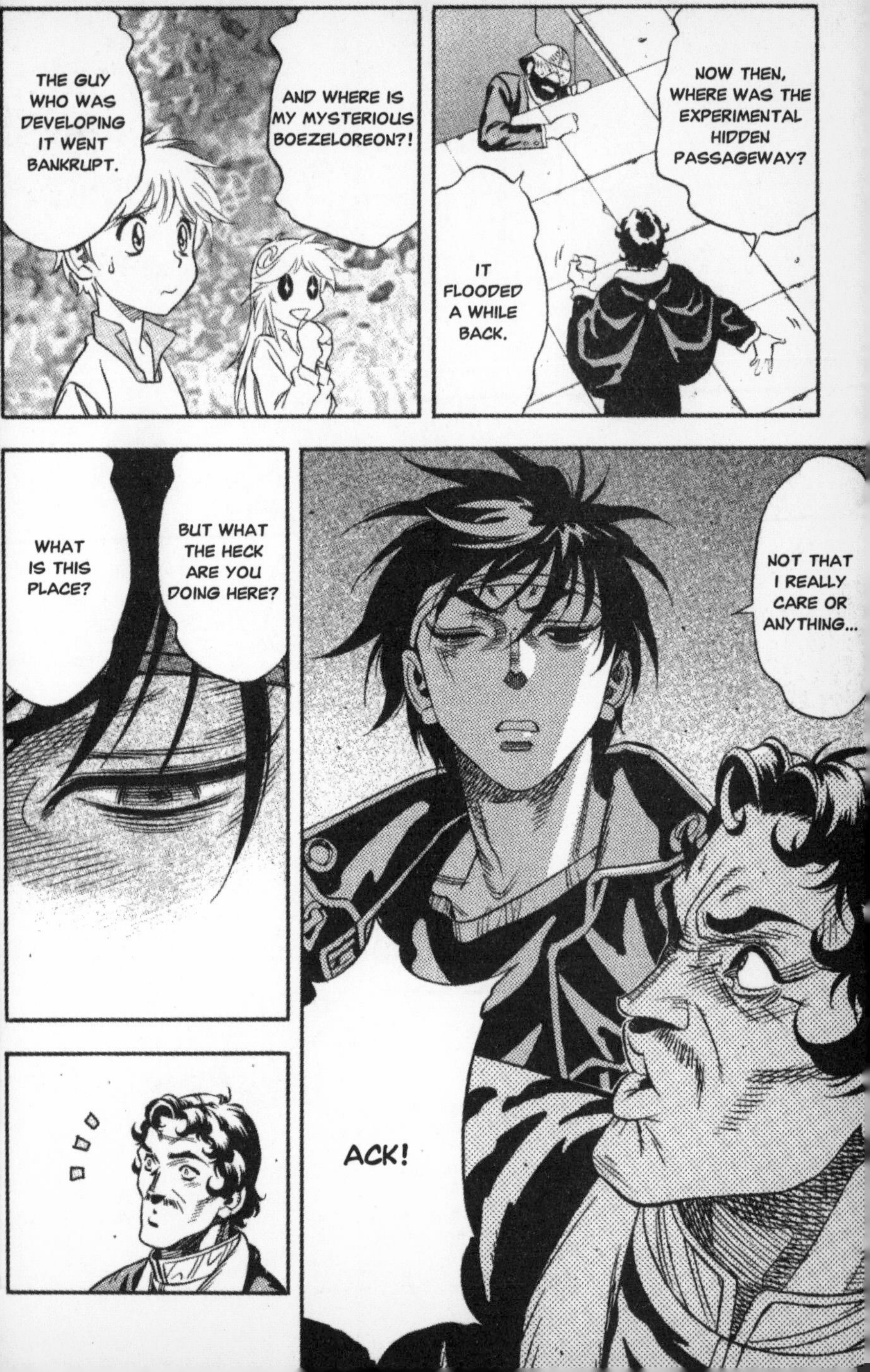
THE GUY WHO WAS DEVELOPING IT WENT BANKRUPT.
AND WHERE IS MY MYSTERIOUS BOEZELOREON?!
NOW THEN, WHERE WAS THE EXPERIMENTAL HIDDEN PASSAGEWAY?
IT FLOODED A WHILE BACK.
WHAT IS THIS PLACE?
BUT WHAT THE HECK ARE YOU DOING HERE?
NOT THAT I REALLY CARE OR ANYTHING...
ACK!

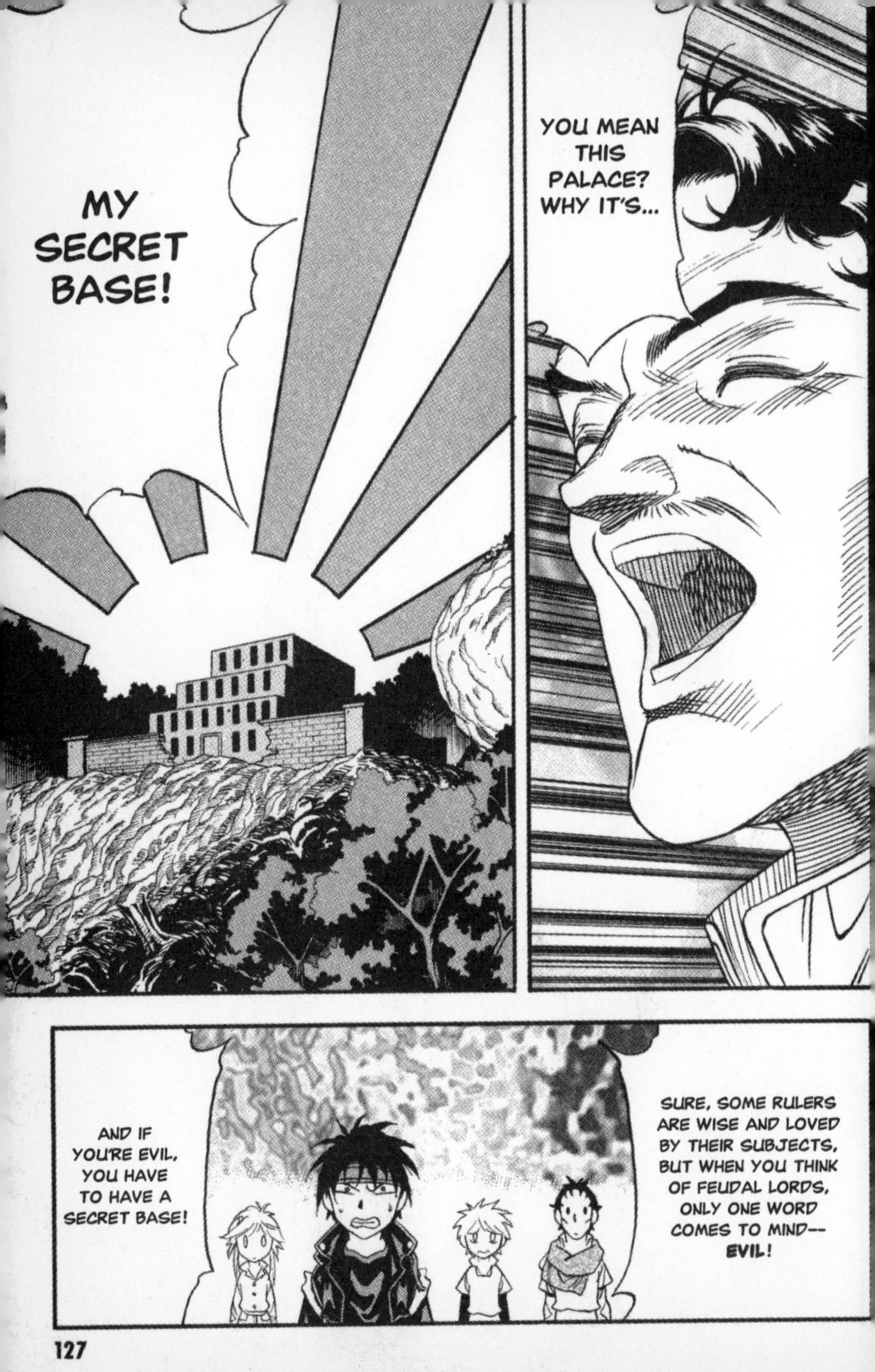
YOU MEAN THIS PALACE? WHY IT'S...
MY SECRET BASE!
SURE, SOME RULERS ARE WISE AND LOVED BY THEIR SUBJECTS, BUT WHEN YOU THINK OF FEUDAL LORDS, ONLY ONE WORD COMES TO MIND-- EVIL!
AND IF YOU'RE EVIL, YOU HAVE TO HAVE A SECRET BASE!

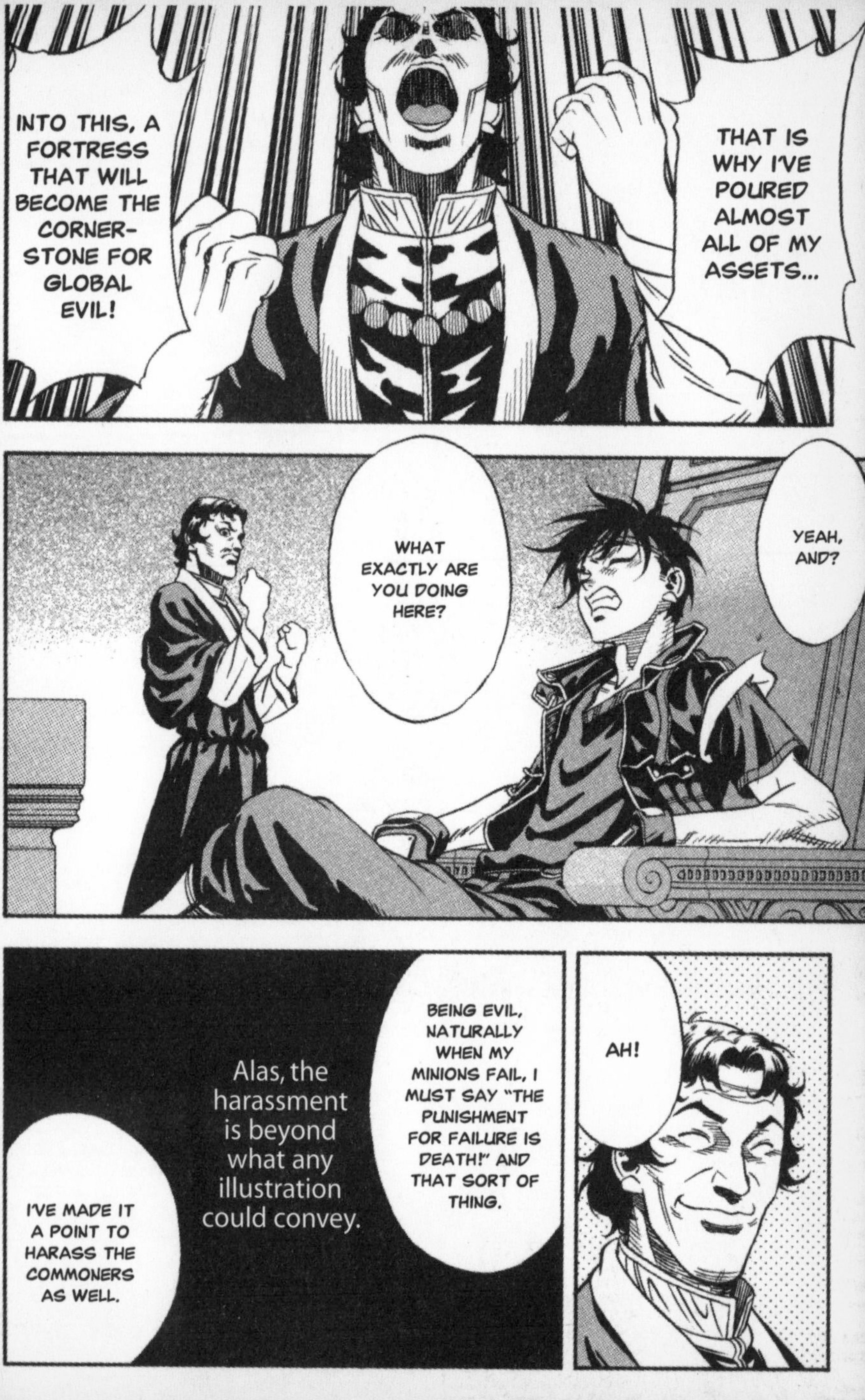
THAT IS WHY I'VE POURED ALMOST ALL OF MY ASSETS...
INTO THIS, A FORTRESS THAT WILL BECOME THE CORNER-STONE FOR GLOBAL EVIL!
YEAH, AND?
WHAT EXACTLY ARE YOU DOING HERE?
AH!
BEING EVIL, NATURALLY WHEN MY MINIONS FAIL, I MUST SAY "THE PUNISHMENT FOR FAILURE IS DEATH!" AND THAT SORT OF THING.
I'VE MADE IT A POINT TO HARASS THE COMMONERS AS WELL.
Alas, the harassment is beyond what any illustration could convey.

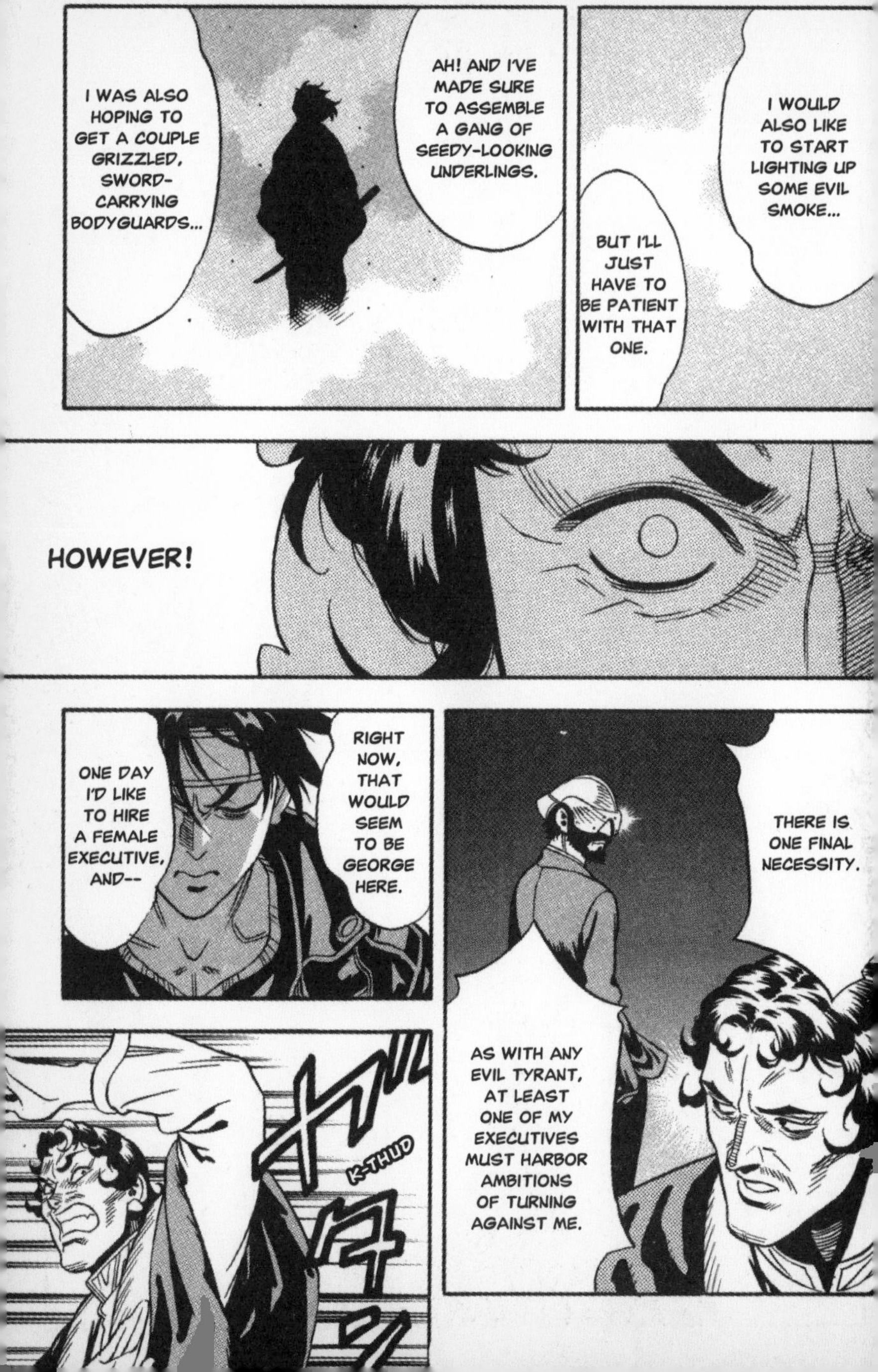
I WAS ALSO HOPING TO GET A COUPLE GRIZZLED, SWORD-CARRYING BODYGUARDS...
AH! AND I'VE MADE SURE TO ASSEMBLE A GANG OF SEEDY-LOOKING UNDERLINGS.
I WOULD ALSO LIKE TO START LIGHTING UP SOME EVIL SMOKE...
BUT I'LL JUST HAVE TO BE PATIENT WITH THAT ONE.
HOWEVER!
ONE DAY I'D LIKE TO HIRE A FEMALE EXECUTIVE, AND--
RIGHT NOW, THAT WOULD SEEM TO BE GEORGE HERE.
THERE IS ONE FINAL NECESSITY.
AS WITH ANY EVIL TYRANT, AT LEAST ONE OF MY EXECUTIVES MUST HARBOR AMBITIONS OF TURNING AGAINST ME.
K-THUD

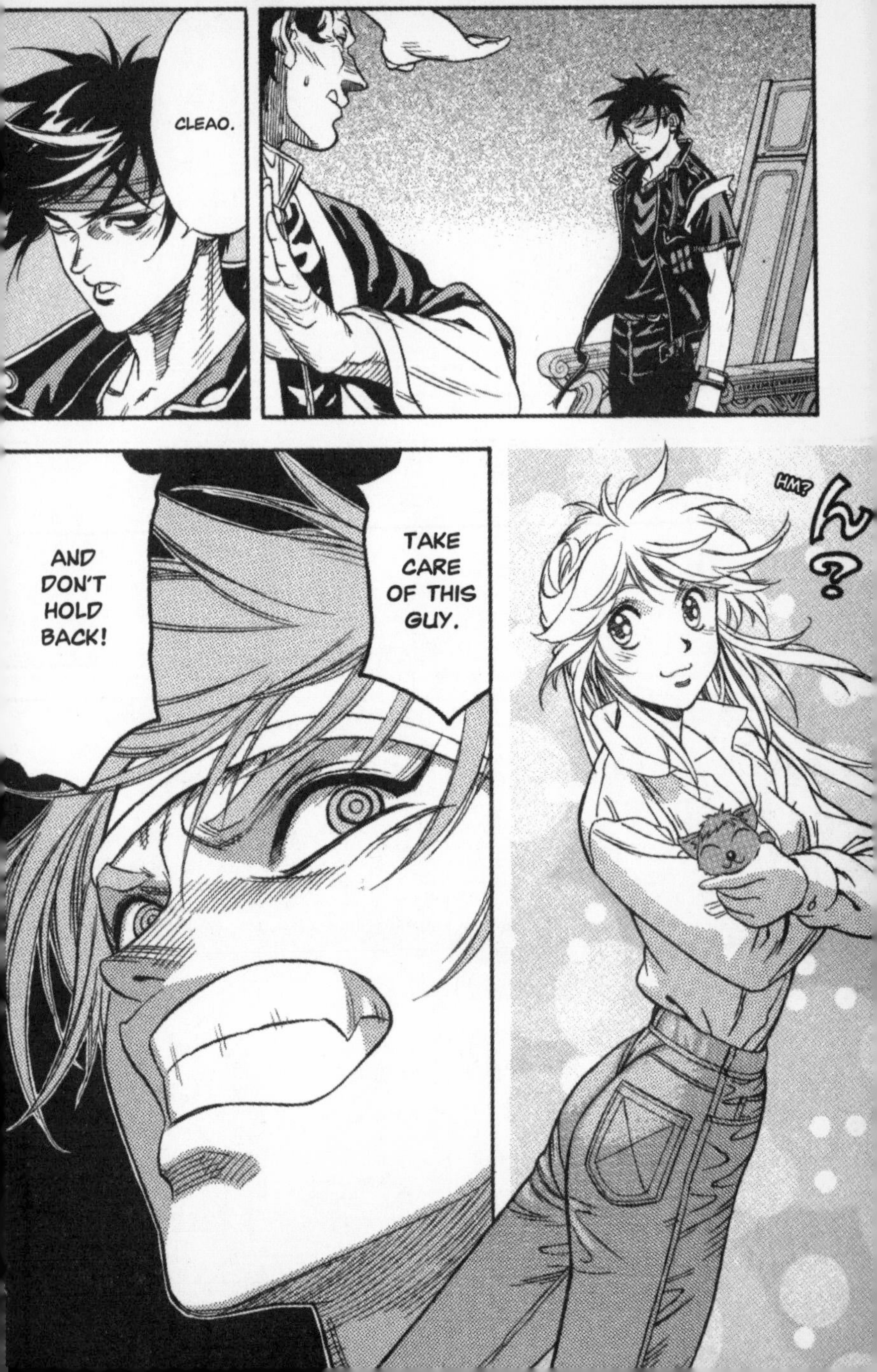
CLEAO.
HM?
ん?
TAKE CARE OF THIS GUY.
AND DON'T HOLD BACK!

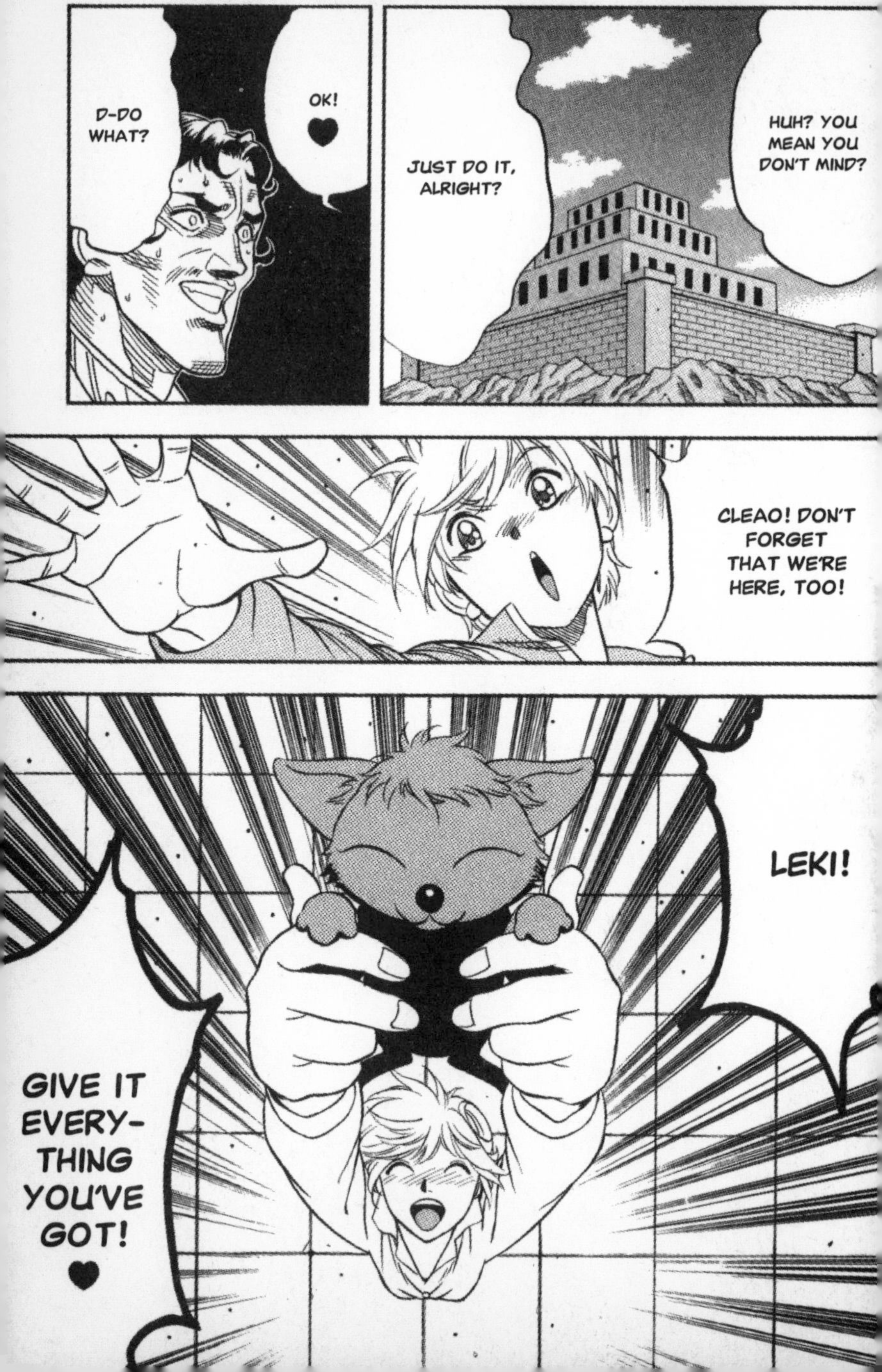
HUH? YOU MEAN YOU DON'T MIND?
JUST DO IT, ALRIGHT?
OK! ♥
D-DO WHAT?
CLEAO! DON'T FORGET THAT WE'RE HERE, TOO!
LEKI!
GIVE IT EVERY-THING YOU'VE GOT! ♥

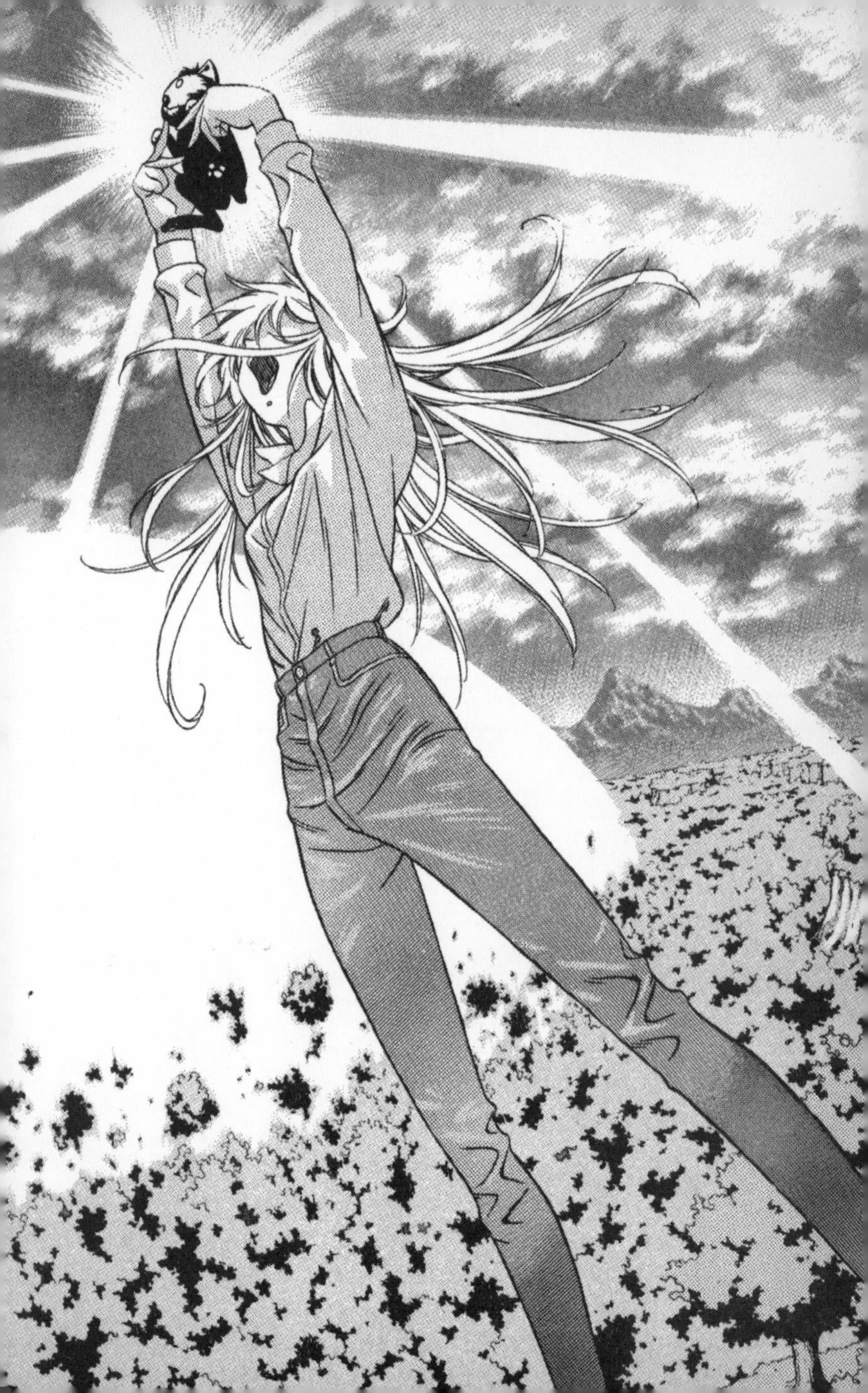

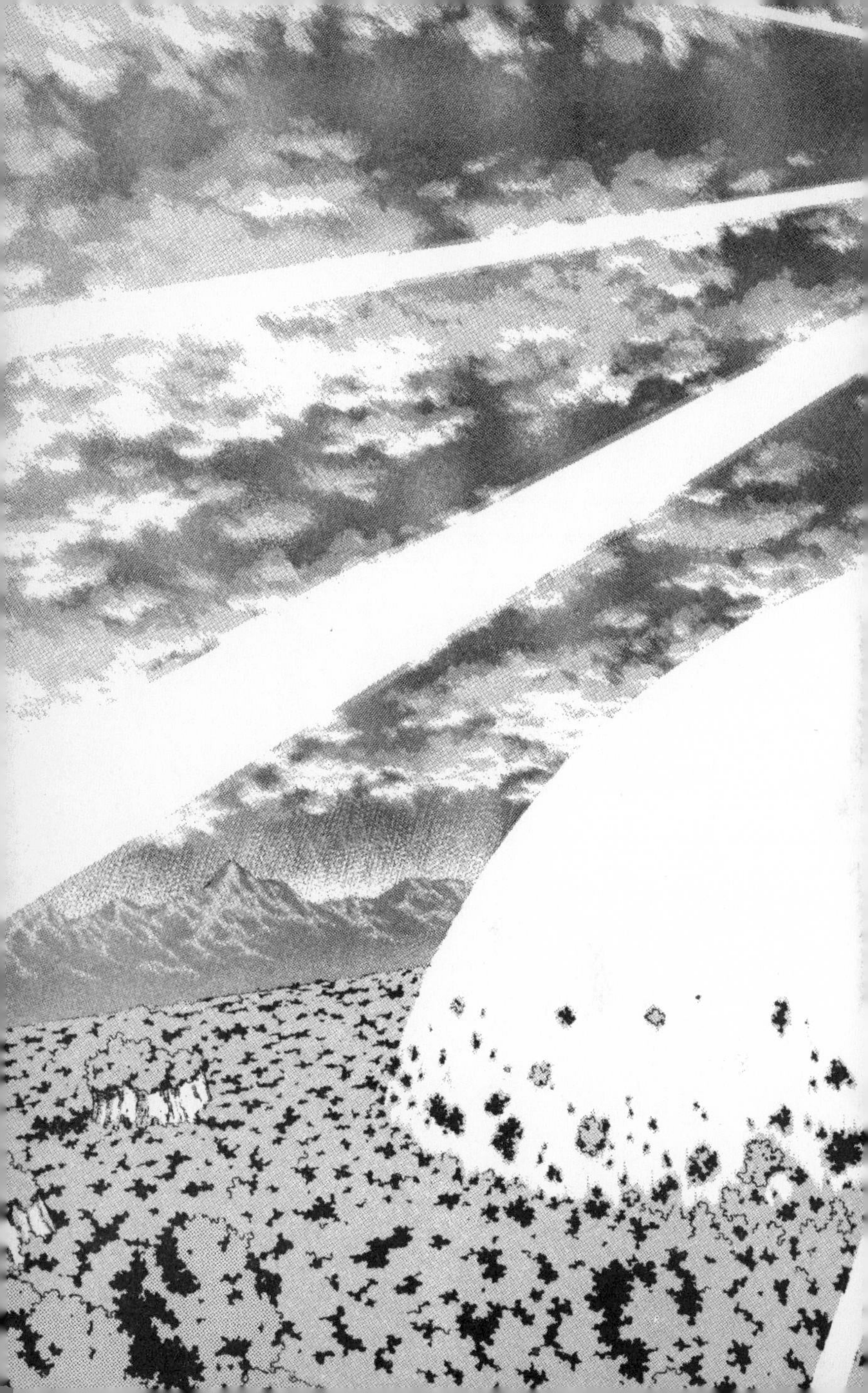

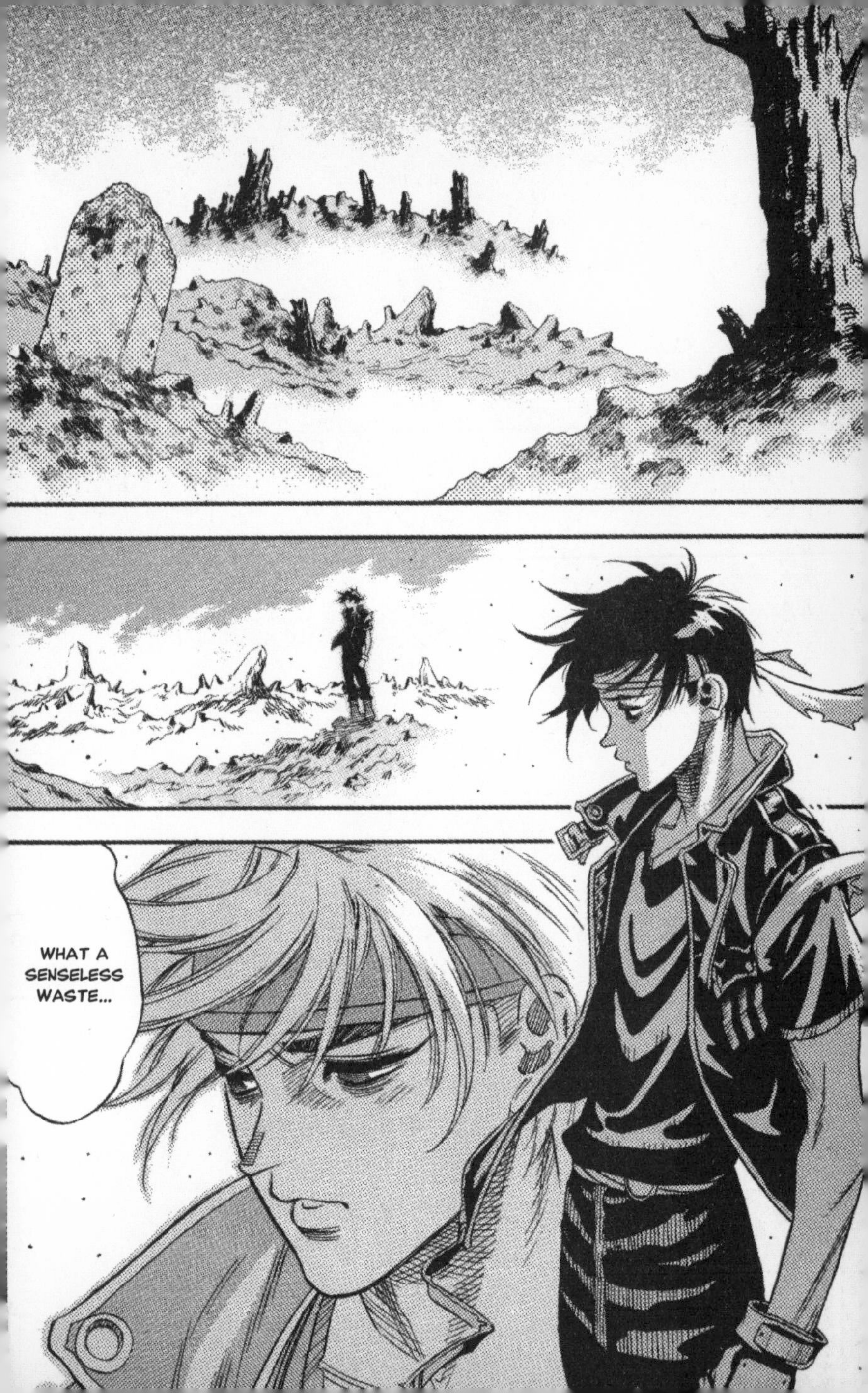
WHAT A SENSELESS WASTE...

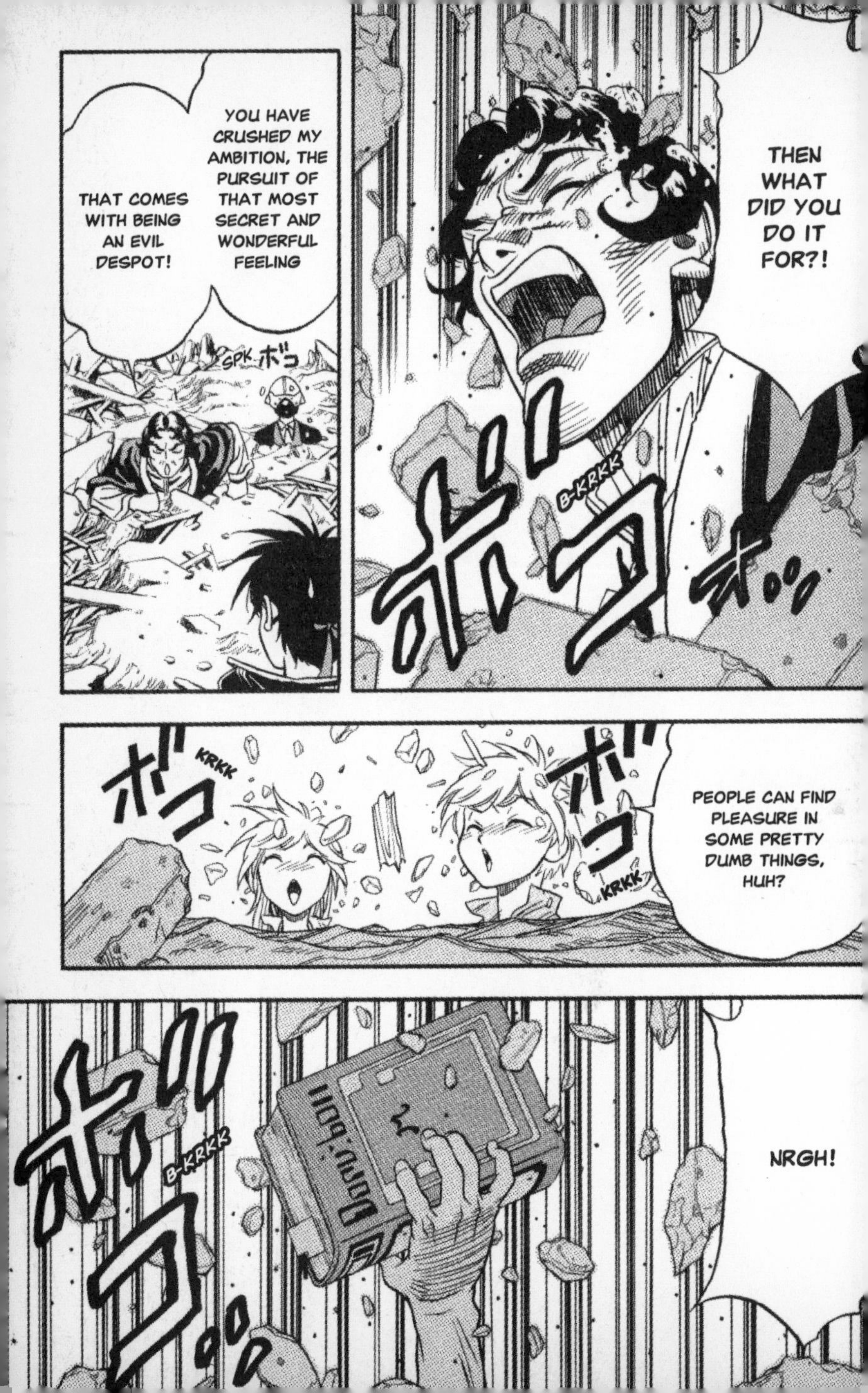
THEN WHAT DID YOU DO IT FOR?!
B-KRKK
YOU HAVE CRUSHED MY AMBITION, THE PURSUIT OF THAT MOST SECRET AND WONDERFUL FEELING
THAT COMES WITH BEING AN EVIL DESPOT!
SPK
PEOPLE CAN FIND PLEASURE IN SOME PRETTY DUMB THINGS, HUH?
KRKK
KRKK
NRGH!
B-KRKK

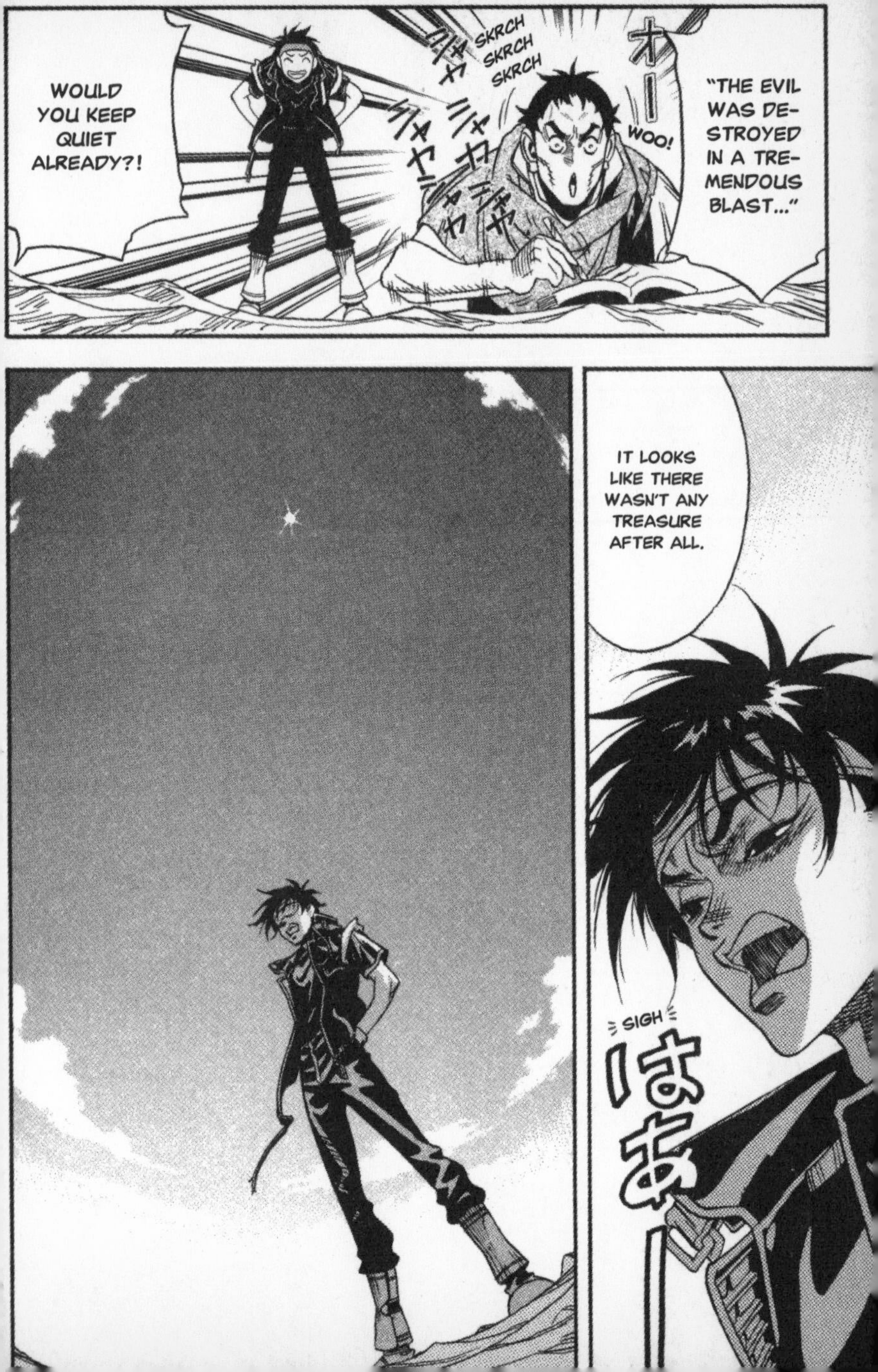
"THE EVIL WAS DE-STROYED IN A TRE-MENDOUS BLAST..."
WOO!
SKRCH SKRCH SKRCH
WOULD YOU KEEP QUIET ALREADY?!
IT LOOKS LIKE THERE WASN'T ANY TREASURE AFTER ALL.
SIGH

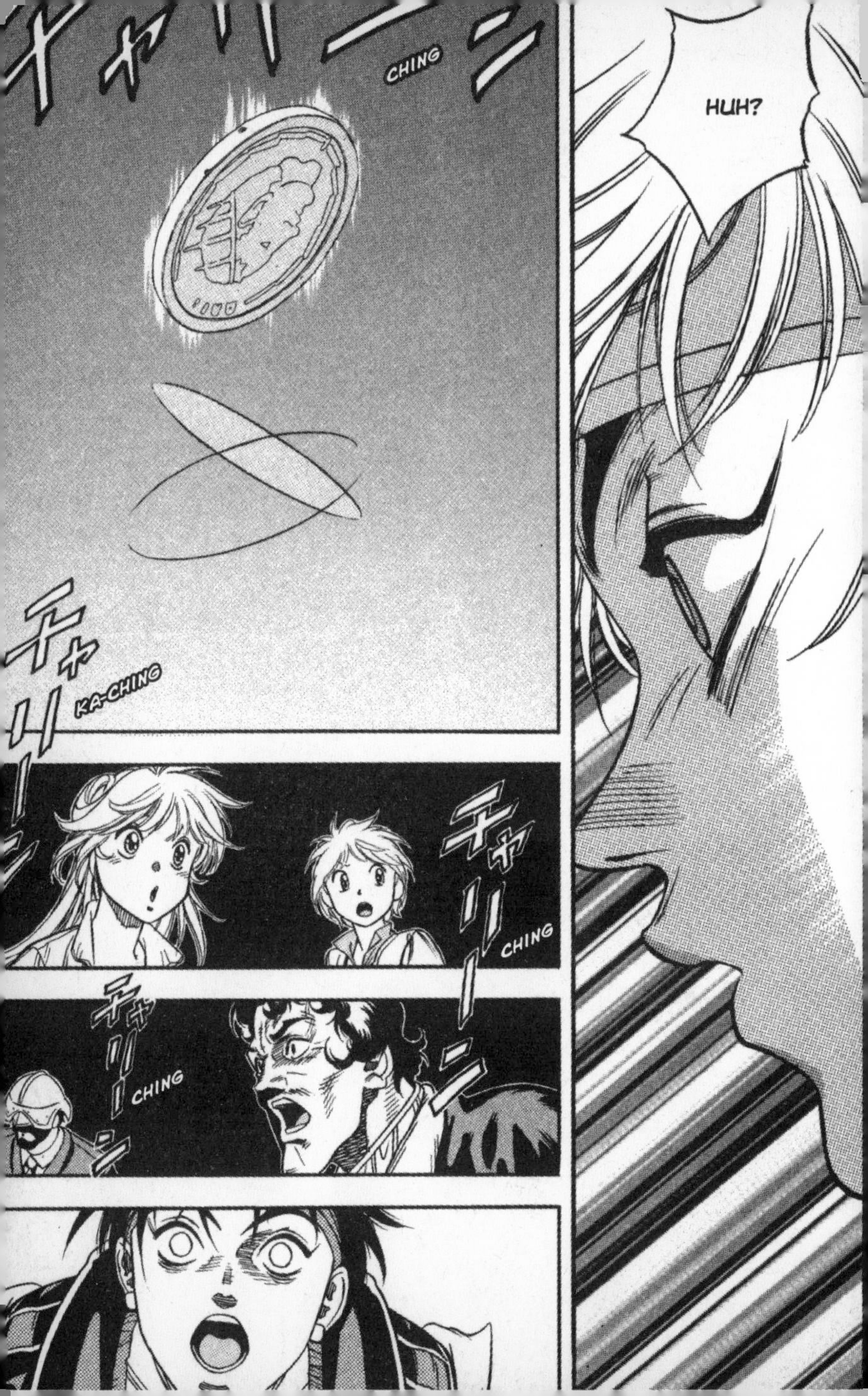
HUH?
CHING
KA-CHING
CHING
CHING

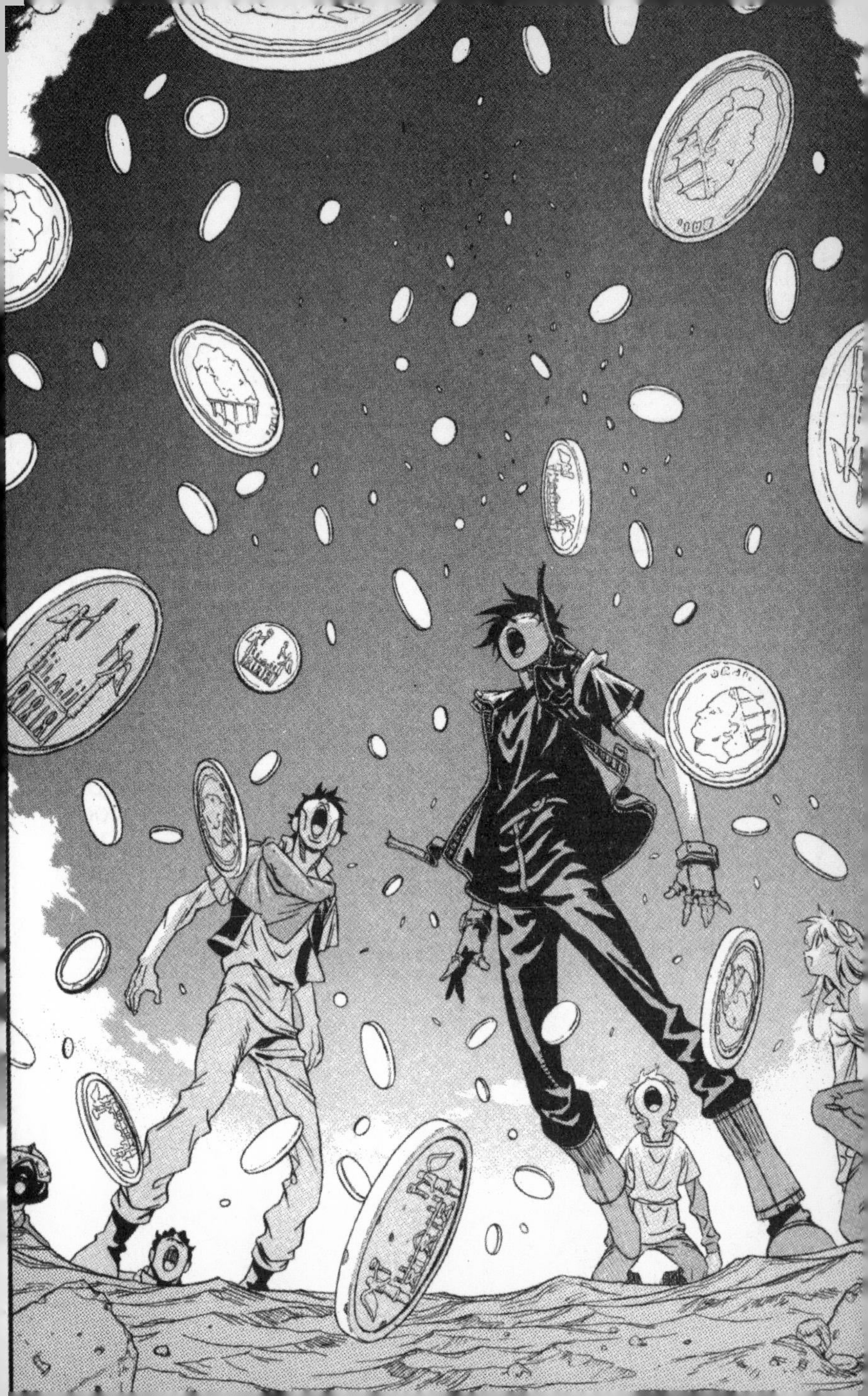

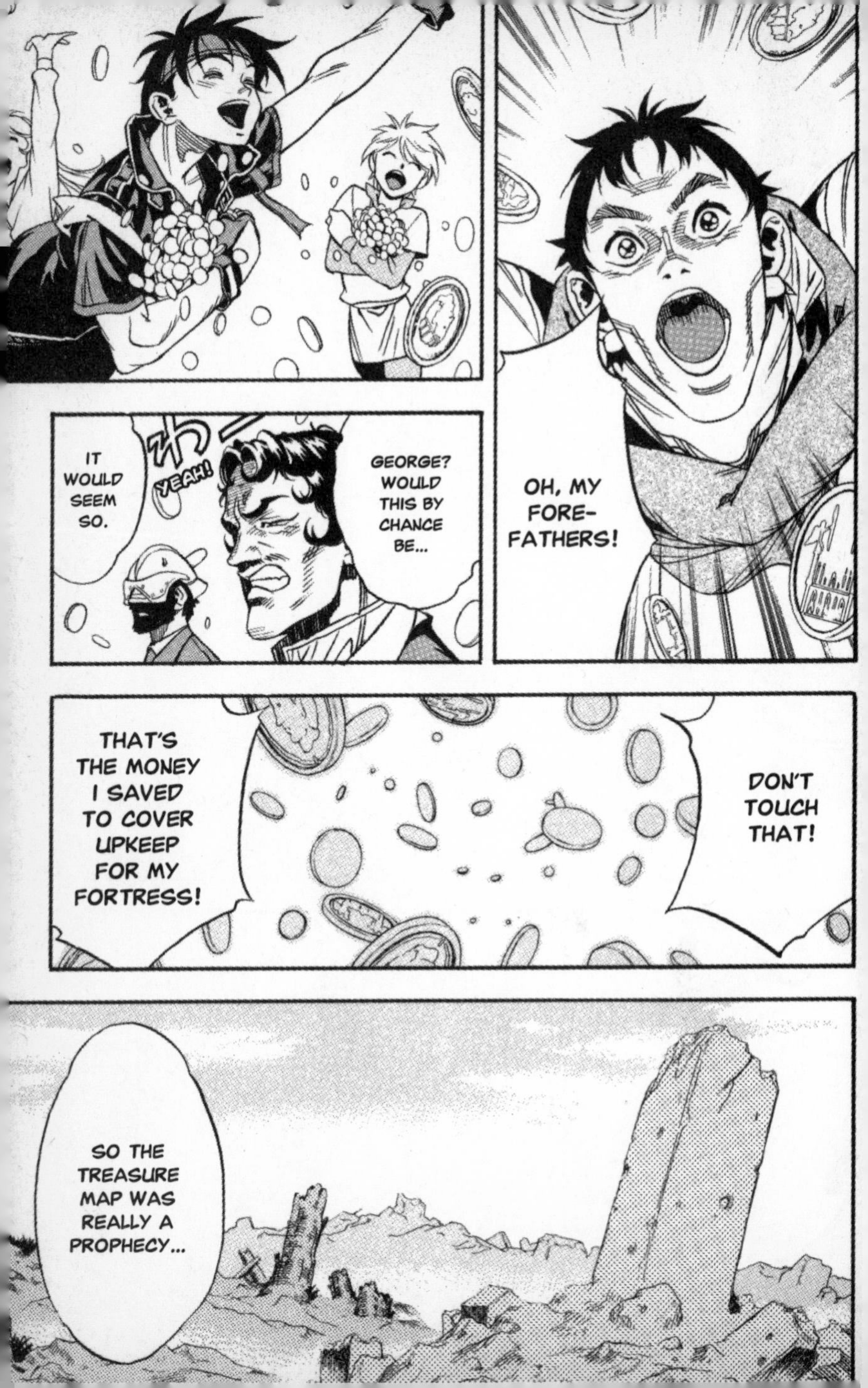
OH, MY FORE-FATHERS!
YEAH!
GEORGE? WOULD THIS BY CHANCE BE...
IT WOULD SEEM SO.
DON'T TOUCH THAT!
THAT'S THE MONEY I SAVED TO COVER UPKEEP FOR MY FORTRESS!
SO THE TREASURE MAP WAS REALLY A PROPHECY...

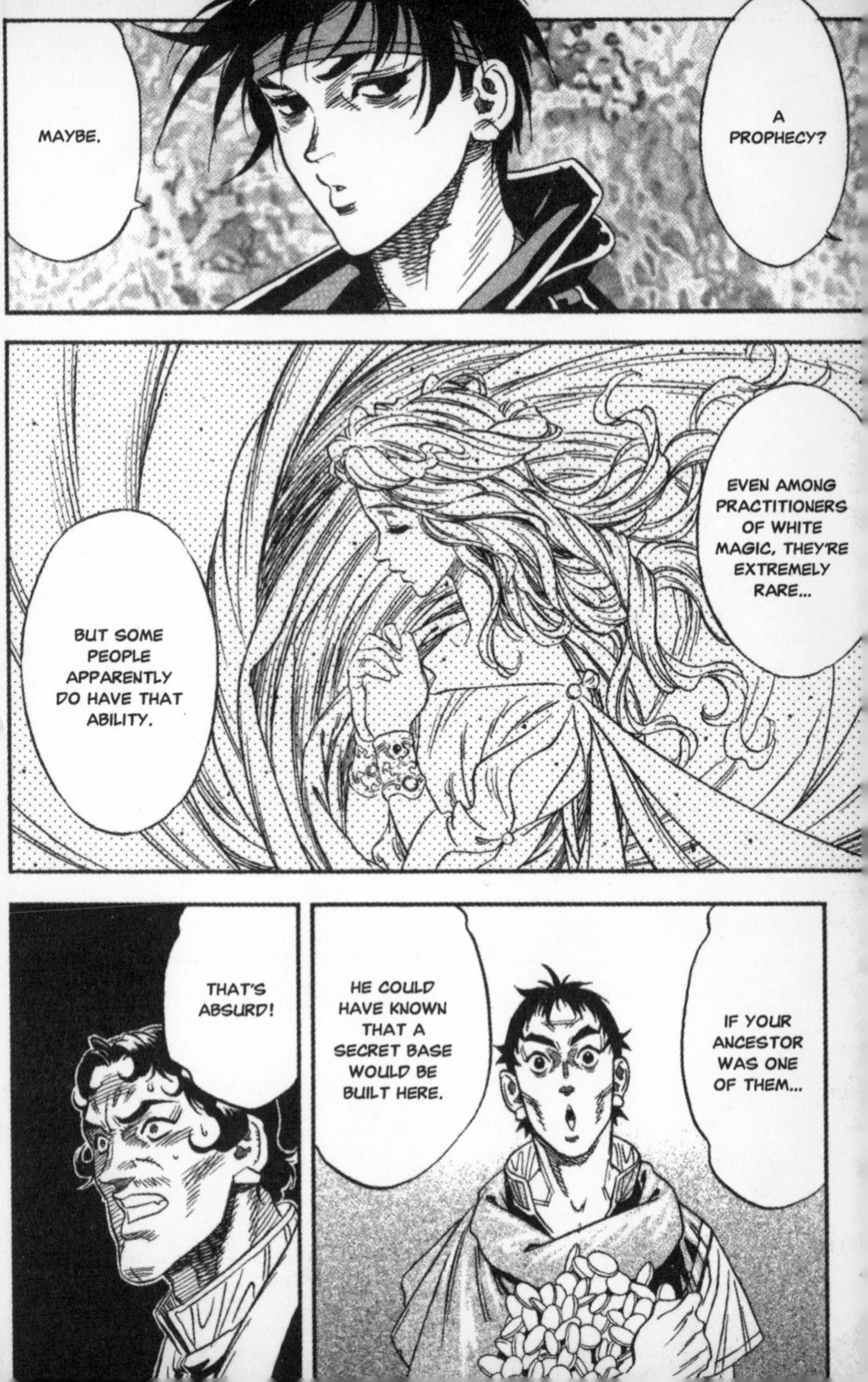
A PROPHECY?
MAYBE.
EVEN AMONG PRACTITIONERS OF WHITE MAGIC, THEY'RE EXTREMELY RARE...
BUT SOME PEOPLE APPARENTLY DO HAVE THAT ABILITY.
IF YOUR ANCESTOR WAS ONE OF THEM...
HE COULD HAVE KNOWN THAT A SECRET BASE WOULD BE BUILT HERE.
THAT'S ABSURD!

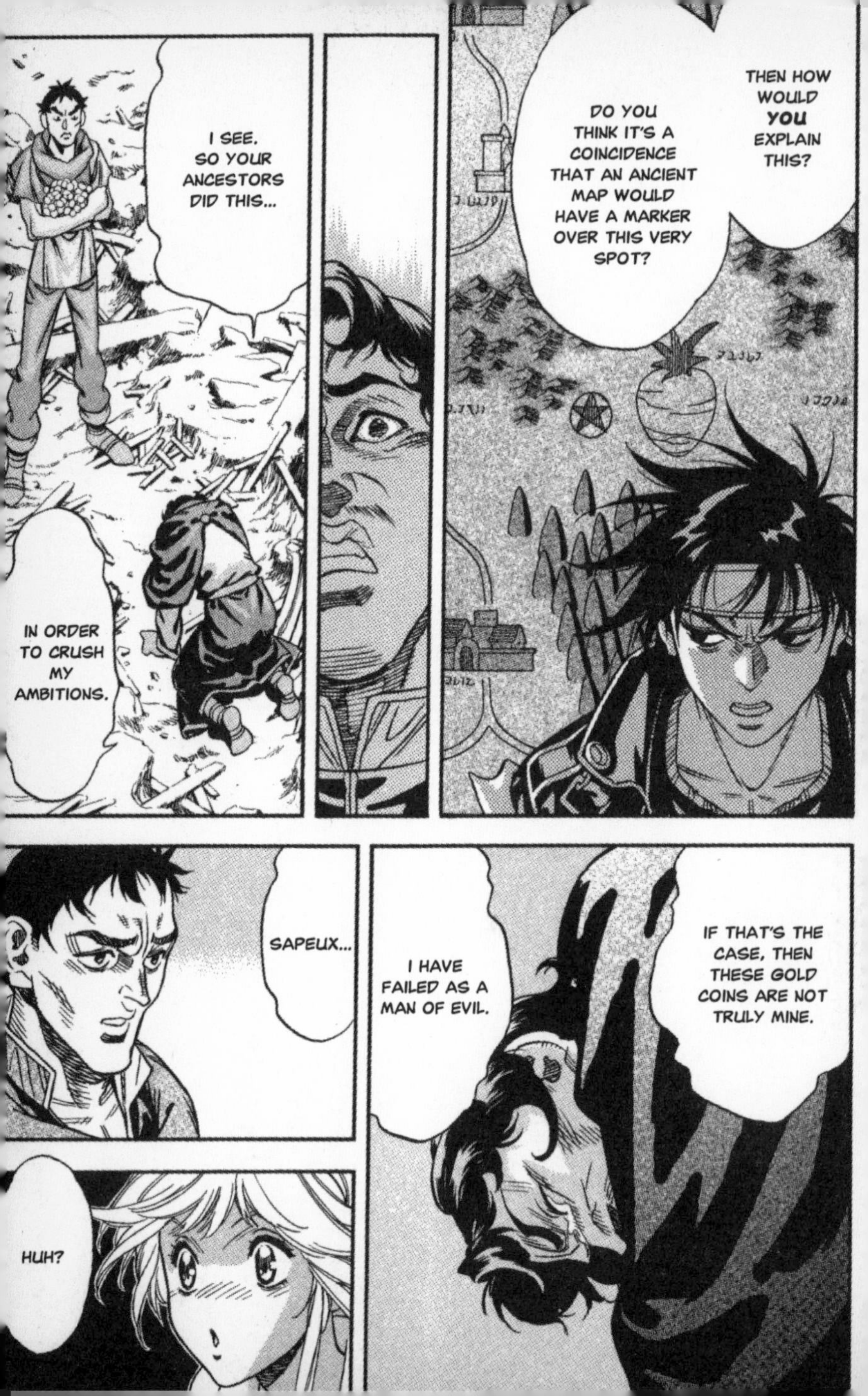

I SEE. SO YOUR ANCESTORS DID THIS...
IN ORDER TO CRUSH MY AMBITIONS.
DO YOU THINK IT'S A COINCIDENCE THAT AN ANCIENT MAP WOULD HAVE A MARKER OVER THIS VERY SPOT?
THEN HOW WOULD **YOU** EXPLAIN THIS?
SAPEUX...
I HAVE FAILED AS A MAN OF EVIL.
IF THAT'S THE CASE, THEN THESE GOLD COINS ARE NOT TRULY MINE.
HUH?

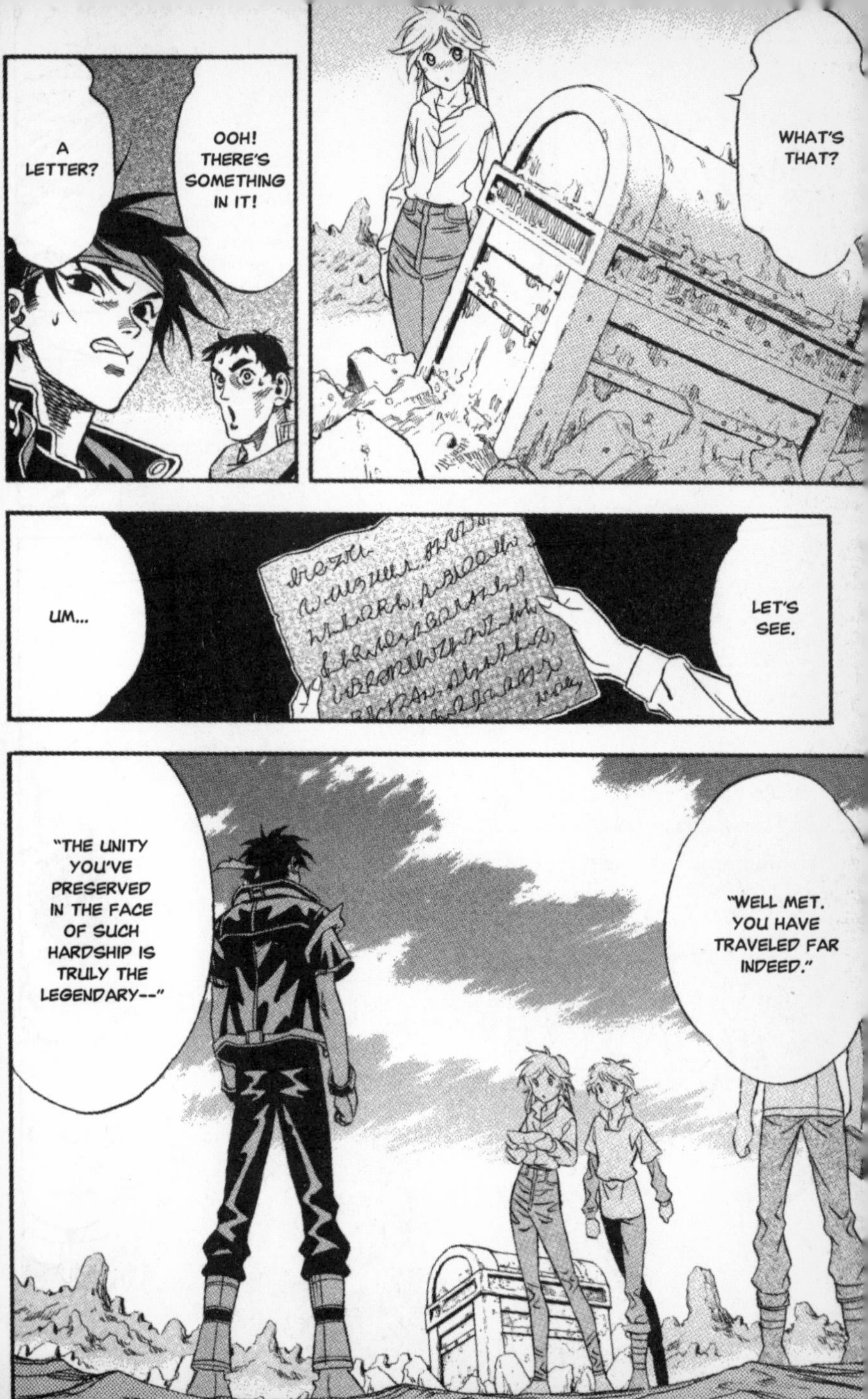
WHAT'S THAT?
OOH! THERE'S SOMETHING IN IT!
A LETTER?
LET'S SEE.
UM...
"WELL MET. YOU HAVE TRAVELED FAR INDEED."
"THE UNITY YOU'VE PRESERVED IN THE FACE OF SUCH HARDSHIP IS TRULY THE LEGENDARY--"

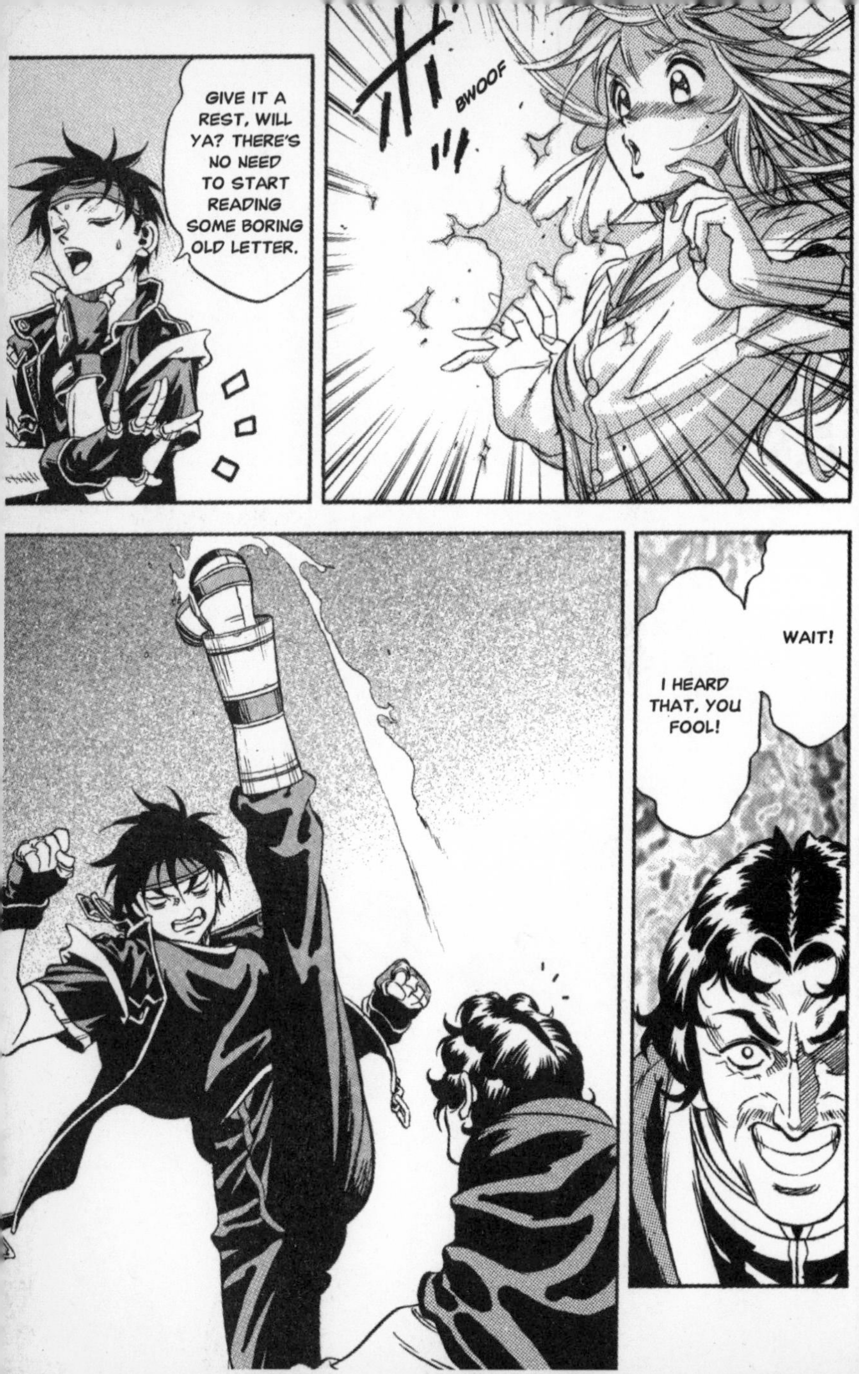
GIVE IT A REST, WILL YA? THERE'S NO NEED TO START READING SOME BORING OLD LETTER.
BWOOF
WAIT!
I HEARD THAT, YOU FOOL!

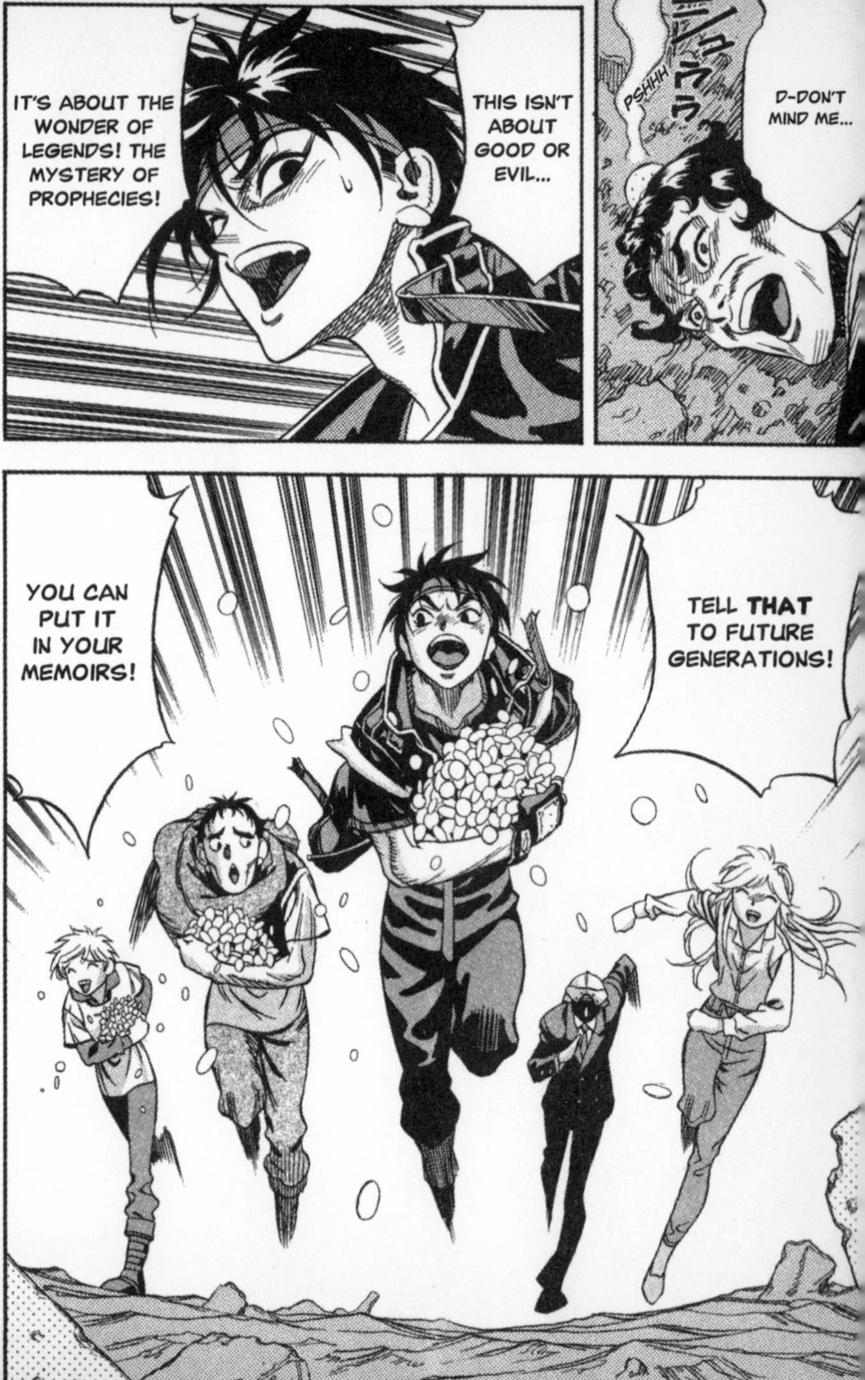
D-DON'T MIND ME...
PSHHH
THIS ISN'T ABOUT GOOD OR EVIL...
IT'S ABOUT THE WONDER OF LEGENDS! THE MYSTERY OF PROPHECIES!
TELL **THAT** TO FUTURE GENERATIONS!
YOU CAN PUT IT IN YOUR MEMOIRS!

ORPHEN

ん?
HM?

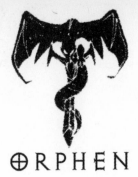

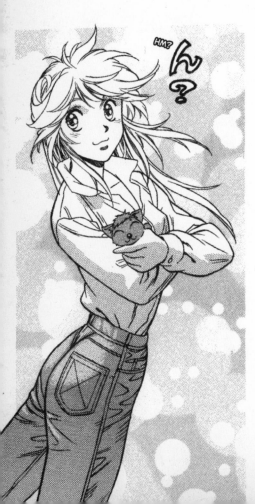

ORPHEN

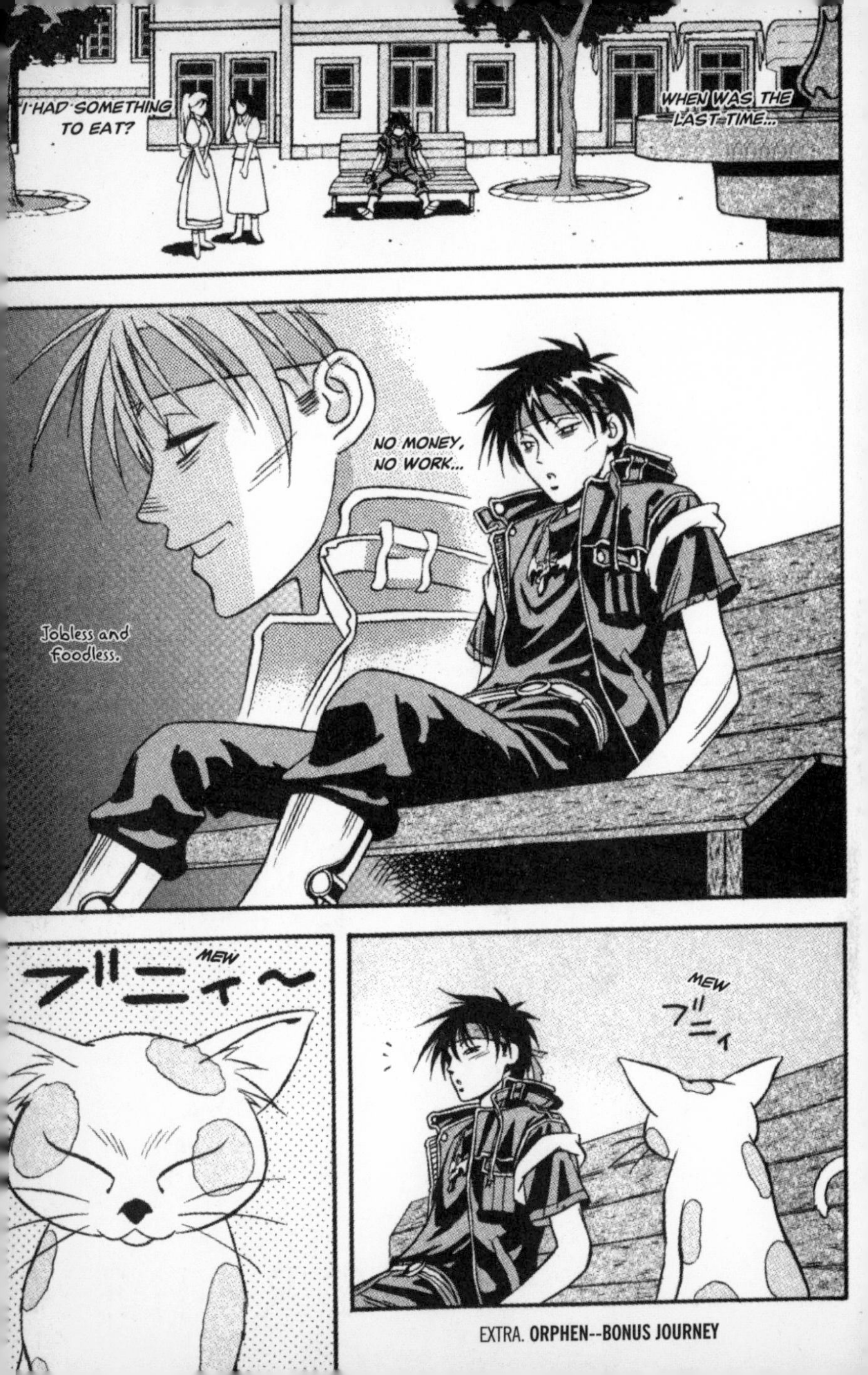
WHEN WAS THE LAST TIME...
I HAD SOMETHING TO EAT?
NO MONEY, NO WORK...
Jobless and foodless.
MEW
ブニィ
MEW
ブニィ〜

EXTRA. **ORPHEN--BONUS JOURNEY**

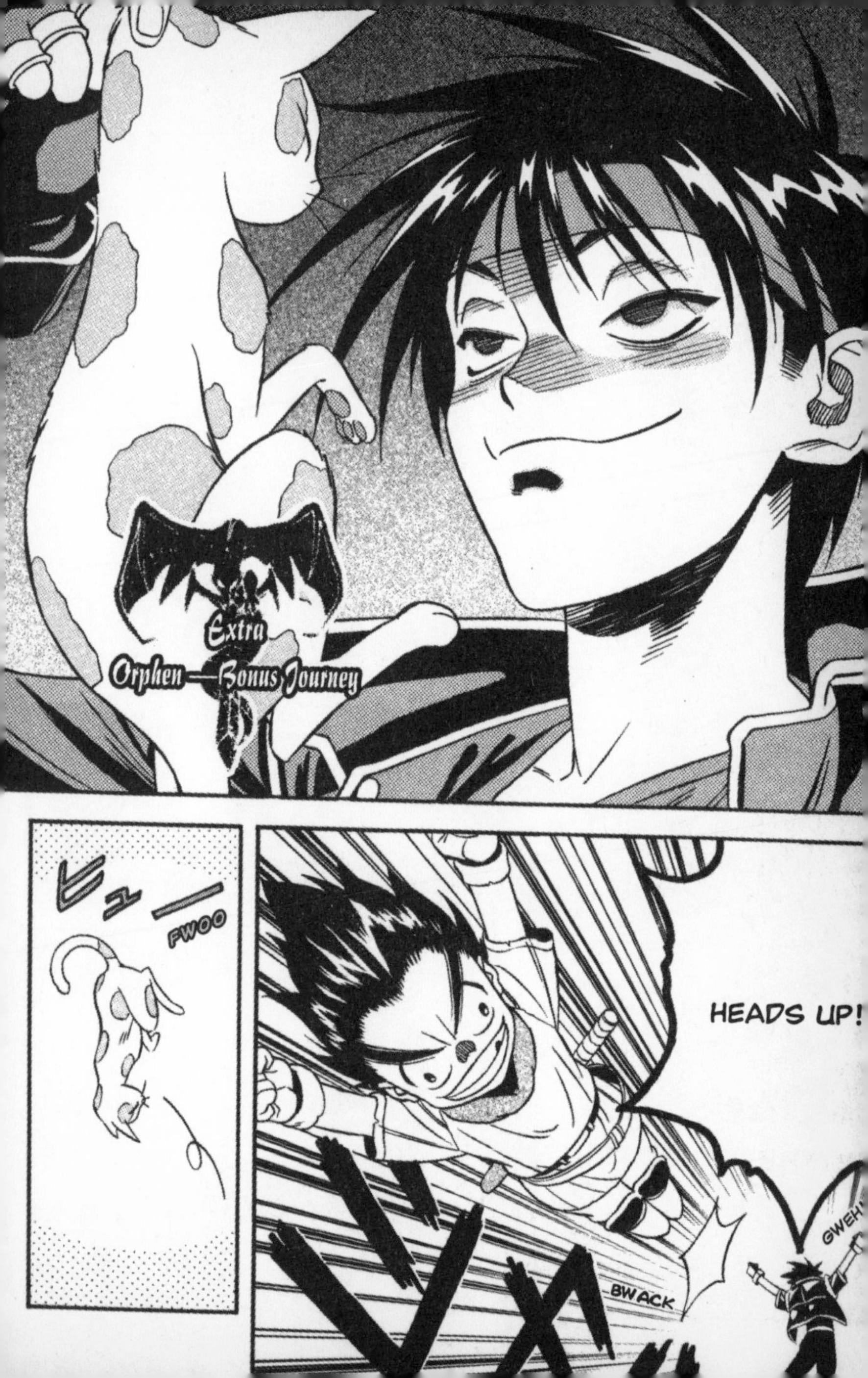
Extra
Orphen—Bonus Journey
HEADS UP!
BWACK
GWEH!
ヒュー
FWOO

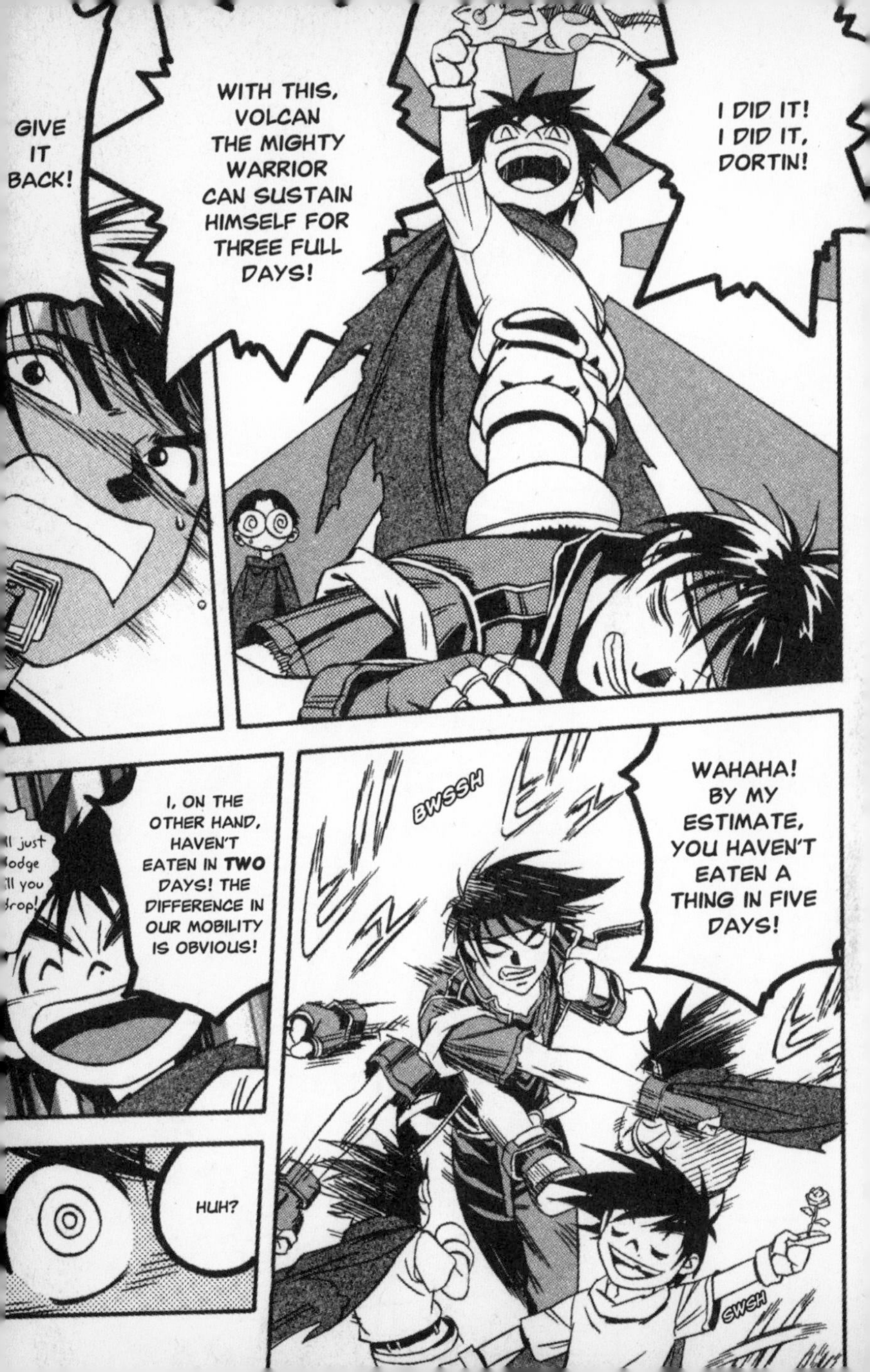
I DID IT! I DID IT, DORTIN!
WITH THIS, VOLCAN THE MIGHTY WARRIOR CAN SUSTAIN HIMSELF FOR THREE FULL DAYS!
GIVE IT BACK!
WAHAHA! BY MY ESTIMATE, YOU HAVEN'T EATEN A THING IN FIVE DAYS!
BWSSH
I, ON THE OTHER HAND, HAVEN'T EATEN IN TWO DAYS! THE DIFFERENCE IN OUR MOBILITY IS OBVIOUS!
HUH?
SWSH

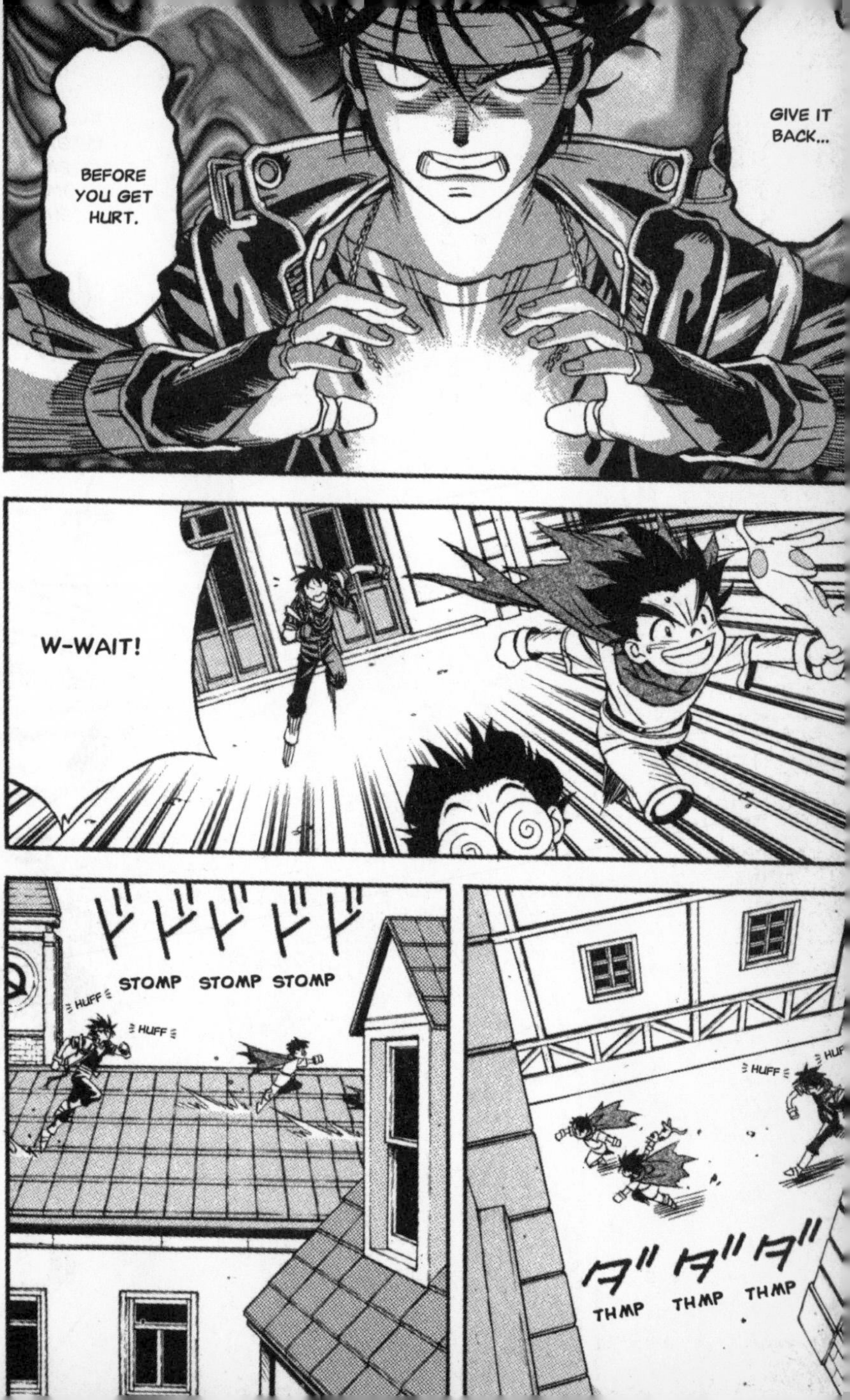
GIVE IT BACK...
BEFORE YOU GET HURT.
W-WAIT!
ダ"ダ"ダ"
THMP THMP THMP
HUFF
HUFF
ドドドドド
STOMP STOMP STOMP
HUFF
HUFF

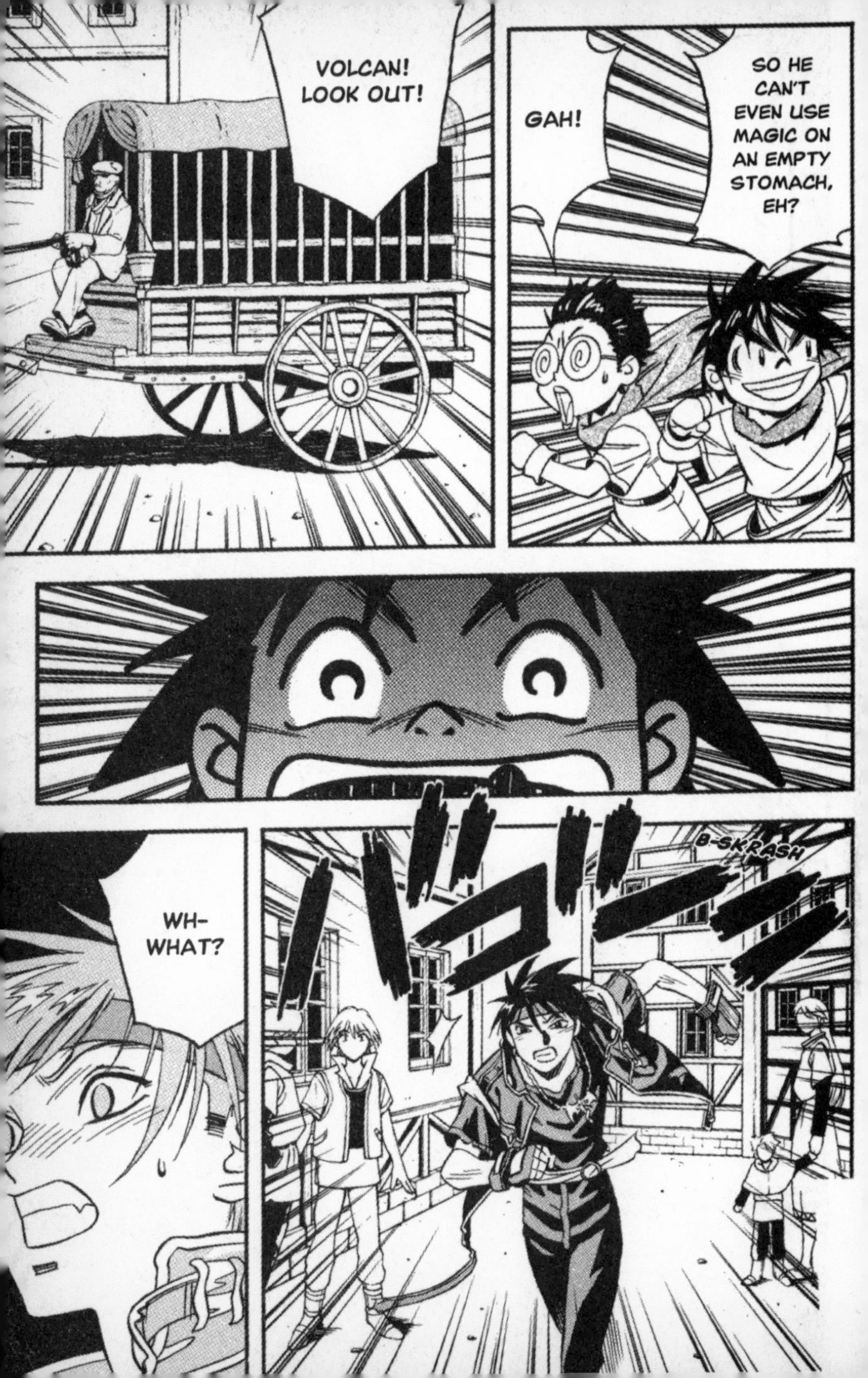
VOLCAN! LOOK OUT!
SO HE CAN'T EVEN USE MAGIC ON AN EMPTY STOMACH, EH?
GAH!
B-SKRASH
WH- WHAT?

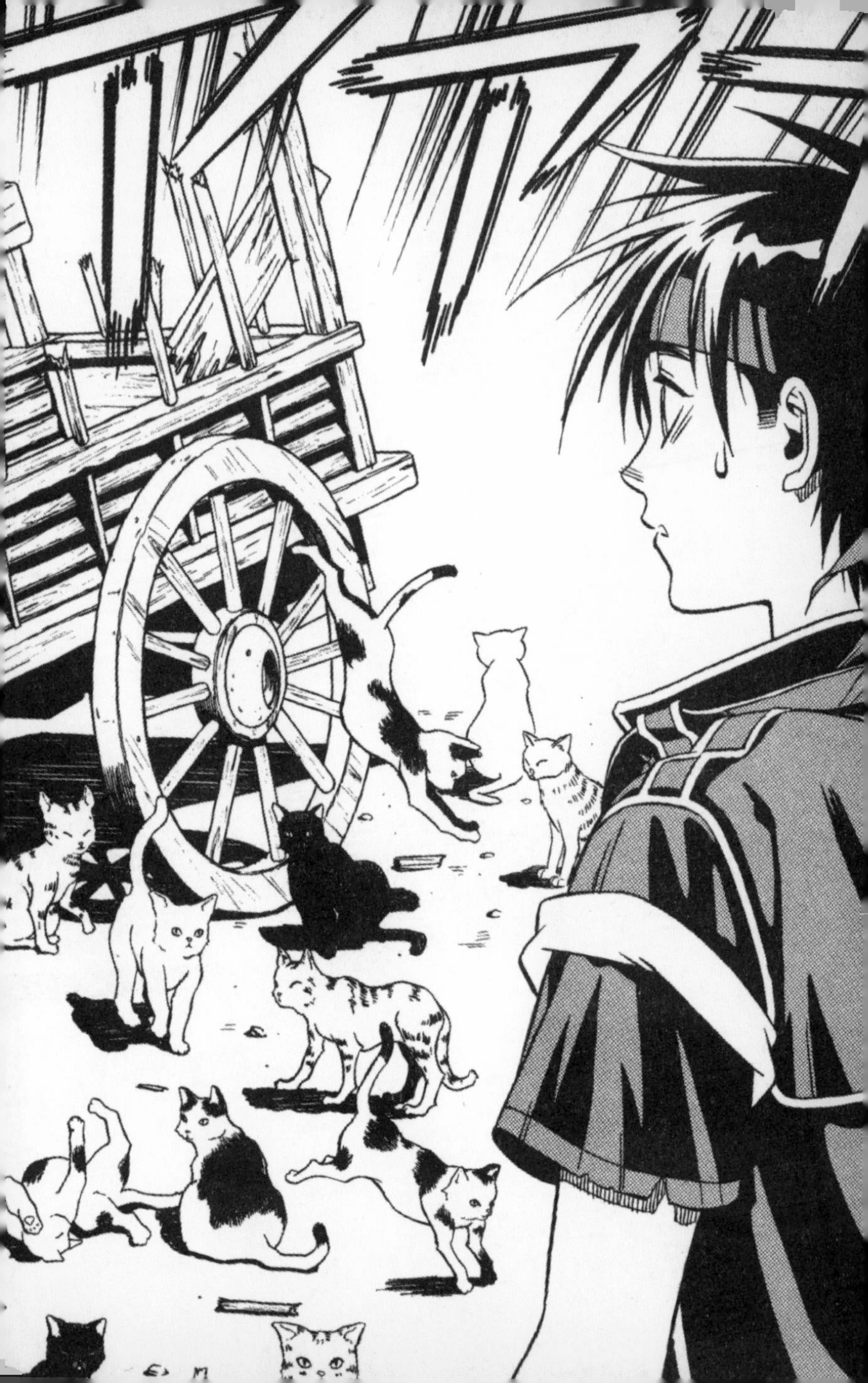

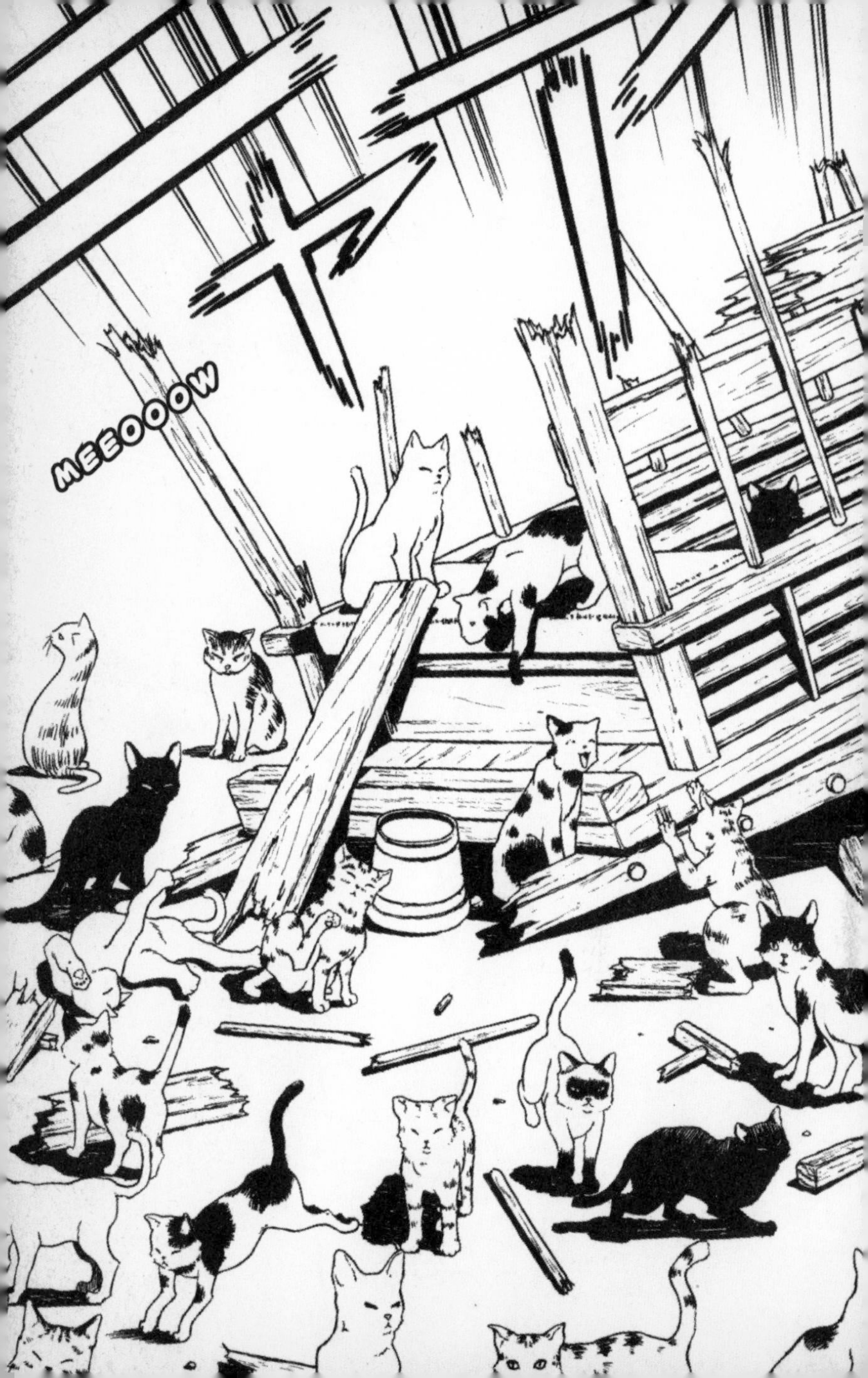
MEEOOOW

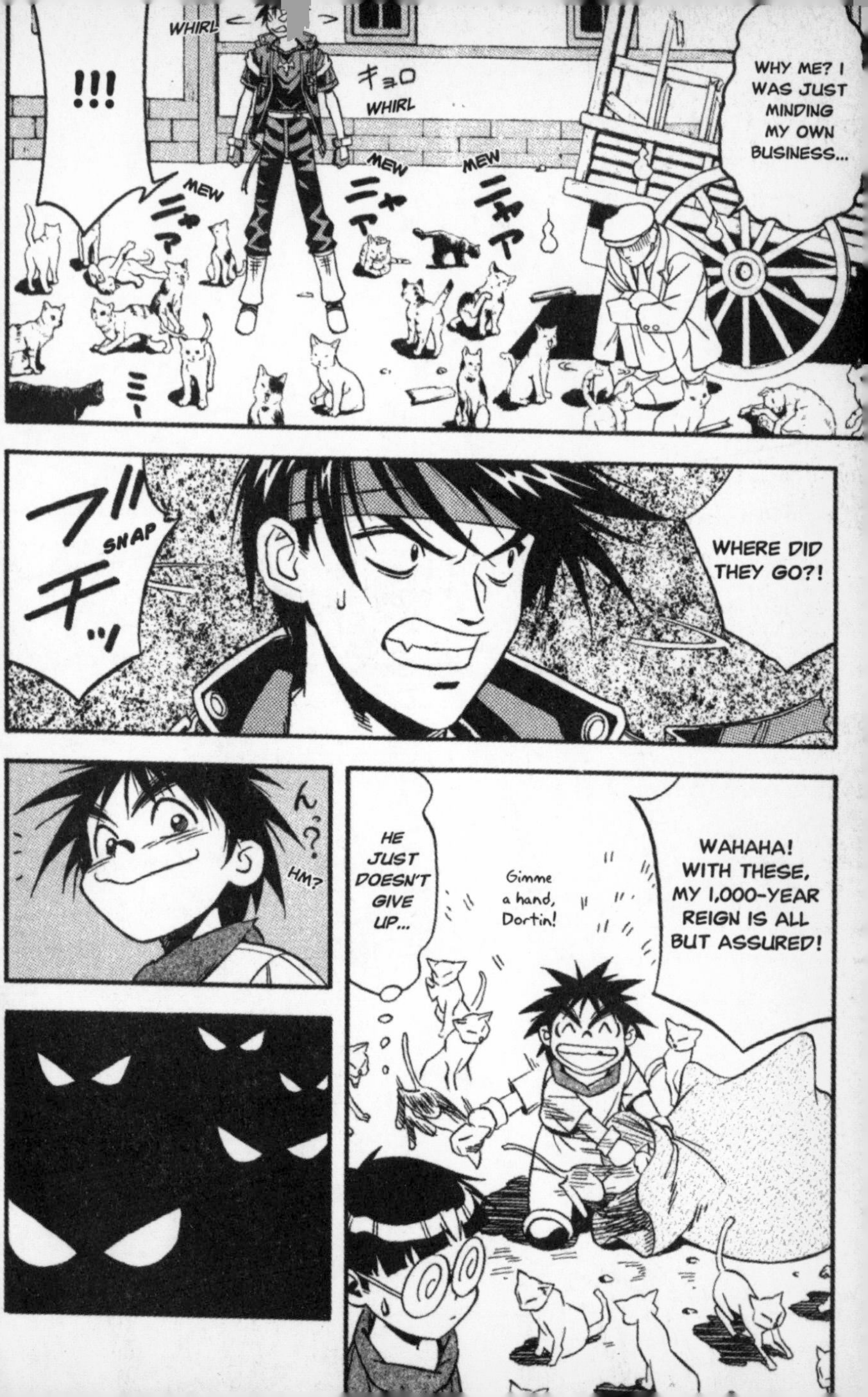
WHY ME? I WAS JUST MINDING MY OWN BUSINESS...
WHIRL
キョロ
WHIRL
!!!
MEW
MEW
MEW
WHERE DID THEY GO?!
SNAP
WAHAHA! WITH THESE, MY 1,000-YEAR REIGN IS ALL BUT ASSURED!
Gimme a hand, Dortin!
HE JUST DOESN'T GIVE UP...
HM?

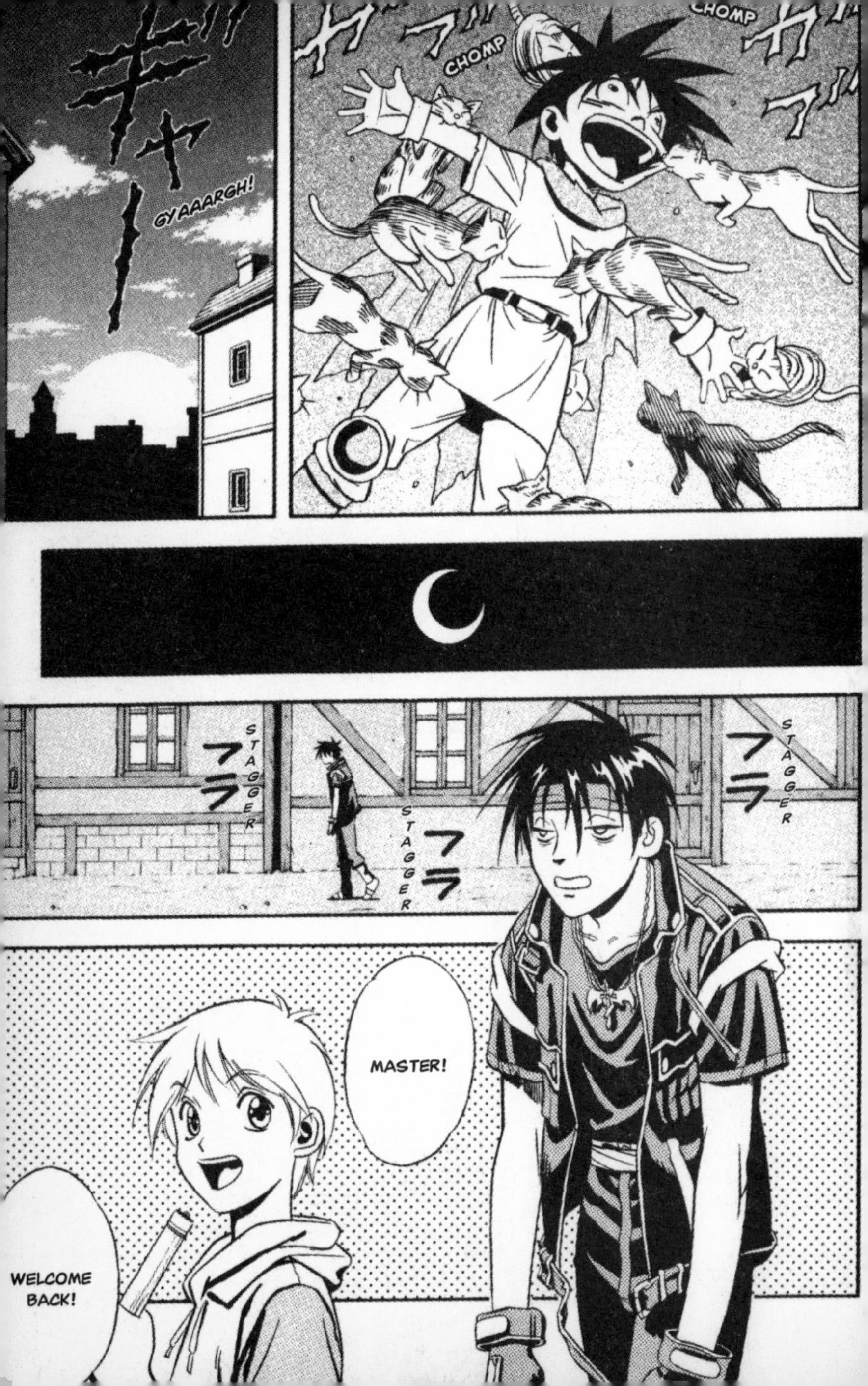

CHOMP
CHOMP
GYAAARGH!
STAGGER
STAGGER
STAGGER
MASTER!
WELCOME BACK!

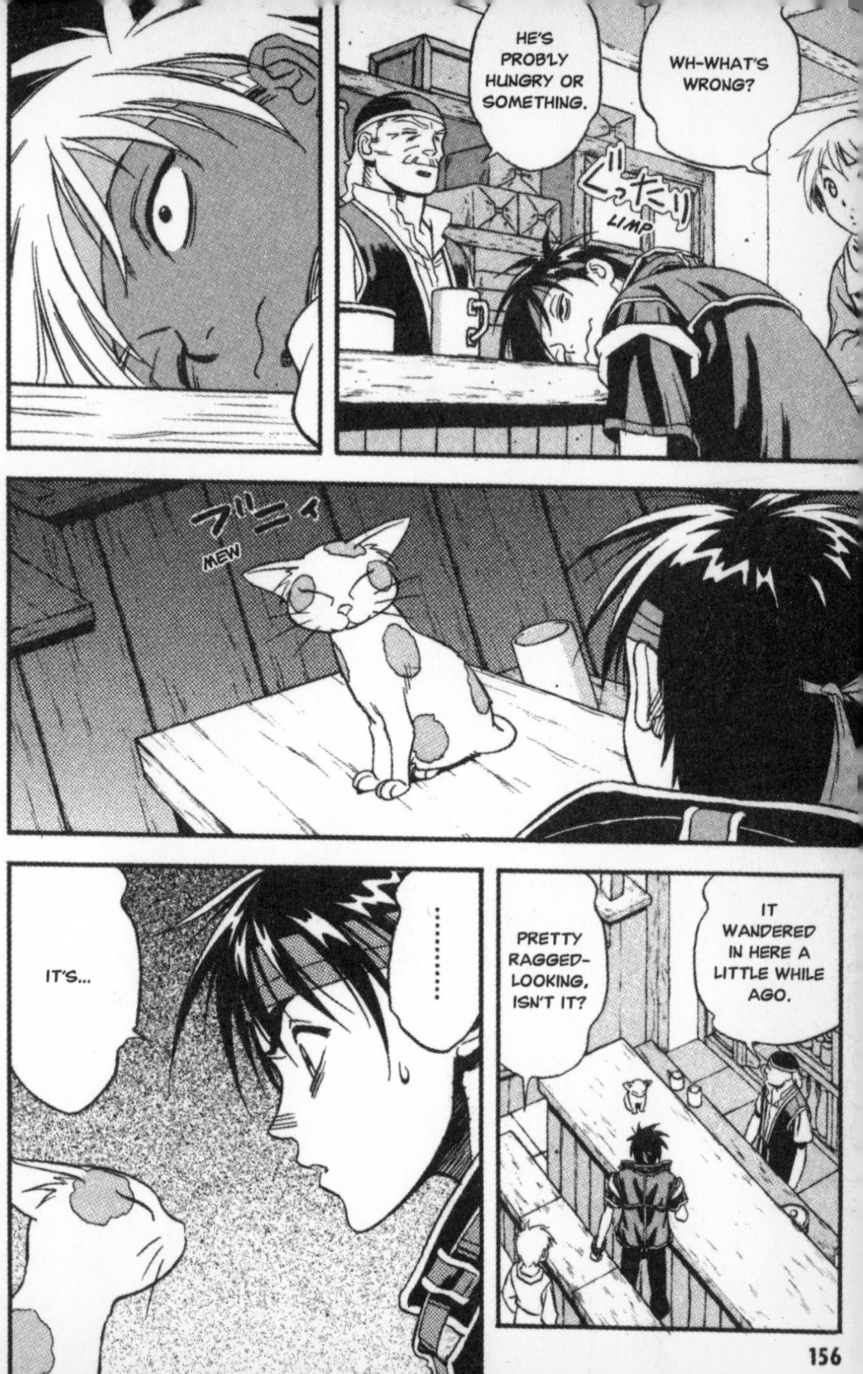
WH-WHAT'S WRONG?
HE'S PROB'LY HUNGRY OR SOMETHING.
ぐったり
LIMP
MEW
IT WANDERED IN HERE A LITTLE WHILE AGO.
PRETTY RAGGED-LOOKING, ISN'T IT?
....
IT'S...

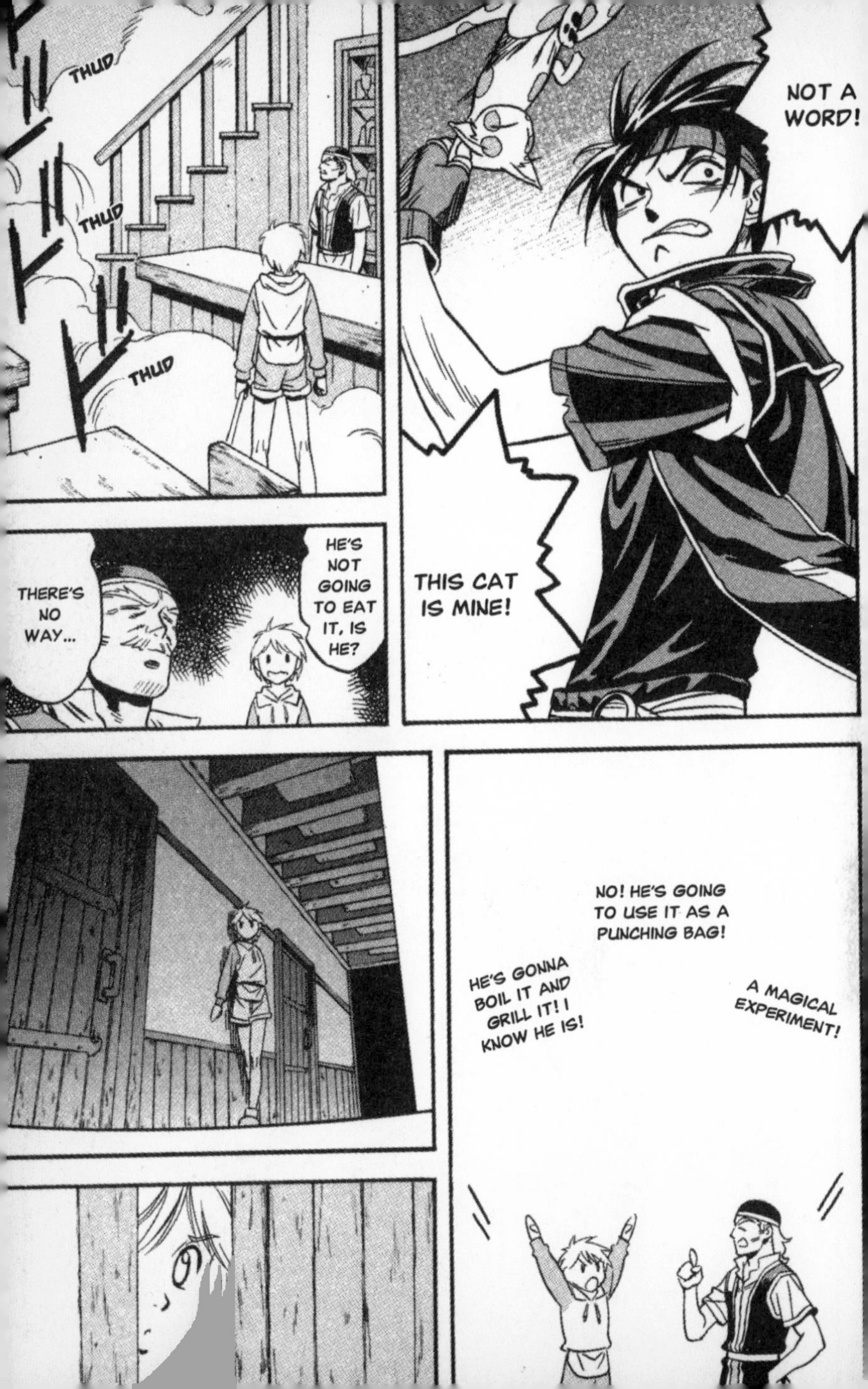
THUD
THUD
THUD
NOT A WORD!
THIS CAT IS MINE!
THERE'S NO WAY...
HE'S NOT GOING TO EAT IT, IS HE?
NO! HE'S GOING TO USE IT AS A PUNCHING BAG!
HE'S GONNA BOIL IT AND GRILL IT! I KNOW HE IS!
A MAGICAL EXPERIMENT!

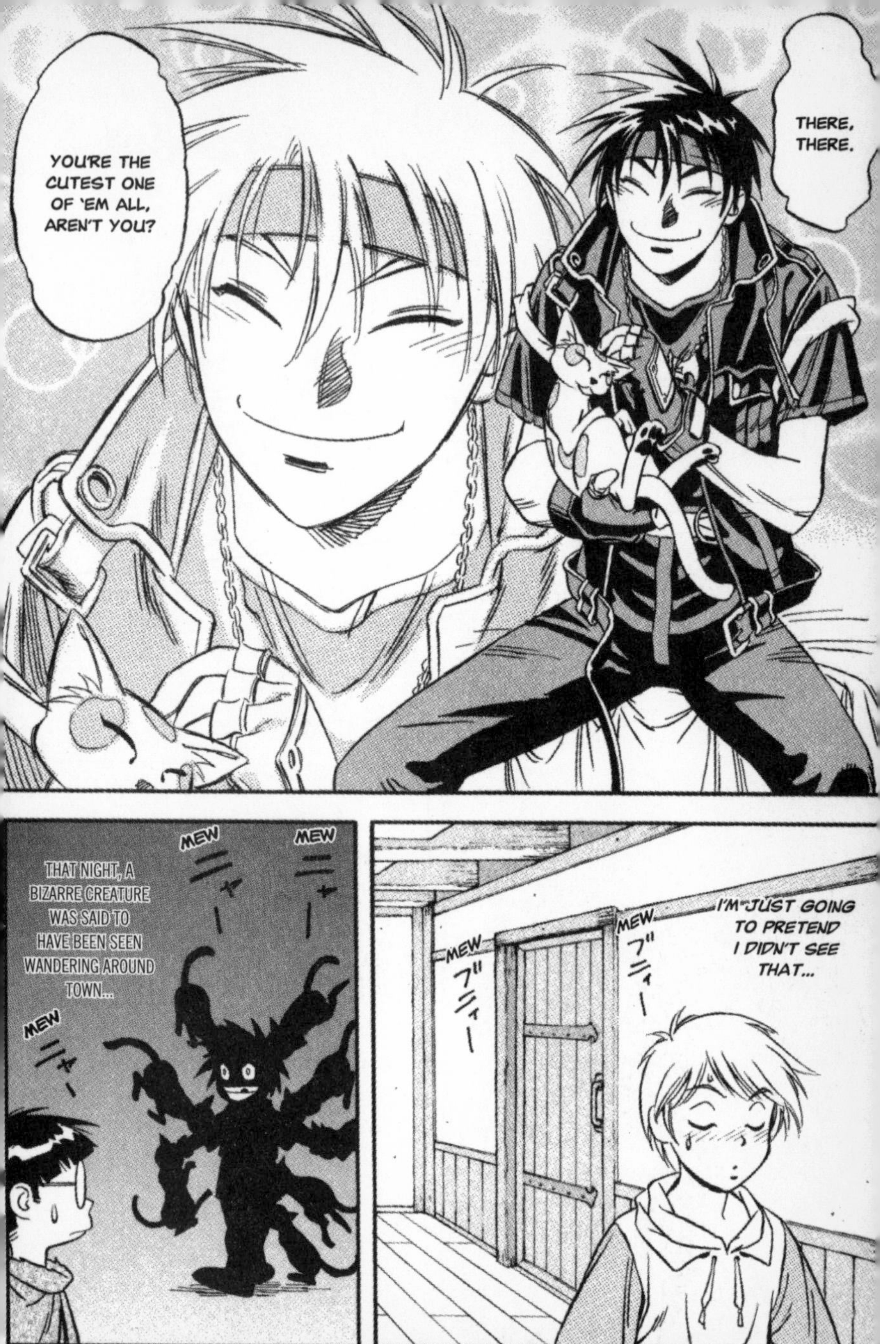
THERE, THERE.
YOU'RE THE CUTEST ONE OF 'EM ALL, AREN'T YOU?
I'M JUST GOING TO PRETEND I DIDN'T SEE THAT...
MEW
MEW
MEW
MEW
THAT NIGHT, A BIZARRE CREATURE WAS SAID TO HAVE BEEN SEEN WANDERING AROUND TOWN...
MEW

To be continued in Volume 5...

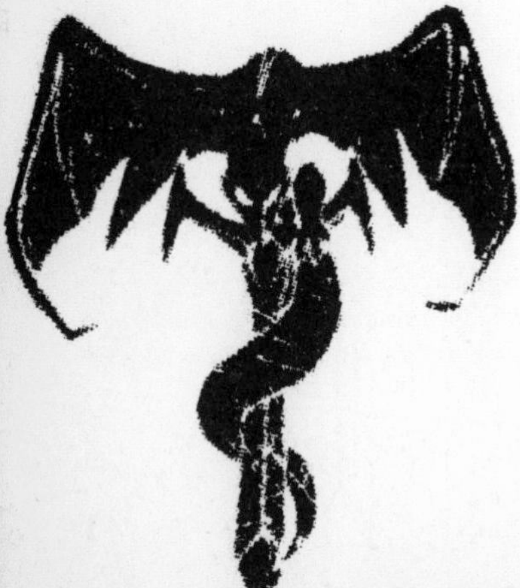

ORPHEN

Orphen Volume Four

© 2000 Yoshinobu Akita/Hajime Sawada
© 2000 Yuuya Kusaka
Originally published in Japan in 2000 by
KADOKAWA SHOTEN PUBLISHING CO., LTD., Tokyo.
English translation rights arranged with
KADOKAWA SHOTEN PUBLISHING CO., LTD., Tokyo.

Editor JAVIER LOPEZ
Translator BRENDAN FRAYNE
Graphic Artist SCOTT HOWARD

Editorial Director GARY STEINMAN
Creative Director JASON BABLER
Sales and Marketing CHRIS OARR
Print Production Manager BRIDGETT JANOTA

International Coordinators TORU IWAKAMI & MIYUKI KAMIYA

President, CEO & Publisher JOHN LEDFORD

Email: editor@adv-manga.com
www.adv-manga.com
www.advfilms.com

For sales and distribution inquiries please call 1.800.282.7202

 is a division of A.D. Vision, Inc.
5750 Bintliff Drive, Suite 210, Houston, Texas 77036

ISBN: 1-4139-0269-3
First printing, January 2006
10 9 8 7 6 5 4 3 2 1
Printed in Canada

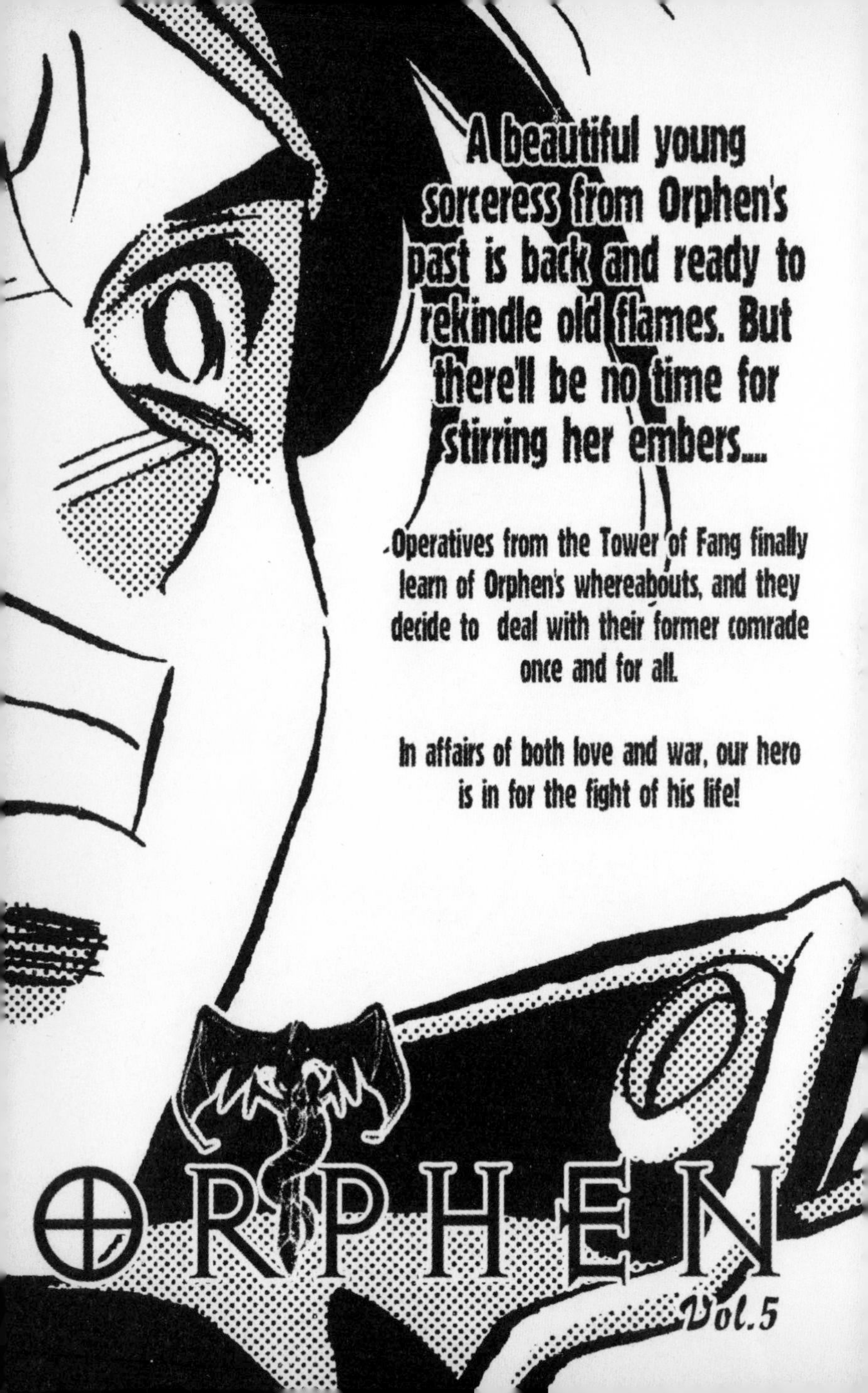
A beautiful young sorceress from Orphen's past is back and ready to rekindle old flames. But there'll be no time for stirring her embers...
Operatives from the Tower of Fang finally learn of Orphen's whereabouts, and they decide to deal with their former comrade once and for all.
In affairs of both love and war, our hero is in for the fight of his life!
ORPHEN
Vol.5

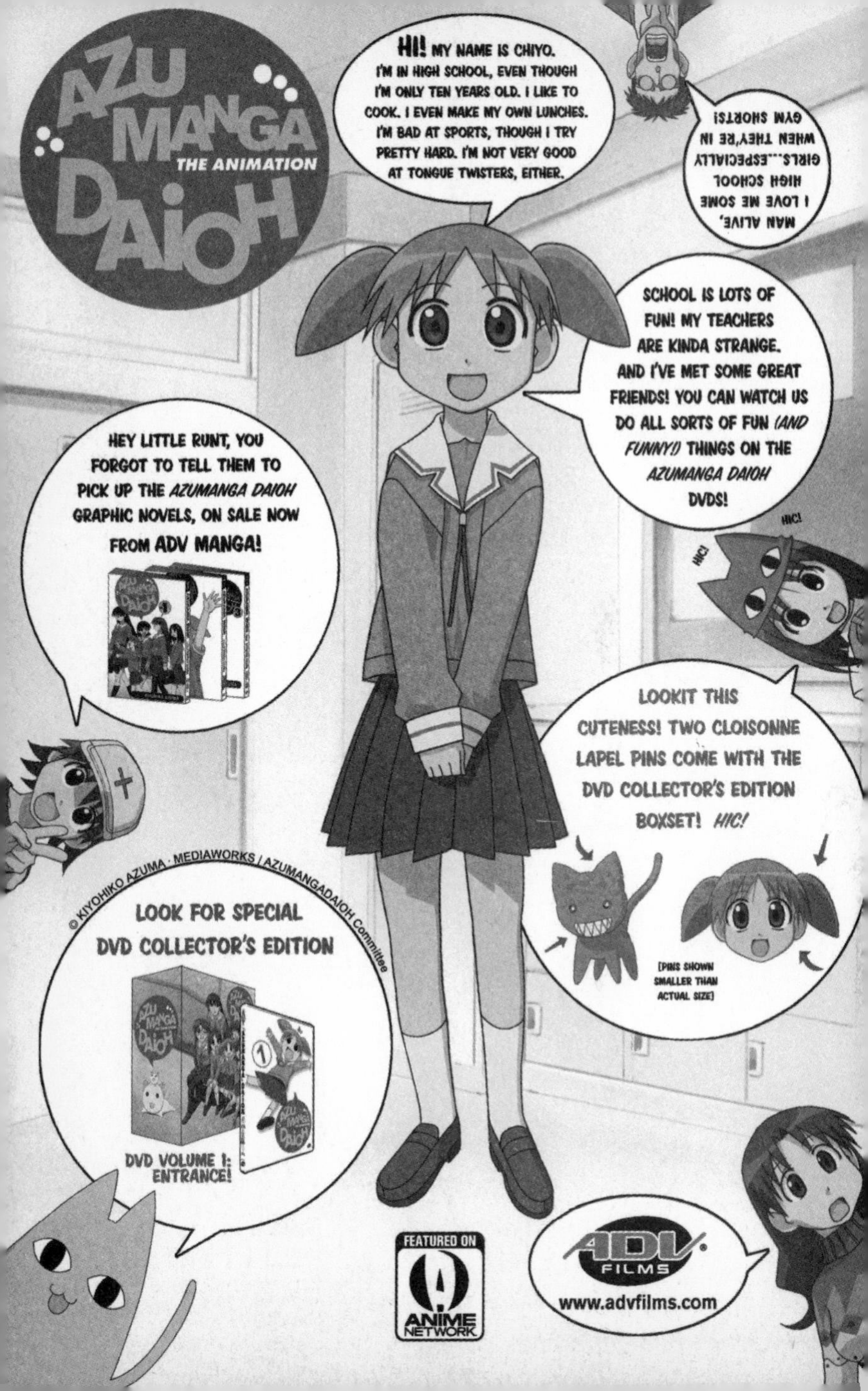
AZUMANGA DAIOH THE ANIMATION
HI! MY NAME IS CHIYO. I'M IN HIGH SCHOOL, EVEN THOUGH I'M ONLY TEN YEARS OLD. I LIKE TO COOK. I EVEN MAKE MY OWN LUNCHES. I'M BAD AT SPORTS, THOUGH I TRY PRETTY HARD. I'M NOT VERY GOOD AT TONGUE TWISTERS, EITHER.
MAN ALIVE, I LOVE ME SOME HIGH SCHOOL GIRLS...ESPECIALLY WHEN THEY'RE IN GYM SHORTS!
SCHOOL IS LOTS OF FUN! MY TEACHERS ARE KINDA STRANGE. AND I'VE MET SOME GREAT FRIENDS! YOU CAN WATCH US DO ALL SORTS OF FUN *(AND FUNNY!)* THINGS ON THE *AZUMANGA DAIOH* DVDS!
HEY LITTLE RUNT, YOU FORGOT TO TELL THEM TO PICK UP THE *AZUMANGA DAIOH* GRAPHIC NOVELS, ON SALE NOW FROM ADV MANGA!
HIC!
HIC!
LOOKIT THIS CUTENESS! TWO CLOISONNE LAPEL PINS COME WITH THE DVD COLLECTOR'S EDITION BOXSET! *HIC!*
[PINS SHOWN SMALLER THAN ACTUAL SIZE]
© KIYOHIKO AZUMA · MEDIAWORKS / AZUMANGADAIOH Committee
LOOK FOR SPECIAL DVD COLLECTOR'S EDITION
DVD VOLUME 1: ENTRANCE!
FEATURED ON ANIME NETWORK
ADV FILMS
www.advfilms.com

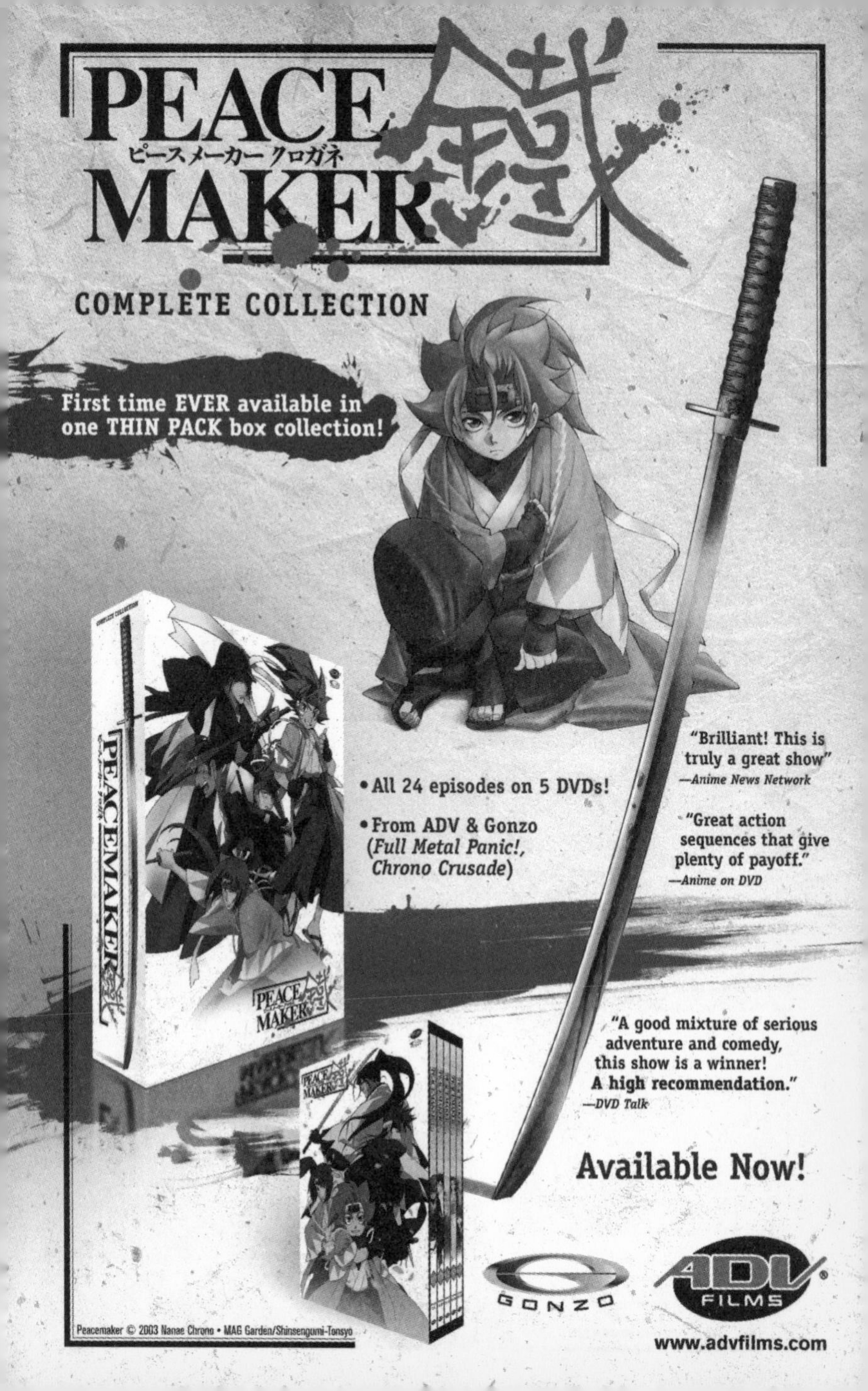
PEACE MAKER 鐵
ピースメーカー クロガネ
COMPLETE COLLECTION
First time EVER available in one THIN PACK box collection!
• All 24 episodes on 5 DVDs!
• From ADV & Gonzo (Full Metal Panic!, Chrono Crusade)
"Brilliant! This is truly a great show"
—Anime News Network
"Great action sequences that give plenty of payoff."
—Anime on DVD
"A good mixture of serious adventure and comedy, this show is a winner! A high recommendation."
—DVD Talk
Available Now!
GONZO
ADV FILMS
www.advfilms.com
Peacemaker © 2003 Nanae Chrono • MAG Garden/Shinsengumi-Tonsyo

DO YOU HAVE WHAT IT TAKES TO MAKE IT IN CROMARTIE HIGH?

Do you have a tough nickname?

❑ Yes ❑ No

How many fights have you been in?

❑ None ❑ More than 100

❑ 5-10 ❑ None – no one ever had the stones to challenge me

What's in your bookbag?

❑ My homework ❑ Porn ❑ A metal plate

How tough do you look? Check all that apply.

❑ Pompadour ❑ Handlebar mustache ❑ Shaved eyebrows

❑ Carpet of chest hair ❑ Lazy swagger ❑ Menacing glare

Say you checked out eleven adult videos. Three of those were new releases, so you had to return them the next day. How many videos do you have left?

❑ 3 ❑ 8 ❑ 11 – I would never give them back.

How did you rate?

10 points or less	**Errand Boy**
10 – 15	**Wannabe Punk**
30 – 40	**One Badass Dude**
More than 100	**Champ by Default**

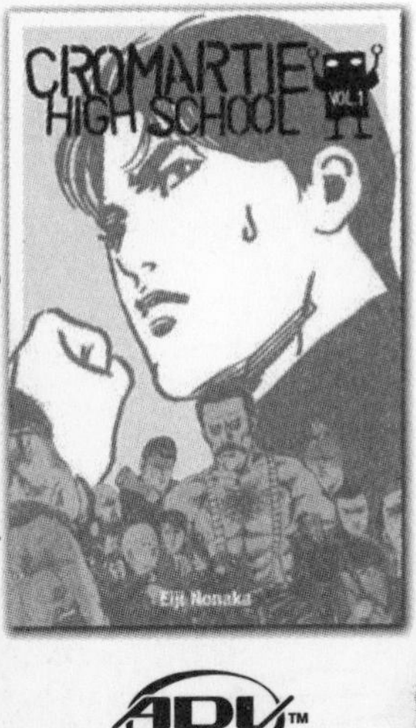
CROMARTIE HIGH SCHOOL
VOL.1
Eiji Nonaka

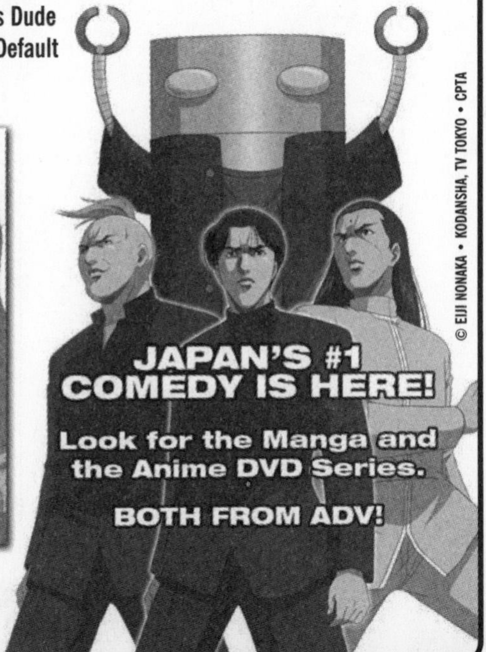

JAPAN'S #1 COMEDY IS HERE!

Look for the Manga and the Anime DVD Series.

BOTH FROM ADV!

ADV Manga™

www.adv-manga.com

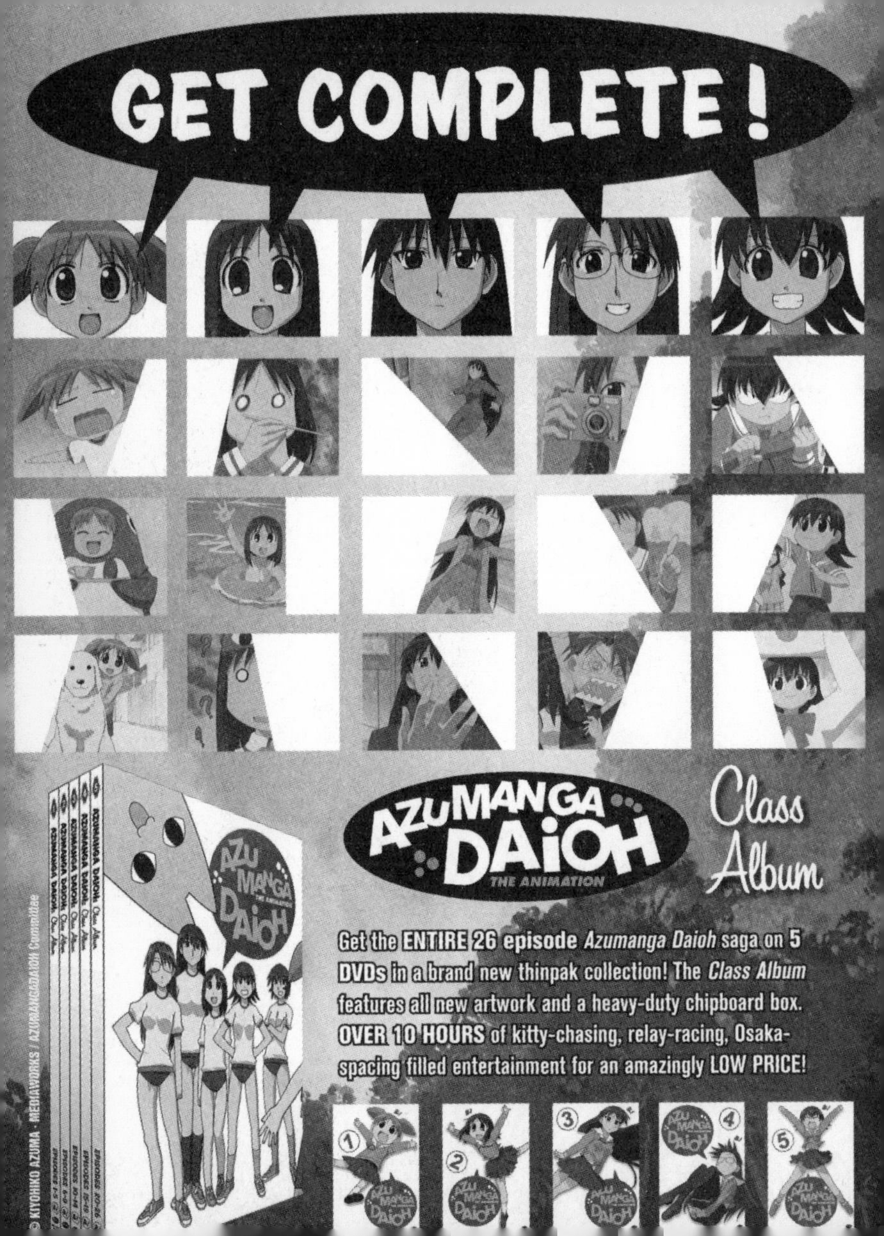
GET COMPLETE !
AZUMANGA DAIOH
THE ANIMATION
Class Album
Get the ENTIRE 26 episode Azumanga Daioh saga on 5 DVDs in a brand new thinpak collection! The Class Album features all new artwork and a heavy-duty chipboard box. OVER 10 HOURS of kitty-chasing, relay-racing, Osaka-spacing filled entertainment for an amazingly LOW PRICE!
1
2
3
4
5
© KIYOHIKO AZUMA · MEDIAWORKS / AZUMANGADAIOH Committee

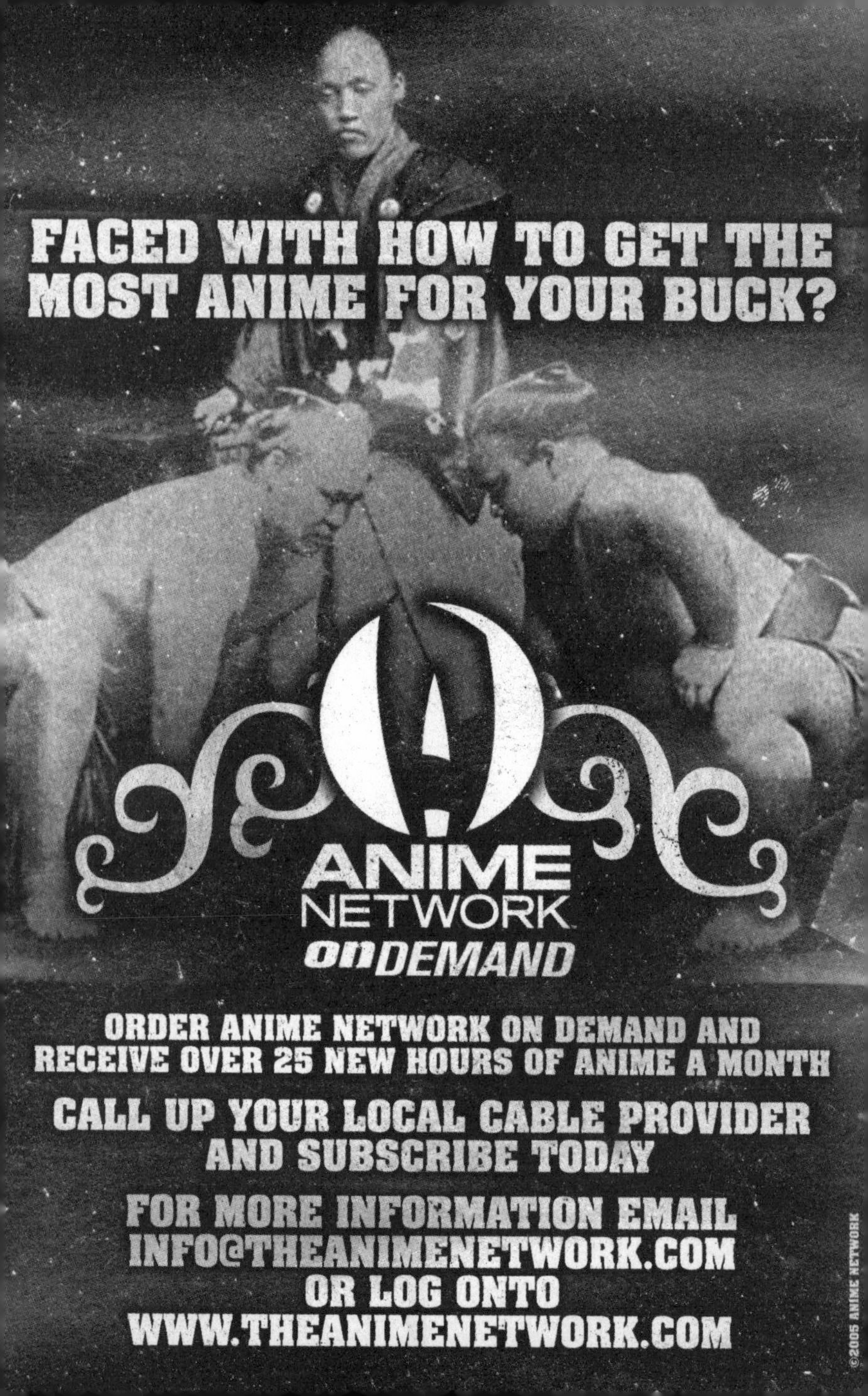
FACED WITH HOW TO GET THE MOST ANIME FOR YOUR BUCK?
ANIME NETWORK
ONDEMAND
ORDER ANIME NETWORK ON DEMAND AND RECEIVE OVER 25 NEW HOURS OF ANIME A MONTH
CALL UP YOUR LOCAL CABLE PROVIDER AND SUBSCRIBE TODAY
FOR MORE INFORMATION EMAIL INFO@THEANIMENETWORK.COM OR LOG ONTO WWW.THEANIMENETWORK.COM
©2005 ANIME NETWORK